Occasions of State

C000149006

This sixth volume in the European Festival Studies series stems from a joint conference (Venice, 2013) between the Society for European Festivals Research and the European Science Foundation's PALATIUM project. Drawing on up-to-date scholarship, a Europe-wide group of early-career and experienced academics provides a unique account of spectacular occasions of state which influenced the political, social and cultural lives of contemporary societies. International pan-European turbulence associated with post-Reformation religious conflict supplies the context within which the book explores how the period's rulers and élite families competed for power – in a forecast of today's divided world.

J.R. Mulryne is Professor Emeritus at the University of Warwick, UK.

Krista De Jonge is Professor of Architectural History at the University of Leuven.

R.L.M. (Richard) Morris is a Supervisor in History at the University of Cambridge.

Pieter Martens is Assistant Professor at the Vrije Universiteit Brussel.

European Festival Studies: 1450–1700

Series Editors:

J.R. Mulryne
University of Warwick, UK
Margaret Shewring
University of Warwick, UK
Margaret M. McGowan
CBE, FBA, University of Sussex, UK

This series, in association with the Society for European Festivals Research, builds on the current surge of interest in the circumstances of European Festivals – their political, religious, social, economic and cultural implications as well as the detailed analysis of their performance (including ephemeral architecture, scenography, scripts, music and soundscape, dance, costumes, processions and fireworks) in both indoor and outdoor locations.

Festivals were interdisciplinary and, on occasion, international in scope. They drew on a rich classical heritage and developed a shared pan-European iconography as well as exploiting regional and site-specific features. They played an important part in local politics and the local economy, as well as international negotiations and the conscious presentation of power, sophistication and national identity.

The series, including both essay collections and monographs, seeks to analyse the characteristics of individual festivals as well as to explore generic themes. It draws on a wealth of archival documentary evidence, alongside the resources of galleries and museums, to study the historical, literary, performance and material culture of these extravagant occasions of state.

Occasions of State

Early Modern European Festivals
and the Negotiation of Power

**Edited by J.R. Mulryne,
Krista De Jonge, R.L.M. Morris
and Pieter Martens**

Routledge
Taylor & Francis Group

LONDON AND NEW YORK

EUROPEAN
SCIENCE
FOUNDATION

First published 2019
by Routledge
2 Park Square, Milton Park, Abingdon, Oxon OX14 4RN

and by Routledge
605 Third Avenue, New York, NY 10017

First issued in paperback 2022

Routledge is an imprint of the Taylor & Francis Group, an informa business

British Library Cataloguing-in-Publication Data
A catalogue record for this book is available from the British Library

Library of Congress Cataloging-in-Publication Data
A catalog record has been requested for this book

ISBN: 978-1-03-240172-0 (pbk)
ISBN: 978-1-4724-3197-4 (hbk)
ISBN: 978-1-315-57845-3 (ebk)

DOI: 10.4324/9781315578453

Typeset in Sabon
by Apex CoVantage, LLC

Contents

Figures

Plates

Editors and contributors

Editors

J.R. Mulryne is Professor Emeritus at the University of Warwick, UK. He was previously Pro-Vice-Chancellor of the University and Director of the Centre for the Study of the Renaissance. He has been a co-convenor of the Society for European Festivals Research since its inception. His publications are mainly on Elizabethan and Jacobean Theatre, Shakespeare, and modern theatre and theatre buildings. He has edited and contributed to *Europa Triumphans: Court and Civic Festivals in Early Modern Europe* (2004); *Court Festivals of the European Renaissance* (2002), with Elizabeth Goldring; and with Margaret McGowan and Margaret Shewring is General Editor of the European Festival Studies: 1450–1700 series. He is also Co-Editor of two recent books in the series, *Ceremonial Entries in Early Modern Europe* (2015) and *Architectures of Festival: Fashioning and Re-Fashioning Urban and Courtly Space in Early Modern Europe* (2017). He was Principal Investigator, in collaboration with the British Library, of the collection of 273 digitised Festival Books in the ownership of the Library, subsequently accessible on the Library's website under 'Renaissance Festival Books'.

Krista De Jonge is Professor of Architectural History at the University of Leuven. She is a member of the Royal Academy of Archaeology and Art History of Belgium, and of the Royal Flemish Academy of Arts and Science. She advises numerous national and international institutions and research programmes and chaired the European Science Foundation Research Networking Programme 'PALATIUM'. She is Series Editor of Architectura Moderna (Brepols). Her main field of research is early modern architecture of the Low Countries in a European context, especially the architecture of the Burgundian and early Habsburg court. Her publications include: 'El Emperador y las fiestas flamencas de su época', in A.J. Morales (ed.), *La fiesta en la Europa de Carlos V* (2000); De Jonge, K. *et al.* (eds), *Jacques Du Broeucq de Mons (1505–1584). Maître artiste de l'empereur Charles Quint* (Mons 2005); 'Antiquity Assimilated: Court Architecture 1530–1560', in K. De Jonge and K.A. Ottenheym, *Unity* *and Discontinuity. Architectural Relations between the Southern and Northern Low Countries 1530–1700*, Architectura Moderna 5 (2007); and 'Marie de Hongrie, maître d'ouvrage (1531–1555), et la Renaissance dans les anciens Pays-Bas', in B. Federinov and G. Docquier (eds), *Marie de Hongrie, Politique et culture sous la Renaissance aux Pays-Bas* (2008).

R.L.M. Morris studied history as a member of Trinity College, University of Cambridge, where he was elected a Senior Scholar in 2011. He completed his doctoral research on 'German identity in the court festivals of the late sixteenth and early seventeenth century Holy Roman Empire' in 2017. He sits on the advisory board of the Society for European Festivals Research, and is a Supervisor in History at the University of Cambridge. In addition to this volume, he is Co-Editor of *Architectures of Festival: Fashioning and Re-Fashioning Urban and Courtly Space in Early Modern Europe* (Abingdon, UK, and New York: Routledge, 2018).

Pieter Martens is Assistant Professor at the Vrije Universiteit Brussel. His research centres on sixteenth-century military architecture, siege warfare and urban iconography. He graduated in architectural engineering at the University of Leuven and also studied in Rome at the Università La Sapienza. His PhD thesis (Leuven, 2009) received awards for its use of archival sources and for its contribution to military history. A laureate of the Royal Flemish Academy of Belgium for Science and the Arts, he has held postdoctoral fellowships at the universities of Leuven and Louvain-la-Neuve, and was the co-ordinator of the European Science Foundation Research Networking Programme 'PALATIUM' (2010–2015). His recent publications include contributions on city views in the exhibition catalogue *Hieronymus Cock. The Renaissance in Print* (2013); an edited volume with Nicolas Faucherre and Huges Paucot (eds), *The Genesis of the Bastioned System in Europe 1500–1550* (2014); and an essay on the language of military architecture in the Low Countries in Marie Madeleine Fontaine and Jean-Louis Fournel (eds), *Les mots de la guerre dans l'Europe de la Renaissance* (2015).

Contributors

Francesca Barbieri is *Cultore della Materia* in Theatre Studies at the Università Cattolica of Milan, where she completed her PhD in 2012. Her studies involve investigating theatricality in the seventeenth and eighteenth centuries in Milan and focus on public events, theatrical performances and stage design. She did research on iconographic sources for the exhibitions *Festa, rito e teatro nella "gran città di Milano" nel Settecento* in 2010 and *Virtù, scene, supplizi. Rappresentazioni della Giustizia nella Milano del Settecento* in 2015 (Milan, Pinacoteca Ambrosiana). She has also researched the theatre designs by the Galliari brothers kept in the collections of Accademia di Belle Arti di Brera of Milan. Her recent publications include contributions to A. Cascetta and D. Zardin (eds), *Giustizia e ingiustizia a Milano tra Cinque e Settecento* (2016); I. Mauro, M. Viceconte, J. Palos (eds), *Visiones cruzadas. Los virreyes de Nápoles y la imagen de la Monarquía de España en el Barroco 1400-1800* (2018). She is currently publishing the monograph *I significati dell'apparenza. La scenografia teatrale a Milano nel secondo Settecento (1765–1792).*

Berta Cano-Echevarría is Associate Professor of English Literature and Culture and Head of the Department of English Philology at the University of Valladolid, Spain. Her main research area is Anglo-Spanish cultural relations and textual transmission. She has published widely on the English College in Valladolid and, with Mark Hutchings, on the cultural manifestations of the Anglo-Spanish peace of 1603–1605.

Chantal Grell is Professor of Early Modern History at the University of Versailles Saint-Quentin. Her publications are on the history of knowledge and visual culture in the modern period, and on courts. Her best-known publications are: with Christian Michel, *L'Ecole des Princes ou Alexandre disgracié. Essai sur la mythologie monarchique de la France absolutiste* (Belles Lettres, 1988); *Le Dix-Huitième siècle et l'Antiquité en France*, 2 vols (Oxford: SVEC, 1995); a contribution to the joint publication *Anne d'Autriche, Infante d'Espagne et Reine de France* (Madrid: CEEH, 2009); and with Robert Halleux, *Sciences, techniques, pouvoirs et sociétés du XVe au XVIIIe siècle* (A. Colin, 2016). She is the editor of the Correspondence of Hevelius (1611–1687). Volume two, *Correspondance avec la Cour de France* (Turnhout: Brepols International Publishers, 2017), deals with the Financing of Scientific Research.

Borbála Gulyás is Research Fellow of the Institute of Art History at the Research Centre for the Humanities of the Hungarian Academy of Sciences, Budapest. She was awarded the Isabel and Alfred Bader Prize for Art History of the Hungarian Academy of Sciences in 2011. She received her PhD in Art History from Eötvös Loránd University, Budapest, in 2013 for a thesis on the art of the Hungarian calligrapher George Bocskay (†1575), who served at the court of Habsburgs Ferdinand I and Maximilian II in Vienna. Her tutor was Dr Géza Galavics, MHAS. Her research interests include art, court festivals and tournaments in Europe, especially in the Kingdom of Hungary, during the early modern period.

Robert Halleux founded, and has over a long period directed, the CHST (Centre d'Histoire des Sciences et des Techniques (Liège, 1982–2015)) and was curator of the exhibition devoted to Ernest de Bavière (Liège, 2011–2012). He is a member of the Académie royale de Belgique and of the Institut de France (Académie des inscriptions et Belles Lettres). With Michel Blay he has edited the *Dictionnaire de la science classique, XVIe – XVIIIe siècles* (Flammarion, 1998) and contributed to the catalogue of the exhibition 'Sciences et curiosités à la cour de Versailles' (Versailles,

2010). He has collaborated with Chantal Grell on *Sciences, techniques, pouvoirs et sociétés du XVe au XVIIIe siècle* (A. Colin, 2016).

Mark Hutchings is Lecturer in English Literature at the University of Reading, UK. His main research interests lie in theatre history and performance and Anglo-Spanish diplomatic relations. He is currently editing a collection of essays on *The Changeling* (Bloomsbury), and a monograph on repertory Turks is forthcoming from Palgrave; with Berta Cano-Echevarría he has published on the Anglo-Spanish peace of 1603–1605.

Robert J. Knecht is Emeritus Professor of French History at the University of Birmingham. A former Chairman of the Society of Renaissance Studies and of the Society for the Study of French History, he is the author of several works on sixteenth- and seventeenth-century France, including *Richelieu* (1991), *Renaissance Warrior and Patron: The Reign of Francis I* (1994), *Catherine de' Medici* (1998), *The French Civil Wars* (2000), *The Rise and Fall of Renaissance France* (revised edn. 2001), *The Valois* (2004) and *The French Renaissance Court* (2008).

Margaret M. McGowan is a Fellow of the British Academy and Research Professor at the University of Sussex. Her research interests centre on the intellectual, cultural and artistic concerns of early modern Europe. Her publications include: *L'Art du Ballet de cour en France, 1581–1643* (1963); *Montaigne's Deceits* (1974); *Ideal Forms in the Age of Ronsard* (1985); *The Vision of Rome in Late Renaissance France* (2000); and *Dance in the Renaissance: European Fashion, French Obsession* (2008). Her recent chapters on Renaissance festivals include 'Lyon: A Centre for Water Celebrations', in Margaret Shewring (ed.), *Waterborne Pageants and Festivities in the Renaissance: Essays in Honour of J.R. Mulryne* (2013), pp. 37–49; and 'Henri IV as Architect and Restorer of the State: His Entry into Rouen, 16 October 1596', in J.R. Mulryne, with Maria Ines Aliverti and Anna Maria Testaverde (eds), *Ceremonial Entries in Early Modern Europe. The Iconography of Power* (2015), pp. 53–75. She edited *Dynastic Marriages 1612/1615. A Celebration of the Habsburg and Bourbon Unions*, the first published volume in the series European Festival Studies: 1450–1700 (2013). She gave the Leopold Delisle lectures in 2012 and was awarded the Wolfson Prize in 2008 and the CBE for services to French Studies in 1998.

Joanna Norman is Director of the V&A Research Institute at the Victoria and Albert Museum, London. Her research interests lie principally in early modern Italy and France, and include the history of performance, furniture and period rooms. Most recently she was Lead Curator for the Scottish Design Galleries at V&A Dundee (opened September 2018) and Project Curator for the critically acclaimed redevelopment of the V&A's Europe 1600–1815 permanent galleries (opened 2015). Previous exhibitions include *Baroque 1620–1800: Style in the Age of Magnificence*

(V&A, 2009) and *Treasures from Budapest: European Masterpieces from Leonardo to Schiele* (Royal Academy of Arts, 2010). Her publications include *Handmade in Britain* (2011) and *The Story of Scottish Design* (co-edited with Philip Long, 2018) as well as contributions to Michael Snodin and Nigel Llewellyn (eds), *Baroque 1620–1800: Style in the Age of Magnificence* (2009); Sarah Medlam and Lesley Ellis Miller (eds), *Princely Treasures: European Masterpieces 1600–1800* (2010); and Elizabeth Miller and Hilary Young (eds), *The Arts of Living: Europe 1600–1815* (2015).

Fabian Persson completed his doctoral thesis 'Servants of Fortune' in Lund and is now Lecturer and Associate Professor in History at Linnaeus University in Sweden. His main expertise lies in the history of the early modern Swedish court and aristocracy, but he has also written on patronage, corruption, elites, aristocratic marriage and duelling. His publications in English include contributions to Nadine Akkerman and Birgit Houben (eds), *The Politics of Female Households* (2013); Dries Raeymaekers and Sebastiaan Derks (eds), *The Key to Power? The Culture of Access in Early Modern Courts* (2016); and John Adamson (ed.), *The Princely Courts of Europe* (1999).

Nikola Piperkov completed his doctoral thesis, 'Les visages de Mercure: eloquence, commerce, alchimie et arts d'imitation à l'époque moderne', in July 2018, in History of Art at the University of Paris I, Panthéon-Sorbonne. His research focuses on the iconography of Mercury in the early modern period, with a particular emphasis on hermetic, alchemical and hieroglyphic theory in Renaissance Florence, Paris, Prague, Antwerp and Haarlem. Nikola was awarded a scholarship by the French School in Rome in 2015, and was granted a doctoral position by the University of Paris I, Panthéon-Sorbonne, where he supervised courses on Italian Renaissance art and theory. He also worked as a teaching assistant at the University of Lyon II Lumière, where he took responsibility for courses on Italian Renaissance and mannerism, early modern numismatics, French academic art and historiography. Currently, Nikola is president of the Association of Art et Histoire de Lyon Philibert de L'Orme.

Paul Schuster is an art historian and, since 2009, curator for Schloss Eggenberg and the Eggenberg Mausoleum at Universalmuseum Joanneum, Graz, Austria. He studied art history and Italian at the University of Graz. His diploma thesis was 'The late Gothic chapel of the Virgin Mary in Schloss Eggenberg'. Since 2009, his doctoral studies have been in philosophy and art history. His doctoral dissertation is entitled 'Schloss Eggenberg. A study of its architectural history and former functions'. His current responsibilities and professional specialisms include building research, residence studies and conservation of historical monuments; historical interiors and interior decoration (seventeenth to eighteenth centuries); history of interior lighting and historical light fixtures; the Eggenberg family as patrons and founders; management of the collection inventory and of the library; digital media in museums and historic sites, museum education and museology.

Maartje van Gelder is Associate Professor in Early Modern History at the University of Amsterdam. Her work concentrates on sixteenth- and seventeenth-century Italy and the Mediterranean, with a particular interest in urban history and the social history of politics and diplomacy. Her first book, *Trading Places. The Netherlandish Merchants in Early Modern Venice*, was published with Brill in 2009. She published on the role Dutch converts to Islam played in early modern Dutch–North African diplomacy in the *Journal of Early Modern History*. Her current research focuses on social unrest and popular politics in early modern Venice. Recently her article "The People's Prince. Popular Politics in Early Modern Venice" was published in the *Journal of Modern History* 90.2 (2018).

Tim White is Principal Teaching Fellow in Theatre and Performance Studies at the University of Warwick, having previously held a full-time post at Central Saint Martins in London. He currently teaches modules on practical video, experimental music, performing online and food and performance. Publications include *Diaghilev to the Pet Shop Boys* (Lund Humphries, 1996) as well as articles for *Contemporary Theatre Review, Dance Theatre Journal* and *Performance Research*. He has contributed to the recent volume *Theatre Noise* and is a founder member of the International Federation of Theatre Research (IFTR) working group on Performance in Public Spaces. Current research interests include video production, music, online performance and immersive strategies.

Preface and acknowledgements

The present volume, the sixth in our *European Festival Studies* series, differs, like its immediate predecessors *Architectures of Festival in Early Modern Europe* (2018) and Felicia Else, *The Politics of Water* (2019), from earlier volumes in the series, in the important respect that these volumes are published under the Routledge imprint of the Taylor and Francis Group. This follows the sale in late 2015 of the former Ashgate Publishing Limited to Taylor and Francis, bringing to an end a long and fruitful relationship between Ashgate and ourselves, not only taking in the beautifully produced, thoroughly edited scholarly books in the series but also others which preceded them, including the two-volume *Europa Triumphans* (2004), published in collaboration with MHRA, which has since become an indispensable resource for students and scholars working in the field. It would be inexcusable if we did not reiterate here our appreciation of Ashgate's work, and especially the encouragement and expertise of the firm's Managing Director, Rachel Lynch. We now anticipate equally cordial relations with staff and agents of Routledge, an anticipation which has been confirmed, as acknowledgements below attest, by the experience of working with this volume and its predecessors.

The volume published here takes its origin from a collaboration between the Society for European Festivals Research, responsible for the first three volumes in the series, and the European Science Foundation's Research Network, PALATIUM. This collaboration, encouraged by the ESF, led to a joint conference of the two organisations under the title 'Making Space for Festival 1400–1700: Interactions of Architecture and Performance in Late Medieval and Early Modern Festivals'. This was held in March 2013 in the Palazzo Pesaro Papafava, the University of Warwick's research and teaching facility in Venice. The conference proved a fruitful collaboration between PALATIUM's interests in – among much else – the architectural features of European palaces, great houses and outdoor locations and SEFR's main concern with festivals of the courts and cities of fifteenth-, sixteenth- and seventeenth-century Europe, their staging, their texts and the historical and cultural circumstances which shaped them and to which they responded. A great deal of common ground emerged at the conference, leading to a decision by an editorial group drawn from both organisations to publish two volumes of related essays in our series, after contributors had undertaken further research, presented their conclusions in an appropriate scholarly format on the basis of editorial guidance and comment and secured permission for the illustrations which now enhance and further extend the book's scholarship. It has been rewarding to work with contributors to the two volumes, who include both early-career and experienced researchers and those whose professional background lies in museums, archives and libraries, as well as those whose prime affiliation lies in universities.

Books like these accumulate many debts. I should like to repeat here an acknowledgement of our special debt to Margaret Shewring (University of Warwick; Co-Convenor of SEFR), whose many hours of sustained and meticulous work have extended from the *Architectures* volume into and throughout the present book. Without her otherwise unacknowledged and expert labours, the present volume, like its predecessor, would not have been published, and certainly not in a timely fashion, given the disruption caused by the sale of Ashgate. It is no exaggeration to say that Margaret's meticulous editorial and scholarly work has made the continued viability of the series possible. Alongside her we should acknowledge the co-editors of the two associated volumes, Krista De Jonge, Richard Morris and Pieter Martens. Their work has contributed very greatly to ensuring the maintenance of high scholarly standards throughout both volumes. We would also like to thank the conference's Scientific Committee: Brigitte Bøggild Johansen (National Museum of Denmark); Monique Chatenet (Centre André Chastel, INHA, Paris); Iain Fenlon (King's College, University of Cambridge); PALATIUM Co-Chair Bernardo J. García (Fundación Carlos de Amberes); PALATIUM Coordinator Pieter Martens (Vrije Universiteit Brussel); Co-Convenor SEFR, Margaret M. McGowan (University of Sussex); and Co-Convenor of SEFR, Margaret Shewring.

As with *Architectures*, we have acquired new obligations as this volume has gone through the press. We have been exceptionally fortunate to work with Jennifer Morrow (Routledge) and as an agent for Taylor and Francis with Autumn Spalding of Apex CoVantage. We could not have hoped for more encouraging and expert collaborators, both of whom went beyond the extra mile to ensure that our books were treated with the greatest care and with enthusiastic commitment to become beautifully produced volumes. Behind them – from our perspective – have stood the colleagues from both organisations, who have worked so well to take our volumes through the press. We must also thank Mr Max Novick of Taylor and Francis, who expertly steered our volumes into the otherwise unfamiliar publishing network of his firm.

The work collected in this volume has been financially supported by the European Science Foundation (ESF) through its support of the Research Network 'PALATIUM. Court Residences as Places of Exchange in Late Medieval and Early Modern Europe (1400–1700)'. Financial and in-kind support has also come from the University of Leuven; Trinity College, University of Cambridge; and from the University of Warwick's Humanities Research Centre, Institute of Advanced Studies, Department of Theatre Studies, Centre for the Study of the Renaissance and Early Modern Forum. At the time of the conference we were the beneficiaries of hard and willingly given work by staff of the Palazzo Pesaro Papafava, especially Chiara Croff, and by postgraduate students (at the time) Tracy Cattell, Leila Zammar, Melanie Zefferino and Pesala Bandara (all University of Warwick). We are particularly pleased and encouraged that several of these former students have continued to contribute to Festival studies, three to the successful completion of a doctorate. We should also like to acknowledge invaluable IT help and guidance from Warwick's Robert Batterbee, and from Matthew Growcoot, who provided a comprehensive audio-visual record of the occasion. Roberta Warman enlivened the conference and its preparation by her sheer delight in taking part and by her experienced knowledge of the inner workings of the University and its research and teaching facility. Sue Rae, also of Warwick, contributed administrative and secretarial skills without complaint, indeed with eager interest, despite the burdens that were sometimes placed on her. Special thanks are due, in addition to Professor Krista De Jonge, to our co-editors Pieter Martens of the Vrije Universiteit Brussel, who helped unstintingly during the preparations for the conference and in the editing of this book, drawing on his longstanding, much-admired work for PALATIUM, and R.L.M. (Richard) Morris of Trinity College, Cambridge, who in addition to his knowledgeable and meticulous work as co-editor of the volume was the first to draw up proposals for its contents and their order.

As we now write, four years have passed since the date of a thoroughly memorable and rewarding conference. Much has happened to both PALATIUM and SEFR during that time. Both have continued to publish their work, with PALATIUM reaching the end of its funding support. SEFR has material for new volumes, both monographs and collections, either based on research conferences, one of which was held as part of the Mons, European City of Culture celebrations, or on the research endeavours of individual scholars, some of whom have investigated their topics for many years. We look forward to a productive future, encouraged by the achievements of the two volumes to which we make reference here.

Ronnie Mulryne
Krista De Jonge
September 2017

Introduction

The power of ceremony

J.R. (Ronnie) Mulryne[1]

This book focuses, as its title indicates, on *Occasions of State*. Both terms are relevant. The festivals about which contributors write are *occasional*, that is to say specially devised to respond to a particular historical moment. Equally, they are state- or municipality-sponsored and therefore intent on exercising authority and demonstrating power. A preoccupation with power – political, military and social – has shadowed, it could be said, every significant development in the history of early modern – and today's – Europe. More to the point, a concern for power underpins every royal or civic entry, every carousel and *giostra*, every negotiation and gift-giving, every extended progress-journey featured here. While objectives and scale vary, common political and social characteristics emerge, from the conspicuous expenditure and spirit-crushing commitment of resources demanded by Charles V's travels to far-flung Habsburg domains, to the local, religious and family issues that prompted extraordinary preparations for the reception in Rome (December 1655) of Queen Christina of Sweden.

Power, and the acquisition of power, is the common theme of the following chapters, ranging from straightforward aggression to more sophisticated and aesthetically highly developed forms of coercion or persuasion. Yet it is the tension and the kinship between power and ceremony which occupy the attention of contributors. Two ways only of exercising power were available – arguably – to the early modern state, that is to say war and ceremony. The present book places emphasis on the second, while recognising common ground between the two. Wars and rumours of war condition our response to almost every occasion of pageantry rooted in the occasions with which these chapters deal. There are moments, perhaps surprisingly, when war and ceremony seem interchangeable, as when, for example, Berta Cano-Echevarría and Mark Hutchings describe in vivid detail how the wily political brains at Philip III's court managed to conceal hostility under the cloak of ceremony. Spanish manipulation, the two authors tell us, turned a politically charged English peace-embassy into 'an extended courtly pageant',

---

1 Quotations in this Introduction, other than those identified in footnotes, are taken from the relevant chapter of this book.

with the whole episode becoming 'an expression of hospitality as power' – a near-symbiotic relationship, as this book explores it, between the apparently antithetical concepts of Ceremony and Power.

The enigma of identity

It would be common ground among today's popular as well as sophisticated commentators that a confident identity serves as 'empowerment' – for individuals, nations or international groupings. The topic is met head-on by Richard Morris, whose assessment of 'German' identity in the book's first chapter draws on specialist disciplines from anthropology via sociology on to the more familiar shores of historical analysis. Morris brilliantly shows how the identity of the German nation remains 'a somewhat fraught and problematic one in historiography'. He develops the discussion, with specific reference to the history of the Holy Roman Empire, into how German self-identity, today as in the past, may be understood as conditioned by prevailing awareness among its people of the country's past. A nation's identity may be closely related to nationalism. The sociologist and political historian, Michael Hechter, quoted by Morris, offers a double view of nationalism as empowering yet fraught with risk. 'Nationalism and its close cousin, ethnicity', Hechter writes, 'currently are the most potent political forces in the world', adding significantly, 'there is a pervasive interest in containing its [nationalism's] dark side'. Morris, for his part, summarises 'the religious upheavals of the Reformation', the 'various political conflicts including the Schmalkaldic War', 'the Thirty Years War', and 'the ever-present Ottoman threat', as a potent brew of ingredients traceable in large part to the competing nations' efforts to establish their national identities. The cost in human lives, cultural artefacts and humane values, when set alongside today's conflicts, may be assessed as comparably great.

Morris takes a benign view of the role played by festive ceremony as a culturally active agent promoting national identity and associated social and political cohesion. Ceremony, ritual action and a common rhetoric may combine, he argues, to underpin an in-state community of rulers, elites and common people. Such community was, undoubtedly, challenged by the day's happenings, by privations and by the dissident views of interested parties. Yet Morris argues persuasively that, *in potentia*, early modern festival served as a rhetorically crafted strategy to bring into being state-centred structures among which in a time of turbulence contemporaries might live – a beneficent role for ceremony and its privileged power.

The sinews of peace

In a book so fully occupied with war and titled *Occasions of State*, it is scarcely surprising that three chapters, by Robert J. Knecht, Nikola Piperkov and (jointly) Berta Cano-Echevarría and Mark Hutchings, are devoted to the celebration of peace – to what, rather loftily, the Irish poet W.B. Yeats, deploring its absence, called 'the ceremony of innocence'.[2] If war and ceremony may be seen as parallel sources of power, peace serves as the alternative to the first and affirmation of the second. Yet, to cite a famous and characterising instance, William Shakespeare's *Henry V* draws on contemporary political experience to foreground the tensions between the two terms. Early spectators thrilled to the play's 'patriotism' – or nationalism – as Henry exhorts his followers at besieged Harfleur to sacrifice their lives willingly in England's cause.[3] The play's climax, however, directly juxtaposes Henry's marriage, the supreme ceremony of political self-fashioning among early modern societies, with the Duke of Burgundy's overwhelmingly powerful plea[4] on behalf of the 'naked, poor and mangled peace' of defeated France. When Henry instructs, 'Do we all holy rites: / Let there be sung *Non nobis* and *Te Deum*',[5] the student of festival will recognise typical elements of early modern festival ceremony. Would the sinews of peace hold firm for Henry V into the following reign? Playgoers of the Elizabethan theatre, aware of history to come, knew they wouldn't – a dramatic rehearsal of the fragility undermining peace in so much dear-bought early modern rhetoric and performance of festival.

Even if the tensions underlying festival celebrations of peace are not given as much emphasis as in Shakespeare's disturbing play, Robert Knecht's vivid examination of the Bastille banquet of December 1518 persuasively demonstrates the instabilities written into what he calls the contemporary requirement for 'a new phase of international diplomacy that called for display and magnificence on an unprecedented scale'. The signing of the Treaty of London promised much towards the delivery of peace between the major powers. Subsequent moments did indeed produce gains, including words spoken at a ceremony before the high altar of St Paul's, when the English king Henry VIII and French ambassadors mutually swore to uphold a perpetual peace between the two lands – though even this scarcely served as the vaunted step towards 'universal' peace. The grand banquet staged at the Bastille in October reflected in fact – consciously or unconsciously – the existence of an undeniable threat level, despite a nervous repeated emphasis in the written text on peace.

As Knecht points out, the Bastille banquet served as part of a prolonged celebration of the 1518 treaty. The Bastille itself, a powerful, silent presence in the celebrations, was by no means associated with peace, given its origin in the English–French Hundred Years War and its capture by Henry V in 1420. The celebrated Field of Cloth of Gold, boasting *détente* via a trial of

2 Easter 1916.
3 *Henry V*, Act 3, scene 1. References to Shakespeare's plays are to *The Oxford Shakespeare: The Complete Works*, eds Stanley Wells and Gary Taylor (Oxford: Clarendon Press, 1988).
4 *Henry V*, Act 5, scene 2.
5 *Henry V*, Act 4, scene 8.

strength, proved the most magnificent of all the festival occasions of the age, inviting comparison, according to one contemporary eyewitness, with 'the miracles of the Egyptian pyramides and the Roman amphitheatres'. Such solid ancient structures sit oddly with the rhetoric of festival, which characteristically combined professions of diplomatic amity with national self-glorification. The ironies in this case, however, proved more accidental and meteorological than scripted. Spectators can scarcely have missed the blow to national prestige that accompanied Henry's defeat in a wrestling match, and *per contra* the fate of the French king's magnificent tent, brought to a premature end by wind and rain. In this as in so many instances, the sinews of peace turned out to be slack: England and France soon reverted to their age-old enmity.

The peaceable city

If Henry VIII and Francis I – and Cardinal Wolsey – aimed by the Treaty of London to secure the peace of Europe, the French silk-manufacturing and publishing city of Lyon (Lyons) was animated a century and a half later by a more modest ambition, summarised by Nikola Piperkov's title as 'the allegorical transformation of Lyon into a city of peace'. Lyon's 1660 celebrations followed the signing the previous year of the Pyrenees Peace Treaty, an event greeted by a wave of optimistic expectation across France and Europe. According to a formal provision, the treaty was to be sealed by the wedding of the Spanish Infanta, Maria Teresa, to Louis XIV of France. The Lyon festival was restricted as it transpired to a *cavalcade*, together with a *Te Deum* in the Cathedral Church of Saint John, but it featured also within the processional celebration a set of enterprising allegories 'invented' by a native of Lyon, the Jesuit antiquary, choreographer and scholar of music and dance, Claude-François Ménestrier. Piperkov focuses on the festival's main allegorical feature, a triumphal arch celebrating the Pyrenees treaty. Notably, even the situation of the arch close to a bridge on the road between Habsburg and Bourbon domains is invested with significance as it figured shared hope for the new peace. According to Ménestrier, a lavish use of fireworks provided a paradoxical means of quenching the flames of war. He tells us that it is peace, not war, that 'makes a monarch worthy of honour'. To the contrary, the modern commentator Olivier Chaline writes that under the Valois and Bourbon administrations of *ancien régime* France, 'the cult of the warrior-prince was one of the central themes of palace iconography, and the business of preparing for and waging war was a recurrent, almost normative, aspect of the business of the court'.[6] Here the values of peace and of war are sharply and controversially set in opposition.

6 John Adamson (ed.), *The Princely Courts of Europe: 1500–1750* (London: Weidenfeld and Nicholson, 1999), p. 82.

A valid commonplace of festival criticism – given new life and pertinence in this book – remarks that 'the point of the festival *is* the audience'.[7] Lyon's celebrations underscore this assertion by including, in line with the occasion's common theme, a surprisingly large number of one-off events foregrounding peace. Ménestrier counts no fewer than twenty-six of these, each sponsored by citizens of private means. Even if many were stimulated by a desire for personal prestige rather than political conviction, such widespread support for the festival's topic speaks of an unusual single-mindedness among the better-off populace. Sir John Hale cites Philip de Commines (*c.* 1500) as his early modern authority when writing that in this period 'Europe was doomed to be fissured by mutual hostilities'.[8] It is against this backdrop that we have to see the brave – or blinkered – optimism of the burghers of Lyon. Within a short period of years, Europe had fallen once again into its customary belligerent ways.

Theatre of peace and hostility

Berta Cano-Echevarría and Mark Hutchings turn their attention to another, largely city-based, set of festivals, though in this case with strong international resonances. Again, as their chapter title declares, the topic is peace: 'Valladolid 1605: a theatre for the peace'. To quote the authors, 'For several weeks the Castilian city of Valladolid, briefly the seat of the Spanish court, served as a theatre for the ratification of the Anglo-Spanish peace, formally bringing to an end twenty years of conflict'. The term 'theatre' is well-chosen, for the story the chapter has to tell is a dramatic one, featuring a narrative that for content, pace and temper echoes the instructions of its royal Spanish director, Philip III, and his court. The English ambassador, the Earl of Nottingham,[9] is cast on occasion as a bit-player, despite his role as deputy for the English king. Wry, often wounding, humour on the part of the Spanish had the effect of separating French theatrical personnel – actor, director, 'inventor' – privy to the concealed aims of the events – from a Spanish and English audience. Cano-Echevarría and Hutchings explain: 'like theatre, with its demarcated space, audience, actors, and script, international relations were conducted through rituals of performance'. It proved easy in this instance to overturn rituals, given Spanish disdain for Anglo-Spanish diplomatic protocol.

King Philip's script-writing tactics emerge from this chapter's story as an exercise in exasperatingly witty manipulation. Ambassador Nottingham's

---

7 See Cano-Echevaría and Hutchings.

8 John Hale, *The Civilization of Europe in the Renaissance* (London: HarperCollins, 1993), p. 94.

9 Charles Howard, who served as Lord High Admiral under Elizabeth I and James VI and I, and had experience as ambassador to France, was a significant figure in England, unused to the cavalier treatment he received on the present embassage.

rage at being (as he saw it) wantonly delayed for two hours in an orchard – following a month side-lined with his followers in Galicia – recognisably mimics an actor's unhappiness with an unsatisfactory script. Philip's provocative treatment of the English climaxed, inevitably, with the question of religion. Sectarian weakness on the part of the visitors was keenly monitored by their Spanish hosts and taken as representing a victory over a confessional enemy: all the guile of Catholic ritual was deployed to tempt unwary Protestants, some of whom fell to temptation. The main event of the embassy visit, however, the entry into Valladolid, managed to reconcile religion and diplomacy by masking its ostentatious Catholicism under the guise of a traditional Pentecost procession, coupled with celebrations for the christening of the royal heir, the future Philip IV. The entry's deliberate confusions were intensified by Philip III going to the length of processing on foot, an unprecedented sign of goodwill. Throughout, Spanish pride struggled with a mischievous spirit of condescension towards the English, rising at times to derision. The sinews of peace survived for the moment, even if under more-than-considerable strain.

When sinews are stretched

Fabian Persson's aptly titled chapter, 'The shield of ceremony', addresses the seeming paradox of its sub-title: 'civic ritual and royal entries in wartime'. Can ceremony be accommodated to war? Are the claims of war so overwhelming that ceremony becomes irrelevant? Spectators of Shakespeare may be reminded – again – of the belligerence that surrounds Henry V's overtures to besieged Harfleur, within the play's troubled preoccupation with power. Persson accepts that 'in early modern Europe, loyalty between ruler and subject was fundamental', but acknowledges too that the political and social contract was 'sometimes' broken. What was to be done? Common sense would suggest that even in times of full-on conflict the bonds represented by customary joyous entries might have at the least a subordinate role to play.

Persson exemplifies the diplomatic role of ceremony, even in wartime, by focusing on the European conquests of Swedish monarchs who into the eighteenth century led military campaigns in person. Captured towns had to be entered. The conquering king and the subject town needed to strike a deal. A mutually binding civic accord confirmed by customary ceremonies offered benefits to both. Persson lays out the alternatives: 'If a town resisted, and was sacked', he writes, 'its citizens would be subject to plunder and violence'; 'consequently, it became all-important to negotiate ways to open the gates [of a besieged city] to foreign rulers that would ensure an orderly take-over'. In the absence of consent, the capitulations of Würzburg (1631) and Lemberg (1704) offered, he indicates, 'dreadful examples of the atrocities that awaited a sacked town', while 'horrific massacre' and 'plunder' occurred at the fall of Frankfurt an der Oder (also 1631). The alternative scenario may be represented, Persson notes, by the settlement negotiated by Gustavus Adolphus at Riga in 1621, when the customary rituals of hand-ing over and return of town keys, kissing of hands and singing *Te Deum* played a role in securing a mutually acceptable peace. The more vexed case in comparison is that of Frankfurt am Main, complicated by the town's alle-giance to Protestantism, set alongside its political loyalty to the Habsburg emperor, which issued eventually, if with difficulty, in shared agreement. If the stretched sinews of peace were to be restored, negotiation and ceremony could, Persson shows, work together even in the most unpropitious circum-stances to secure temporary if not necessarily lasting accord.

Dance to the music of time

Dance is the form of artistic expression which, more than any other, brings together a full range of arts: music (both instrumental and vocal), spectacle (including costume and staging), accomplished verse and the movement of the human body in space. It is said that space serves as an acoustic extension of the performer's voice and the musician's instrument. In another perspec-tive, it serves as the arena which shapes and modifies the steps and figures of dance. Danced festival performances are, in considerable part, products of what today's theatre calls 'found space', that is to say locations which by their physical characteristics and cultural associations inform and delimit performance. Dance, moreover, whether ballet, masque or more inclusive forms, implies, if it does not always achieve, social bonding among partici-pants and spectators. Developed through rehearsal by musicians, actors and dancers – including professional performers – dance has clear social impli-cations for the hierarchical societies which danced performances typically address. Dance therefore serves, like other festival types, as a form of 'soft power' responsive to historical circumstances and prevailing social norms and expectations – in summary, the music of time.

Margaret M. McGowan, *doyenne* of historians of dance in the early modern period, provides in her chapter 'Space for dancing' a wide-ranging account of danced performance in diverse spaces across Europe. These include what she describes as 'routine danced entertainment after dinner', a type that became widespread in countries across the continent, to ambi-tious events such as the *mascarades* danced at Binche in 1549 for the visit of Charles V to his sister Mary of Hungary. Another example mentioned by McGowan is the ten-day celebrations at Amboise featuring 'an enor-mous danced spectacle involving seventy-two performers' for the wedding of Madeleine de la Tour d'Auvergne to Lorenzo, duke of Urbino. The first of these took place indoors in a large hall, the second in a temporarily adapted courtyard. Both demonstrated the willingness of rulers to invest conspicuous human and financial resources in these events. Yet even such performances were outshone by two danced occasions to which McGowan also draws attention. The wedding of Mary Queen of Scots to the Dauphin at the archbishop's palace in Paris in April 1558 was, for magnificence, extraordinary scenographic ingenuity and elaborate dance, well beyond the reach of most royal weddings. Yet even this was in its turn outshone by the *Balet Comique de la Reyne*, performed in 1581 among twenty-three diverse festival events for the marriage of the duc de Joyeuse and the Queen's sister at the Salle du Petit Bourbon, a hall capable of holding 2,500 persons. McGowan, while pointing to the risks attendant on the event's adventurous scenography, calls this 'a pinnacle of danced spectacle in France in the sixteenth century'. On the evidence she presents, dance occupied a central role as a culturally active agent in the noble and royal life of early modern Europe, powerful on the side of the *status quo*.

Procession power

Festival typically moves through urban and courtly space as well as prompting the invention of allegories and images. Its processional features create meaning as surely as references to dynasty or the recollection of ancient festivity. Festival books – printed accounts of festival events – can test a modern reader's patience by recounting at length the participants, the costumes and the order-of-precedence of processions through city streets and piazzas. Yet these too create meaning. We may think of the processional components of festival as marginal, yet a moment's reflection will reveal not only their societal implications but also the logistical skill deployed in marshaling the often very numerous marchers, horses and carriages. Vestiges remain in the modern world of procession power of this kind, including – in Britain – a state opening of parliament, a royal funeral or wedding, or the funeral of a highly regarded statesman. In the USA and other parts of the western world, a similar commitment of resources is devoted to the inauguration or burial of a president. In one-party states (chiefly), parades of military hardware take the place of less overtly belligerent spectacles. On occasions such as these the links between ceremony and power become especially clear.

Paul Schuster's discussion of 'Schloss Eggenberg in Graz and the imperial wedding of 1673' focuses on the elevation of Prince Johann Seyfried, owner of Schloss Eggenberg, to a significant position among contemporary first families. The promotion of Seyfried came about as a result of the prince's successful offer to host Claudia Felicitas of Austria-Tyrol at Eggenberg as she awaited her wedding day as the new bride of Emperor Leopold I. Most remarkable in the present context were the extraordinarily elaborate processional arrangements that escorted Claudia Felicitas's arrival in Graz and the huge parade which marked her wedding day. Her vast travelling party featured more than three hundred and fifty participants. For the wedding day itself, the horse-drawn traffic was even more numerous and to a modern mind almost unmanageable. The luckless Count Oetting, *Unterhofmarschall* for the occasion, was faced with deploying more than ninety coaches, each drawn by six horses, followed by setting them safely on their way along the four-kilometre route from Schloss Eggenberg to the edge of the city. The coaches holding noble participants were 'preceded by small military detachments and accompanied by mounted escorts, the *arcieri* guards, the city councillors, servants, musicians, drummers, trumpeters and countless other people'. Although this was an imperial occasion, the vast procession and its successful management were used as much to advance the reputation of the owner of Schloss Eggenberg as to pay homage to Emperor Leopold I. They thus conjured influence – power – for a noble who, as the castle's restorer and owner, had served his community and its social and political order by investing heavily in his land's architectural and artistic inheritance.

A neutral city

In the early modern period, Liège was one of the great cities of Europe, rich from the manufacture of steel and arms, a city which, in the words of Chantal Grell's and Robert Halleux's chapter 'maintained a position of neutrality in a Europe torn by religious wars'. Ernest of Bavaria's joyous entry into the city in June 1581 may be read principally as an adroit balancing act by which Liège, keenly aware of its neo-independent status, offered its contribution to European peace. Liège contrived to give substance to its profession of neutrality even while exchanging oaths with the zealously Catholic Ernest, thus throwing clear light on how ecclesiastical and state politics might be conducted by skilful players. Ernest on his side assumed his part in the expected rituals of a joyous entry, accepting and returning the keys of the city, and even agreeing to swear an oath guaranteeing the city's rights and privileges. Such trading of power offers a remarkable contrast to the strained relationships of many so-called joyous entries.

Yet perhaps the most memorable aspect of the occasion was the huge procession which accompanied the entry. Ernest's entourage numbered 'more than one thousand cavalrymen, two-hundred-and-fifty infantrymen and two hundred notables' while in his immediate retinue were 'members of his council, more than six hundred common people and in addition to all these a personal escort of six hundred to eight hundred and fifty cavalrymen'. It was in this context that there occurred a slight but significant incident which demonstrated how breaches of expected protocol could take on in these charged circumstances a meaning that might threaten to modify the general climate of consent. Ernest's entourage passed before the assembled company and then, as recorded by the chronicler Théodose Bouille, as Ernest 'tried to dismount at the foot of the steps of Saint Lambert, the cantor of the church, pretending to assist him, puts his hand on the saddle, to mark that it belongs to him and the church'. Processions, as well as ritual actions may, as a result of their formal structure, be charged with political meanings, which the unwary may trigger.

Permanent space and provisional

While by definition ritual is unchanging, its form may respond to prevailing aesthetic styles. The study by Borbála Gulyás of Vienna's so-called *Schweizertor* (Swiss Gate) demonstrates the shared prevalence under Ferdinand I of an *all'antica* style. This style carried allusions both to festivals of the Roman world and to the antiquarianism of the Hofburg, Ferdinand's newly rebuilt main residence. The Swiss Gate had another and more directly political role. Its presence as a permanent structure – though considerably altered today – served to mark, as Gulyás expresses it, 'Ferdinand's fulfilled aspiration for the imperial throne' and, after his proclamation in 1558, 'continued to express the new emperor's power and dignity'. As successor-emperor to the ubiquitous Charles V, Ferdinand needed a mark of imperial status, and this the Gate went some way to conferring – in part as reminiscence of the numerous triumphal arches erected for Charles himself. It therefore extended the customary role of triumphal arches, making permanent reference to an immediate Habsburg past while shoring up in public esteem the present imperial incumbent. It also, by its built form and situation as an integral part of the newly significant Hofburg, lent authority to other, in this case ephemeral, events. These culminated in an astonishing *Feuerwerksschloß*[10] that accompanied Ferdinand's entry to his and the Habsburgs' imperial capital. Evidently, the combination of permanent and ephemeral continued to attract approval, since festival events of a similar kind – foot tournaments, jousts, tilts, a *naumachia* and others – continued in the same location throughout Ferdinand's reign, while also serving to celebrate the entry in 1563 of Maximilian, Ferdinand's son and emperor-to-be. The fact that the complete programme for this last-mentioned event was drawn up by the celebrated humanist Wolfgang Lazius serves to underscore the ambitious structural and stylistic range of a festival series that served a political as well as a social role through a devised combination of permanent and ephemeral elements.

Like Gulyás, Francesca Barbieri focuses on festival events and the temporary and permanent architecture which helped to influence the prevailing political climate, in this case of Milan. Barbieri pays special attention to two royal events, the entry of Margherita of Austria, on her way in 1598–1599 to marry Philip of Spain, son and heir of Philip II, and the entry in 1649 of Maria Anna of Austria, bride of Philip IV. Her main focus falls,[11] however, on the role of theatrical spaces in the politico-cultural life of Milan where, as she notes, 'theatre and theatricality constituted the most important communicative mode during the Baroque era'.[12] The location of a permanent theatre within the Palazzo Regio Ducale, the residence of the city's Spanish

---

10 German for a wooden castle filled with rockets which exploded as part of a programme of fireworks which also included an installation on the spire of St Stephen's Cathedral.

11 See Barbieri's chapter, '*Con grandissima maraviglia*: the role of theatrical spaces in the festivals of seventeenth-century Milan'.

12 Ibid.

governor, itself constituted a political act, whether its source lay in politico-cultural agreement, as in the case of the 1598 theatre, or in implicit challenge. Barbieri recounts how Margherita's entry motivated the construction of temporary and permanent structures in Milan's streets, even though the death of Philip II, father-in-law of the bride, curtailed the celebrations, especially as Margherita was about to become not merely a royal bride but on the accession of her husband as Philip III a Queen-by-marriage. Perhaps the most remarkable aspect of the festival events was the element of through-planning, as a result of which the allegorical significance of the name Margherita, related etymologically to the Latin *margarita* (pearl), was carried through from the seven triumphal arches, including the so-called, stone-built Porta Romana, to the naming of *Salone Margherita*, a hastily constructed permanent theatre in the *palazzo regio ducale*.

The integrally planned festival of 1599, backed by Juan Fernandez de Velasco, the Spanish governor, to celebrate the royal wedding, drew its significance from its service to Hispano-Milanese political and cultural relations in a period otherwise often fraught with hostility. The construction of a successor-theatre to the *Margherita* after an interval of fifty years served, for its part, as a tribute to Maria Anna, but more notably provided opportunities for the development of remarkably ambitious scenographic schemes. Once again, continuities of reference between the ephemeral *apparati* and allusions within the theatre performance proclaimed the festival an integrated whole. On this occasion, the iconographical scheme was in the hands of Jesuits, which may account for the noticeably moral–didactic accents of the allusions, ranging from stress on the bride's anticipated fertility to, as Barbieri notes, references to the moral–political term *magnificentia* (greatness, high-mindedness, magnanimity). Barbieri adds that the third festival event she notices, the wedding in 1672 of Gaspar Téllez-Girón de Osuna, the Spanish Governor of Milan, and Anna Antonia de Benavides, took place in an atmosphere 'complicated by the military and political presence of Spanish foreign powers'. Such a 'complication', fuelled by the unwillingness of the Milanese *Senato* to participate in the ceremony, underlines the cultural–political weight attached to festival and theatre in times of heightened political sensitivity.

Personal space in a public arena

Festival of its essence looks towards its public, whether common or elite. Maartje van Gelder's chapter,[13] while confirming this truism, additionally draws attention to strong private motivations – with distinct political implications – which in this instance informed festival events in the public realm. As festival books abundantly show, the anticipated audience

---

13 Ch. 9, 'Ducal display and the contested use of space in late sixteenth-century Venetian coronation festivals'.

of state-sponsored festivals frequently looked outwards, embracing both national and international observers. Festivals could also address a more local audience. It is unusual, however, even in the proudly republican *Serenissima*, to come across festivals which, as contemporary accounts show, took their origin from such personal, family-oriented sources as the coronation festivals discussed in Van Gelder's absorbing chapter.

The election in 1597 of Marino Grimani as Venetian doge was received with unbounded enthusiasm, Van Gelder tells us, by the *popolani* – everyday people – who in Grimani's case formed a considerable proportion, in today's parlance, of his target audience. Known for his benevolence to the populace, Grimani's election was met, according to contemporary chronicler Giovanni Rota, by a potentially disruptive tide of popular acclaim. The people, Rota tells us, 'as if moved to rapture by ecstasy and out of control with happiness, abandoned their homes, shops, squares and their own businesses', while converging on the ducal palace, singing and shouting in praise of the newly elected doge.[14] Allowance has to be made for commentator's effusiveness, yet the claimed enthusiasm was accompanied, it seems, by a soundscape which could only with the most meticulous forward planning be faked. The continuous ringing of church bells created a deafening noise, fireworks exploded and people lit bonfires on the Grand Canal and in every square and street, 'so that it seemed as if Venice was going up in flames'. The threat to public order, uncharacteristic of Venice, amounted, in van Gelder's words, to 'a festive frenzy that bordered on the riotous'. Grimani and his family, we glean, stoked the potential conflagration by distributing to the masses far more largesse, in money and kind, than the ducal oath promised or festival tradition allowed.

It is scarcely surprising that the privileged class saw these events as a threat to their right – sanctioned by the Venetian constitution – to exercise uncontested power. Grimani's political antennae had evidently failed him, even if he could claim that his actions had been motivated by generosity alone. A more overt challenge to the *status quo*, at the heart of van Gelder's discussion, concerned Grimani's wish to have his wife Morosina Morosini Grimani crowned *dogaressa*, in a ceremony for which there were few precedents. Conscious no doubt of his previous errors, Grimani repeatedly deferred the proposed coronation. His instinct for ostentation nevertheless won out, especially in relation to the presentation to Morosina of the Golden Rose sent to her by Pope Clement VIII as a personal gift. Van Gelder's subsequent discussion of the arch constructed for the butcher's guild on the Piazzetta and, especially, the *naumachia* financed by Grimani and staged by Dutch sailors at short notice, shows how the doge salved Venetian pride by skilful allusion to the city's long-maintained virtues and the abundance which, in a time of widespread dearth, its civic prudence had

14 Translation by Maartje van Gelder.

made available. The whole programme breathed political *nous*. It is perhaps glib to conclude that Grimani earned his posthumous soubriquet of *padre dei poveri*, or attained his long-cherished aim of having Morosina crowned *dogaressa*, as direct results of such *nous*. Yet his establishment of personal space within so volatile an arena as the republican politics of Venice shows a notable ability to profit from the seemingly irreconcilable tension between state and personal power in Venetian public life. At no other point in this book do we come quite so close to festive ceremony as intertwined personal and public expressions of power.

Soft power

The political and family circumstances surrounding the magnificent *giostra* (tournament) staged in Rome (February 1656) for the visit of Queen Christina of Sweden represent an interplay of personal and public reminiscent of Doge Grimani's divided ambitions. Joanna Norman's chapter highlights the 1656 event with particular reference to the fortunes of the Barberini family. As Norman puts it,

> By staging the most complex, splendid and lavish of all the festivities performed for the queen in Rome during this period, they [the Barberini] . . . saw a means of re-establishing their pre-eminence as the leading cultural players on the Roman stage, in the hope of thereby increasing their political importance.

The terms 'cultural' and 'political' are mutually interactive. The Barberini sought to exercise, that is to say, what is today called 'soft power'. In so doing, they responded to prevailing circumstances. Norman explains: Queen Christina

> had converted to Catholicism and abdicated the Swedish throne in the previous year . . . As the daughter of King Gustavus Adolphus, the Swedish monarch who had died for the sake of the Protestant cause during the Thirty Years War, her conversion represented an extraordinary victory for the Catholic Church over the continuing threat of Protestantism.

Some historians have questioned the depth of the unconventional Queen's conversion, but her presence in Rome and the closeness of her friendship at this point with Pope Alexander VII provided sufficient traction to drive the Barberini's family ambitions and justify the otherwise prohibitive cost of the elaborate *giostra*.

The 1656 celebrations included no fewer than three operas staged in the theatre of the Barberini *palazzo alle quattro fontane*. Norman calls the palazzo 'one of the most extraordinary constructions in seventeenth-century

Rome', an assessment underscored by its formidable presence in today's city. She adds that the palace's sheer grandeur allowed the Barberini to 'reassert themselves as a family able to stand alongside a new pope and a queen' – with the *giostra* as an insistence therefore of soft power buttressed by wealth. A related use of location had occurred in 1634 when the Barberini staged a *giostra* for Prince Alexander in the Piazza Navona, a public space with important historic, artistic and social associations situated in the contested, cramped arena of central Rome. Annexing it, therefore, for a family-sponsored artistic event must have struck contemporaries as akin to cultural appropriation. Norman, however, makes an important point. Drawing on the 'extravagant' festival book describing the occasion, she concludes that attendance at the event in the Piazza Navona could only have been available to the seriously wealthy and that 'the patrons of these events were, for all their references to the *popolo*, clearly intent on directing their efforts as much in print as in actuality at a self-selected elite audience'. The motives which prompted festival in the seventeenth century, as in the sixteenth, were rarely pure. Establishing personal space in a public arena entailed a choice of audience that was – with the Barberini and the Grimani – a matter of family ambition as much as political power.

Epilogue

A good play, Shakespeare's Rosalind tells us, 'needs no epilogue', yet, she concedes, 'good plays prove the better by the help of good epilogues'.[15] It was somewhat in this spirit that we invited our colleague Tim White to contribute an epilogue to the present book. This revised version of a previously delivered talk carries forward our book's discussion into a new era and a new topic: into pre- and immediately and more distantly post-revolutionary France and into new perceptions – new to this book – of food and banqueting as in themselves potentially communicating significant cultural and political messages.

White's discussion turns on three Parisian occasions which demonstrate evolving uses of banqueting's social and cultural meanings as they emerge in parallel with the macro-politics of a tumultuous period of French history. The first is the Funeral Supper given by the prominent *gourmand* Grimod de la Reynière the Younger in February 1783; the second, the Feast of the Federation, staged in 1790 through the determination of Charles, Marquis de Villette, to celebrate the fall of the Bastille one year earlier; and the third the so-called Banquet of the Mayors, held in 1900 at the instance of the then President of the Republic, Emile Loubet – after an even more recklessly ambitious banquet proposed by M. Grebauval, President of the Municipal Council, was cancelled. It is true that the three events were not

---

15 *As You Like It*, Epilogue lines 4–5 and 6–7.

directly comparable. Grimod's Funeral Supper offered a bitingly satirical take on the *grand couvert* which in its hierarchical assumptions typified the privileged world of Louis XIV's pre-revolutionary France – and which for informed spectators could trace its lineage to the Hell Banquet staged by the Roman Emperor Domitian many centuries earlier.[16] The Feast of the Federation (also known as 'The Day of the Wheelbarrows') was much more celebratory in intent, entailing astonishingly huge commitments of labour and resources and emphasising enthusiasm and inclusivity rather than the divisiveness characteristic of the Funeral Supper. The Banquet of the Mayors was no less astonishing in its ambition – White spells out the thousands of workmen, waiters and guests involved – but on this occasion reaching out from the metropolitan elite to the sometimes-ill-matched mayors of rural France. Yet, however disparate the aims and execution of the three events, White succeeds in tracing through their chronological sequence an evolving set of assumptions on what he discloses as the culturally significant potential of food to underscore social cohesion or social conflict.

The sense of an ending?

White's Epilogue brings to a conclusion a collection of chapters exploring *Occasions of State* across Europe over an extended period. It is hoped that the volume as a whole is not seen as confined in interest or application to the historic period to which it principally relates. Modern-day successors – if not equivalents – of early modern festivals raise equally teasing questions about society, power and display. We are confident that readers will find parallels in today's world and will read these back with enjoyment and insight into the complex matrix that was the festal world of Europe from the fifteenth to the seventeenth centuries.

16 For further information, see Epilogue (this book) footnote 8.

Part I
Performing diplomacy
Festival and the identity of the state

1   The identity of the state

A new approach to festivals in the early modern Holy Roman Empire

R.L.M. Morris

Rather than focusing on any specific festival occasion, this chapter argues for a new emphasis in festival scholarship, namely the analysis of identity, and suggests theoretical frameworks for this approach. The theories are put forward in relation to the Holy Roman Empire in the mid-sixteenth to seventeenth centuries, although the ideas presented here are applicable to court festivals across Europe throughout the early modern period. In adopting this fresh approach, research on court festivals can gain valuable insights from developments in anthropology, and from theories behind the study of material culture, sociology and other historical sub-disciplines. It is from this perspective that the full importance of festivals to early modern states emerges and that we can appreciate, and reassess our understanding of, the historical contexts in which these festivals occurred, rather than merely using our existing theories about those contexts to colour the way in which we view festival occasions. In the case of the Holy Roman Empire, such a focus on the rhetoric of identity, as it was deployed and fashioned through festival, will enhance our sense of how festivals retained their relevance in the early modern period and thus contribute to an emerging body of scholarship seeking to redress its neglect by broader theories of the state and state emergence.

Using court festival as a means of re-constructing early modern identities and of framing our understanding of early modern societies requires the adoption of a new methodology which departs from much existing historiography. Festival books have, to date, been studied mainly for the details they reveal about how court festivals were staged, the logistics of transforming a city by constructing ephemeral triumphal arches and other structures along the routes of joyous entries, the choreography of processions and the performances of masques, ballets and so on. Much has been learned about the embodied form festivals took. This has been highly instructive in providing a descriptive and narrative framework for festivals, an approach which could be characterised, within the English tradition, as being in the mould of Quentin Skinner's methodology in relation to historical texts, a methodology which built on the theories of the Annales School and was at the forefront of the emerging discipline of the history of political thought – and which centred on the paradigm that texts could, and should, be placed and read within their historical contexts and their relationships to other texts.[1] However, it is possible to push the argument further. Anthropologists such as Clifford Geertz have ascribed a formative role to ceremonies, rituals and festivals – arguing that these interactive occasions were not merely reflective of identities and social hierarchies but played an active part in creating, reinforcing and maintaining them.[2] Rather than simply placing festivals within a corpus of related materials and imposing on them a preconceived historical context, festivals can be studied in such a way as to enrich and inform our understanding of that historical context – to contribute to and reshape our knowledge of the political and social history of the place and time in which they occurred. If texts describing these occasions can be analysed in the light of historical contexts, historical contexts can also be analysed in the light of these texts. The equation is balanced.

A similar approach has been adopted in theoretical writing on material culture. Religion has been an obvious lens through which to analyse and assess material culture, the writing on which attempts to better understand past societies through the material artefacts they produce and use. It has been argued that 'material culture is as much a part of religion as language, thought, or ritual' and that religion may be understood as 'clusters of ideas and practices expressed and embedded within material objects, lived as stimuli to the senses, prompting memory and securing identity'.[3] Stated more broadly, many recent theorists hold that, in the words of Jules David Prown, 'the study of material culture is the study of material to understand culture, to discover the beliefs – the values, ideas, attitudes, and assumptions – of a particular community or society at a given time'.[4] On an even more theoretical level, Arjun Appadurai has contended that 'even though from a *theoretical* point of view human actors encode things with significance, from a *methodological* point of view it is the things-in-motion that illuminate their human and social context'.[5] So it is with festival as with

---

1 Compare Quentin Skinner, *The Foundations of Modern Political Thought*, 2 vols (Cambridge: Cambridge University Press, 1978). For an overview of the Annales School of historiography, see Peter Burke, *The French Historical Revolution: The Annales School, 1929–89* (Cambridge: Polity, 1990); Jean-Pierre V. M. Hérubel, *Annales Historiography and Theory* (London: Greenwood, 1994).

2 See Clifford Geertz, *Negara: The Theatre State in Nineteenth-Century Bali* (Princeton: Princeton University Press, 1980).

3 John Kieschnick, *The Impact of Buddhism on Chinese Material Culture* (Princeton and Oxford: Princeton University Press, 2003), p. 23; Miri Rubin, 'Religion', in Ulinka Rublack (ed.), *A Concise Companion to History* (Oxford: Oxford University Press, 2011), pp. 317–30, p. 330.

4 Jules David Prown, 'The Truth of Material Culture: History or Fiction?', in Steven Lubar and W. David Kingery (eds), *History from Things: Essays on Material Culture* (Washington, DC and London: Smithsonian Institution Press, 1993), pp. 1–19, p. 1.

5 Arjun Appadurai, 'Introduction: Commodities and the Politics of Value', in Arjun Appadurai (ed.), *The Social Life of Things: Commodities in Cultural Perspective* (Cambridge:

material culture – the performance of a festival, its imagery, form, content and choreography can inform a broader understanding of the society in question. It is possible to study identity through court festivals because these events were not merely a spectacular form of elite behaviour or even staged cultural performances of existing identities and social orders – they had agency.

Sociology, too, can inform an analysis of identity as it is revealed through court festivals. The majority of recent sociological research has adopted the 'social constructivist' position – namely that identity is 'produced through social relations'.[6] Following the mid–twentieth-century works of scholars such as George Herbert Mead, Norbert Elias and Erving Goffman, many sociologists now talk about identity as a 'process', constantly formed and reformed through social interactions and cultural influences.[7] Of course, the transitory and illusory nature of the lived experience of identity on an individual level does pose a challenge to those who study it, as many sociologists have observed. Craig Calhoun, for instance, speaks of 'the tension inherent in the fact that we all have multiple, incomplete and/or fragmented identities' and notes that 'there are always internal tensions and inconsistencies among the various identities and group memberships of individuals'.[8] If anything, these problems appear even more evident in attempts to recapture such experiences of self-identity in historical contexts. Yet Steph Lawler has questioned whether this is 'how identities are necessarily experienced', stating that 'as well as fluidity, we see very powerful expressions of fixity around identity', continuing 'I am not arguing that identity *really is* fixed and stable . . . but . . . we cannot simply overlook attempts on the part of social actors to make it *seem* so, to suppress and cover over cracks and instabilities'.[9] Surely such attempts at fixity, to 'cover over cracks' and to present a rhetoric of unified identity, are precisely what we see in early modern festivals.

Another contribution from sociology which is pertinent to festival is the concept of 'habitus' and its relationship to identity. Stephen Mennell employs 'habitus' to mean 'the modes of conduct, taste and feeling which predominate among members of particular groups', continuing that it 'can refer to shared traits of which the people who share them may be largely

---

Cambridge University Press, 1986), pp. 3–63, p. 5. For further, more recent examples of this theoretical approach to material culture, see, for instance, Tara Hamling and Catherine Richardson (eds), *Everyday Objects: Medieval and Early Modern Material Culture and Its Meanings* (Farnham and Burlington, VT: Ashgate, 2010).

6 For example, see Steph Lawler, *Identity: Sociological Perspectives*, 2nd edn (Cambridge: Polity, 2014), p. 3.

7 Ibid., p. 5.

8 Craig Calhoun, 'Social Theory and the Politics of Identity', in Craig Calhoun (ed.), *Social Theory and the Politics of Identity* (Cambridge, MA and Oxford: Wiley-Blackwell, 1994), pp. 9–36, pp. 24, 27.

9 Lawler, *Identity: Sociological Perspectives*, pp. 4, 5, 7.

unconscious', with the result that 'the components of the habitus of one's own group seem to be inherent, innate, "natural", and their absence or difference in the habitus of other groups seems correspondingly "unnatural" and reprehensible'.[10] The difference between this habitus and the closely related notion of 'identity', according to Mennell, 'is perhaps that "identity" implies a higher level of conscious awareness by members of a group, some degree of reflection and articulation'.[11] We, then, as students of festival, may be able to borrow these ideas by seeing generic courtly festival behaviour, the values of conduct, the type of clothing and so on as representing a habitus which fed into a noble identity articulated by the conscious choices of representation on particular occasions.

As already alluded to, this habitus and associated identity necessarily have an oppositional element. Lawler is not alone in declaring that 'all identities are relational in this sense: all rely on *not* being something else'.[12] Stuart Hall uses the term 'constitutive outside' to apply to identity, arguing that 'identities can function as points of identification and attachment only *because* of their capacity to exclude . . . So the "unities" which identities proclaim are, in fact, constructed within the play of power and exclusion'.[13] This raises the issue of identity and ethnicity. Thomas Scheff talks of 'ethnic conflict' based on identity including 'violence between groups with different *cultures*, including differences based on language, religion, race, and class'.[14] This definition of 'ethnic conflict' would certainly encompass the divisions drawn, and represented in festival culture, between the inhabitants of the Holy Roman Empire and the non-Christian culturally 'other' identities of the Turks, the Moors and the inhabitants of the New World. The Turks were frequently represented by characters, images and material culture in festivals, and occasionally by the physical presence of Turkish ambassadors, such as the carefully stage-managed appearance of Ibrahim Bey at the 1562 election of Maximilian II as King of the Romans in Frankfurt, an occasion which could also become incorporated into the rhetoric of the festival.[15] Together with Moors and the inhabitants of the New World, these excluded

---

10 Stephen Mennell, 'The Formation of We-Images: A Process Theory', in Craig Calhoun (ed.), *Social Theory and the Politics of Identity* (Cambridge, MA and Oxford: Wiley-Blackwell, 1994), pp. 175–97, p. 177.

11 Ibid., p. 177.

12 Lawler, *Identity: Sociological Perspectives*, p. 12.

13 Stuart Hall, 'Who Needs Identity?', in Stuart Hall and Paul du Gay (eds), *Questions of Cultural Identity* (London: Sage, 1996), pp. 1–17, p. 5.

14 Thomas J. Scheff, Craig Calhoun, *Social Theory*, pp. 277–303, p. 227.

15 Carina L. Johnson, 'Imperial Authority in an Era of Confessions', in Carina L. Johnson (ed.), *Cultural Hierarchy in Sixteenth-Century Europe: The Ottomans and Mexicans* (Cambridge: Cambridge University Press, 2011), pp. 197–230, esp. pp. 202–5. Other work on the European creation of an 'other' identity includes Nabil Matar, *Turks, Moors, and Englishmen in the Age of Discovery* (New York: Columbia University Press, 1999).

dipoles were connected to rhetoric concerning civilisation as opposed to the 'wild man'.[16] Carolyn Merchant has observed that, in the sixteenth century, 'civilized society' came to be contrasted with 'wilderness' and that 'to become "civilized" was to be brought out of a state of barbarism, to be instructed in the arts of living and to be elevated in the scale of humanity'.[17] Richard Cole, too, has noted the widespread use of 'wild-man folk-lore imagery' in relation to 'non-western peoples', stating that from the point of view of sixteenth-century western Europeans, 'as different as were the Indian and the Turk, both lived in barbaric cultures'. He has also stressed how clothing (or the lack thereof) was important in this 'wild-man' imagery which distinguished 'non-western' culture.[18] Through 'wild-man folk-lore' based partly on appearance, therefore, all 'non-western' peoples could be understood as forming a dipole to German civilisation. One frequently finds characters dressed as these peoples in festivals. The precedent for this can be seen in Hans Burgkmair's depiction of the people of 'Calicut' (a merging of Africans, Americans and Indians) for Emperor Maximilian I's 'Triumph' – a series of woodcuts sent to prominent figures within the Holy Roman Empire. Burgkmair's images showed the people of newly discovered lands displaying few marks of civilisation, being dressed in animal skin or simple feathers and likened visually to animals, thus portraying them as 'easy to subjugate, without pride'.[19] According to Ulinka Rublack, Burgkmair had, therefore, 'created ethnic stereotypes to serve imperial propaganda'.[20]

Another useful distinction to be found in sociological literature lies between 'subjectivity' and 'identity'. This is a distinction drawn by writers such as Venn, whereby 'identity' implies associations with normative and ideologically accepted social categories such as gender or nation. The process of a self, by contrast, being produced by unique formulations which cut across categories in complex ways, through transient lived experience,

16 See William O'Reilly, 'Turks and Indians on the Margins of Europe', in *Belleten, Dört Ayde Bir Çikar* (*Journal of the Turkish Academy of Arts and the Sciences*) LXV.242 (April 2001), 243–56. See also Urs Bitterli, *Die 'Wilden' und die 'Zivilisierten': Grundzüge einer Geistes- und Kulturgeschichte der europäisch-überseeischen Begegnung* (Munich: 1976), 2nd edn (Munich: C.H. Beck, 1991). However, Bitterli's work is limited in scope; see the review by Richard G. Cole in *The American Historical Review* 82.2 (1977), 347–8.
17 Carolyn Merchant, *Reinventing Eden: The Fate of Nature in Western Culture* (New York and London: Routledge, 2003), pp. 68–9.
18 Richard G. Cole, 'Sixteenth-Century Travel Books as a Source of European Attitudes Toward Non-White and Non-Western Culture', *Proceedings of the American Philosophical Society* 116.1 (1972), 59–67, esp. 62–5.
19 Ulinka Rublack, *Dressing Up: Cultural Identity in Renaissance Europe* (Oxford: Oxford University Press, 2010), pp. 178–9.
20 Ibid., p. 180. For another discussion of this theme, see Renate Pieper, *Die Vermittlung einer neuen Welt: Amerika im Nachrichtennetz des Habsburgischen Imperiums 1493–1598* (Mainz: P. von Zabern, 2000).

is referred to as 'subjectivity'.[21] Margaret Wetherell says 'it is "subjectivity" that makes it possible for any particular social identity to be lived either thoroughly or ambivalently, while "identity" helps specify what there is to be lived'.[22] While sources exist which could enable us to begin to reconstruct the subjective personal experience of individuals through their encounters with the identities embodied in festival occasions such as ambassadorial reports, diaries and so on, these sources are sparse and not without significant limitations. However, the study of identity – of what categories were established to be navigated by individuals within a given society – is possible through a close study of festival books and other relevant materials.

The early modern Holy Roman Empire presents a fascinating context within which to study identity as it was fashioned, represented and upheld by court festivals. This is partly because of the complexity of the Empire's political structure of diverse territories and vast geographical scope. Yet it is also because of the challenges to identity posed by the period's social, economic, cultural and political events. Sociological literature repeatedly observes that identity becomes more prominent in response to challenges. Harold Garfinkel shows how rules and norms are seen most clearly when they are breached, and so normative forms of identity are revealed by occasions when identity is seen to be questioned or directly challenged.[23] Similarly, Lawler declares that in popular culture identity 'becomes visible when it is seen to be missing', and that 'it is perhaps when identity is seen to "fail" that we see most clearly the social values that dictate how an identity ought to be'.[24] The elite ranks of the Holy Roman Empire faced an unquestioned crisis of nobility in the sixteenth and seventeenth centuries. Their identity was brought into question by the religious upheavals of the Reformation, the various political conflicts including the Schmalkaldic War, the Thirty Years War and the ever-present Ottoman threat. These conflicts were further exaggerated by the socio-economic changes brought about by the effects of New World trade and banking in raising the status and power wielded by merchant families outside of the established hereditary nobility, and the humanist claims that virtue is true nobility. In the face of such challenges, it was vital for the nobility of the Empire to re-establish their legitimacy through appeals to identity – this lay at the heart of nobility's court festivals.

Indeed, one might characterise the type of rule formulated in response to this crisis of nobility and centred on festivals as 'charismatic' rule reminiscent of the principles of Greek kingship. Lynette Mitchell, in her work on archaic and classical Greece, discusses claims to legitimacy through courage, heroic virtue, demonstrations of competitive skill and even quasi-divine

---

21 C. Venn, *The Postcolonial Challenge: Towards Alternative Worlds* (London: Sage, 2006).
22 Margaret Wetherell, 'Subjectivity or Psycho-Discursive Practices? Investigating Complex Intersectional Identities', *Subjectivity* 22.1 (2008), 73–81, esp. 75.
23 Harold Garfinkel, *Studies in Ethnomethodology* (Cambridge: Polity, 2004).
24 Lawler, *Identity: Sociological Perspectives*, p. 181.

virtue.[25] She cites an example of Dorieus attempting to claim rule over his older half-brother because he had 'manly courage' (*andragathia*) and was the 'first' (*protos*) among his peers.[26] Monarchs were to have more heroic virtues (*aretē*) than anyone else – which they could prove by founding cities, innovation or participation in crown games either in person or through a champion.[27] These virtues could elevate the ruler to almost-divine status. Mitchell observes that by 324BC 'Alexander the Great was openly recognized not just as a hero, but as a god . . . his virtue was enough to make him not just a hero but also divine'.[28] These ideas of nobility are echoed in our period and, particularly through innovation and skill, necessarily supported by learning, feed into humanist ideas of virtue and nobility. Festivals and the associated tournaments and entertainments provided platforms for rulers to demonstrate their skill, manly courage and heroism, by their own participation or that of their champions or representatives, while there were also multiple opportunities to demonstrate innovation as well as learning through the fireworks, machines, elaborate fountains and so forth (as well as classical allusions), and to have these noble virtues proclaimed and lauded publicly at the events and in the festival books commemorating them.[29] Festivals provided the perfect platform for the construction of 'legitimate' noble identity through 'virtue'. Moreover, Tamar Herzog's recent study of disputes over possession and boundaries in Europe and the Americas provides an idea which illuminates the importance of actively asserting and claiming such noble virtue. In discussing the role of civil and canon law in structuring disputes over territory and rights, Herzog shows the way in which the tenets of Roman law permeated society's thought-processes, and especially the concept that silence implied consent, and that rights must be specifically expressed in order to be claimed.[30] This is what happens in festivals, especially triumphal entries. The entries are a performance of legal possession by the entering noble, and a vocalisation of the city's rights. More than that, they are also a performance of, and an active claim to, an identity and its associated legitimacy in a context where silence forfeits such claims – thus giving a vital role to festival and the identity embodied within it.

25 Lynette G. Mitchell, 'The Women of Ruling Families in Archaic and Classical Greece', *The Classical Quarterly* 62.1 (2012), 1–21.
26 Ibid., p. 8.
27 Ibid., p. 16.
28 Ibid., p. 19.
29 On fireworks see, for instance, Simon Werrett, *Fireworks: Pyrotechnic Arts and Sciences in European History* (Chicago: University of Chicago Press, 2010). On fountains and the use of technology as evidence of beneficent rule in early modern Europe see, for instance, Luciano Berti, *Il Principe dello studiolo: Francesco I dei Medici e la fine del Renascimento fiorentino* (Florence: Edam, 1967); J.R. Hale, *Florence and the Medici: The Pattern of Control* (London: Thames and Hudson, 1977).
30 Tamar Herzog, *Frontiers of Possession: Spain and Portugal in Europe and the Americas* (Cambridge, MA and London: Harvard University Press, 2015), pp. 7–8.

The term 'identity' has become a familiar part of the parlance of historians both of early modern Europe and more generally. To take one example, Carter Vaughn Findley states in *The Turks in World History* that 'people throughout history have struggled to assert their identity' and that the history of Turkish 'expansion across Eurasia may shed a valuable light on the processes by which a large and diverse group of people established, transformed, and projected its identity across space and time'.[31] The study of this projection of identity is possible despite Findley's acknowledgement that 'each civilization, however much binds it together, is a site of contestation, difference, and inequality of access to its refinements' and that, while the notion of identity is inherently oppositional, 'diversity and contestation within civilizations . . . stand in the way of their clashing as coherent blocs'.[32]

It may well be true that contemporary 'Germans' and the audiences at court festivals did not consciously engage with their identity. Equally, the term 'Identität' does not feature in primary source material from this time. However, this does not preclude the presence of concepts of identity. For instance, at the festival in Stuttgart in 1609 to celebrate the wedding of Johann Friedrich, Duke of Württemberg, and Barbara Sophia, the sister of the Elector of Brandenburg, a pair of '*Teutsche Singer*' ('German singers') could appeal in song to the '*Teutsche Nation*' ('German nation'), '*Edles Teutsches Blut*' ('noble German blood'), '*Teutsche werde Macht*' ('worthy German might'), and '*Teutsch Hertz*' ('German heart').[33] At the same festival, 'virtues' rode as part of the bridegroom's procession, including '*GERMANA FIDES*' – meaning loyalty and faith.[34] The attribution of 'Teutsche' is indicative of a sense of 'Germanness', and the idea of 'Germana fides' suggests that certain characteristics could be considered as 'German'. Such notions are a foundation of concepts of identity. Moreover, in the study of history more broadly, words are often used which are not contemporary and processes and phenomena of which contemporaries were not necessarily

31 Carter Vaughn Findley, *The Turks in World History* (Oxford: Oxford University Press, 2005), p. 4. For further examples in recent early modern and broader historiography, see Rublack, *Dressing Up*; Alexandra Walsham, *The Reformation of the Landscape: Religion, Identity, & Memory in Early Modern Britain & Ireland* (Oxford: Oxford University Press, 2011); Len Scales, *The Shaping of German Identity: Authority and Crisis, 1245–1414* (Cambridge: Cambridge University Press, 2012). A slightly older example relating to a later period is Harold James, *A German Identity 1770–1990* (London: Weidenfeld and Nicolson, 1989).

32 Findley, *The Turks in World History*, p. 4.

33 Johann Oettinger, *Wahrhaffte Historische Beschreibung Der Fürstlichen Hochzeit . . . Der Durchleuchtig Hochgeborn Fürst . . . Herr Johann Friderich Hertzog zu Würtemberg und Teck . . . Mit Der . . . Fürstin . . . Barbara Sophia Marggrävin zu Brandenburg . . . In der Fürstlichen Haubtstatt Stuttgardten Anno 1609. den 6. Novembris. . .* (Stuttgart: 1610), pp. 109–10, trans. Anna Linton, in J.R. Mulryne, Helen Watanabe-O'Kelly and Margaret Shewring (eds), *Europa Triumphans: Court and Civic Festivals in Early Modern Europe*, 2 vols (Aldershot and Burlington, VT: Ashgate, 2004), vol. 2, pp. 58–73, pp. 62–5.

34 Ibid., pp. 60–61.

aware are described and analysed. Yet this does not, in and of itself, make such studies inherently anachronistic – the sensitive imposition of thematic categories of understanding should be at the heart of good historical analysis, allowing the idiosyncrasies, conflicts and contradictions inherent in past societies to be recognised yet rendered intelligible within an interpretive framework.

Court festivals were not restricted to elites but were devoid of meaning to those outside the court itself. Festivals involved the whole populace of cities, and must be seen not merely as a message delivered by the court to passive recipients from the lower ranks of society, but as a site of interaction between court and society more broadly – with the inevitable tensions which accompanied such encounters. Karl Vocelka has written that *'Feste ein wichtiger Bestandteil des Lebens in den Metropolen waren'* ('festivals were a significant component of urban life').[35] Larsson states, referring to the entry of Maximilian II into Vienna in 1563, that the planning of the entry required *'ein erhebliches Maß an Beratungen und damit an Kommunikation zwischen verschiedenen Instanzen und Individuen'* ('a considerable amount of consultation and moreover of communication between various institutions and individuals') and that this was even more the case for the implementation of these plans in reality. Vocelka continues:

> *Es ist anzunehmen, daß die Mehrzahl, wenn nicht alle Wiener Handwerker an den Vorbereitungen in der einen oder anderen Form beteiligt waren, sei es am Bau und an der Ausschmückung der Ehrenpforten, an der Herstellung des reichhaltigen ephemeren Schmucks in den Straßen und an den Häuserfassaden oder von Kostümen, Waffen, Fahnen etc.*

> [It is accepted, that the majority, if not all Viennese craftsmen were involved in the preparations in one form or another, be it in the construction and decoration of the triumphal arches, in the production of the rich ephemeral ornamentation in the streets and on the fronts of houses or of costumes, ceremonial arms, banners etc.]

Thus, the whole city became involved in the festival over a period of roughly two months.[36] In addition, the burghers and crowds played a significant part

---

35 Karl Vocelka, 'Höfische Feste als Phänomene sozialer Integration und internationaler Kommunikation: Studien zur Transferfunktion habsburgischer Feste im 16. und 17. Jahrhundert', in Andrea Langer and Georg Michels (eds), *Metropolen und Kulturtransfer im 15./16. Jahrhundert: Prag – Krakau – Danzig – Wien* (Stuttgart: Franz Steiner, 2001), pp. 141–50, p. 141.

36 Lars Olof Larsson, 'Höfische Repräsentation als kulturelle Kommunikation: Ein Vergleich der Höfe Maximilians II. in Wien und Rudolfs II. in Prag', in Marina Dmitrieva and Karen Lambrecht (eds), *Krakau, Prag und Wien: Funktionen von Metropolen im frühmodernen Staat* (Stuttgart: Franz Steiner Verlag, 2000), pp. 237–43, p. 238.

in the performances of the festivals themselves. When Princess Elizabeth entered Heidelberg in 1613, having married Friedrich V, Elector Palatine, in London, from the arch erected at the end of the market-place *'bis an das Speyrer Thor hinauß ist die Burgerschafft in zimlicher anzahl und wol staffirt in der Rüstung gestanden'* ('right out to the Speyer Gate a large number of the citizenry stood, well accoutred and armed'). The account added: *'So hatt auch ein Ersamer Rath die Stadtthor renoviren lassen und die Burgerschafft . . . sich frewdig und willig eingestelt'* ('A worthy council also had the City Gate renovated, and the citizenry had joyfully and willingly presented themselves for sentry-duty').[37] These events were about much more than speeches in Latin and elaborate emblems – court festivals and the associated music, processions, fireworks displays, tournaments and physical objects were multisensory events accessible, on one level or another, to the entire audience. The audience was crucial to the efficacy of the festival – without the populace lining the streets, cheering, standing in awe, and thus participating, the events would have had no meaning; a joyous entry was no acclamation of a ruler if no one acclaimed.

Yet, while the populace of a city could become involved with court festivals at every level, this is not to imply that these encounters between court and people were devoid of conflict or were only a means by which the court could project a message to the people at large – festivals could become a symbolically acted dialogue, often only facilitated by the ability of both sides to take their own meanings from the festival events. Thomas Rahn has gone so far as to say that *'Die politische Klugheitslehre der Frühen Neuzeit begreift jede Begegnung hoher Häupter als duellum, als eine Form der kriegerischen Auseinandersetzung, die – stellvertretend – auf dem Feld des Zeremoniells ausgetragen wird'* ('the political wisdom of the early modern period considered every encounter as above all else a duel, as a form of war-like contest, which would be vicariously acted out in the field of ceremonial').[38] Central to understanding the dialogue which could be embodied in a festival is the distinction which Vocelka highlights between *'Feste, die mit dem Hof verbunden waren und von ihm selbst veranstaltet wurden, und Feste, die für den Hof veranstaltet wurden'* ('festivals which were bound up with the court and were organised by the

---

37 *Beschreibung Der Reiß: Empfahung deß Ritterlichen Ordens: Vollbringung des Heyraths: und glücklicher Heimführung . . . Des Durchleuchtigsten Hochgebornen Fürsten und Herrn Herrn Friederichen deß Fünften Pfaltzgraven bey Rhein . . . Mit der auch Durchleuchtigsten Hochgebornen Fürstin . . . Elisabethen. . .* ([Heidelberg]: 1613), p. 136, trans. Anna Linton, in J.R. Mulryne, Helen Watanabe-O'Kelly and Margaret Shewring (eds), *Europa Triumphans*: trans Anna Linton, in J.R. Mulryne *et al.*, *Europa Triumphans*, vol. 2, pp. 80–91, pp. 86–7.

38 Thomas Rahn, 'Grenz-Situationen des Zeremoniells in der Frühen Neuzeit', in Markus Bauer and Thomas Rahn (eds), *Die Grenze: Begriff und Inszenierung* (Berlin: Akademie Verlag, 1997), pp. 177–206, p. 178.

court itself, and festivals which were organised on behalf of the court').[39] Particularly in the case of festivals organised on behalf of the court by local civic elites, court festivals could become a medium through which the burghers of a city could express their concerns and desires to their ruler, often by praising the ruler for qualities they would like him or her to display in future.

Theoretical developments in the field of diplomatic history may offer an insight into how these tensions inherent in ceremonial occasions could be overcome. Michael Talbot remarks that it 'is important to consider that these diplomatic rituals, as with any rituals, were only given meaning by those participating in and viewing them'.[40] Talbot then combines this observation with theory from Pierre Bourdieu and uses the result to argue that, in the case of his study of British diplomacy in the Ottoman Empire, 'polysemy seems to have permitted participation in these rituals largely without an overt expression or manifestation of those tensions, that is, multiple layers of meaning and interpretation enabled equal participation in potentially unequal settings'.[41] Nor is this the only development in diplomatic history which is of significance to festival historians.

Diplomatic historians have debated how central the state should be in historical research. Thomas Zeiler's commentary on 'The Diplomatic History Bandwagon', in which he proclaimed an 'era of innovation' and stated that 'diplomatic history is in the driver's seat when it comes to the study of America and the world', gave central importance to the state, arguing that diplomatic history is identifiable by 'an abiding concern with power – a power that emanates as much from the highest political echelons as it does from contact zones' and that 'maintaining the state . . . is essential to good research'.[42] In reply to this article, Jessica Gienow-Hecht disagreed, declaring that she remained 'less convinced than Zeiler that the state and power constitute the keys to "good research" in diplomatic or any other history'.[43] Diplomatic historians have begun to broaden their methodological approach. Karina Urbach claims that these historians 'have adopted new methods for their work by amalgamating cultural, semiotic, and anthropological ideas as well as by going global through multiarchival research'.[44] John Watkins, too, emphasises the need for

---

39 Vocelka, 'Höfische Feste', p. 142.
40 Michael Talbot, 'British Diplomacy in the Ottoman Empire during the Long Eighteenth Century' (Ph.D. Thesis, Department of History, School of Oriental and African Studies, University of London, 2013), p. 213.
41 Ibid., p. 214.
42 Thomas W. Zeiler, 'The Diplomatic History Bandwagon: A State of the Field', *The Journal of American History* 95.4 (2009), 1053–73, 1053, 1055, 1056, 1072.
43 Jessica C.E. Gienow-Hecht, 'What Bandwagon? Diplomatic History Today', *The Journal of American History* 95.4 (2009), 1083–6, 1084.
44 Karina Urbach, 'Diplomatic History Since the Cultural Turn', *The Historical Journal* 46.4 (2003), 991–7, 991.

diplomatic historians to engage with international relations theory, gender, and material culture in the form of gift-giving.[45] Anthony Cutler has also highlighted the role of material culture in diplomatic exchanges, arguing that there is a false distinction between court ritual and the imagined 'real substance of negotiations'.[46]

A move away from an exclusive focus on state institutions and an acknowledgement of the importance of culture in all its varied forms has also been evident in the development of historiography relating to state formation in recent decades. The concept of 'absolutism' in the sense of a monarch wielding virtually unlimited power through direct, central control has been eroded – this does not necessarily mean that the term must be discarded, but it should be understood in a more nuanced fashion.[47] Understandings of 'absolutism' which equate it with despotism are arguably due to distortion by early modern and subsequent political commentators.[48] The narrative of the rise of the 'nation state' in early modern Europe has also been the subject of revisionist critiques.[49] More recently, these narratives have been replaced by understandings of state formation which attribute a greater role to culture and the representation of monarchical power as essential in maintaining the illusion of absolute authority where it did not in reality exist.[50] In the case of the Reich, Barbara Stollberg-Rillinger's work attempts to answer '*die Frage, wie eine Gesellschaft im Bann einer kollektiven Fiktion gehalten wird*' ('the question, of how a society could be held under the spell of a collective fiction').[51] Henry Kamen has argued more generally for this period

45 John Watkins, 'Toward a New Diplomatic History of Medieval and Early Modern Europe', *Journal of Medieval and Early Modern Studies* 38.1 (2008), 1–14.
46 Anthony Cutler, 'Significant Gifts: Patterns of Exchange in Late Antique, Byzantine, and Early Islamic Diplomacy', *Journal of Medieval and Early Modern Studies* 38.1 (2008), 79–101.
47 For the classic rejection of this notion of 'absolutism', see Nicholas Henshall, *The Myth of Absolutism: Change and Continuity in Early Modern European Monarchy* (London and New York: Longman, 1992).
48 In the English tradition of political thought, Miller observes that Hobbes, in particular, gave the term its negative connotations. See John Miller, 'Introduction', in John Miller (ed.), *Absolutism in Seventeenth-Century Europe* (Basingstoke: Palgrave Macmillan, 1990), pp. 1–20, p. 1. Meanwhile, Burns has noted that in French, the term only entered political language in the decade following the revolution of 1789, either as the hated object of oppression which had been removed, or as an idealised period of order to which France ought to return. See J.H. Burns, 'The Idea of Absolutism', in Miller (ed.), *Absolutism in Seventeenth-Century Europe*, pp. 21–42, p. 21.
49 See J.H. Elliott, 'A Europe of Composite Monarchies', *Past and Present* 137 (1992), 48–71.
50 See, for example, Roy C. Strong, *Art and Power: Renaissance Festivals 1450–1650* (Woodbridge: Boydell Press, 1984); Peter Burke, *The Fabrication of Louis XIV* (New Haven: Yale University Press, 1992); or, focused on a slightly later period but with relevant ideas, T.C.W. Blanning, *The Culture of Power and the Power of Culture: Old Regime Europe, 1660–1789* (Oxford: Oxford University Press, 2002).
51 Barbara Stollberg-Rilinger, *Des Kaisers alte Kleider: Verfassungsgeschichte und Symbolsprache des Alten Reiches* (Munich: C.H. Beck, 2008), p. 8.

that nations were created on the basis of 'a series of shared linkages' which could be 'imagined' and which integrated local identities into a greater sense of 'belonging'.[52]

Kamen's assertion ties in with the approach adopted by the medievalist Gerd Althoff – *Königsherrschaft ohne Staat* – which side-lines a narrative of administrative and legal institutional development in favour of a more cultural approach to early modern rule.[53] Festivals and ceremonial and joyous entries were vital to early modern states. Peter Sahlins has argued that it was the royal presence, illustrating and demonstrating royal jurisdiction, which created territorial borders in the early modern period rather than physical demarcations. Sahlins states that 'the primary function of kings in the Indo-European conception of royalty was not to govern, to wield power, but to take responsibility for the religious act of tracing boundaries', and 'by their presence they *created* the territorial division' since 'in their absence there was nothing to define the precise territorial boundaries of their lands'. Ultimately, Sahlins contends, 'the seventeenth-century state was not, strictly speaking, a territorial state: it was structured instead around "jurisdictions" '.[54] Rulers were present and were seen to be present, and this was vital to state formation, the delineation of their jurisdiction and the creation of identities associated with it.

The question of German identity remains a somewhat fraught and problematic one in historiography. It is bound up with Germany's twentieth-century history and the concept of a German *Sonderweg* leading inevitably to the First World War, the rise of National Socialism, and the Second World War. In his book, *A German Identity 1770–1990*, published in 1989 – the year of the fall of the Berlin Wall – Harold James demonstrates this conflation of the history of German identity with modern concerns.[55] James admits that his account 'tries to point a moral rather than to adorn a tale'.[56] He outlines a 'cycle of German national doctrines' which is 'not just of historical interest', declaring that he hopes 'we can learn something from the first terrifying cycle' as Germany attempted to re-examine a 'painful and even traumatic past' which 'contains the evils and the horrors of National Socialism'. James concludes:

> We may therefore speak of a cycle of answers to the problem which Germans so insistently posed themselves: what constituted national identity? It moved from cultural, to political, to economic, and then

---

52 Henry Kamen, *Early Modern European Society* (London and New York: Routledge, 2000), esp. pp. 6–7.

53 Gerd Althoff, *Die Ottonen: Königsherrschaft ohne Staat* (Stuttgart: Kohlhammer, 2000).

54 Peter Sahlins, *Boundaries: The Making of France and Spain in the Pyrenees* (Berkeley, Los Angeles and Oxford: University of California Press, 1989), pp. 27–8.

55 James, *A German Identity*.

56 Ibid., p. 2.

back to a series of cultural claims. This is the peculiar cycle that justifies a German claim to uniqueness.[57]

As James also observed, the issue became politicised within post-war Germany. From the 1970s especially 'on all parts of the political spectrum, the quest for a substitute for the economic goal – for national identity – became more of a political issue', and the Federal President Richard von Weizsäcker called 'for an open confrontation and reckoning with the past as the only possibility to identify ways in which the "new", post-1945 nation has transcended the social and political limitations of the "old" Germany'.[58] Just over a decade after James's analysis, Heinrich August Winkler's *Der lange Weg nach Westen* charted the development of Germany towards a post-classical nation state which could facilitate a non-threatening German identity, and declared that the specifically German path had ended with the events of 1989–1990.[59] In this account, as in numerous others, the period of the Holy Roman Empire is identified as a crucial element preventing Germany from developing in the same manner as other European nations. Under this shadow of more recent times, fuelled by twentieth-century political concerns, it has been difficult for scholars to analyse 'German' cultural identities, particularly in relation to a time-period in which the Holy Roman Empire spanned vast swaths of Europe. It is only very recently that it has become possible for historians to begin to view the discussion in different terms and, indeed, for historians to be willing to do so. Still, however, the issue of 'German' identity has very rarely been tackled head-on for the early modern period.[60]

The issue of German identity and ideas of a German Nation are also complicated by the historiography relating to nationalism. This historiography, too, has been heavily influenced by contemporary concerns. Michael Hechter declared in his analysis of the subject that 'nationalism and its close cousin, ethnicity, currently are the most potent political forces in the world' and that 'there is a pervasive interest in containing its dark side', while István Deák wrote in 1990 that 'today, as we begin to accommodate the idea of a gradual disappearance of nation-states' the 'supranational Habsburg dynasty' could provide lessons to post-1918 central and east central European nation states.[61] Much of this historiography has restricted nationalism,

57 Ibid., pp. 3, 4, 217.
58 Ibid., pp. 4–5.
59 Heinrich August Winkler, *Der lange Weg nach Westen* (Munich: Beck, 2000).
60 Len Scales has recently attempted to do so for the preceding period. See Scales, *The Shaping of German Identity*. One notable piece relating to the early modern period is Joachim Whaley, 'A German Nation? National and Confessional Identities Before the Thirty Years' War', in R.J.W. Evans, Michael Schaich and Peter H. Wilson (eds), *The Holy Roman Empire 1495–1806* (Oxford: Oxford University Press, 2011), pp. 303–21.
61 Michael Hechter, *Containing Nationalism* (Oxford: Oxford University Press, 2000), pp. 3, 18; István Deák, *Beyond Nationalism: A Social & Political History of the Habsburg Officer Corps 1848–1918* (Oxford and New York: Oxford University Press, 1990), p. 9.

and with it, to an extent, the concept of nations, to the political sphere and, for the most part, to the modern period. Hechter's definition of nationalism as 'collective action designed to render the boundaries of the nation congruent with those of its governance unit' confines nationalism to the modern period. He sees direct rule, where 'the centre assumes full responsibility for governing the entire polity' as a necessary precondition for nationalism, and this only became 'technically possible' with 'modern communications technology . . . and the other accoutrements of the industrial revolution'.[62] Hechter also believes that 'nationalism is, above all, political' and that the 'literary, musical, and artistic aspects of nationalism may be eminently worthy of study, but they ultimately are not responsible for the growing interest in the subject'.[63] Other theorists, however, have been less restrictive. Ernest Renan famously declared that 'the existence of a nation . . . is an everyday plebiscite'; Max Weber observed that 'one may exact from certain groups of men a specific sentiment of solidarity in the face of other groups' and thus concluded that 'the concept belongs in the sphere of values'; and Hans Kohn argued that 'nationalism is first and foremost a state of mind, an act of consciousness'.[64] These definitions are of far greater utility for thinking about early modern proto-nationalism, cultural 'nations' and the 'German' identities revealed in the court festivals of the early modern Holy Roman Empire.

Indeed, studying the court festivals of the Holy Roman Empire with an emphasis on identity, and taking a nuanced approach to state formation and cultural nationhood, can enable us to reintegrate this area into a holistic view of early modern European geopolitics. There have been significant changes in political historiography relating to the Holy Roman Empire, especially since the reunification of Germany. In the nineteenth and early twentieth centuries, the early modern period was characterised by nationalist historiography as one of decline and decay for the Empire.[65] Indeed, Peter Claus Hartmann has vividly described this characterisation of the '*stark föderalistische, militärisch sehr schwache Alte Reich mit wenig ausgeprägter Zentrale als zerrissenes, morsches, kaum lebensfähiges, anachronistisches, veraltetes und schwächliches Gebilde*' ('severely federalist, very militarily weak Old Reich with little pronounced central rule as a fragmented, decayed, scarcely viable, anachronistic, outdated and sickly entity').[66] However, Hartmann's view has

---

62 Ibid., pp. 7, 28, 29.
63 Ibid., p. 6.
64 Ernest Renan, *Qu'est-ce qu'une nation?* (1882), as quoted in John Hutchinson and Anthony D. Smith (eds), *Nationalism* (Oxford: Oxford University Press, 1994), p. 7; Max Weber, *Economy and Society* (1922), eds Guenther Roth and Claus Wittich (Berkeley: University of California Press, 1978), p. 922; Hans Kohn, *The Idea of Nationalism* (New York: Palgrave Macmillan, 1944), p. 11.
65 See Georg Eckert and Gerrit Walther, 'Die Geschichte der Frühneuzeitforschung in der Historischen Zeitschrift 1859–2009', *Historische Zeitschrift* 289 (2009), 149–97.
66 Peter Claus Hartmann, *Das Heilige Römische Reich deutscher Nation in der Neuzeit 1486–1806* (Stuttgart: Philipp Reclam, 2005).

begun to be discredited. In the mid-1980s, Peter Moraw argued that the fourteenth and fifteenth centuries witnessed the foundation and strengthening of an infrastructure which culminated in the reforms of Maximilian I in around 1500, and established a framework for the following three centuries.[67] Furthermore, rather than depicting the empire as a loose, anachronistic, confusing conglomeration of distinct territories, Georg Schmidt went so far as to propose that the early modern Reich should be regarded as a state with many similarities with, as well as some differences from, other contemporary European states.[68] Joachim Whaley has also recently shown that the Holy Roman Empire of this period can be seen in a much more coherent manner, as a 'dynamically evolving polity' rather than a stagnating one.[69] Moreover, Ronald Asch has observed that seventeenth-century legal theorists 'were able to present the Empire as a true state, not too different from the great monarchies of western Europe, without denying the privileges and autonomy of the princes of the Empire'.[70]

The reason, ultimately, that such diverse lands should be considered to be as coherent an entity as other contemporary states is precisely because of the ability and desire of its nobility to create, sustain and propagate a unifying rhetoric of identity and resulting legitimacy of power, superseding the various elements of heterogeneity. To this aim, court festivals were absolutely central. The study of identity construction through court festivals will contribute to this emerging trend in scholarship on the German-speaking lands and allow us, too, to observe a coherent structure in place of the hazily articulated model of bewilderingly heterogeneous elements which has so often been imposed on this region. Historians of early modern Europe may think in terms of territories forged and upheld on the basis of performed identities, as opposed to being guided by ideas of confessional states, linguistic regions, or even composite monarchies. Such territories were not necessarily homogenous states, but ones which existed and acted on the basis of claims to legitimacy, contested or otherwise, which could only exist in the presence of a shared rhetoric of identity.

Bibliography

Primary Printed Sources

Beschreibung Der Reiß: Empfahung deß Ritterlichen Ordens: Vollbringung des Heyraths: und glücklicher Heimführung . . . Des Durchleuchtigsten Hochgebornen

67 Peter Moraw, Von offener Verfassung zu gestalteter Verdichtung: Das Reich im späten Mittelalter 1250 bis 1490 (Berlin: Propyläen, 1985).
68 Georg Schmidt, 'Das Reich und die deutsche Kulturnation', in Heinz Schilling (ed.), Heiliges Römisches Reich Deutscher Nation 962 bis 1806: Altes Reich und neue Staaten 1495 bis 1806 (Dresden: Sandstein, 2006), pp. 105–16.
69 Joachim Whaley, Germany and the Holy Roman Empire, 2 vols (Oxford: Oxford University Press, 2012), vol. 1, p. 6.
70 Ronald G. Asch, The Thirty Years War: The Holy Roman Empire and Europe, 1618–48 (Basingstoke: Palgrave Macmillan, 1997), p. 20.

Fürsten und Herrn Friederichen deß Fünften Pfaltzgraven bey Rhein . . . Mit der auch Durchleuchtigsten Hochgebornen Fürstin . . . Elisabethen . . . ([Heidelberg]: 1613), p. 136, trans. Anna Linton, in J.R. Mulryne, Helen Watanabe-O'Kelly and Margaret Shewring (eds), *Europa Triumphans: Court and Civic Festivals in Early Modern Europe*, 2 vols (Aldershot and Burlington, VT: Ashgate, 2004), vol. 2, pp. 80–91, pp. 86–7.

Johann Oettinger, *Wahrhaffte Historische Beschreibung Der Fürstlichen Hochzeit . . . Der Durchleuchtig Hochgeborn Fürst . . . Herr Johann Friderich Hertzog zu Würtemberg und Teck . . . Mit Der . . . Fürstin . . . Barbara Sophia Marggrävin zu Brandenburg . . . In der Fürstlichen Haubtstatt Stuttgardten Anno 1609. den 6. Novembris . . .* (Stuttgart: 1610), pp. 109–10, trans. Anna Linton, in J.R. Mulryne, Helen Watanabe-O'Kelly and Margaret Shewring (eds), *Europa Triumphans: Court and Civic Festivals in Early Modern Europe*, 2 vols (Aldershot and Burlington, VT: Ashgate, 2004), vol. 2, pp. 58–73, pp. 62–5.

Secondary Sources

Althoff, Gerd, *Die Ottonen: Königsherrschaft ohne Staat* (Stuttgart: Kohlhammer, 2000).

Appadurai, Arjun, 'Introduction: Commodities and the Politics of Value', in Arjun Appadurai (ed.), *The Social Life of Things: Commodities in Cultural Perspective* (Cambridge: Cambridge University Press, 1986), pp. 3–63.

Asch, Ronald G., *The Thirty Years War: The Holy Roman Empire and Europe, 1618–48* (Basingstoke: Palgrave Macmillan, 1997).

Berti, Luciano, *Il Principe dello studiolo: Francesco I dei Medici e la fine del Renascimento fiorentino* (Florence: Edam, 1967).

Bitterli, Urs, *Die 'Wilden' und die 'Zivilisierten': Grundzüge einer Geistes- und Kulturgeschichte der europäisch-überseeischen Begegnung* (Munich: 1976), 2nd edn (Munich: C.H. Beck, 1991).

Blanning, T.C.W., *The Culture of Power and the Power of Culture: Old Regime Europe, 1660–1789* (Oxford: Oxford University Press, 2002).

Burke, Peter, *The French Historical Revolution: The Annales School, 1929–89* (Cambridge: Polity, 1990).

Burke, Peter, *The Fabrication of Louis XIV* (New Haven: Yale University Press, 1992).

Calhoun, Craig, 'Social Theory and the Politics of Identity', in Craig Calhoun (ed.), *Social Theory and the Politics of Identity* (Cambridge, MA and Oxford: Wiley-Blackwell, 1994), pp. 9–36.

Cole, Richard G., 'Sixteenth-Century Travel Books as a Source of European Attitudes Toward Non-White and Non-Western Culture', *Proceedings of the American Philosophical Society* 116.1 (1972), 59–67.

Cutler, Anthony, 'Significant Gifts: Patterns of Exchange in Late Antique, Byzantine, and Early Islamic Diplomacy', *Journal of Medieval and Early Modern Studies* 38.1 (2008), 79–101.

Deák, István, *Beyond Nationalism: A Social & Political History of the Habsburg Officer Corps 1848–1918* (Oxford and New York: Oxford University Press, 1990).

Eckert, Georg and Gerrit Walther, 'Die Geschichte der Frühneuzeitforschung in der Historischen Zeitschrift 1859–2009', *Historische Zeitschrift* 289 (2009), 149–97.

Elliott, J.H., 'A Europe of Composite Monarchies', *Past and Present* 137 (1992), 48–71.

Findley, Carter Vaughn, *The Turks in World History* (Oxford: Oxford University Press, 2005).

Garfinkel, Harold, *Studies in Ethnomethodology* (Cambridge: Polity, 2004).

Geertz, Clifford, *Negara: The Theatre State in Nineteenth-Century Bali* (Princeton: Princeton University Press, 1980).

Gienow-Hecht, Jessica C.E., 'What Bandwagon? Diplomatic History Today', *The Journal of American History* 95.4 (2009), 1083–86.

Hale, J.R., *Florence and the Medici: The Pattern of Control* (London: Thames and Hudson, 1977).

Hall, Stuart, 'Who Needs Identity?', in Stuart Hall and Paul du Gay (eds), *Questions of Cultural Identity* (London: Sage, 1996), pp. 1–17.

Hamling, Tara and Catherine Richardson (eds), *Everyday Objects: Medieval and Early Modern Material Culture and Its Meanings* (Farnham and Burlington, VT: Ashgate, 2010).

Hartmann, Peter Claus, *Das Heilige Römische Reich deutscher Nation in der Neuzeit 1486–1806* (Stuttgart: Philipp Reclam, 2005).

Hechter, Michael, *Containing Nationalism* (Oxford: Oxford University Press, 2000).

Henshall, Nicholas, *The Myth of Absolutism: Change and Continuity in Early Modern European Monarchy* (London and New York: Longman, 1992).

Hérubel, Jean-Pierre V.M., *Annales Historiography and Theory* (London: Greenwood, 1994).

Herzog, Tamar, *Frontiers of Possession: Spain and Portugal in Europe and the Americas* (Cambridge, MA and London: Harvard University Press, 2015).

Hutchinson, John and Anthony D. Smith (eds), *Nationalism* (Oxford: Oxford University Press, 1994).

James, Harold, *A German Identity 1770–1990* (London: Weidenfeld and Nicolson, 1989).

Johnson, Carina L., 'Imperial Authority in an Era of Confessions', in Carina L. Johnson (ed.), *Cultural Hierarchy in Sixteenth-Century Europe: The Ottomans and Mexicans* (Cambridge: Cambridge University Press, 2011), pp. 197–230.

Kamen, Henry, *Early Modern European Society* (London and New York: Routledge, 2000).

Kieschnick, John, *The Impact of Buddhism on Chinese Material Culture* (Princeton and Oxford: Princeton University Press, 2003).

Kohn, Hans, *The Idea of Nationalism* (New York: Palgrave Macmillan, 1944).

Larsson, Lars Olof, 'Höfische Repräsentation als kulturelle Kommunikation: Ein Vergleich der Höfe Maximilians II. in Wien und Rudolfs II. in Prag', in Marina Dmitrieva and Karen Lambrecht (eds), *Krakau, Prag und Wien: Funktionen von Metropolen im frühmodernen Staat* (Stuttgart: Franz Steiner Verlag, 2000), pp. 237–43.

Lawler, Steph, *Identity: Sociological Perspectives*, 2nd edn (Cambridge: Polity, 2014).

Matar, Nabil, *Turks, Moors, and Englishmen in the Age of Discovery* (New York: Columbia University Press, 1999).

Mennell, Stephen, 'The Formation of We-Images: A Process Theory', in Craig Calhoun (ed.), *Social Theory and the Politics of Identity* (Cambridge, MA and Oxford: Wiley-Blackwell, 1994), pp. 175–97.

Merchant, Carolyn, *Reinventing Eden: The Fate of Nature in Western Culture* (New York and London: Routledge, 2003).

Miller, John (ed.), *Absolutism in Seventeenth-Century Europe* (Basingstoke: Palgrave Macmillan, 1990).

Mitchell, Lynette G., 'The Women of Ruling Families in Archaic and Classical Greece', *The Classical Quarterly* 62.1 (2012), 1–21.

Moraw, Peter, *Von offener Verfassung zu gestalteter Verdichtung: Das Reich im späten Mittelalter 1250 bis 1490* (Berlin: Propyläen, 1985).

O'Reilly, William, 'Turks and Indians on the Margins of Europe', *Belleten, Dört Ayde Bir Çikar (Journal of the Turkish Academy of Arts and the Sciences)*, LXV:242 (April 2001), 243–56.

Pieper, Renate, *Die Vermittlung einer neuen Welt: Amerika im Nachrichtennetz des Habsburgischen Imperiums 1493–1598* (Mainz: P. von Zabern, 2000).

Prown, Jules David, 'The Truth of Material Culture: History or Fiction?', in Steven Lubar and W. David Kingery (eds), *History from Things: Essays on Material Culture* (Washington, DC and London: Smithsonian Institution Press, 1993), pp. 1–19.

Rahn, Thomas, 'Grenz-Situationen des Zeremoniells in der Frühen Neuzeit', in Markus Bauer and Thomas Rahn (eds), *Die Grenze: Begriff und Inszenierung* (Berlin: Akademie Verlag, 1997), pp. 177–206.

Rubin, Miri, 'Religion', in Ulinka Rublack (ed.), *A Concise Companion to History* (Oxford: Oxford University Press, 2011), pp. 317–30.

Rublack, Ulinka, *Dressing Up: Cultural Identity in Renaissance Europe* (Oxford: Oxford University Press, 2010).

Sahlins, Peter, *Boundaries: The Making of France and Spain in the Pyrenees* (Berkeley, Los Angeles and Oxford: University of California Press, 1989).

Scales, Len, *The Shaping of German Identity: Authority and Crisis, 1245–1414* (Cambridge: Cambridge University Press, 2012).

Scheff, Thomas J., 'Emotions and Identity: A Theory of Ethnic Nationalism', in Craig Calhoun (ed.), *Social Theory and the Politics of Identity* (Cambridge, MA and Oxford: Wiley-Blackwell, 1994), pp. 277–303.

Schmidt, Georg, 'Das Reich und die deutsche Kulturnation', in Heinz Schilling (ed.), *Heiliges Römisches Reich Deutscher Nation 962 bis 1806: Altes Reich und neue Staaten 1495 bis 1806* (Dresden: Sandstein, 2006), pp. 105–16.

Skinner, Quentin, *The Foundations of Modern Political Thought*, 2 vols (Cambridge: Cambridge University Press, 1978).

Stollberg-Rilinger, Barbara, *Des Kaisers alte Kleider: Verfassungsgeschichte und Symbolsprache des Alten Reiches* (Munich: C.H. Beck, 2008).

Strong, Roy C., *Art and Power: Renaissance Festivals 1450–1650* (Woodbridge: Boydell Press, 1984).

Talbot, Michael, 'British Diplomacy in the Ottoman Empire During the Long Eighteenth Century' (Ph.D. Thesis, Department of History, School of Oriental and African Studies, University of London, 2013).

Urbach, Karina, 'Diplomatic History Since the Cultural Turn', *The Historical Journal* 46.4 (2003), 991–7.

Venn, C., *The Postcolonial Challenge: Towards Alternative Worlds* (London: Sage, 2006).

Vocelka, Karl, 'Höfische Feste als Phänomene sozialer Integration und internationaler Kommunikation: Studien zur Transferfunktion habsburgischer Feste im 16. und 17. Jahrhundert', in Andrea Langer and Georg Michels (eds), *Metropolen und Kulturtransfer im 15./16. Jahrhundert: Prag – Krakau – Danzig – Wien* (Stuttgart: Franz Steiner, 2001), pp. 141–50.

Walsham, Alexandra, *The Reformation of the Landscape: Religion, Identity, & Memory in Early Modern Britain & Ireland* (Oxford: Oxford University Press, 2011).

Watkins, John, 'Toward a New Diplomatic History of Medieval and Early Modern Europe', *Journal of Medieval and Early Modern Studies* 38.1 (2008), 1–14.

Weber, Max, *Economy and Society* (1922), eds Guenther Roth and Claus Wittich (Berkeley: University of California Press, 1978).

Werrett, Simon, *Fireworks: Pyrotechnic Arts and Sciences in European History* (Chicago: University of Chicago Press, 2010).

Wetherell, Margaret, 'Subjectivity or Psycho-Discursive Practices? Investigating Complex Intersectional Identities', *Subjectivity* 22.1 (2008), 73–81.

Whaley, Joachim, 'A German Nation? National and Confessional Identities Before the Thirty Years War', in R.J.W. Evans, Michael Schaich and Peter H. Wilson (eds), *The Holy Roman Empire 1495–1806* (Oxford: Oxford University Press, 2011), pp. 303–21.

Whaley, Joachim, *Germany and the Holy Roman Empire*, 2 vols (Oxford: Oxford University Press, 2012), vol. 1.

Winkler, Heinrich August, *Der lange Weg nach Westen* (Munich: Beck, 2000).

Zeiler, Thomas W., 'The Diplomatic History Bandwagon: A State of the Field', *The Journal of American History* 95.4 (2009), 1053–73.

2   The Bastille banquet, 22 December 1518

Robert J. Knecht

A banquet held within the medieval fortress of the Bastille in Paris on 22 December 1518 is almost a tailor-made example of how architecture could be adapted to the needs of a new phase of international diplomacy that called for display and magnificence on an unprecedented scale. Few, if any, royal *châteaux* in early sixteenth-century France could offer a space large enough to accommodate a full-blown court festival. This required a surface area of between 350 and 600 square metres. The largest hall at Amboise measured only 168 square metres, as did the halls at Saint-Germain and Madrid.[1] On the face of it, the Bastille – a grim fortress built to defend Paris – seems a singular choice for a festive occasion involving a distinguished English embassy and the court of King Francis I, but it had two important advantages over other possible sites. Firstly, it was conveniently situated close to the royal palace of the Tournelles and the rue Saint-Antoine – a broad street often turned into a tournament field – and secondly, it had an inner courtyard of the size required to accommodate a large crowd of people. Furthermore, this was enclosed by high walls, sturdy enough to support an awning needed to provide shelter from rain. I am not aware of the existence of a comparable space in Paris at that time. There was the salle Saint-Louis in the Palais on the Ile de la Cité, but this was the home of the Parlement of Paris, the highest court of justice under the king. It had become detached from the court in the Middle Ages and had settled in Paris while the king and his entourage continued to travel around the kingdom. The hall was occasionally used for banquets, as in 1540 when the Emperor Charles V visited Paris on his way to the Netherlands, but it may not have been available or suited to what Francis had in mind in 1518.[2] His relations with the Parlement at that time were also strained, and one cannot imagine the magistrates, who were

---

1 Monique Chatenet, *La cour de France au XVIe siècle: Vie sociale et architecture* (Paris: Picard, 2002), p. 231.

2 R.J. Knecht, " '*Haulse (Paris) haulse bien hault ta porte*": The Entry of the Emperor Charles V into Paris, 1540', in Pauline M. Smith and Trevor Peach (eds), *Renaissance Reflections* (Paris: Champion, 2002), pp. 99–100. See also Margaret M. McGowan, *Dance in the Renaissance: European Fashion, French Obsession* (New Haven and London: Yale University Press, 2008), pp. 64–5.

noted for their pride, being willing to move for a banquet. There was also a courtyard at the Louvre, but this was largely filled by the medieval keep which Francis was to demolish in 1527 precisely to create space. The *Journal d'un Bourgeois de Paris* tells us that this was done at the cost of 2,500 *livres 'pour appliquer le chasteau du Louvre, logis de plaisance, et pour soy y loger'* ('to turn the castle of the Louvre into a pleasure palace where he might stay').[3] The courtyard was used for a banquet and a tournament during the Emperor Charles V's visit in 1540. A golden statue of Vulcan, 15 feet high and holding a flaming torch, was erected there as well as a golden hand also holding a flaming torch in each corner.[4]

The need for additional space must have been acutely felt as the French court grew in size and became ever more luxurious. In April and May 1518, the courtyard of the *château* of Amboise was transformed for the celebrations prompted by the dauphin's baptism and the marriage of Lorenzo de' Medici, duke of Urbino and Madeleine de La Tour d'Auvergne. The courtyard was covered with sheets strewn with gold *fleur-de-lys* and supported by ropes attached to three tall masts. The surrounding walls were hung with tapestries depicting scenes from antiquity. A month later, on 18 June, Francis I is said to have offered a banquet and ball at the manor of Clos-Lucé, near Amboise, which he had placed at the disposal of Leonardo da' Vinci. The old man was still living there, but there is no evidence that he had any say in the arrangements. The impresario was Galeazzo Visconti, a Milanese nobleman who had fought Francis at the battle of Marignano in 1515 but had since been pardoned by the king as well as knighted. In 1518 he was living at the French court with his wife and daughters. Around the courtyard were columns on two levels entwined with ivy; a wooden floor was covered with sheets bearing the king's device, and the roof consisted of blue sheets adorned with golden stars, planets and signs of the zodiac. The concept of celebrating an event on the basis that it was predestined and written in the heavens, originated in Florence under the Medici, but in France astrological speculations of this kind were deemed too pagan to form part of the permanent decoration of a royal palace. They were thought acceptable, however, as the festive decoration of an improvised venue. At one end of the courtyard at Clos-Lucé was a dais or *tribunal* reserved for the ladies. Lighting was provided by 400 torches. Each man at the banquet sat between two ladies.[5]

---

3 *Le Journal d'un Bourgeois de Paris sous le règne de François Ier*, ed. V-L. Bourrilly (Paris: Picard, 1910), p. 274.

4 Knecht, 'The Entry of the Emperor Charles V into Paris, 1540', p. 101.

5 The date given by Sanudo is questionable as Francis was at Angers on 18 June, having left Amboise on 22 May after spending some five months there. During his time at Angers he was given a feast at the *château* of Plessis-Bourré – which is noted for its regular architectural plan, including two courtyards, introduced into France by Jean Bourré between 1462 and 1478. See *Actes de François Ier*, vol. VIII (Paris: Imprimerie nationale, 1905),

The Bastille banquet of 1518 repeated, on a much grander scale, some of the festive arrangements previously seen at Amboise, Galeazzo Visconti being once again the impresario. It was the culmination of a series of diplomatic encounters between ambassadors of France and England which resulted in the signing of the Treaty of London – whose main provisions were for the return of the town of Tournai to France and for the eventual marriage of Francis I's infant son, François, with Henry VIII's equally young daughter, Mary. It was also part of a more ambitious treaty, including all the major powers, which was meant to achieve universal peace. The two kings at that time were in the flower of manhood, each determined to outdo the other in hospitality. The French embassy which travelled to England in September 1518 was led by the Admiral of France, Sebastian Guillaume Bonnivet. It caused a great stir in France as it was thought to be the finest that had ever left the country.[6] The ambassadors, according to one observer, were accompanied by thirty noblemen, fifty archers and companies of wrestlers, musicians and tennis-players.[7] They made their formal entry into London on 23 September. According to the Venetian, Giustiniani, such a display had never been seen before in England or possibly anywhere else.[8] The chronicler, Edward Hall, puts the numbers at eighty or more noblemen and 'young fresh galants of the court of France', accompanied by a 'great number of rascals and pedlars, and jewellers', who brought 'hats and caps and divers merchandise uncustomed, all under the colour of the trussery [baggage] of the ambassadors'.[9] Their train included '600 horses, seventy mules and seven baggage wagons'. [10] They were met at Blackheath by Bonnivet's opposite number, the Earl of Surrey, who was High Admiral, and a large number of English nobles. They escorted the Frenchmen triumphantly to London. In the days that followed, the negotiators on both sides got down to business while the young French courtiers danced in the Queen's chamber with English ladies. The merchants, who had smuggled their wares in the ambassadors' baggage, set up stall in Taylors' Hall, much to the disgust of English merchants, who could not compete with their duty-free prices.

---

pp. 424–5; Jean-Pierre Babelon (ed.), *Le château en France* (Paris: Berger-Levrault, 1986), pp. 128–9. I am grateful to Monique Chatenet for alerting me to the confusion over the date of the Clos-Lucé banquet.

6 *Le Journal d'un bourgeois de Paris*, ed. V-L. Bourrilly, pp. 62–3; C.G. Cruickshank, *The English Occupation of Tournai, 1513–1519* (Oxford: Oxford University Press, 1971), p. 230.

7 *Letters and Papers, Foreign and Domestic, of the Reign of Henry VIII*, eds J.S. Brewer, J. Gairdner, R.H. Brodie, *et al.*, vol 2 (London: Public Record Office, 1862–1932), p. 4356.

8 *Calendar of State Papers . . . in the Archives and Collections of Venice 1202–1603*, trans. and ed. Rawdon Lubbock Brown, 7 vols (London: Longmans, Green, Reader, and Dyer, 1864-- 1898), vol. 2, 1509--1519 (London, 1867), pp. 458–9, section 1074.

9 Edward Hall, *Henry VIII*, ed. C. Whibley (London: T.C. and E.C. Jack, 1904), vol. 1, p. 168. I have modernized the spelling.

10 *Calendar of State Papers, Venetian*, vol. 2, pp. 458-9, section 1074.

Henry VIII formally received the French ambassadors at Greenwich on 26 September. According to Nicolo Sagudino, the king sat at the end of the hall more splendidly dressed than he had ever seen before. Facing him were four hundred English lords, knights and gentlemen wearing silk and cloth of gold. On Henry's right sat Cardinals Wolsey and Campeggio and behind the English courtiers the French gentlemen who had accompanied the embassy. The ambassadors were presented to the king, who embraced them lovingly. The bishop of Paris delivered a speech in Latin to which the bishop of Ely replied, following which Henry, Wolsey and the ambassadors supped privately.[11] On Sunday, 3 October, Wolsey proclaimed in St Paul's cathedral the successful outcome of the Anglo–French talks and celebrated mass 'with unusual splendour'. This was followed by an oration delivered by Richard Pace, Henry VIII's secretary. The king and the ambassadors then swore perpetual peace between England and France at the high altar. Onlookers were much impressed by Henry VIII's magnificent attire. He wore a robe of crimson satin lined with brocade, a tunic of purple velvet peppered with pearls and precious stones and a collar studded with garnets as big as walnuts.[12]

Immediately after the ceremony in St Paul's cathedral, the whole company was entertained to midday dinner at the bishop of London's palace. This was followed in the evening by 'a most sumptuous supper' served in Wolsey's palace. There was so much gold and silver in the banqueting hall that the Venetian ambassador, Giustiniani, imagined himself in the tower of Croesus. After supper, minstrels came 'richly disguised' followed by three gentlemen in long gowns of crimson satin carrying gold cups filled with money, dice and playing cards. As they played at mumchance, the minstrels 'blew up'. Twelve couples then appeared all dressed alike. After dancing, they put off their masks to reveal the leading couple as Henry himself and his sister, Mary, dowager queen of France. Bonnivet and the French lords thanked Henry for giving them 'such disport'. They were then 'banqueted and had high cheer' before 'they all departed every man to his lodgings'.[13]

On 4 October, various treaties were signed and on the next day Princess Mary and the Dauphin were betrothed, Bonnivet acting as proxy for the latter. Mary, who was still only two years old, wore cloth of gold covered with jewels and a black velvet cap. She provided the assembled company with light relief by saying to Bonnivet: 'Are you the Dauphin of France? If you are, I wish to kiss you'.[14] The marriage contract was then signed at the high altar. On 7 October, jousts were held in which Henry VIII shivered eight lances. His prize was a richly caparisoned horse given to him by Bonnivet.[15] That evening, the final banquet exceeded all the other entertainments in

11 Ibid., section 1085.
12 Hall, *Henry VIII*, vol. 1, p. 170.
13 Ibid., p. 171.
14 *Calendar of Sate Papers . . . Venetian*, vol 2, p. 465, section 1085.
15 *Le Journal d'un Bourgeois de Paris*, p. 63.

splendour. Henry sat at the head of a table shaped like an enormous horse-shoe, flanked, on his right, by Queen Catherine and, on his left, by his sister, Mary. On Catherine's right sat Wolsey, a duchess, Bonnivet, a lady, the Spanish ambassador, another lady, and the Venetian ambassador, in that order. On Mary's left was Cardinal Campeggio, the bishop of Paris, another French ambassador, the Danish ambassador and so on, each man paired by a lady of the English court. An Italian observer noted that

> on the side-board were 82 vases of pure gold of various sorts, the smallest being the size of a tall glass, one foot high, and among them were four drinking cups two feet high, and four similar flasks, and two salt cellars, which were not used for the service of the table, though all the guests drank out of gold, and the silver vessels were innumerable.[16]

Hall tells us that two hundred and sixty dishes were served at the banquet and that a collation of wine and spices followed.

After supper, a masque, specially written for the occasion, was given in the great hall. It began with a man riding a winged horse which, he explained, was Pegasus. He had come to announce to the world the peace and the forthcoming marriage of Mary and the Dauphin. Two children sang a song in praise of these events. A curtain was then drawn back, revealing a castle standing on a rock in which was a cave containing nine beautiful maidens. Outside sat nine youths, while minstrels played off stage. On the rock grew an olive tree, a rose bush, a fir tree, a pomegranate and a lily. Between the olive and the rose sat a small girl with a dolphin in her lap. Pegasus's rider explained that the rock was the rock of peace and the plants were gifts to various rulers: the olive was for the pope as it signified peace, the fir tree was for the Emperor as it was the tallest and strongest, the lily for the king of France as it was beautiful and scented, the pomegranate was for the king of Spain as it was round and golden like the globe, and the rose was for Henry VIII for obvious reasons. But not everyone rejoiced. A Turk suddenly appeared with fifteen armed men who engaged in a fight, an equal number of men representing the allies. The youths and maidens then danced to the accompaniment of lutes and other instruments.

The end of the masque was the signal for another feast. 'One hundred courses of eatables, made neither of meat, nor of eggs, nor of cheese, nor of fish, though how made would be long to narrate, were served'.[17] After Henry and the nobles had partaken of them, there was a scramble for the rest and for comfits which Henry threw among the French guests. At the end of the evening, he distributed silver drinking cups to them and presented the robe he was wearing to Bonnivet. Before he and his companions left London,

16 *Calendar of Sate Papers . . . Venetian*, vol 2, p. 466, section 1088.
17 Ibid., p. 467, section 1088.

however, more gifts were showered on them. Bonnivet received three horses' load of plate worth 3,000 crowns. The bishop of Paris and other ambassadors received generous gifts of plate. The gentlemen in waiting had plate and apparel worth 500 crowns each, and the other gentlemen of the embassy were given 4,000 crowns to share between them. Finally, the ambassadors were given a fine suit of armour for Francis I, their royal master.

The warm and lavish reception given to Bonnivet and his companions by Henry VIII posed a serious challenge to the prestige of Francis I: he had to do better for the English ambassadors, led by the Earl of Worcester, who were soon despatched to France to hand over Tournai in return for a payment of 50,000 crowns. The English decision to return Tournai was part of a larger agreement which included a general treaty of peace, the contract of marriage between Mary and the Dauphin, a proposal that Henry and Francis should meet face to face and that French attacks on English shipping in the Channel should cease.[18] All of these elements were to inspire the iconography that was to animate the French hospitality.

The English ambassadors were received by Francis at the Palais on the Île-de-la-Cité on 11 December. Removing his bonnet, the king stepped down from his throne to embrace each of them. Three days later, the treaty was signed at Notre-Dame and a mass and *Te Deum* were sung. A stone screen between the choirs and high altar had been demolished to make way for a tent of cloth of gold adorned with a large embroidered salamander and supported by four pillars of silver gilt. The service was preceded by a procession through the streets of Paris described by the Bourgeois de Paris as '*la plus belle triumphe que on vit jamais*' ('the finest triumph ever seen').[19] The princes of the blood, nobility, five cardinals, household officials and troops took part, as all the church bells of the capital rang. This was followed by dinner at the Episcopal palace. During the next few days, the English ambassadors were received in turn by the king's mother, the queen, the mayor and aldermen of Paris and several high-ranking nobles.

The climax of the celebrations was the banquet at the Bastille on 22 December. In the words of Edward Hall: 'After all things concluded the French king made a banket house in the bastill of Parys between iiii. Olde walles'.[20] His description, to which we shall return, was only one of several published at the time. Among them, one is particularly informative: published immediately after the event and commonly known as the *Sylva*. The author was Bernardino Rincio, an Italian doctor of medicine from Milan who was attached to the *clientèle* of the French chancellor, Antoine Duprat. He had previously published an *Epithalamium* celebrating the forthcoming Anglo–French nuptials. The *Sylva*, which alone concerns us here, was the first work of its kind to appear in France. Festival books had previously all been in French and

---

18 Cruickshank, *The English Occupation of Tournai*, pp. 239–40.
19 *Le Journal d'un Bourgeois de Paris*, pp. 65–6.
20 Hall, *Henry VIII*, vol. 1, p. 173.

concerned with civic ceremonies, such as a royal entry, laid on by ordinary townspeople. The *Sylva*, written in a humanistic Latin, set out to inform the public of a court festival held in the privacy of a royal castle. The author tells us that it had been organised by Count Galeazzo Visconti.[21]

Entry to the Bastille in the early sixteenth century was through a gateway in the rue Saint-Antoine. For the ambassadors' visit, this had been adorned with pillars and pilasters. A Latin inscription above the gateway read in translation: 'Praise the Lord, all the nations'. Beyond it a path running alongside a moat led to a forecourt. This was transformed into a gallery 90 metres long and 7.20 metres wide, consisting of a trellis box supported by sixty wooden columns painted silver and supporting busts of famous men. Springing from the columns were wooden hoops, entwined with ivy, which formed a vault from which hung wreaths containing the arms of England and France. The gallery led to a forecourt, a bridge and another gateway. This, too, was adorned with flanking columns and pilasters that supported, on the right, the two lions of England and, on the left, a dolphin. Above were the arms of France framed by the collar of the order of St Michael. A Latin inscription read: 'The Temple of Peace comes into view'. This was the courtyard of the Bastille, which was 60 metres long by 24 metres wide. A number of alterations were carried out in preparation for the banquet. The sides were regularised by means of panels and the central area was given a wooden floor. At a height of about 16 metres, ropes were attached to the extremities of the walls, on which large linen sheets were suspended so as to form a pitched roof. At the cost of much effort, this was given gutters which were to prove a blessing on the night of the banquet when it rained heavily. Below the roof was a ceiling made of blue sheets, from which hung thirty large candelabra. Rincio tells us that the sheets were meant to represent heaven's vault. They offered a concave surface on which the signs of the zodiac were displayed. According to another account, these signs were fixed 'all around the hall'. It seems that there were two layers of blue sheets. Edward Hall describes the ceiling as follows:

> this house was covered with cords strained by craft, and every cord was wound about with box, and so laid crosswise one over another in fret, and at the meetings a great knob gilt with gold foil: over the cords was strained woollen cloths of light blue: this roof was 80 feet high . . . the roof was set full of stars gilt furnished with glasses between the frets: and in this house was 212 branches gilt hanged, and on every branch a great number of lights of white wax.[22]

21 Anne-Marie Lecoq, 'Une fête italienne à la Bastille en 1518', in *'Il se rendit en Italie' Études offertes à André Chastel* (Rome, Paris: Ediziioni dell'Elefante and CNRS, 1987), pp. 149–68; Stephen Bamforth and Jean Dupèbe, 'The *Silva* of Bernardino Rincio (1518)', *Renaissance Studies* VIII (1994), 256–315.
22 Hall, *Henry VIII*, vol. 1, p. 173.

Each candelabrum consisted of three superimposed rows of horns of plenty containing wax candles. Pulleys had to be substituted for thirty of the golden knobs to enable the candelabra to be lit more easily. The illumination they provided was reflected, it seems, by mirrors attached to the sheets above.

The hall itself was divided into three parts which the *Sylva* calls the *theatrum*, *orchestra* and *tribunal*. The *theatrum*, according to Lecoq, consisted of three superimposed galleries for spectators on three sides of the hall; the *orchestra* was the central part of the hall; and the *tribunal* was a raised platform filling the end of the hall opposite the entrance. Bamforth and Dupèbe disagree with Lecoq. They take *theatrum* to mean the festival arena as a whole, the *orchestra* as the platform and the *tribunal* as part of this platform. I shall follow Lecoq for the sake of simplicity and because her distribution makes more sense. Adjoining the platform and running along three sides of the hall were three superimposed galleries for spectators supported by sixty wooden pillars on which torches contained in horns of plenty were attached. Hanging from the balustrades were *chapeaux de triomphe* (wreaths) containing the arms of the two kings, the queens and the dauphin. According to Lecoq, the galleries on the right side stopped short of the platform to allow the insertion of a royal box lined with cloth of gold that was reserved for Queen Claude, the king's mother, Louise of Savoy and Antonia, the wife of Galeazzo Visconti. This would have enabled them to watch the events on the *tribunal* and in the *orchestra* without actually taking part. Bamforth and Dupèbe discount the box. They believe the three ladies were seated at the end of the right-hand gallery nearest the platform. Lecoq thinks the *orchestra* was filled with long tables and benches for the guests which would have been cleared for dancing after the banquet.

We can imagine that all eyes at the banquet were focused on the *tribunal* or raised platform at the far end of the hall where the king sat with his sister, Marguerite, the English ambassadors and other distinguished guests. Framing the *tribunal* were five columns bearing trophies whose capitals and bases were painted gold and silver. The space between them was wide enough for three persons standing next to each other. The walls of the *tribunal* were adorned with box, red and white roses above and cloth of gold below. Each side also carried three inscriptions. Covering the *tribunal* was a trellis of box and ivy entwined, more red and white roses and fruit hanging from each intersection. Lecoq argues plausibly that the trellis must have been supported by three more columns on each of three sides. Rincio tells us that there were also many green trees on the tribunal: cedars, olive trees, laurels, lemon trees and orange trees. They must have been on the sides of the *tribunal* so as not to obstruct the banquet and dancing. There were also four large *buffets* (sideboards) in the hall: two displaying gold plate and two displaying silver plate. Lecoq places the former at the rear of the *tribunal* and the latter in two corners of the *orchestra*. Bamforth and Dupède place them all in the four corners of the *orchestra*. It seems to me more likely that the sideboards laden with gold plate would have formed the background of the *tribunal* where the king, his sister and guests would have been eating. Rincio hails the *tribunal* as an island of earthly delights. It was a garden where the king and his guests entertained their English visitors amid trees that were still green despite the season and roses, red and white, symbolising England.

Rincio does not give us the fifty maxims written on tablets attached to the walls, but he does cite some others. At the back of the *tribunal*, behind the king's throne, a sun shone brightly and a Latin inscription read: 'Here is the true and serene day brightly lit by God's torch'. Inscriptions displayed on different parts of the *theatrum* and *tribunal* celebrated the Anglo–French peace. Above the king's throne a bright sun carried the words: *HOC EST DIES VERUS DEI CLARO SERENUS LUMINE* ('Here is the true serene day under the brilliant light of God'). A panel showing Eolus sleeping in the house of Morpheus bore the inscription: *NEC ME SOPOR ISTE GRAVA-BIT* ('This sleep will do me no harm'). Both inscriptions referred to the peace. Other images – a rider-less horse and a philosopher – pointed to the royal virtues of physical endurance and wisdom which had made the peace possible. Francis I's personal responsibility was underlined by a floor covering in his own colours of white, tawny and black. Other inscriptions adorning the *tribunal* claimed that the kings had secured the peace of their own free will; they had not allowed themselves to be manipulated by the goddess Fortune. A famous quote from the *Bucolics* acclaimed the peace as a return to the Age of Gold; another, this time from Scripture, implied that divine Providence was also responsible for the peace. As for the stars and signs of the zodiac, they celebrated a happy conjunction of the planets pointing to present and future happiness. A huge fire-breathing salamander, occupying the place normally accorded to the bear, served to remind guests at the banquet of Francis I's recent victory over the Swiss at Marignano. The idea of representing the signs of the zodiac as they appeared in the sky at a precise moment originated in Italy around the mid-fifteenth century. Decorations executed for the Medici often took their horoscopes into account.

At 4.30 p.m., Francis I entered the hall accompanied by the four English ambassadors, the papal legate, Cardinal Bibbiena, with his personal escort of bishops, and French princes. Queen Claude, Louise of Savoy, the duchess of Alençon and some thirty young ladies were already on the *tribunal* awaiting their arrival. The tables had yet to be laid. The musicians performed a *pavane* and the king danced twice with several persons. At 7 p.m., tables were set up on the *tribunal* and in the *orchestra*. The thirty or so guests on the *tribunal* sat with their backs to the wall and were served from the front as was the custom at court; the two hundred and fifty guests in the *orchestra*, including English lords and Italian ladies, sat on both sides of long tables. An important innovation was the mingling of the sexes: men and women sat alongside each other as they would do today. This had never been seen before at the French court: men and women had always sat at separate tables. The arrangement at the Bastille appears to have been an Italian importation. In Book III of Castiglione's *Il Cortegiano*, a cultivated lady converses on equal terms with male courtiers. The next stage of the banquet reverted to French tradition. This was the procession of the royal viands: twenty-five pages, preceded by trumpeters, archers, heralds and officials of the household led by the Grand Master, carried them on large gold platters. The procession made its way to the *tribunal* slowly along the full length of the hall. While Francis and his guests were served, two-hundred archers and twenty *prévôts* served the guests in the *orchestra* off silver dishes. Fifty *échansons* were also in attendance. At 9 p.m., after nine courses had been served, the tables were removed and dancing began. Most of the guests took up positions in the galleries of the *theatrum* whence they could watch the dancers in the *orchestra*. Groups of maskers wearing costumes, which Italian observers found baffling yet sumptuous, succeeded each other on the floor. Among the dancers were prominent courtiers and, of course, Francis I, who wore a long gown of white satin 'closed back and front like Christ's robe' and embroidered with gold astrological symbols. As the musicians struck up a *pavane*, the maskers were joined by ladies so as to form forty couples. The *pavanes* were performed in the 'Milanese manner' by an orchestra consisting of flutes, some made of wood and others of copper. The female dancers wore berets and very *décolletées* Milanese dresses made by ladies of the court under the direction of Visconti's two daughters. The dancing was new and Italianate. The king and his male courtiers had long been known to dance wearing disguise. A novelty at the Bastille was the way in which they invited ladies from among the spectators to dance with them. This had been seen in England on New Year's Day in 1512 when Henry VIII and eleven of his courtiers had invited ladies to dance with them. Some had accepted but others had refused, perhaps out of a sense of decorum. According to Hall, the masque was 'after the manner of Italy', and new to England. After the dancing at the Bastille which continued far into the night, young ladies offered the chief guests sweetmeats and preserves as Ethiopian perfumes wafted across the hall. The *fête* ended around 2 a.m.[23]

The Bastille banquet has to be seen as part of a prolonged celebration of the peace of London that culminated in the meeting of the two kings of England and France at the Field of Cloth of Gold. This took place on open ground near Calais. This time the problem was too much space rather than too little. Henry VIII ordered the construction of a temporary palace, which was shipped across the Channel prefabricated for assembly in France. Francis ordered three houses to be built in Ardres, and Henry VIII is known to have dined in one of them. The French king also put up an enormous tent outside the town which Florange describes in his memoirs as 'covered with sheets as had been done for the banquets at the Bastille'. He tells us that it resembled a Roman theatre, had stone foundations, and was completely

---

23 Marino Sanudo, *I Diarii*, vol. XXVI (Venice: Visenti, 1889), col. 348–49, cited by Lecoq, 'Une fête italienne', p. 167; McGowan, *Dance in the* Renaissance, p. 137.

round with 'rooms, halls, galleries, on three floors', but he adds that it was never used. The reference to the Bastille is interesting and the rest puzzling.[24] What is certain is that Francis erected a huge tent supported by two ship's masts lashed together. It is said to have measured sixteen paces across in the middle and to have been surrounded by a gallery eight paces wide. The whole was covered in cloth of gold with three lateral stripes of blue velvet 'powdered' with golden *fleur-de-lys*. On the top was a life-size statue, carved in walnut, of St Michael trampling on a serpent and an apple. Around this tent French noblemen had put up some three hundred smaller tents, which an eyewitness described as more magnificent than 'the miracles of the Egyptian pyramids and the Roman amphitheatres'. Unlike the Bastille awning, however, the king's tent was not weather-proof. After only four days it was brought down by wind and rain, the mast being shattered. Francis had to shelter within Ardres.[25]

The Bastille formula was repeated at least twice later in the reign of Francis I. It was used on 15 June 1541 for the marriage of the duke of Cleves with the princess of Navarre at the *château* of Châtellerault. A tall mast was erected in the centre of the courtyard to which were fastened blue sheets covering it completely. At one end of the courtyard were a few tiers of seats for the ladies and, in the centre, a canopy of cloth of gold beneath which mass was sung. Hanging in the courtyard were panels displaying the arms of the duke, the princess and the king.[26] In 1546, on the occasion of the baptism of Catherine de Medici's daughter, the Cour Ovale at Fontainebleau was used to exhibit royal treasures that had been assembled from all corners of the kingdom. In the middle of the courtyard, which was adorned with rich tapestries, a kind of theatre made of wood was erected. It had several doorways and was decorated with foliage of different kinds and wreaths containing the arms of England and France. Ropes attached to a tall mast rising from the middle of the theatre supported an awning of blue silk covering the courtyard. A tall pyramid at the foot of the mast had nine shelves on which gold plate and other precious objects were displayed. Guides stood by to explain their provenance to visitors, including many from England. Some, they explained, had been brought to France by Charlemagne; others were the gifts of foreign princes. The courtyard was also the setting for an entertainment lasting three days which comprised a banquet and a ball. Margaret McGowan gives a vivid account of the various dances and of the extraordinary costumes worn by the participants in her book on *Dance in the Renaissance*.[27]

24 *Mémoires du Maréchal de Florange*, eds R. Goubaux and P-A. Lemoisne, vol. 1 (Paris: Librairie Renouard, 1913), p. 263.
25 Joycelyne Gledhill Russell, *The Field of Cloth of Gold* (London: Routledge & Kegan Paul, 1969), pp. 30–31.
26 Chatenet, *La cour de France au XVIe siècle*, p. 231.
27 Félix Herbet, *Le château de Fontainebleau* (Paris: Champion, 1937), pp. 240–41; McGowan, *Dance in the Renaissance*, pp. 66, 139–41.

The building of permanent architectural spaces large enough to contain major court festivals did not begin till the end of Francis I's reign. The ballroom at Saint-Germain-en-Laye was completed during the reign of Henry II, and that at Fontainebleau in 1550. Originally this was to be a loggia of some 350 square metres on the first floor of the *château* above a portico between the Cour Ovale and the garden. It was to have a flat ceiling and to be lit on two sides by five arcades. The loggia was completed by Philibert Delorme and turned into the ballroom as we know it today by the wood-carver, Francisque Scibec. The great ballroom at the Louvre, measuring almost 600 square metres, was only finished in April 1551. Brightly lit on two sides by large windows, it had a *tribunal* at one end and an entrance surmounted by a gallery for musicians at the other. The *tribunal*, entirely surrounded by a colonnade, was longer than the width of the hall and five steps above its floor. It was where the high table was placed as well as the sideboard and royal plate. An important innovation was the separation of feasting from dancing. Under Henry III, the Louvre had two halls: a lower one for feasting and an upper one for dancing.[28] Things had moved on since those clever but makeshift arrangements half a century before at the Bastille.

Bibliography

Primary Sources

Actes de François Ier, vol. VIII (Paris: Imprimerie nationale, 1905).
Calendar of State Papers . . . in the Archives and Collections of Venice 1202--1603, trans. and ed. Rawdon Lubbock Brown, 7 vols (London: Longmans, Green, Reader, and Dyer, 1864--1898), vol. 2, 1509--1519 (London, 1867).
Edward Hall, *Henry VIII*, ed. C. Whibley (London: T.C. and E.C. Jack, 1904), vol. 1.
Le Journal d'un Bourgeois de Paris sous le règne de François Ier, ed. V-L. Bourrilly (Paris: Picard, 1910).
Letters and Papers, Foreign and Domestic, of the Reign of Henry VIII, eds J.S. Brewer, J. Gairdner, R.H. Brodie, *et al.* (London: Public Record Office, 1862–1932), vol. 2.
Mémoires du Maréchal de Florange, eds R. Goubaux and P-A. Lemoisne (Paris: Librairie Renouard, 1913), vol. 1.
Sanudo, Marino, *I Diarii*, vol. XXVI (Venice: Visentini, 1889).

Secondary Sources

Babelon, Jean-Pierre (ed.), *Le château en France* (Paris: Berger-Levrault, 1986).
Bamforth, Stephen and Jean Dupèbe, 'The *Silva* of Bernardino Rincio (1518)', *Renaissance Studies* VIII (1994), 256–315.
Chatenet, Monique, *La cour de France au XVIe siècle: Vie sociale et architecture* (Paris: Picard, 2002).

28 Chatenet, *La cour de France*, pp. 233–43.

Cruickshank, C.G., *The English Occupation of Tournai, 1513–1519* (Oxford: Oxford University Press, 1971).

Herbet, Félix, *Le château de Fontainebleau* (Paris: Champion, 1937).

Knecht, R.J., ' "*Haulse (Paris) haulse bien hault ta porte*": The Entry of the Emperor Charles V into Paris, 1540', in Pauline M. Smith and Trevor Peach (eds), *Renaissance Reflections* (Paris: Champion, 2002), pp. 99–100.

Lecoq, Anne-Marie, 'Une fête italienne à la Bastille en 1518', in *'Il se rendit en Italie' Études offertes à André Chastel* (Rome, Paris: Edizioni dell Elefante and CNRS, 1987).

McGowan, Margaret M., *Dance in the Renaissance: European Fashion, French Obsession* (New Haven and London: Yale University Press, 2008).

Russell, Joycelyne Gledhill, *The Field of Cloth of Gold* (London: Routledge & Kegan Paul, 1969).

Smith, Pauline M. and Trevor Peach (eds), *Renaissance Reflections* (Paris: Champion, 2002).

3 Triumphal arches in court festivals under the new Holy Roman Emperor, Habsburg Ferdinand I

Borbála Gulyás

The Habsburg prince Ferdinand I was proclaimed Holy Roman Emperor in 1558.[1] Until his death in 1564, his court put an emphasis on elements *all'antica* for several festivities. The ancient style was most apparent in classically inspired triumphal arches, which played an important role in the antiquarianism of the Viennese court.[2] The revival of interest in antiquity around the middle of the sixteenth century also significantly influenced the rebuilding of Ferdinand I's main residence, the Hofburg, the development of his collection of antiquities and the style of artworks *all'antica* he commissioned during this period.[3]

1 I would like to express my gratitude to Edit András, Miranda Blank, Renate Holzschuh-Hofer, Géza Pálffy and Friedrich Polleroß for help lent towards completion of this chapter and, for generous support of my research, to the Short Visit Grant of the PALATIUM Research Programme of the European Science Foundation (ESF), the "Lendület" Holy Crown of Hungary Research Project (2012–2017) of the Institute of History, Research Centre for the Humanities of the Hungarian Academy of Sciences, the Ernst Mach Research Grant of the Foundation Aktion Österreich-Ungarn (AÖU) and the Österreichischer Austauschdienst (ÖAD). The author is affiliated with the Research Centre for the Humanities of the Hungarian Academy of Sciences, Institute of Art History.

2 Friedrich Polleroß, '*Romanitas* in der habsburgischen Repräsentation von Karl V. bis Maximilian II.', in Richard Bösel, Grete Klingenstein and Alexander Koller (eds), *Kaiserhof – Papsthof: (16. – 18. Jahrhundert)*, Publikationen des Historischen Instituts beim Österreichischen Kulturforum in Rom, Abhandlungen, 12 (Vienna: Verlag der Österreichischen Akademie der Wissenschaften, 2006), p. 216. For court festivals under Ferdinand I, see Helen Watanabe-O'Kelly and Anne Simon, *Festivals and Ceremonies: A Bibliography of Works Relating to Court, Civic and Religious Festivals in Europe, 1500–1800* (London and New York: Mansell, 2000), pp. 2–5; Andreas Gugler, 'Feiern und feiern lassen: Festkultur am Wiener Hof in der zweiten Hälfte des 16. und der ersten Hälfte des 17. Jahrhunderts', *Frühneuzeit-Info* 11 (2000), 77–9; Matthias Pfaffenbichler, 'Das Turnier zur Zeit Ferdinands I. in Mitteleuropa', in Wilfried Seipel (ed.), *Kaiser Ferdinand I.: 1503–1564: Das Werden der Habsburgermonarchie* (Vienna: Kunsthistorisches Museum; Milan: Skira, 2003), pp. 277–81.

3 Polleroß, '*Romanitas*', pp. 211–20; Renate Holzschuh-Hofer, 'VI.7.1. Die Hofburg und ihre Ikonologie im 16. Jahrhundert', in Herbert Karner (ed.), *Die Wiener Hofburg, 1521–1705: Baugeschichte, Funktion und Etablierung als Kaiserresidenz*, Österreichische Akademie der Wissenschaften Denkschriften der Philosophisch-Historischen Klasse, 444, Veröffentlichungen zur Kunstgeschichte, 13, Veröffentlichungen zur Bau- und Funktionsgeschichte der

In general, ephemeral or permanent arches were based on architectural structures originally erected for the triumphal processions of ancient Rome. From the very beginning of the Renaissance, their historical reference widely attracted humanists, princely patrons and artists, who in turn examined and applied the original sources to reveal a knowledge of the ancient world. During the sixteenth century, the Roman triumph was also frequently discussed both in scholarship and literature as well as represented in various artworks, or imitated by the dramaturgy and decorations of *all'antica* festivities.[4] The ephemeral triumphal arches of court festivals, especially of entries, were frequently associated, as architectural symbols, with the victory parades of ancient Rome.[5]

'Paper pageants'

So far as the practice of the Holy Roman Empire[6] is concerned, the 'paper pageants'[7] of Emperor Maximilian I, the imperial predecessor of both Charles V and Ferdinand I, should be initially mentioned. The allegorical scenes of

---

Wiener Hofburg, 2 (Vienna: Österreichische Akademie der Wissenschaften, 2014), pp. 533–44; Borbála Gulyás, 'Inscriptions "all'antica" of the Sepulchral Monument of Emperor Maximilian I in Innsbruck by the Calligrapher George Bocskay', *Frühneuzeit-Info* 26 (2015), 219.

4 Werner Weisbach, *Trionfi* (Berlin: G. Grote, 1919); Roy Strong, *Art and Power: Renaissance Festivals 1450–1650* (Woodbridge: Boydell, 1984), pp. 44–50. Robert Baldwin, 'A Bibliography of the Literature on Triumph', in Barbara Wisch and Susan Scott Munshower (eds), *'All the World's a Stage. . .': Art and Pageantry in the Renaissance and Baroque: Triumphal Celebrations and the Rituals of Statecraft*, Papers in Art History from Pennsylvania State University, 6 (University Park, PA: Pennsylvania State University, 1990), vol. 1, pp. 359–85; Margaret M. McGowan, 'The Renaissance Triumph and Its Classical Heritage', in J.R. Mulryne and Elizabeth Goldring (eds), *Court Festivals of the European Renaissance: Art, Politics and Performance* (Aldershot: Ashgate, 2002), pp. 26–47; Veronika Sandbichler, 'Die Bedeutung hinter dem Sichtbaren: Allegorie – Trionfo – Visuelle Propaganda', in Wilfried Seipel (ed.), *Wir sind Helden: Habsburgische Feste in der Renaissance* (Vienna: Kunsthistorisches Museum, 2005), pp. 45–6; Randolph Starn, 'Renaissance Triumphalism in Art', in John Jeffries Martin (ed.), *The Renaissance World* (New York and London: Routledge, 2007), pp. 326–46; Veronika Sandbichler, '*Identifikationen*: antike Helden, Götter und Triumphe: Die Habsburger und ihre antiken Vorbilder im 16. Jahrhundert', in Sabine Haag (ed.), *All'Antica: Götter und Helden auf Schloss Ambras* (Vienna: Kunsthistorisches Museum, 2011), pp. 122–3.

5 Herta Blaha, 'Österreichische Triumph- und Ehrenpforten der Renaissance und des Barock' (Dissertation, Universität Wien, 1950); Hans Martin von Erffa, 'Ehrenpforte', in *Reallexikon zur deutschen Kunstgeschichte*, vol. 4 (Stuttgart: J. B. Metzlersche Verlagsbuchhandlung, 1958), columns 1443–1504.

6 For an overview of the entries of the Holy Roman Empire, see Helen Watanabe O'Kelly, 'Entries, Fireworks and Religious Festivals in the Empire', in Pierre Béhar and Helen Watanabe O'Kelly (eds), *Spectacvlvm Europævm: Theatre and Spectacle in Europe: Histoire du spectacle in Europe: (1580–1750)*, Wolfenbütteler Arbeiten zur Barockforschung, 31 (Wiesbaden: Harrassowitz, 1999), pp. 721–30.

7 Larry Silver, 'Paper Pageants: The Triumphs of Emperor Maximilian I', in Wisch and Munshower (eds), *"All the World's a Stage. . ."*: *Art and Pageantry in the Renaissance and Baroque*, pp. 293–331.

the enormous Arch of Honour (*Ehrenpforte*) and Triumphal Procession (*Triumphzug*), more than 50 metres long, together with Dürer's Great Triumphal Chariot (*Der Große Triumphwagen*) were personally commissioned by the emperor.[8] This 'memorial' project was labelled by Maximilian I in short as 'The Triumph',[9] designed in sections by his court humanists and several outstanding German artists including Albrecht Altdorfer, Hans Burgkmair the Elder, Albrecht Dürer, Jörg Kölderer and Hans Springinklee. Nevertheless, the triumphal elements *all'antica* represented in the monumental compositions were only realised as preliminary drawings, miniatures and woodcuts and did not materialise in Maximilian I's actual festivities.[10] Even so, the large, widely disseminated woodcuts vividly incorporated several main elements of ancient triumphs which followed the triumphal traditions of ancient Rome – besides the inheritance of Burgundian festive culture – in the visual imagery of the Habsburg emperor's court of the early sixteenth century.

Until Maximilian I's death in 1519, only the Arch of Honour had been published, since the Triumphal Procession and the Great Triumphal Chariot remained as yet unfinished. It is noteworthy that a few years later Archduke Ferdinand I ordered that the finished parts of the works should be collected from Augsburg and Nuremberg to be delivered to Vienna for printing.[11] Ferdinand I's instructions led to the first entire printed edition of the Procession in 1526, as well as a reprint of the Arch of Honour in 1526–1528.[12]

Charles V

It is noteworthy that ephemeral triumphal arches were introduced into the festivities of the Holy Roman Empire by Charles V, the immediate

---

8 Jan-Dirk Müller, *Gedechtnus: Literatur und Hofgesellschaft um Maximilian I.*, Forschungen zur Geschichte der älteren deutschen Literatur, 2 (Munich: Wilhelm Fink, 1982), pp. 148–59; Thomas Ulrich Schauerte, *Die Ehrenpforte für Kaiser Maximilian I.: Dürer und Altdorfer im Dienst des Herrschers*, Kunstwissenschaftliche Studien, 95 (Munich and Berlin: Deutscher Kunstverlag, 2001); Larry Silver, *Marketing Maximilian: The Visual Ideology of a Holy Roman Emperor* (Princeton: Princeton University Press, 2008); Starn, 'Renaissance Triumphalism in Art', pp. 327–30.

9 Szilvia Bodnár, 'Die Verklärung Kaiser Maximilians I.: Der Triumphzug, der Triumphwagen und die Ehrenpforte', in Szilvia Bodnár (ed.), *Dürer és kortársai: Művészóriások óriásmetszetei, I. Miksa császár diadala: Dürer und seine Zeitgenossen: Riesenholzschnitte hervorragender Künstler: Der Triumph Kaiser Maximilians I* (Budapest: Museum of Fine Arts, 2005), p. 27.

10 Schauerte, *Die Ehrenpforte*, p. 58.

11 Eduard Chmelarz, 'Die Ehrenpforte des Kaisers Maximilian I', *Jahrbuch der Kunsthistorischen Sammlungen des Allerhöchsten Kaiserhauses* 4 (1886), 311–12; Schauerte, *Die Ehrenpforte*, pp. 423–5.

12 Schauerte, *Die Ehrenpforte*, pp. 455–8.; Wilfried Seipel (ed.), *Werke für die Ewigkeit: Kaiser Maximilian I. und Erzherzog Ferdinand II.* (Vienna: Kunsthistorisches Museum, 2002), Cat. Nr. 1. (Veronika Sandbichler); Bodnár (ed.), *Dürer*, Cat. Nr. II. (Szilvia Bodnár). The finished *Great Triumphal Chariot* was first published by Albrecht Dürer in 1522 and 1523: see Seipel (ed.), *Werke für die Ewigkeit*, Cat. Nr. 46. (Veronika Sandbichler); Bodnár (ed.), *Dürer*, Cat. Nr. III. (Szilvia Bodnár).

predecessor of Ferdinand I. It is well known that during his reign Charles entered numerous cities throughout Europe, including principal cities of the German-speaking territories of the Holy Roman Empire, and cities in Italy, the Low Countries, England, France and Spain, providing spectacular models for future festivities in his own lands. These entries were based on both the traditions of the late medieval festivals of Burgundy and the imitation of ancient classical triumphs.[13] On such spectacular occasions as those on which Charles made his entries, temporary arches were erected with a frequency never previously seen in any princely European court, effectively stimulating the revival of the triumphal processions of antiquity within the Empire.[14] Ephemeral arches were featured for the first time in the Austrian hereditary lands of the Habsburg dynasty due also to Charles, who entered the cities of the Tyrol on the way from his imperial coronation in Bologna to the Diet of Augsburg in 1530. To greet him in Innsbruck – where he met Ferdinand I on 11 May – six triumphal arches were erected, while in Schwaz on 13 May there were a further seven.[15]

Ferdinand I, the Hofburg and the Swiss Gate

Eventually, Ferdinand I succeeded Charles V on the imperial throne. The proclamation of the new emperor was a result of an intense political debate in the Holy Roman Empire that had begun more than a decade earlier.[16] Since the late 1540s, Charles intended his son Philip to be recognised as his heir, in spite of the fact that his younger brother Ferdinand was his elected successor from the time of his coronation as king of the Romans in Aachen in 1531. By the end of the 1540s, due to altered political circumstances, especially the opposition of Protestant electors, Charles V's ambitious plans failed, and eventually the entire debate was concluded by the Treaty of Passau in 1552, negotiated by Ferdinand on behalf of Charles. This led to the Peace of Augsburg in 1555, which gave Lutherans religious freedom and established both Ferdinand I and the Habsburg dynasty's Austrian line as successors to imperial power.[17]

Obtaining the imperial title around the middle of the sixteenth century served to increase the antiquarianism of the Viennese court. The rebuilding

---

13 Strong, *Art and Power*, pp. 75–97; Watanabe O'Kelly and Simon, *Festivals and Ceremonies*, pp. 1–2; Gugler, 'Feiern', pp. 77–8.

14 Polleross, '*Romanitas*', pp. 208–9.

15 Blaha, *Österreichische Triumph- und Ehrenpforten*, pp. 12, 132.

16 Renate Holzschuh-Hofer, 'Radikal elitär oder schlicht bescheiden? Zur Ikonologie der Wiener Hofburg im 16. Jahrhundert unter Ferdinand I.', in Werner Paravicini and Jörg Wettlaufer (eds), *Vorbild – Austausch – Konkurrenz: Höfe und Residenzen in den gegenseitigen Wahrnehmung: 11. Symposium der Residenzen-Kommission der Akademie der Wissenschaften Göttingen*, Residenzenforschung, 23 (Ostfildern: J. Thorbecke, 2010), pp. 270–71; Holzschuh-Hofer, 'Die Hofburg und ihre Ikonologie', pp. 534–5.

17 Holzschuh-Hofer, 'Radikal', p. 271; Holzschuh-Hofer, 'Die Hofburg und ihre Ikonologie', pp. 534–5.

of the Hofburg, the main residence of Ferdinand I, offers an initial example. From 1521 Ferdinand was archduke of Austria and, since 1526, king of Bohemia as well as king of Hungary. As noted earlier, since 1531 he was also king of the Romans and his permanent residence within the Austrian hereditary lands of the Habsburg dynasty became Vienna.[18]

Located in the centre of the city, the rebuilding of his ducal and royal, later imperial, residence the Hofburg offers a prime example of the antiquarianism of Ferdinand I's court. Following the confirmation of succession to the crown of the Holy Roman Empire by the Treaty of Passau, the first significant artwork commissioned by Ferdinand was the Swiss Gate (*Schweizertor*)[19] (see Figure 3.1).

Located on the façade of the Hofburg, this imitated a Doric-order Roman triumphal arch. Besides its very central location, it is noteworthy that the Gate was erected in 1552–1553, after the promulgation of the Treaty of Passau but before Charles V's abdication (1555–1556), death (1558) and Ferdinand's actual proclamation as Emperor (1558). In this way, the Swiss Gate represented Ferdinand's fulfilled aspiration for the imperial throne, and after 1558 continued to express the new emperor's power and dignity.[20] Additionally, at the same moment, a well was built to the right of the Gate to serve the inner courtyard. This also related to the achievement of the title of emperor, with its stone curb decorated by a carved relief of the two-headed imperial eagle bearing the date 1552.[21]

The Swiss Gate was located on the façade of the newly built North-West Wing of the Hofburg[22] and served as the main entrance to the wing through the inner courtyard. The Gate's *all'antica* architecture was moreover

18 Christiane Thomas, 'Wien als Residenz unter Kaiser Ferdinand I.', *Studien zur Wiener Geschichte* 49 (1993), 106–10; Renate Holzschuh-Hofer, 'Die Wiener Hofburg im 16. Jahrhundert. Festungsresidenz Ferdinands I.' *Österreichische Zeitschrift für Kunst und Denkmalpflege* 61/2–3 (2007), 308–16; Renate Holzschuh-Hofer, 'IV.1.1. Die Alte Burg (Schweizerhof): 1521–1619', in Herbert Karner (ed.), *Die Wiener Hofburg*, pp. 84–6.

19 Wilfried Seipel (ed.), *Kaiser Ferdinand I.*, Cat. Nr. III.21. (Georg Kugler); Eckart Vancsa, 'Wien I.: Hofburg', in Artur Rosenauer (ed.), *Geschichte der bildenden Kunst in Österreich vol. 3.: Spätmittelalter und Renaissance* (Vienna: Österreichische Akademie der Wissenschaften, Munich, Berlin, London and New York: Prestel, 2003), pp. 275–6; Renate Holzschuh-Hofer, 'Die renaissancezeitliche Hofburg und das Schweizertor mit seiner Programmatik im Lichte der neuen Erkenntnisse durch die Bauforschung', *Österreichische Zeitschrift für Kunst- und Denkmalpflege* 62/4 (2008), 643–60; Susanne Beseler, 'Das Schweizertor und die Metamorphosen seiner Oberfläche', *Österreichische Zeitschrift für Kunst- und Denkmalpflege* 62/2 (2008), 660–71; Holzschuh-Hofer, 'Radikal', pp. 270–71; Holzschuh-Hofer, 'Die Alte Burg', pp. 111–22.; Holzschuh-Hofer, 'Die Hofburg und ihre Ikonologie', pp. 536–7.

20 Holzschuh-Hofer, 'Die renaissancezeitliche Hofburg', pp. 652–3; Holzschuh-Hofer, 'Radikal', pp. 271–2; Holzschuh-Hofer, 'Die Hofburg und ihre Ikonologie', pp. 536–7.

21 Holzschuh-Hofer, 'Die renaissancezeitliche Hofburg', p. 652; Holzschuh-Hofer, 'Die Alte Burg', p. 111.

22 Holzschuh-Hofer, 'Die Wiener Hofburg', p. 319; Holzschuh-Hofer, 'Die Alte Burg', pp. 109–11.

Figure 3.1 The front façade of the Swiss Gate of the Hofburg in Vienna (1552–1553).
Photo: Borbála Gulyás.

eye-catching, due to the fact that it considerably differed from the new façade, divided by regularly spaced and decorated rectangular windows.

At this point, it should be emphasised that the appearance of the Swiss Gate in the sixteenth century differed from its appearance today. Its present-day red and dark grey surface stems only from later periods.[23] Discoveries made during its recent restoration show that the Gate was originally built of a bluish-grey sandstone (the so-called *Flyschsandstein*) with only a few coloured and gilded areas. Holzschuh-Hofer's new reconstruction[24] shows these details were confined to the upper parts of the Gate on both façades, to be precise to their figural and inscribed details only. This kind of partial colouring highlighted in particular the figural elements and inscriptions *all'antica* of the entablature and attic. The large, variously coloured and gilded coat of arms of Ferdinand I, centred on the middle of the attic, decorated both façades of the passageway. It was flanked by two plain surfaces within profiled and gilded framing and bearing gilded inscriptions. On the outer façade was Ferdinand's name, current titles and the date of construction, 'MDLII', and on the rear the completion date, 'MDLIII'.

On the entablatures of both façades, the metopes of the frieze were filled with gilded stone reliefs. The symbol of a fire-iron with a flint and the St Andrew's Cross occupied the centre of both façades; together with the flames on the sides of the friezes these represented the Order of the Golden Fleece and the Burgundian inheritance of Ferdinand I and the Habsburg dynasty. (The same symbols were used for the carved frames of windows of the new wing.) In the metopes were grotesque heads and votive vessels, the symbols of Jupiter as the god of thunder, the 'combined' eagles of Jupiter and the Empire and bucrania (grotesque heads of cattle), together with various trophies standing for victory and visually evoking the traditions of Roman triumphs. According to Sebastiano Serlio, the Doric order of the whole edifice alluded to the ancient gods Mars and Jupiter, and the hero Hercules.[25]

The lettering of the Swiss Gate

The letter type of the inscriptions as well as their special technique also recalled ancient style. The inscriptions were written in classical square capitals, as frequently used in Roman monumental architecture, among other

---

23 Holzschuh-Hofer, 'Die renaissancezeitliche Hofburg', p. 658; Beseler, 'Das Schweizertor', p. 669; Holzschuh-Hofer, 'Die Alte Burg', pp. 114–15.

24 Holzschuh-Hofer, 'Die Alte Burg', Fig. IV.27.

25 Holzschuh-Hofer, 'Die renaissancezeitliche Hofburg', pp. 649–53, 658–60; Renate Holzschuh-Hofer, 'Feuereisen im Dienst politischer Propaganda von Burgund bis Habsburg: Zur Entwicklung der Symbolik des Ordens vom Goldenen Vlies von Herzog Philipp dem Guten bis Kaiser Ferdinand I.', *RIHA Journal* 0006 (16 August 2010). (www.riha-journal.org/articles/2010/holzschuh-hofer-feuereisen-im-dienst-politischer-propaganda, date of access: 10 December 2013), 67–83; Holzschuh-Hofer, 'Die Alte Burg', pp. 116, 119–20.

instances on the attic of a Roman-derived triumphal arch, such as the Swiss Gate. The construction of the Roman capitals was based on the perfect forms of square and circle. This concept was also applied to the ideal proportions of the human body, in which every part is considered in relation to the whole, as stated in the *De Architectura* of Vitruvius. The concept became widespread in the Renaissance from the fifteenth century on, due to the writings of Italian humanists, especially those collecting and studying ancient epigraphy. Such capitals *all'antica* were later popularised throughout Italy, and subsequently north of the Alps, by treatises on mathematics, geometry, architecture and calligraphy, each offering a variety of designs for ideal Roman alphabets.[26]

It is also remarkable that, despite all architectural details of the Swiss Gate being made of stone, the letters of the inscriptions were made of gilded bronze,[27] and each was separately fixed to the painted surface of the framed stone plates of the attic. The classical type and the golden colouring of the inscriptions with their special technique – oversized metal letters attached to a painted stone surface – imitated the bronze-inlaid inscriptions on marble of the Romans, as used also for inscriptions on permanent triumphal arches.[28] Similar examples will be provided to show that the colouring of ephemeral arches discussed here usually resembled marble, which was considered a noble material in antiquity.

Architects and theorists

Archival sources indicate that an Italian master, Pietro Ferrabosco, can be identified in connection with the Swiss Gate. Ferrabosco, an architect and painter, originated from Lombardy and served for a long period at the Viennese court, from as early as the 1540s to the 1580s.[29] Primary sources show that he painted the Gate's coats of arms, the background of the surfaces carrying the inscriptions in metal and the ceiling of the passageway.[30] This last consisted of depictions of the coats of arms of Austrian hereditary lands,

---

26 Millard Meiss, 'Alphabetical Treatises in the Renaissance', in Millard Meiss (ed.), *The Painter's Choice: Problems in the Interpretation of Renaissance Art* (New York, Hagerstown, San Francisco, London: Harper and Row, 1976), pp. 176–86.

27 Holzschuh-Hofer, 'Die Alte Burg', p. 111.The letters were gilded by a local master, Valthin Kraus: see Holzschuh-Hofer, 'Die renaissancezeitliche Hofburg', p. 645.

28 Holzschuh-Hofer, 'Die Alte Burg', p. 120.

29 Harry Kühnel, 'Beiträge zur Geschichte der Wiener Hofburg im 16. und 17. Jahrhundert', *Anzeiger der Österreichischen Akademie der Wissenschaften, Philosophische-Historische Klasse* (1958), 272–6; Péter Farbaky, 'Pietro Ferrabosco in Ungheria e nell'impero asburgico', *Arte Lombarda* 139 (2003), 127–34; Herbert Karner, 'Pietro Ferrabosco', in Artur Rosenauer (ed.), *Geschichte der bildenden Kunst Österreichs vol. 3: Spätmittelalter und Renaissance* (Vienna: Österreichische Akademie der Wissenschaften, Munich, Berlin, London and New York: Prestel, 2003), pp. 274–5.

30 Holzschuh-Hofer, 'Die renaissancezeitliche Hofburg', p. 645; Holzschuh-Hofer, 'Die Alte Burg', pp. 111, 114.

together with diverse grotesque ornaments.[31] Ferrabosco was also possibly involved in the architectural design of the Gate.[32]

The architectural projects Ferdinand I commissioned, as well as written sources, confirm that he was familiar with, and interested in, both the ancient architectural theories of Vitruvius and the contemporary works of Sebastiano Serlio. Primarily, the Swiss Gate imitated examples provided by Serlio's treatise.[33] The Books of his architectural manual, illustrated by outstanding visual material, were published from 1537 onwards, and by the middle of the sixteenth century its Italian editions and their translations were widespread throughout Europe.[34] In this regard it is noteworthy that the first German edition of Book 4 was dedicated to Ferdinand I as early as 1542 and that on its title page the rich grotesque decoration was surmounted by his coat of arms.[35] A special copy with hand-coloured illustrations, owned apparently by Ferdinand I, is now kept in Vienna, with its leather binding decorated by depictions of antique coins and bearing a dedicatory text to him made up of golden-coloured Roman square capitals.[36] The volume was published in Antwerp, not by the Italian architect, but by the Flemish artist Pieter Coecke van Aelst, who was court advisor to the governess of the Low Countries, Mary of Hungary, sister of Ferdinand I and Charles V, and also involved in the publication of the illustrated account of the well-known Antwerp Entry of Philip of Spain in 1549. At that time, besides the German edition, Coecke published Dutch and French translations of different Books of Serlio's treatise, some dedicated to Mary.[37]

31 The motifs of the ceiling are interpreted as a starting point for Ferdinand I's rule in order to obtain the imperial title, which is also represented here by the symbols of the Swiss Gate and its architectural forms as an end point: see Holzschuh-Hofer, 'Radikal', p. 272.

32 Géza Galavics, 'The Hungarian Royal Court and Late Renaissance Art', *Hungarian Studies* 10/2 (1995), 308. ⟨http://epa.oszk.hu/01400/01462/00017/pdf/307-332.pdf, date of access: 10 December 2013⟩; Péter Farbaky, 'Pietro Ferrabosco', p. 129.

33 Polleross, '*Romanitas*', pp. 215, 218; Holzschuh-Hofer, 'Die Alte Burg', pp. 116–22.

34 Herman de la Fontaine Verwey, 'Pieter Coecke van Aelst and the publication of Serlio's book on architecture', *Quaerendo* 6/2 (1976), 169–72, 194; John Bury, 'Serlio: Some Bibliographical Notes', in Christof Thoenes (ed.), *Sebastiano Serlio: Sesto Seminario Internazionale di Storia dell'Architettura* (Milan: Electa, 1989), pp. 100–101; Sylvie Deswarte-Rosa (ed.), *Sebastiano Serlio a Lyon: Architecture et imprimerie vol. 1. Le traité d'architecture de Sebastiano Serlio, une grande entreprise éditoriale au XVIe siècle* (Lyon: Mémoire active, 2004).

35 [Sebastiano Serlio], Pieter Coecke van Aelst (ed.), *Die gemaynen reglen von der architectur uber die funf manieren der gebeu. . .* (Antwerp, 1542), see Polleross, '*Romanitas*', pp. 214–1215; Holzschuh-Hofer, 'Die Alte Burg', pp. 117, 121.

36 Österreichische Nationalbibliothek, Vienna, Sammlung für Handschriften und alten Drucken, Alt Einb 72.O.57 (see Polleross, '*Romanitas*', pp. 214–15, Fig. 5).

37 Krista De Jonge, 'Vitruvius, Alberti and Serlio: Architectural Treatises in the Low Countries: 1530–1620', in Vaughan Hart and Peter Hicks (eds), *Paper Palaces: The Rise of the Renaissance Architectural Treatise* (New Haven and London: Yale University Press, 1998), pp. 281–90; Krista De Jonge, 'The Architectural Enterprises of the Emperor and His Court

The German translation by Jacob Rechlinger, published in Antwerp in 1542 and dealing with columns, was one of the most popular volumes of Serlio. Coecke van Aelst also added to it useful materials for readers, for instance a Roman capital alphabet mentioned above.[38]

The Swiss Gate and the entry of Ferdinand I

The Swiss Gate adopted the style promoted by Serlio and therefore featured as a permanent architectural sign of the revival of antiquity at the Viennese court, as well as depicting the triumph *all'antica* of the new emperor. Due to its central placement on the façade of the Hofburg, the Gate also played a part, in place of ephemeral decoration, for festivities such as tournaments. On 14 April 1558, following the imperial proclamation of Ferdinand I in Frankfurt on 14 March,[39] the city of Vienna organised a ceremonial entry for the new emperor.[40] The poet Petrus Rotis wrote of the imperial 'triumph' in his Latin account published during the same year as the celebration; another related work edited by Georg Eder, rector of the University of Vienna, featured panegyric addressed by several humanists to the new emperor, and also called the entry a 'triumph'.[41]

---

in the Low Countries: The European Context', in Fernando Checa Cremades (ed.), *Carolus* (Toledo: Museo de Santa Cruz, 2000), pp. 44–6; Jochen Becker, 'Greater than Zeuxis and Apelles: Artists as Arguments in the Antwerp Entry of 1549', in J.R. Mulryne and Elizabeth Goldring (eds), *Court Festivals of the European Renaissance*, pp. 175–80; Krista De Jonge, 'Les éditions du traité de Serlio par Pieter Coecke van Aelst', in Sylvie Deswarte-Rosa (ed.), *Sebastiano Serlio a Lyon*, pp. 262–8.

38 Verwey, 'Pieter Coecke van Aelst', pp. 183–6; Bury, 'Serlio', p. 100; De Jonge, 'Vitruvius, Alberti and Serlio', pp. 282–4; Krista De Jonge, 'L'édition de la traduction allemande du Livre IV par Jacob Rechlinger chez Pieter Coecke van Aelst à Anvers en 1542 [1543]', in Sylvie Deswarte-Rosa (ed.), *Sebastiano Serlio a Lyon: Architecture et imprimerie vol. 1. Le traité d'architecture de Sebastiano Serlio, une grande entreprise éditoriale au XVIe siècle* (Lyon: Mémoire active, 2004), pp. 278–9. A second edition of the German translation of Book 4 by Serlio was published by the widow of Coecke van Aelst, Mayken Verhulst, in Antwerp in 1558: see Verwey, 'Pieter Coecke van Aelst', pp. 191–2; Bury, 'Serlio', p. 100.

39 Harriet Rudolph, *Das Reich als Ereignis: Formen und Funktionen der Herrschaftsinszenierung bei Kaisereinzügen (1558–1618)*, Norm und Struktur, 38 (Cologne, Weimar and Vienna: Böhlau, 2011), pp. 152–5.

40 Joseph Feil, *Kaiser Ferdinand's I. Einzug in Wien: 14. April 1558* (Vienna: Karl Ueberrenter, 1853); Karl Vocelka, 'Die Wiener Feste der frühen Neuzeit aus waffenkundlicher Sicht', *Jahrbuch des Vereins für Geschichte der Stadt Wien* 34 (1978), 135–8; Harriet Rudolph, 'Humanistische Feste?' in Thomas Maissen and Gerrit Walther (eds), *Funktionen des Humanismus: Studien zum Nutzen des Neuen in der humanistischen Kultur* (Göttingen: Wallstein, 2006), pp. 186–7; Andrea Sommer-Mathis, 'VI.4. Residenz und öffentlicher Raum: Höfisches Fest in Wien im Wandel vom 16. zum 17. Jahrhundert', in Herbert Karner (ed.), *Die Wiener Hofburg*, p. 495.

41 Petrus a Rotis, *Triumphi, quo D. Ferdinandus I. Ro. Imperator . . . Viennae a suis exceptus est: Descriptio* (Vienna, 1558); Georg Eder, *Triumphus D. Ferdinando I. Ro. imperatori. . .* (Vienna, 1558).

The route Ferdinand I took through the city started at the gate on the bank of the Danube and paused at St Stephen's Cathedral. After listening to a *Te Deum*, Ferdinand progressed to the Hofburg. Significant ephemeral decorations along the processional route are not mentioned in the sources. However, it was noted that the Emperor's progress ended at the Hofburg, where his final reception took place. At last, in the evening, he and his family saw a tournament and fireworks from the windows of the residence. This ended with an astonishing siege and the explosion of a wooden castle filled with rockets (in German '*Feuerwerksschloß*'), accompanied by fireworks mounted on the spire of St Stephen's Cathedral.[42] The tournament field was situated directly in front of the North-West façade of the Hofburg and the Swiss Gate, and was laid out in order to provide space for such chivalric spectacles.[43] In the case of the two tournaments of 1558 celebrating the proclamation of the new emperor in Vienna, the permanent triumphal arch of the Swiss Gate offered an *all'antica* feature evoking the ancient style of the Roman Empire.

Other tournaments and spectacles

During the reign of Emperor Ferdinand I, other tournaments took place in the same field as in 1560 and 1563. In May and June 1560 in Vienna and its surroundings, a one month–long series of tournaments took place – foot tournaments, jousts, tilts, folia, a sea battle and the siege of a firework fortress – together with entertainments such as banquets and hunts organised by Archduke Maximilian in honour of his father, the emperor and his brother-in-law, the Duke of Bavaria Albert V.[44] This was the '*Wiener*

---

42 Rotis, *Triumphi*, fols FIVr–GIr.

43 Holzschuh-Hofer, 'Die Wiener Hofburg', pp. 320–1; Markus Jeitler, 'IV.3. Der Burgplatz ("In der Burg")', in Herbert Karner (ed.), *Die Wiener Hofburg*, pp. 185–6; Sommer-Mathis, 'Residenz und öffentlicher Raum', p. 495.

44 Thomas DaCosta Kaufmann, *Variations of the Imperial Theme in the Age of Maximilian II and Rudolf II*, Outstanding dissertations in the fine arts (New York and London: Garland, 1978), pp. 24–6; Vocelka, 'Die Wiener Feste', pp. 143–4; Matthias Pfaffenbichler, 'Das Turnier als Instrument der Habsburgischen Politik', *Waffen- und Kostümkunde* 34/1–2 (1992), 24–8; Pfaffenbichler, 'Das Turnier zur Zeit Ferdinands I.', pp. 279–81; Seipel (ed.), *Kaiser Ferdinand I.*, Cat. Nr. III.21. (Matthias Pfaffenbichler), III.23–7. (Georg Kugler); Seipel (ed.), *Wir sind Helden*, Cat. Nr. 3.9–3.10. (Veronika Sandbichler), 3.12–3.14. (Matthias Pfaffenbichler); Rudolph, 'Humanistische Feste?', p. 176; Borbála Gulyás, "gegen den Bluedthunden und Erbfeindt der Christenhait": Die Thematisierung der Türkengefahr in Wort und Bild im Rahmen der höfischen Feste der Habsburger im 16. Jahrhundert', in Robert Born and Sabine Jagodzinski (eds), *Türkenkriege und Adelskultur in Ostmitteleuropa vom 16. bis zum 18. Jahrhundert*, Studia Jagellonica Lipsiensia, 14 (Ostfildern: Thorbecke, 2014), p. 224; Borbála Gulyás, 'The Fight Against the Ottomans in Hungary and the Court Festivals of the Habsburgs in the Sixteenth Century', in Pál Fodor and Pál Ács (eds), *Identity and Culture in Ottoman Hungary*, Studien zur Sprache, Geschichte und Kultur der Türkvölker, 24 (Berlin: Klaus Schwarz, 2017), pp. 287–91.

Turnier' ('Viennese Tournament') described among others in the richly illustrated printed account by Hans Francolin, the Hungarian herald of Ferdinand I. His popular work was published several times in German as well as
in Latin, accompanied by seven large-scale detailed engravings.[45]

According to Francolin's comprehensive account, on 12 and 17 June two
chivalric spectacles were staged in the field in front of the Swiss Gate, a
foot tournament and a tilt respectively.[46] These were organised without any
large ephemeral decorations or architectural structures, with the exception
of some small-scale settings providing the allegorical–mythological framework of the tournament. For example, a 'magic hill' of the goddess Isabella
of Carthage and her ladies-in-waiting was set up for the first foot combat
featuring the ladies rescued by knights.[47] According to the engravings by
Hans Sebald Lautensack, the stands for the princely spectators were on both
occasions placed next to the Swiss Gate (see Figure 3.2).

In this fashion, the permanent triumphal arch appeared as the main festive decoration of the chivalric event, demonstrating imperial power to
ordinary viewers. It is also known that three years later, in March 1563, a
tournament was organised in the same field for the entry of Maximilian II
into Vienna, which finished with the spectacular siege of a wooden fortress
and fireworks.[48] Its decorations *all'antica* will be discussed later.

A few months afterwards, on 8 November 1558, Ferdinand I made his sol-
emn entry into Prague as the recently proclaimed emperor and also as king
of Bohemia.[49] Prague, the capital of the Bohemian Kingdom, was an important venue for the people of the Empire, particularly after the suppression

45 Hans Francolin, *Thurnier Buch. . .* (Vienna, 1560); Hans Francolin, *Rerum praeclare
    gestarum. . .* (Vienna, 1560); see Gerhard Winkler, 'Das Turnierbuch Hans Francolins',
    Wissenschaftliche Mitteilungen aus dem Niederosterreichischen Landesmuseum 1 (1980),
    105–120; Watanabe-O'Kelly and Simon, *Festivals and Ceremonies*, p. 4. For another
    printed account of the Tournament, see Prospero Brutto, *Le giostre, i trionfi et gli apparati
    mirabili fatti in Viena alla corte de . . . Ferdinando imperatore* (Bologna, 1560), pp. 4–5.
46 Seipel (ed.), *Wir sind Helden*, Cat. Nr. 3.12, 3.14. (Matthias Pfaffenbichler).
47 It was a small rectangular-shaped wooden edifice covered by canvas painted as a rocky
    hill; see its depiction on the left of the engraving of Lautensack (see Figure 3.2) and on a
    fragment of a miniature representing some participants of the event such as the goddess
    Isabella, the court giant Giovanni Bona dressed as a Wild Man and Archduke Rudolf. See
    Seipel (ed.), *Wir sind Helden*, Cat. Nr. 3.9. (Matthias Pfaffenbichler).
48 See the woodcut by Donat Hübschmann in Caspar Stainhofer, *Gründtliche und khurtze
    beschreibung des alten unnd jungen Zugs. . .* (Vienna, 1566), fol. 17r; see also Josef
    Wünsch, 'Der Einzug Kaiser Maximilians II. in Wien 1563', *Berichte und Mittheilungen
    des Alterthums-Vereines zu Wien* 46 (1914), 22; Marina Dmitrieva-Einhorn, 'Ephem-
    eral Ceremonial Architecture in Prague, Vienna and Cracow in the Sixteenth and Early
    Seventeenth Centuries', in J.R. Mulryne and Elizabeth Goldring (eds), *Court Festivals of
    theEuropean Renaissance*, p. 369; Gulyás, 'Die Thematisierung der Türkengefahr', p. 228.
49 Kaufmann, *Variations*, pp. 22–4; Pfaffenbichler, 'Das Turnier als Instrument', p. 24; Dmitrieva-
    Einhorn, 'Ephemeral Ceremonial Architecture', pp. 363–5, 381, 385–6; Rudolph, 'Human-
    istische Feste?' pp. 172–3, 184–5; Václav Bůžek, *Ferdinand von Tirol zwischen Prag und*

Figure 3.2 Hans Sebald Lautensack, Foot tournament in front of the Hofburg (Hans Francolin, *Rerum praeclare gestarum . . .* (Vienna, 1560)), engraving.

of the rebellion of the protestant Bohemian estates against the Habsburgs in 1547. The entire event, including the entry and a spectacular tournament on the following day, was organised by the emperor's son, Archduke Ferdinand, the recent governor of Prague, who also commissioned both Latin and Italian printed accounts of the festivities.[50]

The entry into Prague was dominated by temporary arches *all'antica* erected to complement the gates of the city, which were similarly decorated with inscriptions, banners and coats of arms. For instance, the entrance gates at the Charles Bridge were adorned 'as in Italy' with laurel wreaths, greeting tags, banners displaying the imperial eagle and depictions of the Bohemian and imperial crowns.[51]

Ferdinand I passed by all the ceremonial edifices, including several ephemeral arches. The first of them was erected by the Jesuits at St Clement's Church and was decorated with allegorical figures of Peace and Justice, in addition to a statue of Mars as a victorious mythological counterpart of the emperor. The second and most impressive triumphal arch was commissioned by Archduke Ferdinand himself. Raised near the castle area, the enormous Corinthian-order edifice was as high as the surrounding buildings. It was richly decorated with Ferdinand I's coat of arms, showing the imperial eagle bearing the imperial crown, several Latin inscriptions and numerous figural elements such as sculptures. These last included two large, possibly moving colossi[52] representing the Biblical giants Samson and Gedeon (or Gideon), and allegorical figures of the virtues (among others, Faith, Religion, Justice, Temperance, Nobility, Power, Magnanimity, Goodness and Piety), portraits of preceding Habsburg emperors (Charles V, Maximilian I, Rudolf I and Frederick III) and reliefs representing the former emperors' famous battles. The third arch was erected next to St Vitus Cathedral and adorned with the allegorical figure of Concord set beside depictions of Ferdinand I's lands, and a related inscription that declared that the emperor ruled over his lands as a second Jupiter. Finally, two arches were decorated with various trophies: the first by the allegorical figure of Peace with several

---

Innsbruck: *Der Adel aus den böhmischen Ländern auf dem Weg zu den Höfen der ersten Habsburger* (Vienna, Cologne and Weimar: Böhlau, 2009), pp. 168–88.

50 Matthaeus Collinus and Martin Cuthenus, *Ad invictissimum ac potentissimum imperatorem Ferdinandum ode gratulatoria continens brevem descriptionem pompae in ingressu suae majestatis in urbem Pragam instructae ab archiduce Ferdinando VIII. die Novembris Anni 1558* (Prague, 1558) and its German translation, Ignaz Cornova (ed.), *Beschreibung des feyerlichen Einzugs Kaiser Ferdinands I. in die Hauptstadt Prag den 8. November 1558* (Prague: Haase und Widtmann, 1802); Pierandrea Mattioli, *Le solenni pompe, i superbi et gloriosi apparati, i trionfi, i fuocchi, et gli altri splendidi et diletteuoli spettacoli fatti alla venuta dell' invittisimo imperatore Ferdinando primo. . .* (Prague, 1559), see Seipel (ed.), *Wir sind Helden*, Cat. Nr. 1.8. (Veronika Sandbichler); Bůžek, *Ferdinand von Tirol*, pp. 168–9, n. 497.

51 Mattioli, *Le solenni pompe*, fol. CIVr; Bůžek, *Ferdinand von Tirol*, pp. 177–8; Dmitrieva-Einhorn 'Ephemeral Ceremonial Architecture', p. 365.

52 Mattioli, *Le solenni pompe*, fol. DIIv.

banners and weapons, and the second bearing Turkish weapons and harnesses evoking the hoped-for triumph of the Holy Roman Empire over the Ottomans.[53]

Alongside the antique architectural structures, the entry was also supported by dramaturgical episodes *all'antica*, for instance when the emperor was greeted by the songs of the nine muses, among others the Muse Calliope, who invoked the Greek and Roman gods to protect the Habsburg dynasty, or when red and white wine streamed from a well in the form of a large statue of Silenus.[54] The tournament performed in ancient costumes the next evening, also devised by Archduke Ferdinand, was intended to provide a mythological framework for the festivities. According to surviving accounts, it was staged in the castle garden as – evoking the famous Binche festivities of 1549 – the Gigantes were to besiege Jupiter while he was standing on Mount Vesuvius, armed with actual fireworks representing his thunder. The god's final victory was intended to symbolise the emperor's glorious triumph.[55]

Painted decoration of the arches

Particular attention should be drawn to the fact that contemporary accounts regularly notice the imitation of marble in the case of ephemeral structures, as a way of underlining their allusion to antiquity. The large, Corinthian-order arch in Prague, discussed above, was made, according to the accounts, of wood, canvas and stucco, with the colouring of the chiaroscuro stucco details of the sculptures and reliefs resembling bronze, and the colouring of the drapery imitating marble.[56]

On the occasion of the coronation in September 1563 of Maximilian II – as Hungarian King Maximillian I – in Pozsony (today Bratislava, Slovakia), one of the sources emphasised that the temporary arches appeared like marble: *'le porte . . . erano con somma magnificenza quasi di marmo fabbricate'* ('the arches were with the greatest magnificence constructed as though of marble').[57]

---

53 Mattioli, *Le solenni pompe*, fols CIIIv–EIVr; Cornova, *Beschreibung*, pp. 75–80, 85–8; Dmitrieva-Einhorn 'Ephemeral Ceremonial Architecture', pp. 365, 381; Bůžek, *Ferdinand von Tirol*, pp. 177–83.

54 Mattioli, *Le solenni pompe*, fol. DIv; Bůžek, *Ferdinand von Tirol*, pp. 174, 179.

55 Pfaffenbichler, 'Das Turnier als Instrument', p. 24; Pfaffenbichler, 'Das Turnier zur Zeit Ferdinands I.', p. 279; Veronika Sandbichler, 'Habsburgische Feste in der Renaissance', in Wilfried Seipel (ed.), *Wir sind Helden: Habsburgische Feste in der Renaissance* (Vienna: Kunsthistorisches Museum, 2005), pp. 11–13.

56 Mattioli, *Le solenni pompe*, fols DIIr–DIIv; Cornova, *Beschreibung*, p. 75.

57 Natale Conti, *Delle historie de' suoi tempi* (Venice, 1589), fol. 381v (cited by Farbaky, 'Pietro Ferrabosco', p. 130.)

Figure 3.3 Donat and Martin Hübschmann, Ephemeral triumphal arches by Pietro Ferrabosco erected for the coronation of Maximilian II as Hungarian king in Pozsony, 1563 (leaflet by Johannes Sambucus bound with Caspar Stainhofer, *Gründtliche und khurtze beschreibung . . .* (Vienna, 1566)), woodcut.

© Bayerische Staatsbibliothek, München, Rar. 250, fol. 20r, detail.

According to written accounts and an illustrated leaflet depicting the events of the Hungarian king's coronation,[58] two arches decorated in this way were erected along the route of his ceremonial entry into the centre of the city (see Figure 3.3).[59]

Both arches were similar 'marble-like' structures with one central round-topped archway only. The two edifices were to be set up at the ends of a temporary floating bridge, flanked by young trees, built out over the Danube

---

58 It was published by Caspar Stainhofer and contains a text by the Hungarian humanist Johannes Sambucus and a woodcut by Donat and Martin Hübschmann: see Zuzana Ludiková, 'Zsámboky János röplapja Miksa magyar királlyá koronázásáról' [A Leaflet by Johannes Sambucus of the Coronation of Maximilian as Hungarian king], *Századok* 143 (2009), 975–80.
59 Galavics, 'The Hungarian Royal Court', pp. 308–309; Farbaky, 'Pietro Ferrabosco', p. 130.

for the royal procession. They were similarly decorated: the coat of arms of Emperor Ferdinand I was placed in the middle, accompanied by the coats of arms of Maximilian II (I of Hungary) and his spouse, Maria, about to be crowned Hungarian king and queen consort. Archival material sets out the names of the Italian and German masters involved, the stages of construction and the costs. The two structures were made of seasoned wood, later painted and gilded. In addition, the same sources tell us that both arches were designed by Pietro Ferrabosco,[60] the Italian master mentioned above in connection with the Swiss Gate.

The entry of Maximilian II

As noted previously, in relation to the tournament field in front of the Hofburg and the Swiss Gate, Maximilian II made an entry into Vienna in the same year, on 16 March 1563.[61] His triumphal procession into Vienna, as the Empire's principal city of residence, celebrated his coronation as king of the Romans in Frankfurt in November 1562, an event which implied that, as the heir of his father, Ferdinand I, who had himself been crowned as king of the Romans in the past, Maximilian would in turn be Ferdinand's immediate successor as emperor.

A key figure of the overt antiquarianism of the Viennese court, the humanist Wolfgang Lazius devised the entire programme and decorations *all'antica* of the spectacular event. Lazius, as court historian, was an experienced antiquarian at Emperor Ferdinand I's court.[62] He published his elaborate programme and a large number of classical Latin inscriptions for the triumphal arches in a separate explanatory volume in Vienna in 1563, together with other panegyrics.[63]

---

60 Galavics, 'The Hungarian Royal Court', pp. 308–309; Farbaky, 'Pietro Ferrabosco', p. 130; Árpád Mikó, 'Pietro Ferrabosco számadása a Miksa magyar királlyá koronázására épített pozsonyi diadalkapuról (1563) [Pietro Ferrabosco's bill of costs concerning the triumphal arches erected for the coronation of Maximilian I of Hungary (1563)]', *Művészettörténeti Értesítő* 62 (2013), 323–8.

61 Wünsch, 'Der Einzug', pp. 18–34; Blaha, *Österreichische Triumph- und Ehrenpforten*, pp. 41–8, 102–104, 132–3, 169–79; Kaufmann, *Variations*, p. 27; see Vocelka, 'Die Wiener Feste', pp. 144–6; Howard Louthan, *The Quest for Compromise: Peacemakers in Counter-Reformation Vienna*, Cambridge Studies in Early Modern History (Cambridge: Cambridge University Press, 1997), pp. 35–42; Dmitrieva-Einhorn, 'Ephemeral Ceremonial Architecture', pp. 363, 365, 369–74, 381, 385; Rudolph, 'Humanistische Feste?' pp. 173–5, 180–81, 186; Sommer-Mathis, 'Residenz und öffentlicher Raum', pp. 495–6.

62 Max Kratochwill, 'Wolfgang Lazius', *Wiener Geschichtsblätter* 20 (1965), 449–52; Renate Kohn, *Wiener Inschriftensammler vom 17. bis zum beginnenden 19. Jahrhundert*, Forschungen und Beiträge zur Wiener Stadtgeschichte 32 (Vienna: Franz Deuticke, 1998), pp. 9–11.

63 Wolfgang Lazius, 'Periphrasis solenniorum, atque arcuum triumphalium. . .', in *Epitome solenniorum, quæ in auspicatum adventum . . . Maximiliani, Bohemiæ Regis et Archiducis*

Along the triumphal route of the emperor-to-be, Maximilian II, three temporary arches were erected, adorned with numerous inscriptions written in Roman squared capitals, as well as statues and reliefs. The first arch was dedicated to Austria, the second to Bohemia and Hungary and the third and largest edifice to the Holy Roman Empire and the transfer of imperial power from Ferdinand I to Maximilian II. According to Lazius, they were named 'Porta Austriaca', 'Porta Bohemica' and 'Porta Romana'. In addition, the series of temporary structures was accompanied by three wine wells streaming red and white wine. The arches and wine wells were designed in accordance with the scheme drawn up by Lazius, and their preparation was supervised by the Danish painter and printmaker Melchior Lorck, who was also involved in their final painting. Drawing on models by Lorck, other masters, for instance the German architect Hans Saphoy working at St Stephen's Cathedral, constructed them.[64]

Besides the publication by Lazius, the ephemeral arches were also described, as well as depicted in detail, by the text and woodcuts of Caspar Stainhofer's account printed in German. (See Figures 3.4–3.6.)[65] It is worth noting that, as with examples discussed above, the German text emphasised in every case that the colouring of the arches resembled marble. This can also be traced in woodcuts by Donat Hübschmann. For instance, the 'Porta Austriaca' was described as *'ain herrliche Ehren portten gewaltig aufgericht, von Seulen, in gueter proportion, als ob sy mit Märbl und andern dergleichen stainen Gemaurt und außgesetzt wäre'* ('a magnificent arch of honour erected with columns of good proportion as if it had been built of, and covered by, marble and other similar stones').[66]

The first arch, the 'Porta Austriaca', was erected next to the Waaghaus. This Doric-order edifice was surmounted by a peacock symbolising Austria, flanked by allegorical figures representing the virtues Charity and Hope. Its decoration was dominated by two large silvered colossi, dressed as Roman warriors holding flags and the coats of arms of the city of Vienna and of the emperor. Besides these, among the several Latin inscriptions, can be found the city's greetings to Ferdinand I and Maximilian II. The next temporary arch, the 'Porta Bohemica', erected at the Roßmarkt, was similar to the

---

Austriæ etc. una cum quatuor arcuum triumphalium constitutione, eorumque explicatione . . . (Vienna, 1563), fols AIVr–CIv.

64 Blaha, *Österreichische Triumph- und Ehrenpforten*, pp. 102–104; Werner Kayser, 'Melchior Lorich's Ehrenpforten und Weinbrunnen zum Einzug Kaiser Maximilians II. in Wien, insbesondere die Ehrenpforte beim Waaghaus', *Philobiblon* 23 (1979), 279–95, and see Mikael Bøgh Rasmussen, 'Vienna: A Habsburg Capital redecorated in Classical Style for the Entry of Maximillian II as King of the Romans in 1563', in J.R. Mulryne *et al.* (eds), *Architectures of Festival in Early Modern Europe: Fashioning and Re-Fashioning Urban and Courtly Space* (Abingdon and New York: Routledge, 2017), pp. 53–72.

65 Stainhofer, *Gründtliche*.

66 Stainhofer, *Gründtliche*, fol. 6r.

Figure 3.4 Donat Hübschmann, Porta Austriaca in Caspar Stainhofer, *Gründtliche und khurtze beschreibung* . . . (Vienna, 1566), woodcut.

© Bayerische Staatsbibliothek, München, Rar. 250, fol. 5r.

Figure 3.5 Donat Hübschmann, Porta Bohemica in Caspar Stainhofer, *Gründtliche und khurtze beschreibung* . . . (Vienna, 1566), woodcut.

Figure 3.6 Donat Hübschmann, Porta Romana in Caspar Stainhofer, *Gründtliche und khurtze beschreibung . . .* (Vienna, 1566), woodcut.

'Porta Austriaca' in structure and size, built with one semicircular archway and two top storeys, but still a Corinthian-order edifice.

The 'Porta Bohemica' was dedicated to the Bohemian Kingdom and the Hungarian Kingdom, both of which had recently, since 1562 and 1563 respectively, been ruled by Maximilian II as king. On the top of the upper storey, in the middle, the figure of the Bohemian lion embraced the coats of arms of Hungary, accompanied by female figures of the virtues Constantia and Wisdom.

The largest and most spectacular Corinthian-order arch, the 'Porta Romana', was located at the Kohlmarkt. Its Latin inscriptions declared the transfer of Emperor Ferdinand I's power to his successor, the new king of the Romans, Maximilian II. On the top, centred between the allegorical figures of the virtues Faith and Justice, was the imperial eagle, which nodded three times when the arch was passed by the emperor's heir. Below this, on the third level, above a globe of the world in the centre and the life-size figures of Ferdinand I and Maximilian II, Latin inscriptions celebrated the transfer of power and others praised the Habsburg predecessors of the emperor-to-be and Maximilian himself. The transfer was symbolically strengthened by the presence of Jupiter brandishing his thunder, with the imperial eagle and Saturn in armour flanking the globe, the emperor and his heir. In addition, other statues of the ancient gods of the planets (Mars, Apollo, Juno and Mercury) were situated on both sides of the archway.

Finally, on the processional route two ephemeral statues or colossi were erected. The available sources do not provide information allowing us to identify their costumes, except that they were possibly covered with silver paper and that each held a crown over his or her head.[67] According to one of the illustrations of the printed account of the Viennese Tournament in 1560, mentioned above, they probably represented the ancient gods Venus and Mars. To be specific, the final chivalric spectacle in 1560 took place next to the city boundary, in a field dedicated to Mars and Venus. On a related engraving, two colossi representing these ancient gods may be seen lifting the imperial crown.[68]

To summarise, the triumphal arches of the Swiss Gate, and the similar ephemeral structures employed as architectural decorations for the festivities of Ferdinand I, were inspired by ancient Rome and played an important part in imperial antiquarianism. Alongside other features *all'antica*, they effectively served the *repraesentatio maiestatis* of the new imperial court of Vienna.

---

67 Johann Evangelist Schlager, *Wiener Skizzen aus dem Mittelalter* (Vienna: Gerold, 1835–46), vol. 3 (1839), p. 51.

68 *Kaiser Ferdinand I.*, Cat. Nr. III.26. (Matthias Pfaffenbichler). Similarly, three colossal statues described by Ferdinand I in his letter to Archduke Ferdinand as '*Riesenbilder*' ('statues of giants') and formerly used at the Prague Entry of Ferdinand I in 1558, were still in 1563 stored in the gardens of the castle of Prague; see Franz Kreyczi, 'Urkunden und Regesten aus dem K. und K. Reichs-Finanz-Archiv [2]', *Jahrbuch der Kunsthistorischen Sammlungen des Allerhöchsten Kaiserhauses* 5 (1887), Reg. Nr. 4340. (cited by Dmitrieva-Einhorn, 'Ephemeral Ceremonial Architecture', p. 387).

Bibliography

Primary Sources

Brutto, Prospero, *Le giostre, i trionfi et gli apparati mirabili fatti in Viena alla corte de . . . Ferdinando imperatore* (Bologna, 1560).

Collinus, Matthaeus and Martin Cuthenus, *Ad invictissimum ac potentissimum imperatorem Ferdinandum ode gratulatoria continens brevem descriptionem pompae in ingressu suae majestatis in urbem Pragam instructae ab archiduce Ferdinando VIII. die Novembris Anni 1558* (Prague, 1558).

Conti, Natale, *Delle historie de' suoi tempi* (Venice, 1589).

Cornova, Ignaz (ed.), *Beschreibung des feyerlichen Einzugs Kaiser Ferdinands I. in die Hauptstadt Prag den 8. November 1558* (Prague, 1802).

Eder, Georg, *Triumphus D. Ferdinando I. Ro. imperatori. . .* (Vienna, 1558).

Feil, Joseph, *Kaiser Ferdinand's I. Einzug in Wien: 14. April 1558* (Vienna: Karl Ueberrenter, 1853).

Francolin, Hans, *Rerum praeclare gestarum. . .* (Vienna, 1560).

Francolin, Hans, *Thurnier Buch. . .* (Vienna, 1560).

Lazius, Wolfgang, 'Periphrasis solenniorum, atque arcuum triumphalium. . .', in *Epitome solenniorum, quæ in auspicatum adventum . . . Maximiliani, Bohemiæ Regis et Archiducis Austriæ etc. una cum quatuor arcuum triumphalium constitutione, eorumque explicatione . . .* (Vienna, 1563), fols AIVr–CIv.

Mattioli, Pierandrea, *Le solenni pompe, i superbi et gloriosi apparati, i trionfi, i fuocchi, et gli altri splendidi et diletteuoli spettacoli fatti alla venuta dell' invittisimo imperatore Ferdinando primo . . .* (Prague, 1559).

Rotis, Petrus a, *Triumphi, quo D: Ferdinandus I. Ro. Imperator . . . Viennae a suis exceptus est: Descriptio* (Vienna, 1558).

[Selio, Sebastiano], Pieter Coecke van Aelst (ed.), *Die gemaynen reglen von der architectur uber die funf manieren der gebeu. . .* (Antwerp, 1542).

Stainhofer, Caspar, *Gründtliche und khurtze beschreibung des alten unnd jungen Zugs . . .* (Vienna, 1566).

Secondary Sources

Baldwin, Robert, 'A Bibliography of the Literature on Triumph', in Barbara Wisch and Susan Scott Munshower (eds), *"All the World's a Stage . . .": Art and Pageantry in the Renaissance and Baroque: Triumphal Celebrations and the Rituals of Statecraft*, Papers in Art History from Pennsylvania State University, 6 (University Park, PA: Pennsylvania State University, 1990), vol. 1, pp. 359–85.

Becker, Jochen, 'Greater than Zeuxis and Apelles: Artists as Arguments in the Antwerp Entry of 1549', in J.R. Mulryne and Elizabeth Goldring (eds), *Court Festivals of the European Renaissance: Art, Politics and Performance* (Aldershot: Ashgate, 2002), pp. 171–95.

Béhar, Pierre and Helen Watanabe-O'Kelly (eds), *Spectacvlvm Europævm: Theatre and Spectacle in Europe: Histoire du spectacle in Europe: (1580–1750)*, Wolfenbütteler Arbeiten zur Barockforschung, 31 (Wiesbaden: Harrassowitz, 1999).

Beseler, Susanne, 'Das Schweizertor und die Metamorphosen seiner Oberfläche', *Österreichische Zeitschrift für Kunst- und Denkmalpflege* 62/2 (2008), 660–71.

Blaha, Herta, 'Österreichische Triumph- und Ehrenpforten der Renaissance und des Barock' (Dissertation, Universität Wien, 1950).

Bodnár, Szilvia, 'Die Verklärung Kaiser Maximilians I.: Der Triumphzug, der Triumphwagen und die Ehrenpforte', in Szilvia Bodnár (ed.), *Dürer és kortársai: Művészóriások óriásmetszetei, I. Miksa császár diadala: Dürer und seine Zeitgenossen: Riesenholzschnitte hervorragender Künstler: Der Triumph Kaiser Maximilians I* (Budapest: Museum of Fine Arts, 2005), pp. 23–76.

Bodnár, Szilvia (ed.), *Dürer és kortársai: Művészóriások óriásmetszetei, I. Miksa császár diadala: Dürer und seine Zeitgenossen: Riesenholzschnitte hervorragender Künstler: Der Triumph Kaiser Maximilians* (Budapest: Museum of Fine Arts, 2005).

Bøgh Rasmussen, Mikael, 'Vienna: A Habsburg Capital Redecorated in Classical Style for the Entry of Maximillian II as King of the Romans in 1563', in J.R. Mulryne *et al.* (eds), *Architectures of Festival in Early Modern Europe: Fashioning and Re-Fashioning Urban and Courtly Space* (Abingdon and New York: Routledge, 2017), pp. 53–72.

Born, Robert and Sabine Jagodzinski (eds), *Türkenkriege und Adelskultur in Ostmitteleuropa vom 16. bis zum 18. Jahrhundert*, Studia Jagellonica Lipsiensia, 14 (Ostfildern: J. Thorbecke, 2014).

Bösel, Richard, Grete Klingenstein and Alexander Koller (eds), *Kaiserhof – Papsthof: (16. – 18. Jahrhundert)* (Vienna: Österreichischen Akademie der Wissenschaften, 2006).

Bury, John, 'Serlio: Some Bibliographical Notes', in Christof Thoenes (ed.), *Sebastiano Serlio: Sesto Seminario Internazionale di Storia dell'Architettura* (Milan: Electa, 1989), pp. 92–101.

Bůžek, Václav, *Ferdinand von Tirol zwischen Prag und Innsbruck: Der Adel aus den böhmischen Ländern auf dem Weg zu den Höfen der ersten Habsburger* (Vienna, Cologne and Weimar: Böhlau, 2009).

Checa Cremades, Fernando (ed.), *Carolus* (Toledo: Museo de Santa Cruz, 2000).

Chmelarz, Eduard, 'Die Ehrenpforte des Kaisers Maximilian I', *Jahrbuch der Kunsthistorischen Sammlungen des Allerhöchsten Kaiserhauses* 4 (1886), 289–319.

De Jonge, Krista, 'Vitruvius, Alberti and Serlio: Architectural Treatises in the Low Countries: 1530–1620', in Vaughan Hart and Peter Hicks (eds), *Paper Palaces: The Rise of the Renaissance Architectural Treatise* (New Haven and London: Yale University Press, 1998), pp. 281–96.

De Jonge, Krista, 'The Architectural Enterprises of the Emperor and His Court in the Low Countries: The European Context', in Fernando Checa Cremades (ed.), *Carolus* (Toledo: Museo de Santa Cruz, 2000), pp. 35–53.

De Jonge, Krista, 'L'édition de la traduction allemande du Livre IV par Jacob Rechlinger chez Pieter Coecke van Aelst à Anvers en 1542 [1543]', in Sylvie Deswarte-Rosa (ed.), *Sebastiano Serlio a Lyon: Architecture et imprimerie vol. 1. Le traité d'architecture de Sebastiano Serlio, une grande entreprise éditoriale au XVIe siècle* (Lyon: Mémoire active, 2004), pp. 278–9.

De Jonge, Krista, 'Les éditions du traité de Serlio par Pieter Coecke van Aelst', in Sylvie Deswarte-Rosa (ed.), *Sebastiano Serlio a Lyon: Architecture et imprimerie vol. 1. Le traité d'architecture de Sebastiano Serlio une grande entreprise éditoriale au XVIe siècle* (Lyon: Mémoire active, 2004), pp. 262–8.

Deswarte-Rosa, Sylvie (ed.), *Sebastiano Serlio a Lyon: Architecture et imprimerie vol. 1. Le traité d'architecture de Sebastiano Serlio, une grande entreprise éditoriale au XVIe siècle* (Lyon: Mémoire active, 2004).

Dmitrieva-Einhorn, Marina, 'Ephemeral Ceremonial Architecture in Prague, Vienna and Cracow in the Sixteenth and Early Seventeenth Centuries', in J.R. Mulryne and Elizabeth Goldring (eds), *Court Festivals of the European Renaissance: Art, Politics and Performance* (Aldershot: Ashgate, 2002), pp. 363–90.

Erffa, Hans Martin von, 'Ehrenpforte', in *Reallexikon zur deutschen Kunstgeschichte*, vol. 4 (Stuttgart: J. B. Metzlersche Verlagsbuchhandlung, 1958), columns 1443–1504.

Farbaky, Péter, 'Pietro Ferrabosco in Ungheria e nell'impero asburgico', *Arte Lombarda* 139 (2003), 127–34.

Fodor, Pál and Pál Ács (eds), *Identity and Culture in Ottoman Hungary*, Studien zur Sprache, Geschichte und Kultur der Türkvölker 24 (Berlin: Klaus Schwarz, 2017).

Fontaine Verwey, Herman de la, 'Pieter Coecke van Aelst and the publication of Serlio's book on architecture', *Quaerendo* 6/2 (1976), 167–94.

Galavics, Géza, 'The Hungarian Royal Court and Late Renaissance Art', *Hungarian Studies* 10/2 (1995), 307–32. (http://epa.oszk.hu/01400/01462/00017/pdf/307-332.pdf, date of access: 10 December, 2013).

Gugler, Andreas, 'Feiern und feiern lassen: Festkultur am Wiener Hof in der zweiten Hälfte des 16. und der ersten Hälfte des 17. Jahrhunderts', *Frühneuzeit-Info* 11 (2000), 68–176.

Gulyás, Borbála, ' "gegen den Bluedthunden und Erbfeindt der Christenhait": Die Thematisierung der Türkengefahr in Wort und Bild im Rahmen der höfischen Feste der Habsburger im 16. Jahrhundert', in Robert Born and Sabine Jagodzinski (eds), *Türkenkriege und Adelskultur in Ostmitteleuropa vom 16. bis zum 18. Jahrhundert*, Studia Jagellonica Lipsiensia, 14 (Ostfildern: J. Thorbecke, 2014), pp. 217–36.

Gulyás, Borbála, 'Inscriptions "all'antica" of the Sepulchral Monument of Emperor Maximilian I in Innsbruck by the Calligrapher George Bocskay', *Frühneuzeit-Info* 26 (2015), 219–227.

Gulyás, Borbála, 'The Fight Against the Ottomans in Hungary and the Court Festivals of the Habsburgs in the Sixteenth Century', in Pál Fodor and Pál Ács (eds), *Identity and Culture in Ottoman Hungary*, Studien zur Sprache, Geschichte und Kultur der Türkvölker, 24 (Berlin: Klaus Schwarz, 2017), pp. 277–300.

Haag, Sabine (ed.), *All'Antica: Götter und Helden auf Schloss Ambras* (Vienna: Kunsthistorisches Museum, 2011).

Hart, Vaughan and Peter Hicks (eds), *Paper Palaces: The Rise of the Renaissance Architectural Treatise* (New Haven and London: Yale University Press, 1998).

Holzschuh-Hofer, Renate, 'Die Wiener Hofburg im 16. Jahrhundert. Festungsresidenz Ferdinands I', *Österreichische Zeitschrift für Kunst und Denkmalpflege* 61/2–3 (2007), 307–25.

Holzschuh-Hofer, Renate, 'Die renaissancezeitliche Hofburg und das Schweizertor mit seiner Programmatik im Lichte der neuen Erkenntnisse durch die Bauforschung', *Österreichische Zeitschrift für Kunst- und Denkmalpflege* 62/4 (2008), 643–60.

Holzschuh-Hofer, Renate, 'Feuereisen im Dienst politischer Propaganda von Burgund bis Habsburg: Zur Entwicklung der Symbolik des Ordens vom Goldenen Vlies von Herzog Philipp dem Guten bis Kaiser Ferdinand I.', *RIHA Journal* 0006 (16 August, 2010). (www.riha-journal.org/articles/2010/holzschuh-hofer-feuereisen-im-dienst-politischer-propaganda, date of access: 10 December, 2013).

Holzschuh-Hofer, Renate, 'Radikal elitär oder schlicht bescheiden? Zur Ikonologie der Wiener Hofburg im 16. Jahrhundert unter Ferdinand I.', in Werner Paravicini and Jörg Wettlaufer (eds), *Vorbild – Austausch – Konkurrenz: Höfe und*

Residenzen in den gegenseitigen Wahrnehmung: 11. Symposium der Residenzen-Kommission der Akademie der Wissenschaften Göttingen, Residenzenforschung, 23 (Ostfildern: J. Thorbecke, 2010), pp. 257–73.

Holzschuh-Hofer, Renate, 'IV.1.1. Die Alte Burg (Schweizerhof): 1521–1619', in Herbert Karner (ed.), *Die Wiener Hofburg: 1521–1705: Baugeschichte, Funktion und Etablierung als Kaiserresidenz*, Österreichische Akademie der Wissenschaften Denkschriften der Philosophisch-Historischen Klasse, 444, Veröffentlichungen zur Kunstgeschichte, 13, Veröffentlichungen zur Bau- und Funktionsgeschichte der Wiener Hofburg, 2 (Vienna: Österreichische Akademie der Wissenschaften, 2014), pp. 80–143.

Holzschuh-Hofer, Renate, 'VI.7.1. Die Hofburg und ihre Ikonologie im 16. Jahrhundert', in Herbert Karner (ed.), *Die Wiener Hofburg: 1521–1705: Baugeschichte, Funktion und Etablierung als Kaiserresidenz*, Österreichische Akademie der Wissenschaften Denkschriften der Philosophisch-Historischen Klasse, 444, Veröffentlichungen zur Kunstgeschichte, 13, Veröffentlichungen zur Bau- und Funktionsgeschichte der Wiener Hofburg, 2 (Vienna: Österreichische Akademie der Wissenschaften, 2014), pp. 530–548.

Jeitler, Markus, 'IV.3. Der Burgplatz ("In der Burg")', in Herbert Karner (ed.), *Die Wiener Hofburg: 1521–1705: Baugeschichte, Funktion und Etablierung als Kaiserresidenz*, Österreichische Akademie der Wissenschaften Denkschriften der Philosophisch-Historischen Klasse, 444, Veröffentlichungen zur Kunstgeschichte, 13, Veröffentlichungen zur Bau- und Funktionsgeschichte der Wiener Hofburg, 2 (Vienna: Österreichische Akademie der Wissenschaften, 2014), pp. 184–187.

Karner, Herbert, 'Pietro Ferrabosco', in Artur Rosenauer (ed.), *Geschichte der bildenden Kunst in Österreich vol. 3.: Spätmittelalter und Renaissance* (Vienna: Österreichische Akademie der Wissenschaften, Munich, Berlin, London and New York: Prestel, 2003), pp. 274–5.

Karner, Herbert (ed.), *Die Wiener Hofburg, 1521–1705: Baugeschichte, Funktion und Etablierung als Kaiserresidenz*, Österreichische Akademie der Wissenschaften Denkschriften der Philosophisch-Historischen Klasse, 444, Veröffentlichungen zur Kunstgeschichte, 13, Veröffentlichungen zur Bau- und Funktionsgeschichte der Wiener Hofburg, 2 (Vienna: Österreichische Akademie der Wissenschaften, 2014).

Kaufmann, Thomas DaCosta, *Variations of the Imperial Theme in the Age of Maximilian II and Rudolf II*, Outstanding dissertations in the fine arts (New York and London: Garland, 1978).

Kayser, Werner, 'Melchior Lorich's Ehrenpforten und Weinbrunnen zum Einzug Kaiser Maximilians II. in Wien, insbesondere die Ehrenpforte beim Waaghaus', *Philobiblon* 23 (1979), 279–95.

Kohn, Renate, *Wiener Inschriftensammler vom 17. bis zum beginnenden 19. Jahrhundert*, Forschungen und Beiträge zur Wiener Stadtgeschichte, 32 (Vienna: Franz Deutlicke, 1998).

Kratochwill, Max, 'Wolfgang Lazius', *Wiener Geschichtsblätter* 20 (1965), 449–52.

Kreyczi, Franz, 'Urkunden und Regesten aus dem K. u. K. Reichs-Finanz-Archiv [vol. 2.]', *Jahrbuch der Kunsthistorischen Sammlungen des Allerhöchsten Kaiserhauses* 5 (1887), XXV–CXIX.

Kühnel, Harry, 'Beiträge zur Geschichte der Wiener Hofburg im 16. und 17. Jahrhundert', *Anzeiger der Österreichischen Akademie der Wissenschaften, Philosophische-Historische Klasse* (1958), 268–83.

Louthan, Howard, *The Quest for Compromise: Peacemakers in Counter-Reformation Vienna*, Cambridge Studies in Early Modern History (Cambridge: Cambridge University Press, 1997).

Ludiková, Zuzana, 'Zsámboky János röplapja Miksa magyar királlyá koronázásáról' [A leaflet by Johannes Sambucus describing the coronation of Maximilian as Hungarian king], *Századok* 143 (2009), 975–80.

Maissen, Thomas and Gerrit Walther (eds), *Funktionen des Humanismus: Studien zum Nutzen des Neuen in der humanistischen Kultur* (Göttingen: Wallstein, 2006).

Martin, John Jeffries (ed.), *The Renaissance World*, The Routledge Worlds (New York and London: Routledge, 2007).

McGowan, Margaret M., 'The Renaissance Triumph and Its Classical Heritage', in J.R. Mulryne and Elizabeth Goldring (eds), *Court Festivals of the European Renaissance: Art, Politics and Performance* (Aldershot: Ashgate, 2002), pp. 26–47.

Meiss, Millard, 'Alphabetical Treatises in the Renaissance', in Millard Meiss (ed.), *The Painter's Choice: Problems in the Interpretation of Renaissance Art* (New York, Hagerstown, San Francisco and London: Harper & Row, 1976), pp. 176–86.

Meiss, Millard (ed.), *The Painter's Choice: Problems in the Interpretation of Renaissance Art* (New York, Hagerstown, San Francisco and London: Harper & Row, 1976).

Mikó, Árpád, 'Pietro Ferabosco számadása a Miksa magyar királlyá koronázására épített pozsonyi diadalkapuról (1563) [Pietro Ferabosco's bill of costs concerning the triumphal arches erected for the coronation of Maximilian I of Hungary (1563)]', *Művészettörténeti Értesítő* 62 (2013), 323–8.

Müller, Jan-Dirk, *Gedechtnus: Literatur und Hofgesellschaft um Maximilian I.*, Forschungen zur Geschichte der älteren deutschen Literatur, 2 (Munich: Wilhelm Fink, 1982).

Mulryne, J.R. and Elizabeth Goldring (eds), *Court Festivals of the European Renaissance: Art, Politics and Performance* (Aldershot: Ashgate, 2002).

Mulryne, J.R., Krista De Jonge, Pieter Martens and R.L.M. Morris, *Architectures of Festival in Early Modern Europe: Fashioning and Re-Fashioning Urban and Courtly Space* (Abingdon and New York: Routledge, 2017).

Paravicini, Werner and Jörg Wettlaufer (eds), *Vorbild – Austausch – Konkurrenz: Höfe und Residenzen in den gegenseitigen Wahrnehmung: 11. Symposium der Residenzen-Kommission der Akademie der Wissenschaften Göttingen*, Residenzenforschung, 23 (Ostfildern: J. Thorbecke, 2010).

Pfaffenbichler, Matthias, 'Das Turnier als Instrument der Habsburgischen Politik', *Waffen- und Kostümkunde* (1992), 13–36.

Pfaffenbichler, Matthias, 'Das Turnier zur Zeit Ferdinands I. in Mitteleuropa', in Wilfried Seipel (ed.), *Kaiser Ferdinand I.: 1503–1564: Das Werden der Habsburgermonarchie* (Vienna: Kunsthistorisches Museum, Milan: Skira, 2003), pp. 277–81.

Polleross, Friedrich, '*Romanitas* in der habsburgischen Repräsentation von Karl V. bis Maximilian II.', in Richard Bösel, Grete Klingenstein and Alexander Koller (eds), *Kaiserhof – Papsthof: (16. – 18. Jahrhundert)*, Publikationen des Historischen Instituts beim Österreichischen Kulturforum in Rom, Abhandlungen, 12 (Vienna: Österreichischen Akademie der Wissenschaften, 2006), pp. 207–23.

Reallexikon zur deutschen Kunstgeschichte, vol. 4 (Stuttgart: Metzler, 1958).

Rosenauer, Artur (ed.), *Geschichte der bildenden Kunst in Österreich vol. 3: Spätmittelalter und Renaissance* (Vienna: Österreichische Akademie der Wissenschaften, Munich, Berlin, London and New York: Prestel, 2003).

Rudolph, Harriet, 'Humanistische Feste?' in Thomas Maissen and Gerrit Walther (eds), *Funktionen des Humanismus: Studien zum Nutzen des Neuen in der humanistischen Kultur* (Göttingen: Wallstein, 2006), pp. 166–90.

Rudolph, Harriet, *Das Reich als Ereignis: Formen und Funktionen der Herrschaftsinszenierung bei Kaisereinzügen (1558–1618)*, Norm und Struktur, 38 (Cologne, Weimar and Vienna: Böhlau, 2011).

Sandbichler, Veronika, 'Die Bedeutung hinter dem Sichtbaren: Allegorie – Trionfo – Visuelle Propaganda', in Wilfried Seipel (ed.), *Wir sind Helden: Habsburgische Feste in der Renaissance* (Vienna: Kunsthistorisches Museum, 2005), pp. 45–7.

Sandbichler, Veronika, 'Habsburgische Feste in der Renaissance', in Wilfried Seipel (ed.), *Wir sind Helden: Habsburgische Feste in der Renaissance* (Vienna: Kunsthistorisches Museum, 2005), pp. 11–3.

Sandbichler, Veronika, '*Identifikationen*: Antike Helden, Götter und Triumphe: Die Habsburger und ihre antiken Vorbilder im 16. Jahrhundert', in Sabine Haag (ed.), *All'Antica: Götter und Helden auf Schloss Ambras* (Vienna: Kunsthistorisches Museum, 2011), pp. 120–3.

Schauerte, Thomas Ulrich, *Die Ehrenpforte für Kaiser Maximilian I.: Dürer und Altdorfer im Dienst des Herrschers*, Kunstwissenschaftliche Studien, 95 (Munich and Berlin: Deutscher Kunstverlag, 2001).

Schlager, Johann Evangelist, *Wiener Skizzen aus dem Mittelalter* (Vienna: Gerold, 1835–46), vol. 3. (1839).

Seipel, Wilfried (ed.), *Werke für die Ewigkeit: Kaiser Maximilian I. und Erzherzog Ferdinand II.* (Vienna: Kunsthistorisches Museum, 2002).

Seipel, Wilfried (ed.), *Kaiser Ferdinand I.: 1503–1564: Das Werden der Habsburgermonarchie* (Vienna: Kunsthistorisches Museum, Milan: Skira, 2003).

Seipel, Wilfried (ed.), *Wir sind Helden, Habsburgische Feste in der Renaissance* (Vienna: Kunsthistorisches Museum, 2005).

Silver, Larry, 'Paper Pageants: The Triumphs of Emperor Maximilian I', in Barbara Wisch and Susan Scott Munshower (eds), *"All the World's a Stage. . .": Art and Pageantry in the Renaissance and Baroque: Triumphal Celebrations and the Rituals of Statecraft*, Papers in Art History from the Pennsylvania State University, 6 (University Park, PA: Pennsylvania State University Press, 1990), vol. 1, pp. 293–331.

Silver, Larry, *Marketing Maximilian: The Visual Ideology of a Holy Roman Emperor* (Princeton: Princeton University Press, 2008).

Sommer-Mathis, Andrea, 'VI.4. Residenz und öffentlicher Raum: Höfisches Fest in Wien im Wandel vom 16. zum 17. Jahrhundert', in Herbert Karner (ed.), *Die Wiener Hofburg: 1521–1705: Baugeschichte, Funktion und Etablierung als Kaiserresidenz*, Österreichische Akademie der Wissenschaften Denkschriften der Philosophisch-Historischen Klasse, 444, Veröffentlichungen zur Kunstgeschichte, 13, Veröffentlichungen zur Bau- und Funktionsgeschichte der Wiener Hofburg, 2 (Vienna: Österreichische Akademie der Wissenschaften, 2014), pp. 494–508.

Starn, Randolph, 'Renaissance triumphalism in art', in John Jeffries Martin (ed.), *The Renaissance World*, The Routledge Worlds (New York and London: Routledge, 2007), pp. 326–46.

Strong, Roy C., *Art and Power: Renaissance Festivals: 1450–1650* (Woodbridge: Boydell, 1984).

Thoenes, Christof (ed.), *Sebastiano Serlio: Sesto Seminario Internazionale di Storia dell'Architettura* (Milan: Electa, 1989).

Thomas, Christiane, 'Wien als Residenz unter Kaiser Ferdinand I.', *Studien zur Wiener Geschichte* 49 (1993), 101–17.

Vancsa, Eckart, 'Wien I.: Hofburg', in Artur Rosenauer (ed.), *Geschichte der bildenden Kunst in Österreich: Vol. 3: Spätmittelalter und Renaissance* (Vienna: Österreichische Akademie der Wissenschaften, Munich, Berlin, London and New York: Prestel, 2003), pp. 275–7.

Vocelka, Karl, 'Die Wiener Feste der frühen Neuzeit aus waffenkundlicher Sicht', *Jahrbuch des Vereins für Geschichte der Stadt Wien* 34 (1978), 133–48.

Watanabe-O'Kelly, Helen, 'Entries, Fireworks and Religious Festivals in the Empire', in Pierre Béhar and Helen Watanabe-O'Kelly (eds), *Spectacvlvm Europævm: Theatre and Spectacle in Europe: Histoire du spectacle in Europe: (1580–1750)*, Wolfenbütteler Arbeiten zur Barockforschung, 31 (Wiesbaden: Harrassowitz, 1999), pp. 721–41.

Watanabe-O'Kelly, Helen and Anne Simon, *Festivals and Ceremonies: A Bibliography of Works Relating to Court, Civic and Religious Festivals in Europe, 1500–1800* (London and New York: Mansell, 2000).

Weisbach, Werner, *Trionfi* (Berlin: G. Grote, 1919).

Winkler, Gerhard, 'Das Turnierbuch Hans Francolins', *Wissenschaftliche Mitteilungen aus dem Niederosterreichischen Landesmuseum* 1 (1980), 105–20.

Wisch, Barbara and Susan Scott Munshower (eds), *"All the World's a Stage . . .": Art and Pageantry in the Renaissance and Baroque: Triumphal Celebrations and the Rituals of Statecraft*. Papers in Art History from Pennsylvania University, 6, vol. 1 (University Park, PA: Pennsylvania State University, 1990).

Wünsch, Josef, 'Der Einzug Kaiser Maximilians II. in Wien 1563', *Berichte und Mittheilungen des Alterthums-Vereines zu Wien* 46 (1914), 11–34.

4 Ernest of Bavaria's joyous entry into Liège, 15 June 1581

Chantal Grell and Robert Halleux

The election of Ernest of Bavaria

Following the death of Gerard of Groesbeek, prince-bishop of Liège (1564–1580), a new election had to be organised on 29 December 1580. The candidates were Archduke Matthias, brother of the Emperor Rudolf II, and Ernest of Bavaria, a Wittelsbach by his father and a Habsburg by his mother. (See Figure 4.1.)

Ernest, appointed as coadjutor a few days before Groesbeek's death, was 27 years old and combined various titles: appointed Bishop of Freising at the age of 11 in 1565, and Bishop of Hildesheim in 1575, he was ordained priest in Cologne in 1577. On 28 January 1581, he was elected prince-bishop of Liège by the canons of the chapter of the Cathedral of Saint Lambert, with the support of Philip II of Spain and of Alexander Farnese in Brussels. He was the first Bavarian candidate since John of Bavaria in the fifteenth century, also known as 'John the merciless'. His career was not over: in 1583, he became Elector of Cologne, and in 1585 Bishop of Münster. He was at that date one of the most prominent figures in the Empire.

The Prince-Elector was the head of a mosaic of strategically located territories (see Plate 1).[1] A Catholic country under the authority of the Holy Roman Empire in the centre of a conflict zone, the Principality of Liège maintained a position of neutrality in a Europe torn by religious wars. The election of Ernest came as the result of a family strategy of territorial domination. His predecessor had aggressively eradicated Protestantism. Ernest further strengthened the role of the Jesuits from 1582, and in 1592 founded a seminary for the education of the clergy.

---

1 The Country of Liège, the County of Hoorn (in today's nomenclature, Dutch Limburg), the city of Maastricht, the County of Loon (in today's Belgian nomenclature, Limburg), the Marquisate of Franchimont, the Duchy of Bouillon, the Barony of Herstal, and twenty-two *bonnes villes* ('good cities'), including twelve Flemish- and ten French-speaking, where the citizenry managed day-to-day affairs.

Figure 4.1 Portrait of Ernest of Bavaria by Dominicus Custos, *Atrium heroicum Caesarum, regum imaginibus illustratum*, Augsbourg, M. Manger, J. Praetorius, 1600–1602, in fol.

© cliché CHST.

The exhibition devoted to him in Liège in 2011–2012[2] focused on the paradoxes and the strong personality of Ernest. We learn that he completed his studies in Rome at the Roman College, where he had been a pupil of the mathematician Christopher Clavius. An intransigent defender of the Council of Trent, a slayer of witches, by inclination an alchemist, he was a priest who married in secrecy, took many mistresses and legitimised his children. He was also a cultivated man who was acquainted with the humanists Lævinius Torrentius, Jean Chapeauville and Justus Lipsius, was interested in Copernican astronomy and took a keen interest in all things technical.

Ernest of Bavaria made his joyous entry to Liège on 15 June 1581 and formally took possession of his capital on 18 June. At that time, Liège was a rich city whose economy was based on coal, steel and the arms trade, though it remained a neutral city. The city had about 20,000 inhabitants. The Principality consisted of twenty-two *bonnes villes*, all with privileges. In the following year, Ernest had to make an entry to each of them. The grand entry to Liège is therefore the first in a long chain of entries, undoubtedly an exhausting undertaking.

2 'Ernest de Bavière (1554–1612). Un prince de Liège dans l'Europe moderne.' Grand Curtius, 18 November 2011/20 May 2012. See G. Xhayet and R. Halleux (eds), *Ernest de Bavière (1554–1612) et son temps. L'automne flamboyant de la Renaissance entre Meuse et Rhin* (Turnhout: Brepols, 2011).

The sources

The sources are numerous. Ernest's entry to Liège was exceptional because there had been no election of a foreign candidate to this role for more than a century. Three contemporary eyewitness reports in Latin were published during Ernest's lifetime:

1   The highly detailed *Inauguratio Principis Ernesti, utriusque Bavariæ Ducis* by Jean Polit was published in 1583.[3] A lawyer, scholar and court poet from Liège, Polit (1554–1601) had written poems which he dedicated to Gerard of Groesbeek. Ernest appointed him historiographer in 1588, when Polit's *Panegyrici ad Christiani orbis principes* appeared in Cologne. Of the same age as Ernest, whom he did not know before the entry to Liège, Polit accompanied him everywhere from then on. His account has the character of an official description by a Liégeois who understands the precise meaning of each element of the occasion.

2   Born around 1530–1540 in Devon, Robert Turner (d. 1599) studied rhetoric and philosophy at Oxford. In 1569, he taught rhetoric in Douai and wrote pamphlets for Mary Stuart. He resided in Paris, then in Rome in 1575, where he chose to study theology at the Collegium Germanicum, at the period when Ernest was also a student there. Under the direction of the Jesuits, he went to Bavaria where he created the Eichstadt seminary. In 1582, he served as professor of eloquence in Ingolstadt. He obtained a prebend (stipend) and joined the Faculty in 1584, to teach cases of conscience. He was rector there in 1585 and in 1593 became a canon in Breslau. A close associate of Ernest of Bavaria, he became his advisor and theologian. His *Triumphus Bavaricus*, published in 1584, is modelled on the panegyrics of ancient rhetoricians.[4] It narrates Ernest's entire journey from Munich to Liege and quotes *in extenso* the lengthy Latin harangue delivered by Turner on behalf of the Duke of Bavaria.

3   Jean Chapeauville (1551–1617) studied philosophy at Cologne and Louvain, followed by theology at Louvain, was ordained priest and was appointed by Groesbeek in 1578 as one of the synod examiners. In 1579, he became priest of St Michel and canon of St Peter. He was appointed inquisitor of the Faith by Ernest in 1582. In 1587, he became canon of

---

3 *Inauguratio Principis Ernesti, utriusque Bavariæ Ducis, in Leodiensium principem, illiusque in suam civitatem, ac reliquas Leodinæ Patriæ Urbes* (Cologne: Jean Gymnicus, 1583), pp. 1–102.

4 'Triumphus Bavaricus', *Panegyrici de duobus triumphis clarissimis . . . hoc Leodio in inauguratione Ernesti ducis Bavariæ*, published by Sartorius in Ingolstadt in 1584. As the title indicates, there are two panegyrics, one on the translation of the relics of Gregory of Naziance to Rome, which does not concern Ernest, the other on the grand entry to Liège. The text can be found in *Roberti Turneri Oratoris et Philosophi Ingolstadiensis orationes XIV* (Ingolstadt: Sartorius, 1584), pp. 91–187.

the Cathedral of Liège and first penitentiary at the behest of Pope Sixtus V, who was impressed by his zeal. Ernest appointed him vicar general for spiritual matters in 1598. He left a *Collection of the most important historians of the bishops of Liege*,[5] published in 1599–1601.

Eighteenth-century historians mention, in addition to these eyewitness reports, the testimony of Barthélemy Honoré at Liège, a work which was printed but is now lost. Four chronicles written in the vernacular are preserved in the library of the University of Liège.[6] These civic chronicles stress Ernest's reception by the city authorities; as short manuscripts, for private use and thus unpublished, they may include a few previously unknown details but are unlikely to vary substantially from the main accounts discussed here. There are, finally, subsequent compilations – by Fisen, Foulon and Bouille (in French) – which base their accounts on the narratives of Polit and Chapeauville.[7] Some nineteenth-century accounts are in effect compilations. Baron de Chestret de Haneffe, a numismatist, bibliophile, and biographer of Jean Polit, paraphrases the works of both Polit and Turner, of which he owned a copy.[8] The account by the liberal anticlerical historian Ferdinand Hénaux presents Ernest as spendthrift and luxurious.[9] Joseph Daris, a history professor at the Seminary, offers a very brief narrative.[10] From 1929 to 1938 a long series of articles by Eugène Polain devoted twenty pages to Ernest's Grand Entry.[11]

Although Liège was a country of engravers, we do not have any drawing or engraving of Ernest's entry, nor an official *recueil*. It is the same for the entries of his predecessors, Erard de la Marck, Georges of Austria, Corneille de Berghes, Georges-Louis de Berghes and Gerard of Groesbeek, and for the entries of the nephews who succeeded him, Ferdinand, Maximilian Henry and Joseph Clément. Illustrations of entries were often commissioned by the cities (or municipalities) as testimony to their own glory. Here, the context is different: this foreign prince was elected by the chapter of the Cathedral, and municipal authorities could not therefore take advantage of his appointment for their own prestige.

5 *Qui Gesta Pontificum Trajectensium Tungrensium et Leodiensium scripserunt Auctores Praecipui* (Liège, 1611).

6 Manuscripts 179, fol. 247r and v; 174, pp. 142–3; 543, fol. 573v; 630, pp. 494–501.

7 Bartholomé Fisen, S.J., *Sancta Legia Romanæ Ecclesiæ filia sive Historiarum Ecclesiæ Leodiensis partes duæ* (Liège: G.H. Streel, 1696). Erasme Foullon, S.J., *Historia Leodiensis per Episcoporum et Principum seriem digesta, ab origine populi usque ad Ferdinandi Bavari tempora* (Liège: Everard Kints, 1736), II, pp. 317–18. Théodose Bouille, *Histoire de la ville et pays de Liège* (Liège: Barnabé, 1732), III, pp. 4–10.

8 *Bulletin de l'Institut archéologique liégeois* 24 (1878), 123ff.

9 Ferd Henaux, *Histoire du pays de Liège* (Liège: Desoer, 1856), II, pp. 132–9.

10 *Histoire du diocèse et de la principauté de Liège pendant le XVIe siècle, réimpression de l'édition de 1880* (Brussels: Culture et Civilisation, 1974), pp. 459–63.

11 Eugène Polain, 'Ernest de Bavière, évêque et prince de Liège 1581–1612' in *Bulletin de l'Institut archéologique liégeois*, LIII (1929), 23–167.

The itinerary and the stages

For the historian, Ernest's entry has interest as a political event that connects a prince of the Church, who never came to Liège in that capacity, to a city jealous of its traditions and privileges. The printed and manuscript descriptions allow us to analyse the emblematic decoration and costumes, highlighting the city's very special profile: a profile that was political, conveying an affirmation of the city's identity and neutrality, and ecclesiastical, as well as economic, given that Liège was a major industrial metropolis.

Ernest will have had to pass, throughout his journey, a series of real and symbolic gates and triumphal arches, and will have had to stop at each stage to confirm the rights of the mayors and aldermen, the trades organisations, the various ecclesiastical chapters and civic institutions, so that when entering the Cathedral of Saint Lambert, he had already signed a whole series of so-called capitulations.

The entry may be discussed by treating its component parts in succession:

The prince and his cortege

Having left Visé in the morning, Ernest arrived in Liège from the east at two o'clock. He had crossed the duchies of Kleve, Jülich and Berg, with each prince providing him with an escort. By adding up the numbers mentioned, we find that he was accompanied by more than one thousand cavalrymen, two hundred and fifty infantrymen and two hundred notables, together with, in his retinue, members of his council, more than six hundred common people and, in addition to all these, a personal escort of six hundred to eight hundred and fifty cavalrymen. Ernest took his place in the centre of a procession composed as follows:

1   At the head, the lancers (Polit) or halberdiers (Bouille) sent by the governors of the fourteen major districts and fortresses of the country.
2   These were accompanied by representatives of the Noble Estate of the Principality, including twenty-six earls and barons, who took part in a personal capacity, dignitaries of the cities 'who wore silk mantles lined with blue [a present from the Prince], decorated with silver fringes' and enriched with the insignia of the Golden Fleece worn as necklaces. The colour palette was appropriate, as blue, white and silver are the colours of Bavaria.
3   Next came the foreign delegations and the princes: Philippe de Croÿ, Prince of Chimay, with a following of one-hundred-and-fifty horses; the Prince of Arenberg, followed by one hundred and sixty-six horses; William of Bavaria, the Duke of Jülich, with a retinue of three hundred and fifty-four cavalrymen, sixty-four footmen and the governors of his territories and court advisors; Duke Ferdinand of Bavaria, with a following

of more than two hundred horses and a hundred men on foot (two hundred and five horses and ten infantrymen, according to Polit); Charles de Croÿ, Duke of Aarschot, followed by about a hundred horses and many men on foot.

Ernest's retinue, positioned as noted in the middle of the procession, was made up as follows:

1   Fourteen pages of the court dressed in silk, with hats decorated with peacock feathers and pearls; the prince's personal guard (twenty-four men) dressed in blue and white silk; two drummers on horseback in the 'Hungarian fashion'; Ernest's close circle, Charles de Ligne Prince of Arenberg, Philippe de Croÿ, Landgrave of Leuchtenberg, the Grand Duke Ferdinand of Bavaria, Charles de Croÿ Duke of Aarschot as ambassador of the King of Spain, between Ferdinand and William of Jülich; eight of the prince's trumpeters; the flag-bearer Adolph of Schwarzenberg, carrying the prince's red flag embroidered with his coat of arms and with the coats of arms of the different parts of the country of Liège; the grand mayor carrying the rod of justice; the Count of Duras carrying the silver sword.
2   Ernest himself, in civilian clothes, processed between the two burgomasters. His costume is not described.
3   He was followed by his Privy Council and all his officials, senators, archdeacons, secretaries, the commissioners of the city, singers (the choir) and his servants, in total six hundred people and, in long columns, six hundred mercenary cavalry comprising the prince's personal guard.[12]

As Polit noted, the splendour of the silk clothing worn by those from Liège and their neighbours contrasted with the garments of black silk and gold necklaces of the German princes (Polit, p. 42).

The prince and the city

The various processional stages are shown on the city map (see Plates 2 and 3: from East to West, numbers 1–7).

As soon as scouts on the ramparts caught sight of the prince, cannons were fired three times 'so that the earth trembled'. Each of the processional stages was designed and set up in the following ways:

N°1, at the Faubourg Saint Léonard. At two o'clock, Ernest was welcomed, at a convent outside the walls, by the mayors, who dismounted at his approach. He was addressed in laudatory terms in both French and German by both mayors, who offered him the keys to the city. He held them a

---

12 Bouille counts eight hundred and fifty horsemen and thirty-seven infantry (Bouille, p. 6).

moment and then returned them, praising the mayors for their loyalty, 'not doubting they would continue to keep them fairly, adding that, as for him, he wanted to live and die with his subjects' (Boulle, p. 5).

Three companies of ten men lined the quay. The fourth row was formed by a boundary hedge outside the city wall. Ernest was required to swear to maintain the privileges and liberties of the city. The text of the oath, which his predecessors 'had been accustomed to swear on this day', was presented by the mayors and read by Ernest. The mayors re-mounted their horses and returned to the city, with the prince in their midst. Confronted by a multitude of petitions for clemency from 'criminals', the 'wise and prudent' mayors required that requests be made in writing to avoid excess. Between the convent and the city gate there was a distance of 500 metres, which took two hours for the procession to cover.

N°2. The Gate of Saint Léonard was decorated with the coats of arms of the Empire, the house of Bavaria, Ernest's predecessors and the city, with Latin mottoes including Ernest's own: *Audiatur altera pars* (let the other party be heard) (Polit, pp. 42–5). The gate was guarded by archers, who closed it. The mayors ordered its opening in vain. They dispatched one of the city servants, who opened the gate on their behalf, after three attempts (Bouille, p. 5). The leaders of the crossbowmen offered their flag to the Prince, who swore to preserve the rights, privileges and freedoms of the company of archers. At four o'clock, the last occasion on which time is indicated, the procession advanced to Saint Lambert, between the thirty-two trades in arms and the four companies of musketeers under their flags, standing in their ranks with the crowd behind them. This itinerary, along the current Féronstrée street, measures 1 kilometre, with a further 300 metres up to the church of S. George.

N°3. A triumphal arch constructed solely for Ernest's benefit. The arch was located opposite the Church of St George and was 50 feet or 15 metres high (Turner), with three Doric porticoes adorned with emblems and devices testifying to Ernest's glory and surrounded by girls 'of a chosen beauty, and magnificently dressed' (Polit, p. 45). At the top, the imperial eagle held the globe in its claws. In the centre, the arms of Ernest and the mayors appeared, with a poem referring to Ernest's personal device. Above were figures (*simulacra*) representing Stability, Nobility and Authority. Below were figures (*effigies*) representing Prudence and Temperance, and paintings depicting Mucius Scaevola and Horatius Cocles, accompanied by verses. Still further below, at one side, were effigies of two girls, Honour and Glory, and at the other *Abundantia* and *Fama*. Around the arch were the insignia of the twenty *bonnes villes* of the principality (Polit, pp. 46–7).

When half of the procession had passed, and Ernest arrived under the arch, a machine lowered the *perron de Liège* (a column with a pine cone, symbol of the freedom of the city). At the sound of a melodious concert of instruments, a girl of rare beauty, dressed in a purple garment like a goddess, recited verses in French, proclaiming the betrothal of the prince and the city. This poem functioned both as a eulogy and an epithalamium. Ernest, it stated, would be inspired by it as he increased his dealings with young Liégeoises. The girl offered Ernest a garland of flowers (Polit, pp. 48–9; Turner). An artificial castle, standing at the side of the river Meuse, showed the river on fire, while a cannon's thunder was heard on land. The prince continued in the direction of the market square, a route which led him to plunge into the crowd for about 300 metres. According to Polit, windows in this locality were leased for six pieces of gold (Polit, p. 50). Ernest removed his hat in order to be better seen: 'He had a handsome face, full of eagerness, good-humoured, caring and laughing with the happiness of his people' (Polit, p. 51).

N°4. At the Market Square Ernest came upon four stages, separated by pyramids 18–20 metres high:

- On the first of these, four young men were dressed as girls, representing the Ecclesiastical Estate under the figures of Church, Faith, Hope and Charity. The young men praised Ernest and offered him a golden figure representing Faith (Bouille). They explained what the Church expected from the prince, that is to say, the restoration of a religion that was currently faltering, and a defence of the faith (p. 52).
- On the second stage, young men represented the Estate of the Nobility. Ernest received a golden sword 'to reward the good and punish the wicked' (Polit).
- At the third stage, which represented the Third Estate, that is to say the people, Ernest was offered a golden heart and was urged not to neglect the cause of an afflicted people. Instead, he should, like another Gideon, use the sword given by God to suppress injustice and peace-breaking. He was exhorted to be 'he who holds in his hand the heart of the multitude' (Polit, p. 53).
- On the fourth stage, a common man accused of *lèse-majesté* (treason), adopted a begging posture at the feet of a judge, who held in his hands an inscription in gold letters: *Audiatur altera pars* ('let the other party be heard') – a motto, as noted above, familiar to the prince (Bouille, p. 7).
- Polit explains that between these stages were pyramids 20 metres high, with at the top naked children who decorated the pyramids with olive branches, played the lyre and poured out white and red wine at the central pyramids.

N°5: Ernest entered the City Hall ('*le détroit*'). He received the text of a new oath, to which he consented and was offered sweets and drinks.[13]

---

13 He agreed to respect the decisions of the Court of Aldermen, and also convened the Court of the Twenty-Two. Polit gives the oath and names all the aldermen.

The Prince and the chapter

1 The provost, the dean and the cathedral canons were placed sitting on the steps of the church of St Lambert (N°6). They wore silk vestments given by the prince, with furs and an '*almucium*' ('a shoulder cape'). Some wore crosses, others carried relics (Polit names all the canons, pp. 55–7). Ernest passed in front of them, then 'as he tried to dismount at the foot of the steps of Saint Lambert, the church cantor, pretending to assist him, put his hand on the saddle, to mark that it and the horse belonged to him' and the church (Bouille, p. 7).

2 Ernest was stripped of his coat and dressed in a cassock and 'ratchet', a long jacket embroidered with flowers of gold, adorned with gems and pearls (Polit); he was then dressed in his *almucium* and ermine. He was next taken to the high altar in S. Lambert's (Polit, p. 61). The provost lauded him on behalf of the chapter. He was taken further into the church and at the entrance rang a bell 'as churchwarden of Alken, an office with a significant relation to the bishops, without which he could not insist on allegiance' (Bouille, p. 7).

3 In front of the altar he read an ancient capitulation (or oath), which he swore on his knees to observe. (Bouille gives the full text, pp. 7–10; Polit, however, does not mention this detail.)

   On the steps of St Lambert, money was thrown to the crowd.

4 Ernest was finally led in triumph to the episcopal palace (N°7). Polit writes that this was followed by a lavish banquet.

The next day the Grand Entry closed with a High Mass followed by a procession, of which Polit describes the organisation.

Conclusion

In the order of the main procession, of its various stages, the decoration of the city and the colours and sounds of the joyous entry, there is a conflation of various traditions. The splendour of Burgundian joyous entries mixes with observance of antique precedent and characteristic Jesuit practices, together with the overt symbolism of the city's privileges. Each step along the processional route had the effect of ritualising the abandonment of a portion of Ernest's power.[14]

Bibliography

Primary manuscript sources

Chronicles (in the vernacular) in Manuscripts 174, 179, 543, and 630 (University of Liège).

---

14 On Ernest's various 'capitulations', see Georges Hansotte, *Les institutions politiques et judiciaires de la principauté de Liège aux temps modernes* (Brussels: Crédit communal, 1987), pp. 59–62.

Primary printed sources

Bouille, Théodose, *Histoire de la ville et pays de Liège* (Liège: Barnabé, 1732), III, pp. 4–10.

Chapeauville, Jean, *Qui Gesta Pontificum Trajectensium Tungrensium et Leodiensium scripserunt Auctores Praecipui* (Liège, 1611).

Fisen, Bartholomé S.J., *Sancta Legia Romanæ Ecclesiæ filia sive Historiarum Ecclesiæ Leodiensis partes duæ* (Liège: G.H. Streel, 1696).

Foullon, Erasme S.J., *Historia Leodiensis per Episcoporum et Principum seriem digesta, ab origine populi usque ad Ferdinandi Bavari tempora* (Liège: Everard Kints, 1736), II, pp. 317–18.

Polit, Jean, *Inauguratio Principis Ernesti, utriusque Bavariæ Ducis, in Leodiensium principem, illiusque in suam civitatem, ac reliquas Leodinæ Patriæ Urbes* (Cologne: Jean Gymnicus, 1583).

Roberti Turneri Oratoris et Philosophi Ingolstadiensis orationes XIV (Ingolstadt: Sartorius, 1584), pp. 91–187.

Turner, Robert, 'Triumphus Bavaricus', *Panegyrici de duobus triumphis clarissimis . . . hoc Leodio in inauguratione Ernesti ducis Bavariæ* (Ingolstadt: Sartorius, 1584).

Secondary sources

Chestret de Haneffe, Baron de, *Bulletin de l'Institut archéologique liégeois* 24 (1878).

Darius, Joseph, *Histoire du diocèse et de la principauté de Liège pendant le XVIe siècle, réimpression de l'édition de 1880* (Brussels: Culture et Civilisation, 1974).

Hansotte, Georges, *Les institutions politiques et judiciaires de la principauté de Liège aux temps modernes* (Brussels: Crédit communal, 1987).

Henaux, Ferdinand, *Histoire du pays de Liège*, vol. II (Liège: Desoer, 1856).

Polain, Eugène, 'Ernest de Bavière, évêque et prince de Liège 1581–1612' in *Bulletin de l'Institut archéologique liégeois*, LIII (1929), 23–167.

Xhayet, G. and R. Halleux (eds), *Ernest de Bavière (1554–1612) et son temps. L'automne flamboyant de la Renaissance entre Meuse et Rhin* (Turnhout: Brepols, 2011).

5 Valladolid 1605

A theatre for the peace

Berta Cano-Echevarría and Mark Hutchings

For several weeks the Castilian city of Valladolid, briefly the seat of the Spanish court, served as a theatre for the ratification of the Anglo–Spanish peace, formally bringing to an end twenty years of conflict. The Earl of Nottingham's (Charles Howard's) embassy to Philip III was the second part of the peacemaking process, a reciprocation of the Spanish mission to England the previous year. In this chapter, we examine the theatricality of diplomatic ceremonial. The scripting of the peace on the city stage illustrates how a public and state understanding of international relations was bound up with the grammar and syntax of theatrical display.

While the importance of ceremony is recognised by historians of diplomacy, its wider implications have not been explored.[1] The semiotics of protocol, for example, tend to be understood primarily in socio-political terms, as a shared code of conduct where each participant knew his 'place', and where placing and movement signified status, role, access and so on.[2] Yet the choreographic character of early modern diplomacy admits of comparison with a form of representation that, perhaps not coincidentally, was also evolving into a 'professional' activity over the course of the sixteenth century. Like theatre, with its demarcated space, audience, actors and script, international relations were conducted through rituals of performance. Just as monarchical and civic authority were displayed – and thus legitimated – in the masque, progresses, urban pageants and city entries, so diplomacy was staged, in public as well as elite spaces. This is not simply metaphor. What is most telling about early modern accounts is the attention paid to the theatrical properties of ceremonial, not as mere details of diplomacy but as its essence. For all that negotiations between (or, properly speaking, on behalf of) monarchs were conducted in private, it would be a mistake to conclude that early modern diplomacy offered public 'fictions' that symbolised

---

1 For a recent exception, see Janette Dillon, *The Language of Space in Court Performance, 1400–1625* (Cambridge: Cambridge University Press, 2010).
2 See especially William Roosen's important essay 'Early Modern Diplomatic Ceremonial: A Systems Approach', *The Journal of Modern History* 52.3 (1980), 452–76.

(and perhaps misrepresented) transactions previously carried out elsewhere. Indeed, the distinction between 'public' and 'private' is misleading, since *all* behaviour was socially and politically coded, regardless of where it took place. Most significantly, much of what to the modern eye appears to be *mere* ceremonial was in fact the *enactment* of diplomatic relations, not its simulation. As such, conceiving of diplomacy as 'theatrical' is not to invoke an analogy but to align this practice of monarchical negotiation by proxy with the kinds of expression of power that monarchy choreographed for itself: appropriately so, since the early modern ambassador was effectively an actor (surrogate for his master) who performed (in the sense of *represented*) his master's power in the presence of the host. This choreographing of diplomacy produced a complex staging of state-to-state diplomacy in Valladolid in 1605.

The Anglo–Spanish peace was a treaty-as-diptych: a Spanish delegation was sent to London (King James had refused Philip III's request that the negotiations be conducted in Brussels), the treaty was signed there in August 1604, and, on Philip's insistence, the peace was ratified in Spain. This format had considerable implications for the nature and interpretation of the various ceremonies laid on by the host country. Indeed, what happened in Spain may only properly be understood in terms of what had preceded it in England. As we have described elsewhere, this two-legged affair was one of 'symmetry and reciprocity'; and yet while the Spanish had been forced to negotiate the peace in England, Philip held the upper hand in Spain, where the festivities were precisely calibrated to restore Habsburg honour in a peace that had not given Spain what it desired.[3]

The peacemaking and the ratification were not of course identical. The hosting of the English embassy took place after the treaty had been agreed. In England the negotiations began tentatively, with courtly entertainments for the ambassador extraordinary who had been sent ostensibly to congratulate James upon his succession but also to lay the foundations for the peace: only then did the Constable of Castile arrive to sign the treaty. The intrigue surrounding the preliminary negotiations at the Stuart court has been described elsewhere.[4] A year later the Spanish reciprocated, but not in kind. Just as Philip III's lavish gift-giving must have embarrassed James and Anna,[5] so the reception of the English embassy was an elaborate festival that outdid England's hospitality the previous year.

---

3 See Mark Hutchings and Berta Cano-Echevarría, 'Between Courts: Female Masquers and Anglo-Spanish Diplomacy, 1603–05', *Early Theatre* 15.1 (2012), 91–108.

4 We discuss the preliminaries to the peace in 'The Spanish Ambassador and *The Vision of the Twelve Goddesses*: A New Document [with text]', *English Literary Renaissance* 42.2 (2012), 223–57.

5 See Gustav Ungerer, 'Juan Pantoja de la Cruz and the Circulation of Gifts', *Sederi* 9 (1998), 59–78.

Nottingham's progress

From arrival to departure the English mission's reception was finely choreographed. Philip's plan was that Nottingham would make landfall at Santander and proceed south via Burgos, where the English would be impressed by the city's remarkable cathedral, and then on to Valladolid. Perhaps the host's intentions are most evident, however, in the improvisation that was required once news reached Philip that the English fleet had sailed west and dropped anchor off La Coruña. Like a subject held in the monarch's gaze, Nottingham was instructed to remain in Galicia for a whole month while new preparations were made to bring him south. In the interval, the governor of 'the Groyne', as the English called La Coruña, improvised, laying on entertainment for the several hundred Englishmen, while horses, mules and supplies were sent north from Valladolid. It was a pattern that was repeated during Nottingham's 'progress', the English accounts recording how, at every stage on this re-arranged itinerary, provincial dignitaries acted as host to the English king's representative.

Even before the formal entry into Valladolid, Philip's design was clear, as Nottingham was once again 'held' initially on the periphery; throughout the following weeks the embassy would follow the royal script to the letter; indeed, Nottingham's list of requests was largely dismissed, as the king's annotations in the original document indicate.[6] As we propose to show, Philip's intention was to incorporate the embassy into an extended courtly pageant, with the city itself appropriated as theatre. Given James's financial difficulties, trumping England's hospitality was not a difficult feat; what Philip desired was to script the ratification on Habsburg terms (as he had been unable to do with the Treaty of London). The challenge, however, was presented by Valladolid itself, which for all its attributes required considerable modification to serve as festival stage. The reasons for the relocation of the *corte* in 1601 remain unclear, but the effect was to transform the city, with the population doubling to 70,000 in five years. An old residence of the Marquis of Camarasa, bought by the Duke of Lerma (who modern historians suspect to have benefited from shady property dealings) was purchased by Philip. This building, situated opposite San Pablo church, and to which a new banqueting hall connected by a gallery specially commissioned for the peace was still under construction in the spring of 1605, would play a key role in the ratification. The scale of the preparations was noted by Tomé Pinheiro da Veiga, a Portuguese visitor, who wryly (though perhaps not inaccurately) remarked that '*de hum dia para o outro, se vem huns Palacios encantados onde era montura*' ('enchanted palaces appear suddenly where once there was a dump').[7] This suggestion of a cityscape transformed into a

---

6 Archivo General de Simancas, E 2557, Fol. 37.
7 Tomé Pinheiro da Veiga, *Fastiginia*, ed. Ernesto Rodrigues (Lisbon: Centro de Literaturas e Culturas Lusófonas e Europeias, 2011, p. 53).

theatre of 'enchant[ment]' neatly captures both the size of the task and the civic or regal nature of the festivities envisaged.

Despite the logistical difficulties the city faced (not least accommodating some six hundred 'heretics'), these festivities were elaborate, large-scale, and citywide. As Dudley Carleton wrote to John Chamberlain in a letter dated 10 June, 'Here have bin feasts and triumphs enough for Stoes chronicle, and some what remaines for every day we stay here'.[8] The comparison with Stowe is instructive: Carleton is drawn to remark on the kinds of civic events his countryman chronicled. While some of the hospitality was of course restricted to high-status figures, such as the ratification ceremony itself, the episode is notable for how the city – and its enlarged population – played a key role in the reception of the Nottingham mission. Philip fully understood that 'the point of the festival *is* the audience',[9] and accordingly set the English visitors on a public stage, their presence bearing witness to the peace as 'actors' of a Habsburg script. But the resulting theatre was rather more complex than this analogy allows, for these events were characterised by a fascinating interplay and transposition of roles between constituencies. Our focus here is on three key outdoor events, each of which features the participation of the citizens of Valladolid and whose 'triangulation' illustrates how the politics of the peace was staged, internationally and domestically, and diplomacy enacted.[10]

The entry into the city

The manner of Nottingham's arrival in Valladolid illustrates the ambiguity that attended the embassy's reception. Philip's desire to choreograph the ratification to the very last detail meant that, despite the arduousness of its fortnight-long progress south, the English party was instructed to continue past Valladolid to Simancas, some seven leagues away, and to rest for two days. The principal reason for this was that an approach from the south-west, through the *Puerta del Campo*, afforded the most impressive view of the city for visitors, as it did for its temporary inhabitants the English entourage: the point of entry would then facilitate the most desirable route into and through the city. This set the tone for what was to follow and enabled the king to assert his authority and control over proceedings. But it also meant that the ratification proper began with a form of ceremonial

---

8 PRO, SP 94/11/123; cited in Gustav Ungerer, 'The Spanish and English Chronicles in King James's and Sir George Buc's Dossiers on the Anglo-Spanish Peace Negotiations', *Huntington Library Quarterly* 61.3/4 (1998), 309–24; 320.

9 Helen Watanabe-O'Kelly, 'Early Modern European Festivals – Politics, Performance, Event and Record', in J.R. Mulryne and Elizabeth Goldring (eds), *Court Festivals of the European Renaissance: Art, Politics and Performance* (Aldershot and Burlington, VT: Ashgate, 2002), pp. 15–25; p. 16.

10 For the dissemination of these texts, see Ungerer, 'The Spanish and English Chronicles'.

that resembled nothing so much as a royal entry.[11] The Constable of Castile had not been accorded a similar honour in London (because James had not been resident there when the constable went to England), though the Spanish ambassador had witnessed James's ceremonial entry into London in March 1604 (delayed because of a particularly severe outbreak of plague); but for many of Nottingham's entourage this occasion may have reminded them of what they had witnessed the previous year, albeit from a rather different perspective. Nottingham himself, appointed Lord High Constable for the entry into London, would effectively reprise that role here.[12] As will become clear, the various entertainments the English visitors enjoyed admitted a range of interpretation, overlaid as they were with the politics of the peace and, indeed, the events that had preceded the signing of the treaty.

The entry is interesting, then, both for its carefully designed theatre and its function as a symbolic (but also actual) enactment of peacemaking. In key respects, it followed the model of royal ceremonials familiar to Europeans, and certainly the rarity of such events explains in part the response of the people of the city. The chief difference, of course, was that here the host was the *king*. Rather than the city admitting the monarch in confirmation of a socio-political contract, as conventionally, in this case the king was overseeing the visit of a foreign, subordinate subject (who nonetheless was a 'substitute' for his brother monarch). Nottingham's 'double' status as both surrogate and representative may explain both the regality of the procession and the ostentatious orchestration of such a privilege by Philip. It represented both his commitment to the peace and an expression of hospitality as power.

While the procession into the city two days later evoked aspects of a royal entry, the embassy's staying at Simancas on Tuesday 14 May was preparatory to that. Valladolid itself would play a chiefly logistical role as Nottingham's civic host, though as we shall see it took an active part in the entertainments arranged; the object of Nottingham's visit was the Spanish king and his *corte*. Thus, elements of the Spanish nobility, by degrees, visited James's emissary prior to the entry, and these visits constituted the earl's first, formal encounter with the *corte*. Instructed on the Tuesday, according to the account of the Somerset Herald, Robert Treswell, 'that it was the Kings pleasure, we should rest at *Simancas* all Wednesday, and not till Thursday come to the Court', the English received on the day following a visit from the son of the current ambassador in England and his designated

11 On the significance of the city entry, see J.R. Mulryne, Maria Ines Aliverti and Anna Maria Testaverde (eds), *Ceremonial Entries in Early Modern Europe: The Iconography of Power* (Farnham and Burlington, VT: Ashgate, 2015).
12 See Mark Hutchings and Berta Cano-Echevarría, 'The Spanish Ambassador's Account of James I's Entry into London, 1604 [with text]' in *The Seventeenth Century*, 33.3 (2018), 255–77.

successor.[13] The identity of Nottingham's guests is clearly symbolic, emissaries to emissary, and just as Spain's ambassador to James arrived in England ahead of the Constable of Castile, so here a meeting served as preliminary to the more formal occasions the following day. On the Thursday, a larger party of more senior nobles met the embassy and escorted it towards the city; such was the scale of the events planned that a delay had to be fashioned: about two miles from Valladolid, Nottingham was invited into 'a certain banqueting house which stood vpon the high way, to see the delicacy of the orchards and gardens, as to tast of the variety of fruits within the same'.[14] It seems, however, that this stop had not been planned initially, but was improvised as a result of the constable being delayed:

> *para juntarse todos en casa del Condestable, de donde salieron, se tardaron más tiempo que fuera razón [. . .] y hubo de esperar el Almirante más de dos horas en una huerta.*
>
> [they took longer than was reasonable to gather in the house of the Constable, from where they were to come out, so that the Admiral (Nottingham) was kept waiting for two hours in an orchard.][15]

Finally, led by the admiral's opposite number, the Constable of Castile, his party of high-ranking nobles passed through the *Puerta del Campo*, crossed the esplanade of *Campo Grande*, and emerged onto the Simancas road through the *Puerta del Carmen*. The constable brought with him a horse which he presented to the admiral, who left his coach and mounted, to enter the city alongside his Spanish counterpart. The symbolism of the gift and the mode of conveying James's representative into Valladolid was obvious: one of the English accounts asserts that 'the King himselfe did vse to ride' it.[16] All the eyewitnesses testify to the scale of the occasion. In addition to the escort of members of the *corte*, the embassy received a less formal but more numerous civic presence as it approached the outer *puerta*. In Pinheiro's account,

> *Á tarde, começou a acudir tanta gente e tantos coches, que eles e os cavalos o ocupavam, de maneira que os que passavam não podiam voltar, e lhes era necessário ir adiante, com que se facia uma vista formosissima por espaço de mais de quatro tiros de espingarda.*[17]

13 Robert Treswell, *A Relation of such\Things as Were Observed to Happen in the Journey of the Right Honourable Charles Earle of Nottingham, L. High Admirall of England, His Highnesse Ambassadour to the King of Spaine* (London, 1605), p. 29.
14 Ibid., p. 30.
15 Luis Cabrera de Cordoba, *Relaciones de las cosas sucedidas en la corte de España desde 1599 hasta 1614* (Valladolid: Junta de Castilla y León, 1997), p. 245.
16 *A Relation*, p. 30.
17 Pinheiro da Veiga, *Fastiginia*, p. 70.

[In the afternoon, there started to come so many people and coaches to this road that it became completely congested so that those that went could not go back and were forced to continue forward, being a beautiful thing to see for a distance of more than four shots of cannon.]

Unfortunately for all concerned, the uncontrollable intervened – the weather. Treswell records how

the weather being all that time extraordinarily hot, suddenly to the great disordering of all the company, there fell so great a shewer of raine as the like was not seene of long time before: and continuing till the company could get to the towne, notwithstanding his Lordship kept still his horse backe, accompanied with many of the chiefe of the company.[18]

Nonetheless, the procession continued, albeit in some disarray. Entering through *La Puerta del Campo*, the English would have been struck by the topography of the Spanish city: instead of a succession of narrow streets, as was the case with London pageants, the route was punctuated by plazas opening out before it, arenas that would come to play key roles in the entertainments to follow. First they crossed the *Campo Grande*, home to most of the embassies, and which would serve as the venue for a military parade towards the end of the visit; passing through *La Puerta del Campo*, Nottingham and the constable then paraded through streets that took them to the Plaza Mayor, which would host the bullfight and the *juego de cañas*, and then 'along by the Court gate' to the royal palace; here 'the King, Queen and Ladies (as it was sa[i]d) [were] standing in seuerall windows to take view of the company',[19] while another source states that the king privately took a coach incognito to observe the English unseen.[20] From this plaza, which would play a key role in later events, Nottingham was escorted to his lodgings nearby, where in the evening he was visited by 'diuers Noble men as also the *Mayordomo* to the Queen', Treswell remarking that this 'was much wondred at by the Spaniards themselues, for that (if they speake true) they neuer knew the like fauour done to any Ambassadour whatsoeuer'.[21]

Philip's desire to observe the fruits of his choreography was in keeping with his predilection for such private viewing (he would later observe the christening of his son from a place of concealment), but it also draws attention to the spectacle of ceremonial entries as doubly significant, both ideologically and theatrically. Rather than distinguish between ceremonial as

18 *A Relation*, p. 31.
19 Ibid., p. 32.
20 Pinheiro da Veiga, *Fastiginia*, p. 72.
21 *A Relation*, p. 32.

enactment and spectacle as theatrical entertainment,[22] we read these events as signifying through the performance which, after all, constitutes them. Moreover, the city entry deconstructs notional identities: Nottingham's embassy is both actor (in the eyes of the fascinated populace) and audience of the city, itself a spectacle, even – newly imagined as setting for the English – to those daily familiar with it. Here, and in the events we consider below, this fluidity between viewer and viewed, subject and object, creates a telling dynamic. Indeed, perhaps curiously, given the usual focus on the monarch, it is in and through the figure of Nottingham in particular that this complexity may be seen to work. His presence in Spain could not but be controversial, given his role in the recent conflict. The grandeur of his entry into Valladolid accorded with his status as former enemy as well as ambassador for the peace, and this dual status was activated at points during his visit. As we show below, for the wider population this facet of the ratification was available through the theatre of diplomacy, in the ways in which political perspectives could be articulated, sometimes silently, always visibly (see Plate 4).

The Pentecost procession

Once inside the city gates, the embassy became an actual, visible presence: anticipation gave way to perception, and the hosting of the embassy began in earnest. It was within the walls of the city that the festival proper would begin, and where, indeed, the inevitable tensions, albeit muted, would be played out. In Spain, the conflict with England had been understood and presented as a war against religious secession; while the English had steadfastly avoided the religious issue during the peace negotiations, for Spaniards this remained the key question, and even though it could be elided at the level of state, it manifested itself in various ways in public.[23] How the English responded to the rites and symbols of Catholicism was observed with keen interest, and much was made of even the slightest hint of reconversion.[24] Pinheiro da Veiga records that

> *me afirmaram que, em chegando esta gente à Corunha, acudiram infinitos às missas, e que o embaixador fizera tornar a embarcar como trinta*

---

22 Watanabe-O'Kelly, pp. 15–16.

23 The articles of the peace were translated from Latin into English and published in London to quieten rumours of concessions made in the treaty to religious toleration: *Articles of Peace, Entercourse, and Commerce* (London, 1605).

24 Conversions there certainly were. Pickering Wotton, whose father (created first Baron Wotton of Marley by James I on 13 May 1613) escorted the Constable of Castile when he arrived in England, was a member of the English embassy to Valladolid, where he converted and, remaining after the departure of the embassy, died there in October 1605. See 'Wotton, Edward, first Baron Wotton (1548–1628), diplomat and administrator', *Oxford Dictionary of National Biography* (Oxford, 2004; online edn. 2013).

deles, para atemorizar os mais. Aquí, vi ir alguns a missa e vésperas, descobertos, não sei si por curiosidade.[25]

[I was told that upon arrival in La Coruña, many of these people went to hear mass and the ambassador ordered thirty of them to re-embark as a warning to the rest. Here I have seen some attend mass and vespers openly, I don't know if merely out of curiosity.]

Such local impressions and encounters surely informed Valladolid's experience of the choreographed events, but they also had a deeper political resonance. Since 1589 the city had hosted a seminary for English Catholic priests who returned to England to minister secretly (and at risk of their lives) to Catholic communities. Understandably, the head of the English College, Joseph Creswell, saw an opportunity and sought to arrange a private interview with Nottingham; he pressed the Council of State to schedule a visit to the college by Philip, accompanied by the admiral: after all, Englishmen were coming to the college in private, '*unos de dia y otros de noche, y yo andando a buscar a los que no atreven venir aca*' ('some during the day, some at night and I myself go to fetch those that don't dare to come here').[26] During the conflict, both Philip and his father had honoured the college with royal visits,[27] but Creswell's suggestion was politically awkward, and it did not take place.[28]

If such a public demonstration of religious reconciliation of compatriots was impossible, the liturgical calendar offered Philip an opportunity to make a more subtle point. The Pentecost feast with its traditional procession through the streets of the city was taking place at the end of May, and Philip made sure that it coincided with the christening of the newborn prince, the future Philip IV. With this combination of celebrations, all the paraphernalia of Roman ritual could be exhibited freely to the higher glory of the Habsburg dynasty. Creswell himself approved, especially as the king in person marched in the procession:

Admirablemente fue traçada la fiesta del bateo, y q su mgd (Dios le guarde) andubiesse en la procession, porque esta gente no ha visto antes

---

25 Pinheiro da Veiga, *Fastiginia*, p. 73.

26 Joseph Creswell's letter to Lerma. Archivo General de Simancas, E 2557, Fol. 40.

27 See Berta Cano-Echevarría *et al.*, ' "Comfort without offence"? The Performance and Transmission of Exile Literature at the English College, Valladolid, 1592–1600', *Renaissance and Reformation / Renaissance et Réforme* 31.1 (Winter/Hiver 2008), 31–67.

28 Although the visit to the English College did not take place, a number of historians and critics, possibly misled by the discussions of the Council, accept it as fact. See for example, Albert J. Loomie, *The Spanish Elizabethans* (New York: Fordham University Press, 1963), p. 216; Robert W. Kenny, 'Peace with Spain, 1605', *History Today* 20.3 (1970), 198–208, 206; and Ungerer, 'The Spanish and English Chronicles', p. 313. Proof that it did not take place is found in a letter of Joseph Creswell to the Council dated 17 September 1605 (Archivo General de Simancas, E 2512, Fol. 48) where he asks for permission to send a letter to King James and include the emblems and poems that the students had devised for the occasion but did not have the chance to display.

las cosas de nuestra religion autorizadas, si no reprobadas y castigadas. El Sr a de premiar la traça y los traçadores.

[The feast of the christening was admirably designed and so that his Majesty (God save him) walked with the procession, because these people have never seen before things of our religion authorized, but condemned and punished. The lord will reward the design and its designers.]

Indeed, a great deal of tact was required because on this occasion the monarch would descend from his characteristically high position to walk along the streets as one more *processante*. The order in which the various participants were to march was carefully planned and meticulously recorded by Treswell:

First went many Friers singing, bearing amongst them diverse crosses, banners, and other ceremonious reliques of the Church, the Sacrament being likewise caried by foure church-officers.

Then followed divers Noblemen according to their degrees.

Next before the Kings owne person went the yonger princes of Savoy.

Then the king himselfe in person: after whom followed the Cardinal being Archbishop of *Toledo*, and with him the Prince of Savoy the elder brother. Then followed together the Prince of *Moroco*, the Emperours Ambassadour: the Ambassadour of France: the Ambassadour of Venice: after whom followed divers Gentlemen of the Kings chamber, and the rest of the traine.[29]

What Treswell does not explain (perhaps intentionally) is Nottingham's position in the procession, as he is not listed among the other ambassadors. The Spanish sources, however, make clear that some English gentlemen, one of them the Count of Perth, a relative of the King of England, and another, Sir Thomas, son of the Count of Suffolk, marched with the Spanish noblemen, while Nottingham enjoyed a position of honour, having been placed at a balcony where he could both watch and be watched. This vantage point, conspicuous on the corner opposite the royal palace and with a view of both the church of San Pablo and the palace, framed the ambassador for the two hours he stood there, dressed magnificently

con la gorra en la mano, y un capotillo con muchos botones de diamantes, casaca guarnecida de la misma manera, y el collar grande de la orden de la jarretera.[30]

[with a cap in his hand, wearing a short cape full of diamond buttons, his doublet decorated in the same manner and the large medallion of the order of the garter]

29 *A Relation*, pp. 35–6.
30 Anon., *Relacion . . . Valladolid*, p. 18.

As the king passed, Nottingham bowed to him, Philip in turn uncovering his head, which was interpreted as a gesture of goodwill by both parties.

But the whole episode had a more complex side to it, as must have been evident to many in the crowd. Just five years before, Valladolid had witnessed the procession of an image of the Virgin desecrated in the English attack on Cadiz in 1596, its deliverance presided over by the queen herself as it was taken to the English College, which had undertaken the task of protecting the 'Vulnerata' as an act of penance on behalf of its countrymen. Now, framed in the balcony was the very man who had commanded the soldiers responsible. His position was not only a vantage point to watch the feast, but (unknowingly) a symbolic act of atonement as he held his hat in his hands and contemplated the various relics and images passing below; the grandeur of the occasion, with the participation of the king, was reminiscent of that other great procession in which the queen had been present, when war with England was brought home to Valladolid.

The bullfight and the *juego de cañas*

On 9 June, the day of Corpus Christi, the peace was finally ratified in a ceremony preceded by another religious procession through the city. The ratification was carefully designed to perform the power of the Habsburg monarchy and the relative inferiority of the English representative (who was invited to sit on a stool for part of the proceedings). The citizens of Valladolid saw nothing of this, save perhaps glimpses of the cortege as it made its way through the specially constructed passage connecting the palace with the new banqueting hall. But the ratification was celebrated publicly the following day, bringing together nobles and commoners, Spaniards and Englishmen, in the centre of the city, the Plaza Mayor.

Unlike in England, where it was essentially a form of popular entertainment confined to the less salubrious parts of London, bullfighting in Spain also attracted nobles and even monarchs to pit their courage against the bull.[31] In 1527, during the festivities for the birth of Philip II in Valladolid, Charles V fought a bull on horseback with a spear; ever since that occasion, bullfighting had become a feature of monarchical festivities.[32] Even more novel to English eyes was the *juego de cañas* that often followed. This dangerous sport, like the faux-medieval tournament, was exclusively played by the nobility, richly attired in the Moorish fashion and mounted on horses, launching their *cañas* high in the air against the defending quadrilles,

31 On the relatively minor popularity of English baiting, see Oscar Brownstein, 'The Popularity of Baiting in England before 1600: A Study in Social and Theatrical History', *Educational Theater Journal* 21.3 (1969), 237–50.
32 Emilio Casares, *Valladolid en la Historia Taurina (1152–1890)* (Valladolid: Diputación Provincial, 1999), pp. 35–67.

protected by shields. This martial display, on the heels of the ratification, served to underline Philip's appropriation of the terms by which the peacemaking might symbolically be understood. (See Plate 5.)

The Plaza Mayor in Valladolid was a perfect stage for such a spectacle. Despite the shortcomings of the city as the seat of the court, it offered a magnificent arena surrounded by uniform buildings with three storeys of balconies and an elegant town hall, all newly built after a fire had destroyed it some forty years before.[33] For occasions such as this, the square would be surrounded by scaffolds, the windows hanging with banners and the ground covered with sand to improve the performance of the animals. The enlargement of the square allowed for an unprecedented number of spectators to attend. The official Spanish *Relacion* gives the astonishing figure of one hundred thousand people,[34] but Pinheiro is more detailed, and perhaps his figure is the more accurate:

> *caberiam neles [os palanques] dez ou doze mil pessoas. Tem a Praça três ordens de janelas nos três sobrados, e em cada orden há cem janelas, e, sobre elas, eirados com seu corrimão, que tomam toda a largura da primeira casa, e, detrás dela, dez com muitas janelas sobre o eirado, que são duzentas janelinhas; [. . .] Estavam todos estes lugares ocupados, e os telhados se destelharam, e estaba a gente em pinha sobre eles. Entram na Praça catorze ruas, e nelas se fizeram tablados de dos sobrados, que as ocupavam: fizemos computaçao da gente que podía já estar sentada e achámos que seriam mais de quarenta mil pessoas; e, com haver tanto lugar, nos custou lugar para amigos duzentos reais, mas valiam a mil e oitocentos os ordinários.*[35]

[The scaffolds could hold between ten and twelve thousand people. The square has three orders of windows in three storeys, with one hundred windows in each, and above, a roof terrace with its corridor, and behind ten attics with many windows over the terrace, totalling two hundred little windows [. . .]. All these were occupied and the tiles were taken off the roofs so that people could stand crammed together on them. Fourteen streets enter the square and here scaffolds of two storeys were placed. We calculated the number of people that could be

---

33 After the fire of 1561, Philip II commissioned the architect Francisco de Salamanca to design a project for the rebuilding of the whole area; this modernised the centre and allowed space for one of the biggest plazas in Spain to be built. See José Altés Bustelo, *La Plaza Mayor de Valladolid: el proyecto de Francisco de Salamanca para la reedificación del centro* (Valladolid: Universidad de Valladolid, 1993).

34 'Adonde se juzgó que avia poco menos de cien mil personas'; *Relacion de lo sucedido en la ciudad de Valladolid, desde el punto del felicissimo nacimiento del Principe Don Felipe Dominico Victor nuestro Señor: hasta que se acabaron las demostraciones de alegria que por el se hizieron* (Valladolid, 1605), p. 32.

35 Pinheiro da Veiga, *Fastiginia*, pp. 135–6.

accommodated and estimated some forty thousand. Despite the abundance of space we had to pay two hundred *reales* for our seats, but the ordinary seats cost one thousand and eight hundred.]

According to the sources, many came from distant places, but despite the number of foreign visitors and the high prices, possibly more than half of the inhabitants of the city were present.

Such an event staged protocol as well as sport. As with a royal occasion, only in this case in the open air, the theatre of court etiquette was on display. Indeed, the event was organised and paid for by the city (in whose jurisdiction it was held), and presided over by the mayor, Don Diego Sarmiento de Acuña, the future Count of Gondomar and ambassador to England. Although the bullfighting did not begin until three in the afternoon the spectacle commenced at noon, with the entrance of the king and queen on horseback, followed (also mounted) by the ladies in waiting, each accompanied by two escorts on foot.[36] Philip and Margaret dined in the town hall, served by the ladies, and then appeared on the balcony to signal the beginning of the feast. By this time everyone was seated, the town hall balconies reserved for the nobility and the English notables, the ladies flanking the monarchs on the left, the gentlemen on the right. Special attention was given to the English: 'and for that his Lordship and all his company from the meanest to the highest, should have the pleasure of the sights, there were some appointed to see every Englishman furnished of convenient roome: which they did'.[37] But just as the event was about to begin, with all eyes on the king, Philip drew everyone's attention to Nottingham by inviting him to sit among the ladies instead. Thus was choreographed a curious moment of theatre as the admiral vacated his seat, exited the balcony and reappeared to take his new place, conspicuously with the Spanish ladies (Pinheiro remarked that he cunningly chose to sit beside the prettiest, Catalina de la Cerda).[38] However this moment might be interpreted, once again, as with the Pentecost procession, attention was being drawn to Nottingham.

The significance of this occasion for the English and Spanish is similarly unclear and, in keeping with the complexity of this episode, contradictory. To a degree this was a question of cultural difference. The English accounts report that men and horses were killed during the bullfighting; the Spanish sources make no mention of this, only that the Constable of Castile suffered

---

36 Pinheiro admits that this entry pleased him most of the whole feast, '*pelo descostume de ver entrar as damas a cavalo e com tanto concerto e magestade; e, assim, destas festas, os accesorios foram o mais principal*' ('because it is very unusual to see the ladies on horseback with such co-ordinated movement and majesty; and so in this feast the unusual features were the most important'), Pinheiro da Veiga, *Fastiginia*, p. 138.

37 *A Relation*, p. 45.

38 Pinheiro da Veiga, *Fastiginia*, p. 140.

a slight head injury in the *juego de cañas*.[39] Whatever the accuracy of these accounts, they betray a certain sensibility which perhaps offers a clue to how such spectacles signified to each party. Both English accounts, the anonymous *The Royal Entertainment* and Robert Treswell's *A Relation of Such Things*, served to promote the peace to a somewhat sceptical English audience, here was a reminder of underlying tensions and, perhaps, cultural stereotyping. But as everyone recognised, such displays of martial power were always doubly coded, as both playful simulations and reminders that the courtier–soldier remained ready to fight: as so often, peacemaking had as its corollary the expression of war-readiness. Importantly, the audience for this performance was not only the English but the Spanish citizens, who were perhaps reassured by the Habsburg prowess they witnessed.

A week later, after a fabulous masque in the new ceremonial hall,[40] the English delegation departed. But the memory of the English visitors left its trace not only in written accounts but also in the private entertainments that the court enjoyed in the summer months that were to follow. A surprising record left by Cabrera de Córdoba describes how during the festivity of Midsummer Night the monarchs enjoyed watching a mock re-representation of the court masque in the gardens of the Duke of Lerma's estate. Men played the role of women, a 'truant' played the queen and a coach man the Cardinal of Toledo, while Nottingham was represented by a eunuch called Sevillano. In the light of this it is tempting to return to the placing of Nottingham among the ladies and read Philip's stagecraft as finely calibrated mockery the Spanish audience would have appreciated.

The festival of 1605 was the culmination of a series of civic and royal events the city would experience, prior to the *corte*'s return to Madrid the following year. Crucially, the war with England had been central to all of them, since the 1600 visit of the king and the procession of the Vulnerata the same year both involved the English College: the presence of the English commander a decade later surely produced a cultural echo of past enmity, however much the present was concerned with the peace. Over all of this hung the issue of religion, and the question of toleration of Catholics in England which the Treaty of London had not resolved, but which the ratification highlighted by the Englishmen's very appearance in the royal city. It may be that Nottingham himself could only have been received ambivalently, given recent history: protocol required that he be treated with respect according to his rank, but collective cultural memory – represented chiefly by the citizenry of Valladolid – could not be so easily overridden. As it happened, Nottingham would be criticised at home for a perceived laxness in

---

39 *A Relation*, p. 46; *The Royal Entertainement of the Right Honourable the Earle of Nottingham, Sent Ambassador from His Maiestie to the King of Spaine* (London, 1605), p. 13; Cabrera de Córdoba, *Relaciones de las cosas sucedidas*, p. 249.

40 See Hutchings and Cano-Echevarría, 'Between Courts: Female Masquers and Anglo-Spanish Diplomacy, 1603–05', *Early Theatre* 15.1 (2012), 91–108.

how he tolerated his charges' exposure to religious temptation, and only months later the Gunpowder Plot would put an end to any question of greater religious toleration in England. And yet despite these tensions the peace would endure for the duration of James's and Philip's reigns, and indeed – though it came to naught – it laid the foundations for a Stuart–Habsburg match in 1623.

Acknowledgments

This work was supported by the Ministerio de Economía y Competitividad [FFI2015–66847-P].

Bibliography

Manuscript Sources

Archivo General de Simancas, E 2557, Fol. 37.
Archivo General de Simancas, E 2557, Fol. 40.
Archivo General de Simancas, E 2512, Fol. 48.
PRO, SP 94/11/123.

Printed Primary Sources

Anonymous, *Relacion de lo sucedido en la ciudad de Valladolid, desde el punto del felicissimo nacimiento del Principe Don Felipe Dominico Victor nuestro Señor: hasta que se acabaron las demostraciones de alegria que por el se hizieron* (Valladolid, 1605).
Anonymous, *A Relation of svch Things as Were Observed to Happen in the Journey of the right Honourable Charles Earle of Nottingham, L. High Admirall of England, His Highnesse Ambassadour to the King of Spaine* (London, 1605).
Articles of Peace, Entercourse, and Commerce (London, 1605).
Cabrera de Córdoba, Luis, *Relaciones de las cosas sucedidas en la corte de Espagña desde 1599 hasta 1614'* (Valladolid: Junta de Castilla y León, 1997).
Tresswell, Robert, *The Royal Entertainement of the Right Honourable the Earle of Nottingham, Sent Ambassador from His Maiestie to the King of Spaine* (London, 1605).

Secondary Sources

Brownstein, Oscar. 'The Popularity of Baiting in England Before 1600: A Study in Social and Theatrical History', *Educational Theater Journal* 21.3 (1969), 237–50.
Bustelo, José Altés, *La Plaza Mayor de Valladolid: el proyecto de Francisco de Salamanca para la reedificación del centro* (Valladolid: Universidad de Valladolid, 1993).
Cano-Echevarría, Berta and Hutchings, Mark, 'The Spanish Ambassador and *The Vision of the Twelve Goddesses*: A New Document [with text]', *English Literary Renaissance* 42.2 (2012), 223–57.

Cano-Echevarría, Berta, *et al.*, ' "Comfort Without Offence"? The Performance and Transmission of Exile Literature at the English College, Valladolid, 1592–1600', *Renaissance and Reformation/Renaissance et Réforme* 31.1 (2008), 31–67.

Casares, Emilio, *Valladolid en la Historia Taurina (1152–1890)* (Valladolid: Diputación Provincial, 1999).

Dillon, Janette, *The Language of Space in Court Performance, 1400–1625* (Cambridge: Cambridge University Press, 2010).

Hutchings, Mark and Cano-Echevarría, Berta, 'Between Courts: Female Masquers and Anglo-Spanish Diplomacy, 1603–05', *Early Theatre* 15.1 (2012), 91–108.

Hutchings, Mark and Cano-Echevarría, Berta, 'The Spanish Ambassador's Account of James I's Entry into London, 1604 [with text]' (forthcoming in *The Seventeenth Century*; online 2017, print 2018).

Kenny, Robert W., 'Peace with Spain, 1605', *History Today* 20.3 (1970), 198–208.

Loomie, Albert J., *The Spanish Elizabethans* (New York: Fordham University Press, 1963), p. 216.

Mulryne, J.R., Aliverti, Maria Ines Aliverti and Anna Maria Testaverde (eds), *Ceremonial Entries in Early Modern Europe: The Iconography of Power* (Farnham and Burlington, VT: Ashgate, 2015).

Oxford Dictionary of National Biography (Oxford: Oxford University Press, 2004; online edn, 2013).

Pinheiro da Veiga, Tomé, *Fastiginia*, ed. Ernesto Rodrigues (Lisbon: Centro de Literaturas e Culturas Lusófonas e Europeias, 2011).

Roosen, William, 'Early Modern Diplomatic Ceremonial: A Systems Approach', *The Journal of Modern History* 52.3 (1980), 452–76.

Ungerer, Gustav, 'Juan Pantoja de la Cruz and the Circulation of Gifts', *Sederi* 9 (1998), 59–78.

Ungerer, Gustav, 'The Spanish and English Chronicles in King James's and Sir George's Buc's Dossiers on the Anglo-Spanish Peace Negotiations', *Huntington Library Quarterly* 61.3/4 (1998), 309–24.

Watanabe-O'Kelly, Helen, 'Early Modern European Festivals – Politics, Performance, Event and Record', in J.R. Mulryne and Elizabeth Goldring (eds), *Court Festivals of the European Renaissance: Art, Politics and Performance* (Farnham and Burlington, VT: Ashgate, 2002), pp. 15–25.

6 The shield of ceremony

Civic ritual and royal entries in wartime

Fabian Persson

In early modern Europe, loyalty between ruler and subject was fundamental. Yet it was a bond that was sometimes broken. A realm would then descend into chaos and civil war, as during the *Fronde* in France, the Civil War in England or the Time of Troubles in Russia. Breakdown of social order threatened citizens, but a refusal to obey could also lead to provinces breaking away, such as the Netherlands and Portugal from Spain. Thus, it was often in the interest of both ruler and subjects to sustain the bonds holding them together. Princes and subjects had to cooperate at least to a certain degree. For society to function, people had to agree on basic rules of conduct. To express such bonds, public rituals were used, among them the joyous entry.[1]

Joyous entries took many different forms in medieval and early modern Europe. They were called *entrée joyeuse*, royal entry, *eriksgata* or *Huldigungsfahrt*, according to local customs, but these ceremonies had a number of important characteristics in common.[2] They were often performed at the beginning of the reign of a new prince and included the ceremonial entry of the prince into a principal town. The prince was extolled and recognised as the legitimate ruler, while he in return confirmed the town's customary rights and privileges.[3] A wide array of forms was used to express the common bond between ruler and subjects, such as ephemeral arches, orations,

---

1 R.J. Knecht, 'Court Festivals as Political Spectacle: The Example of Sixteenth-Century France', in J.R. Mulryne, Helen Watanabe-O'Kelly and Margaret Shewring (eds), *Europa Triumphans: Court and Civic Festivals in Early Modern Europe*, 2 vols (Aldershot and Burlington, VT: Ashgate, 2004), vol.1, pp. 19–31. Peter Arnade, *Realms of Ritual: Burgundian Ceremony and Civic Life in Late Medieval Ghent* (Ithaca, NY and London: Cornell University Press, 1996).

2 For the Swedish *eriksgata*, see the discussion in Fabian Persson 'So that we Swedes are not more swine or goats than they are: Space and Ceremony at the Swedish Court', in Birgitte Bøggild Johannsen (ed.), *Beyond Scylla and Charybdis: European Courts and Court Residences Outside Habsburg and Valois/Bourbon Territories, 1500–1700* (Copenhagen: University Press of Southern Denmark, 2015).

3 Lawrence M. Bryant, *The King and the City in the Parisian Royal Entry Ceremony: Politics, Ritual, and Art in the Renaissance* (Geneva: Droz, 1986).

music, performances of *tableaux vivants* and printed sheets and books.[4] The town would present the prince with both the town keys and some valuable *objets d'art* as a gift, and oaths would be exchanged. The prince could then leave the town having been affirmed as the legitimate ruler, while the citizens had their privileges guaranteed. Joyous entries have been characterised as the most effective form of royal propaganda, reaching a far greater number of people than more ambitious court festivals.[5] This 'ceremonial expression of union' was used both by the prince to ensure his power and by the towns to make privileges iron-clad and proof from challenge.[6]

The ceremony of joyous entries was also used in the New World, in order to emphasise the status of the rulers while simultaneously binding the subjects to them. A Spanish viceroy of Mexico would follow a set route when first arriving in his new territories and would be received with great ceremony by various civil and military representatives. In towns and villages, he would be greeted by 'ceremonial arches, decorated streets, singing and dancing Indians, and effusive orations by Spanish and Indian officials'.[7] Even when the entries were less planned and organised, they could be perceived as akin to European joyous entries. Frenchmen in America interpreted native peoples greeting them as the American version of joyous entries.[8]

Real life, however, complicated these clear-cut aims. To express homage and loyalty to your prince may appear straightforward – but how were such feelings to be expressed when the prince was a foreign conqueror who had captured your town or country? What loyalty could a prince expect from subjects he might soon abandon, leaving someone else to rule? Wars, ever present in early modern society, created such shifting sands of loyalty.

Swedish monarchs continued into the eighteenth century to lead military campaigns in person. Military campaigns such as these would result in Swedish kings entering a number of captured towns. Royal entries of this type were not traditional 'joyous entries', but even so, a number of similarities are obvious. The conquering king and the captured town needed to strike a deal. A mutually binding civic accord benefited both king and town even in wartime. This civic accord was elevated by ceremony to emphasise its importance and strength.

The fact that the monarch entered the captured town in person offered the opportunity for ceremony. He was often accompanied by a court and army,

---

4 Wim Blockmans and Walter Prevenier, *The Promised Lands: The Low Countries Under Burgundian Rule, 1369–1530* (Philadelphia, PA: Pennsylvania State University, 1999), p. 218.
5 Knecht, 'Court Festivals as Political Spectacle', p. 19.
6 Bryant, *passim.*
7 J.H. Elliott, *Empires of the Atlantic World: Britain and Spain in America, 1492–1830* (New Haven and London: Yale University Press, 2006), pp. 125–6.
8 Patricia Seed, *Ceremonies of Possession in Europe's Conquest of the New World 1492– 1640* (Cambridge: Cambridge University Press, 1995), p. 61.

which could make the ceremony suitably impressive, despite its improvised nature in comparison with more traditional entries. Both army and court sometimes reflected the growing ambition of the conquering king, as can be seen by the increase in German and Bohemian courtiers surrounding the successful Gustavus Adolphus in the early 1630s. In such a changing world, new bonds had to be forged quickly and sometimes discarded even more quickly. The alternative was politically unthinkable.

Towns entered by force

In August 1704, Swedish troops sacked Lemberg.

> The king along with the prince of Württemberg was among the first to enter and quickly secured the gate until others could follow; he then marched in closed formation to the other gates and fired at anyone who appeared in the windows or on the streets.[9]

After the town was sacked, it continued to be plundered for some time until the king gave the army the order to cease looting.

During wars, kings could enter towns in different ways. The sack of Lemberg was an example of a less-than-joyous entry. If a town resisted and was sacked, its citizens would be subject to plunder and violence. Consequently, it became all-important to negotiate ways to open the gates to foreign rulers that would ensure an orderly take-over. The falls of Lemberg in 1704 or Würzburg in 1631 were dreadful examples of the atrocities that awaited a sacked town.

In 1631, both Frankfurt an der Oder and Frankfurt am Main fell into Swedish hands. The circumstances were very different. Frankfurt an der Oder provided a salutary warning that for a town to fall into the hands of a hostile army without negotiation was a harrowing experience. In April 1631, Swedish troops stormed the town, and during the following hours the garrison was slaughtered and the citizens plundered. Soldiers who seized a town by force traditionally had the right to plunder, and the king had to allow three hours of unhindered looting.[10] A Scots mercenary noted that he 'did never see officers lesse obeyed' during 'the fury'.[11] To the rest of Germany, this horrific massacre and plunder demonstrated what happened to a town taken by force.[12]

---

9 Jöran Nordburg, *Konung Carl XII:s historia*, vol. 1 (Stockholm, 1740), p. 536.
10 Anders Fryxell, *Berättelser ur svenska historien*, vol.4 (Stockholm, 1846), p. 263.
11 Frank Tallett, *War and Society in Early Modern Europe: 1495–1715* (London: Routledge, 1992), p. 115.
12 Christopher Duffy, *Siege Warfare. The Fortress in the Early Modern World, 1494–1660* (London: Routledge & Kegan Paul, repr. 1996), p. 177.

Civic ceremonies and negotiated royal entries

Ways in which such dreadful consequences could be avoided are illustrated when Gustavus Adolphus in 1621 negotiated the surrender of the important town of Riga in Livonia. On the morning of 12 September 1621, after a month-long siege, he initiated a bombardment, usually heralding imminent slaughter, but anticipated this by sending a trumpeter to warn the citizens of the horrors awaiting if they did not surrender. After some negotiation, the town at last opened its gates to the king. Gustavus Adolphus then entered together with his brother Prince Charles Philip, passing through what later became known as the Swedish Gate (*svenskporten*). Nicolaus Eyke, the oldest mayor of Riga, came to meet them, handing over the keys of the town wrapped in a silk cloth. The king handed the keys back and confirmed the privileges of the town. He also confirmed the rights of Riga to mint its own coins.[13]

The citizens swore an oath of obedience to their new ruler 'under the blue sky'. Councillors, elders and guilds were gathered, along with ordinary burghers, who swore the required oath with their heads bare and their fingers raised.[14] A *Te Deum* was then sung in St Peter's church to give thanks for the town being saved from destruction. By negotiating this accord, king and town reached a peaceable solution. In a letter to the Council in Sweden, the king stated that he had considered storming Riga, but desisted as he wanted to refrain from bloodshed – and furthermore was running out of powder. Consequently, the citizens of Riga kept their privileges and their property, with only the houses belonging to the Jesuit order being confiscated.

The entry into Riga illustrates a number of features representative of how a fallen town might receive its conqueror. The keys of the town and the privileges would be handed over to the new ruler. These would then be handed back with a reassurance of confirmation. The citizens would take a new oath of allegiance and pay homage to their new prince. A *Te Deum* would be sung and the prince would receive gifts and be fêted by the leading burghers.

Further ceremonies could be included, such as the kissing of hands. When Thorn in Poland surrendered to Charles X in 1655, the king 'was with great ceremony received in the town . . . Then the king handed back the keys to the mayor and confirmed the [town's] privileges'.[15] The whole town council kissed the king's hands. This kissing of hands became a set part of royal entries, for instance that of Philip II of Spain.[16]

13 Georg Ericsson, *Gustav II Adolf och Sigismund 1621–1623* (Uppsala: Almqvist and Wiksells, 1928).

14 Johan Hallenberg, *Svea rikes historia Under konung Gustaf Adolf den Stores Regering*, vol. 4 (Stockholm, 1794), p. 976.

15 Samuel Pufendorf, *Sju böcker om konung Carl X Gustafs bragder*, trans. and ed. by Adolf Hillman, vol.1 (Stockholm, 1915), p. 107.

16 Knecht, 'Court Festivals as Political Spectacle', p. 22.

A royal entry while the king was on military campaigning varied between towns. Some represented more overtly hostile territory. Munich, for example, was the residence of the staunchly catholic Elector Maximilian, an implacable foe of both Gustavus Adolphus and Lutherans. The Elector fled the town and in May 1632 the Swedish army approached. The mayor and magistrate of Munich had to meet the king outside the town, kneeling on the ground, as can be seen in a contemporary engraving. The king then entered Munich through the Isar Gate. The town had to pay a tax of 300,000 Gulden, a huge sum, but was spared plunder apart from various trivial items in the collections of the Electoral palace.

Even the great general Gustavus Adolphus could scarcely hope to keep Munich in the long run. However, the ambitions and expectations of a ruler would vary during a long war. Sometimes, the king could hope to incorporate captured towns into Sweden. Riga is such an example. The changing fortunes of war meant that royal ambitions would change over time. In the 1650s, Charles X had plans for dividing Poland and keeping parts for himself. It is reasonable to suppose that these plans offer an explanation as to why the king, after having entered Elbing 'with great pomp' in December 1655, commanded a 'salute – at all places in Poland which had recognised his rule' in order to celebrate the birth of his son.[17]

The fortunes of war were hard to predict, and so ambitions to keep territory would vary over time. Gustavus Adolphus had obviously far-reaching plans in Germany, as did Charles X in Denmark and Poland.[18] Yet these plans were fragile and could easily be reversed. Other towns were newly ceded to Sweden by treaty when the royal entry took place. In March 1658, King Charles X visited a number of towns the Danes had ceded to him in Skåne. Illustrations, including engravings, depict deputations handing over the town keys of, for instance, Landskrona, to a plump king sitting comfortably in his sleigh. The occasion was also celebrated by cannon saluting from the castle in the town. Some towns were allies, at least nominally, at the time of the royal entry. The religious fault lines created by the Thirty Years War meant that predominantly Protestant cities might be classed as allies. They would still, however, be part of the Empire and as such subjects of the Emperor.

An interesting case is the important town of Frankfurt am Main. The town had great symbolic value as the seat of imperial diets and coronations. Efforts to keep Frankfurt out of the war became impossible after the great Swedish victory at Breitenfeld in September 1631. Swedish armies now pushed deeper into Germany, and Frankfurt had to negotiate with the approaching Swedes.[19] The town was reluctant to break its oath to the

---

17 Pufendorf, *Sju böcker om konung Carl X Gustafs bragder*, p. 108.
18 Peter H. Wilson, *Europe's Tragedy: A New History of the Thirty Years War* (London: Penguin, 2010), p. 486.
19 Anja Rieck, *Frankfurt am Main unter schwedischer Besatzung 1631–1635* (Frankfurt am Main and New York: P. Lang, 2005).

emperor openly, as it might result in losing the all-important town privileges. Imperial loyalists inside the town were also reluctant to allow the Swedes to enter. On their side, the Swedes did not want to sack one of the great German Protestant towns aggressively. One of the king's key demands was to place a Swedish garrison in Frankfurt, a demand from which, despite insistent pleas, the king refused to budge. The negotiated outcome was that the Swedish were allowed passage through Frankfurt and the right to garrison nearby Sachsenhausen. The autonomy of Frankfurt within the empire would still be nominally tolerated. At the same time, the Frankfurt authorities sent messages to the emperor saying that the town was in reality captured and coerced.

These negotiations illustrate clearly how towns had to tread a careful, and sometimes double-dealing, path when it came to establishing their political security. For his part, King Gustavus Adolphus wanted to proclaim Frankfurt as an ally in the struggle against the emperor and the Catholic League. Thus, it was in his interest to tie Frankfurt as closely to him as possible. Eventually, an agreement was reached by which the town opened its gates in return for a guarantee of its customary privileges.[20] When Gustavus Adolphus entered the town on 17 November 1631, this news was made widely public through printed broadsheets. His entry has been called 'carefully staged' and had huge symbolic impact. An observer noted that the king 'was now seated . . . in the very same roome, where the emperours at their coronation use to be entertained'.[21] For the entry into Frankfurt, celebratory poetry was composed by Balthasar Schedius.[22] The king even reprised his royal entry by returning to the town for a more sumptuous entry three days later.[23] A third, really magnificent entry was staged in January 1632. By this time, Queen Maria Eleonora had joined her husband and took part in the ceremonies. The royal couple were greeted with bonfires and volleys of ammunition in a Frankfurt that had now had time to 'put on its finest festive clothes'.[24] The burghers of Frankfurt turned out in force and a gift of a precious *objet d'art* was given to the Queen.

When campaigning, royal life was simplified, but still certain complications are worth observing. Even when King Charles XII resided in Turkey for several years, he ordered that his meals should be announced by trumpets and drums. Naturally, circumstances often restricted court life when campaigning. Thus, Charles XII mocks the attempts to organise balls and assemblies when there are only four ladies of quality available. Nevertheless, efforts were made; as for the king's name-day in 1701, when one of his

20 Ibid., p. 352.
21 Wilson, *Europe's Tragedy*, p. 486.
22 Balthasar Schedius, *Vivat Rex Sveciæ: Schwedischer Triumph unnd Dancksagung. Zu Lob und Ehren Dem Ewigen und Allsmächtigen Gott* (n.p.: 1631).
23 Rieck, *Frankfurt am Main unter schwedischer Besatzung 1631–1635*, p. 70.
24 Ibid., p. 72.

generals arranged a *wirtschaft* complete with poetry and a ballet, 'which greatly pleased his Majesty and everyone present'.[25]

Charles XII never married, but married kings who were accompanied by their queens while campaigning would have a more lively court life. The presence of noblewomen or ladies of royal rank would raise the standard of day-to-day social intercourse. When Gustavus Adolphus resided in Augsburg he invited ladies of the Fugger family to court in order to dance 'German and English dances'.[26] During the longer residence in Frankfurt am Main in the winter of 1631–1632, the king was joined by Queen Maria Eleonora. Her presence increased efforts towards more normal forms of courtly festivities. A Frankfurt silk merchant described the Queen as 'a very beautiful woman [. . .] she wears on top of her head a small, gilded crown with shining diamonds'.[27] The king himself began wearing a red cloak in Frankfurt, which may suggest an imitation of imperial garments. An observer of Gustav Adolphus in the city made careful notes about the ceremonies used at royal meals,[28] and compared the high degree of ceremony to ceremonial dining after imperial coronations in the city.

In Frankfurt, the king also organised a traditional German court entertainment.[29] He himself played the host, the Queen a chamberer, Duke Bernhard of Weimar a *Kellner* (Cellar Master), Countess von Solms a *Kellnerin* (Cellar Mistress), the Count von Hanau a fool, a young female relation of Countess von Solms a female fool and the Winter King, Frederick of Bohemia, a Jesuit. Everyone was dressed according to his or her role. As a burgher, the king wore a big collar and a big key, the Queen dressed as a servant girl, and the Winter King in Jesuit garb. Everyday entertainment could take many forms. In Maria Eleonora's Frankfurt accounts can be found, for example, payments made to dancing Jews.

The presence of a queen would set a campaigning court on a more normal courtly footing. In Frankfurt, the queen's household attendants numbered 183 persons.[30] When Maria Eleonora entered Würzburg in the summer of 1632, she was accompanied by her women attendants, twenty-three *hofjunkern*, twenty-three wagons and a thousand cavalry. The queen took delight in outraging Catholics while making her entry to Würzburg, by including as a valued member of her retinue a monkey dressed up as a capuchin monk, with a rosary in its paws and shaved hair.[31]

25 Joran Nordberg, *Konung Carl XII:s historia*, vol. 1 (Stockholm, 1740), p. 147.

26 Carl Grimberg, *Svenska folkets underbara öden*, vol.3 (Stockholm: P.A. Norstedt and Sunors Verlag, 1924), pp. 158–9.

27 Rieck, *Frankfurt am Main unter schwedischer Besatzung 1631–1635*, p. 92.

28 Ibid., p. 75.

29 Ibid., p. 74.

30 Ibid., p. 93.

31 Fritz Arnheim, 'Gustav Adolfs Gemahlin Maria Eleonora von Brandenburg (geb.: 21 November 1599, gest. 28 März 1655). Eine biographische Skizze', *Hohenzollern Jahrbuch (1903–1907)*, 175–213.

For a number of Protestant towns, the Swedish army was a potential, though dangerous and costly, ally against an overbearing and religiously intolerant emperor. We can see how the reception of Gustavus Adolphus in Nürnberg, Augsburg and Erfurt was marked by more enthusiasm and festivity than in Munich. In this connection, on St Benedict's day, 21 March 1632, Gustavus Adolphus rode into Nürnberg through the Spittler Gate (*Spittlerthor*).[32] First came two Nürnberger trumpeters, then the Nürnberger cavalry, then councillors and distinguished visitors. After that, six Swedish trumpeters and a kettle drummer entered.[33] The king himself was followed by the exiled king of Bohemia and a number of German princes. The streets were crammed with spectators and all the overlooking windows were full of people. In his quarters, the king was met and congratulated by the town council. They gave cannons and ammunition as a present as well as precious gold and silver objects. Poetry in both German and Latin celebrated the royal entry.[34] For the oath-taking, Johann Staden had composed a special hymn entitled *Plausus noricus*.

Similar enthusiasm greeted the Swedish monarch in Augsburg a few weeks later.[35] When Augsburg opened its gates to Gustavus Adolphus on 10 April 1632, the burgher militia paraded. The protestant part of the town council welcomed the king by the Jakobertor. Church bells rang and cannons fired salutes. Following this, the king's chaplain held a service and a *Te Deum* was sung. The king then rode to the Weinmarkt and the house of Count Marquard Fugger where he was to stay. There he received gifts from the magistrates, principally a *wunderschrank* (cabinet of curiosities) with its contents, and in addition to that wine and fish.

An important part of the ceremony was the swearing of new oaths of allegiance. An engraving shows the *huldigung* – the oath-taking – of the corporations of Augsburg in April 1632 in the Weinmarkt in front of the Fuggerhaus. Sattler, the king's secretary, took the oath:

> I shall remain loyal to His Majesty and the Crown of Sweden. [I shall] work in their best interests and for their welfare and do everything subjects are obliged to do for their natural master and their rightful superiors, so help me God!

Afterwards, the magistrate wined and dined the king. In the case of Augsburg, the oath-taking created a sensation in Germany, in that the citizens of a free Reichsstadt had to swear allegiance as subjects to a Swedish king.[36]

---

32 Georg Wolfgang Karl Lochner, *Über die Theilnahme der Stadt Nürnberg am dreissigjährigen Kriege* (Nürnberg, 1832).

33 Franz Ludwig Freiherr von Soden, *Gustav Adolph und sein Heer in Süddeutschland von 1631 bis 1635*, vol.1 (Erlangen, 1865), p. 219.

34 Ibid., p. 221.

35 Ibid., p. 239.

36 Marcus Junkelmann, *Gustav Adolf. Schwedens Aufstieg zur Großmacht* (Regensburg: Pustet, 1993), p. 415.

Engravings and *fliegende blätter* (leaflets) also advertised how a king and a city had come to terms. Furthermore, we can see how the Swedes created memorials to mark their presence. The crossing of the Rhine in 1632 near Oppenheim was commemorated by Gustavus Adolphus with a twelve-meter-high obelisk.[37] On top was placed a crowned lion with a sword and an orb. Hugo Grotius wrote a text intended to be carved on the reddish sandstone, but that was never realised.[38] A similar obelisk was later planned at Stettin.[39]

Where did the campaigning king reside?

Naturally, practical considerations presented themselves. Sometimes an empty palace was there for the taking. In Munich, Gustavus Adolphus lived in the electoral palace together with the deposed King Frederick of Bohemia and Count Palatine August. In Mainz the king, similarly, lived in the electoral palace of St Martinsburg.[40] Both in Munich and Mainz this led to the palaces being plundered of precious objects and books. When Charles X captured Warsaw in August 1655, the king also chose to reside in a royal palace.[41] When Denmark was occupied in 1658–1660, the royal castles of Kronborg and Frederiksborg were used to house the court, with Christmas 1658 celebrated at Kronborg.

Quite often guesthouses (*gasthäuser*) or the houses of prominent citizens were used. In Erfurt, Gustavus Adolphus stayed at the *gasthaus* Hohen Lilie. In Augsburg, he stayed at the Fuggerhaus. In Frankfurt, he occupied Braunfels, the house that emperors used to lodge in. This was certainly a conscious choice, sending a signal of future intentions.

Charles XII made a point of not living too comfortably. He would often sleep in a tent rather than a house, though the tent was insulated with straw and heated with hot cannon balls. He adopted this practice because, he said, 'he should himself show both officers and the common soldiers that a soldier should not be particular about his own comfort, as that will soon make him womanish'.[42]

Meeting princes

One occasion when ceremony had to be emphasised during campaigns was when the king met other princes. We can see this in the way Charles X received the Prince of Transylvania, Georg Rakoczy. Engravings show a very humble Transylvanian Prince bowing in front of King Charles. These

37 *Theatrum Europaeum*, vol. 2 (Frankfurt am Main, 1646), p. 492.
38 Victor Granlund, ' "Die Schwedensäule" och Gustafsburg', in *Historiskt Bibliotek* (Stockholm: Klemmings antiqvariat och sortiment, 1875–1880), p. 560.
39 Gerhard Eimer, 'Carl Gustaf Wrangel som byggherre i Pommern och Sverige', *Stockholm Studies in History of Art* 6 (1961).
40 Rieck, *Frankfurt am Main unter schwedischer Besatzung 1631–1635*, p. 85.
41 Pufendorf, *Sju böcker om konung Carl X Gustafs bragder*, p. 76.
42 Nordberg, *Konung Carl XII:s historia*, p. 190.

meetings appear to be staged outdoors. One engraving shows that sumptuous tents were used. It is reasonable to suggest that the king had an interest in spreading the news of his alliance as far as possible.

A little later we can see the campaigning Charles X meeting not an ally, but a defeated foe, Frederik III of Denmark, in March 1658. Here the first meeting also took place outdoors, with the two kings descending from their carriages. Afterwards, they went together to a festive meal at Frederiksborg castle. A similar meeting was arranged between Charles XII and August of Poland and Saxony at the castle of Altranstädt.

Conclusions

Joyous entries were used to confirm a ruler's legitimacy as well as the privileges of his subjects. Such bonds between ruler and subject were at the core of early modern society, meaning that civic ceremonies to celebrate them were extremely important. Normally, such ceremonies marking the common bond between a prince and his people would be planned meticulously long beforehand. Yet, in wartime, time was scarce and the stakes high. In such cases, a royal entry into a formerly hostile town had to be negotiated within weeks or even days. The sacking of Frankfurt an der Oder or Lemberg demonstrated the danger of not reaching a negotiated and orderly transition to the new overlord.

The interaction with captured towns was characterised by a certain realism. The king was received and fêted, but not with such adulation as during a traditional joyous entry. There was no time to organise complex celebrations, and furthermore they might be dangerous in a longer perspective. If a town was recaptured by imperial troops, it was best if the celebrations for Gustavus Adolphus – or a former conqueror – had been suitably modest.

Civic ceremonies modelled on existing joyous entries were used to seal the accord between conquering prince and town. This elevated the ceremony into something orderly and familiar. It also made the accord very public. We can see why courts accompanying the king on campaign often resulted in ceremonies in the open. Everybody, at least those well positioned among the crowds, could see the entries of Gustavus Adolphus into a number of towns. The mayors and the town council would meet the king and hand over the keys to the town; if circumstances were highly charged, as in Munich, they might have to kneel on the wintry ground outside the city gates. This was followed by kissing the king's hand and a celebratory entry into the town, often accompanied by church bells and volleys of cannon fire. Burgher militia might line the streets, and the monarch would be treated to a sumptuous meal where he would receive precious gifts. In his turn, he would confirm the rights and privileges of the town. The citizenry then had to take an oath of loyalty to their new ruler and a *Te Deum* was sung.

The spectacle of these civic ceremonies was orchestrated by Gustavus Adolphus as he entered a large number of German towns. These 'joyous entries' underwent a last twist as the King made his final entry into a German town after his death in 1632. His corpse was transported to the ducal castle at Wolgast in Pomerania, and remained there until everything was prepared. Wolgast and Pomerania were semi-occupied by Sweden despite the wishes of the Pomeranian Duke and the Elector of Brandenburg. Even in death, it could be said, the king forced Germans to wait on him.

Bibliography

Printed Primary Sources

Fryxell, Anders, *Berättelser ur svenska historien*, vol. 4 (Stockholm, 1846).

Hallenberg, Johan, *Svea rikes historia under konung Gustaf Adolf den Stores regering*, vol. 4 (Stockholm, 1794).

Lochner, Georg Wolfgang Karl, *Über die Theilnahme der Stadt Nürnberg am dreissigjährigen Kriege* (Nürnberg, 1832).

Nordberg, Jöran, *Konung Carl XII:s historia*, vol. 1 (Stockholm, 1740).

Pufendorf, Samuel, *Sju böcker om konung Carl X Gustafs bragder*, vol. 1, trans. and ed. by Adolf Hillman (Stockholm, 1915).

Schedius, Balthasar, *Vivat Rex Sveciæ. Schwedischer Triumph unnd Dancksagung. Zu Lob und Ehren Dem Ewigen und Allsmächtigen Gott* (n.p., 1631).

Soden, Franz Ludwig Freiherr von, *Gustav Adolph und sein Heer in Süddeutschland von 1631 bis 1635*, vol. 1 (Erlangen, 1865).

Theatrum Europaeum, vol. 2 (Frankfurt am Main, 1646).

Secondary Sources

Arnade, Peter, *Realms of Ritual: Burgundian Ceremony and Civic Life in Late Medieval Ghent* (Ithaca, NY and London: Cornell University Press, 1996).

Arnheim, Fritz, 'Gustav Adolfs Gemahlin Maria Eleonora von Brandenburg (geb.: 21 November, 1599, gest. 28 März, 1655). Eine biographische Skizze', *Hohenzollern Jahrbuch* (1903–1907), 175–213.

Blockmans, Wim and Walter Prevenier, *The Promised Lands: The Low Countries Under Burgundian Rule, 1369–1530* (Philadelphia, PA: University of Pennsylvania Press, 1999).

Bryant, Lawrence M., *The King and the City in the Parisian Royal Entry Ceremony: Politics, Ritual, and Art in the Renaissance* (Geneva: Droz, 1986).

Duffy, Christopher, *Siege Warfare: The Fortress in the Early Modern World, 1494–1660* (London: Routledge & Kegan Paul, repr. 1996).

Eimer, Gerhard, 'Carl Gustaf Wrangel som byggherre i Pommern och Sverige', *Stockholm Studies in History of Art* 6 (1961).

Elliott, J.H., *Empires of the Atlantic World: Britain and Spain in America, 1492–1830* (New Haven and London: Yale University Press, 2006).

Ericsson, Georg, *Gustav II Adolf och Sigismund 1621–1623* (Uppsala: Almqvist and Wiksells, 1928).

Granlund, Victor, ' "Die Schwedensäule" och Gustafsburg', in *Historiskt Bibliotek* (Stockholm: Klemmings antiqvariat och sortiment, 1875–1880), p. 560.

Grimberg, Carl, *Svenska folkets underbara öden*, vol. 3 (Stockholm: P.A. Norstedt and Sunors Forlag, 1924).

Junkelmann, Marcus, *Gustav Adolf. Schwedens Aufstieg zur Großmacht* (Regensburg: Pustet, 1993).

Knecht, R.J., 'Court Festivals as Political Spectacle: The Example of Sixteenth-Century France', in J.R. Mulryne, Helen Watanabe-O'Kelly and Margaret Shewring (eds), *Europa Triumphans: Court and Civic Festivals in Early Modern Europe*, 2 vols (Aldershot and Burlington, VT: Ashgate, 2004), vol. 1, pp. 19–31.

Persson, Fabian, 'So That We Swedes Are Not More Swine or Goats Than They Are: Space and Ceremony at the Swedish Court', in Birgitte Bøggild Johannsen (ed.), *Beyond Scylla and Charybdis: European Courts and Court Residences outside Habsburg and Valois/Bourbon Territories, 1500–1700* (Copenhagen: University Press of Southern Denmark, 2015).

Rieck, Anja, *Frankfurt am Main unter schwedischer Besatzung 1631–1635* (Frankfurt am Main and New York: P. Lang, 2005).

Seed, Patricia, *Ceremonies of Possession in Europe's Conquest of the New World 1492–1640* (Cambridge: Cambridge University Press, 1995).

Tallett, Frank, *War and Society in Early Modern Europe: 1495–1715* (London: Routledge, 1992).

Wilson, Peter H., *The Thirty Years War: Europe's Tragedy: A New History of the Thirty Years War* (London: Penguin, 2010).

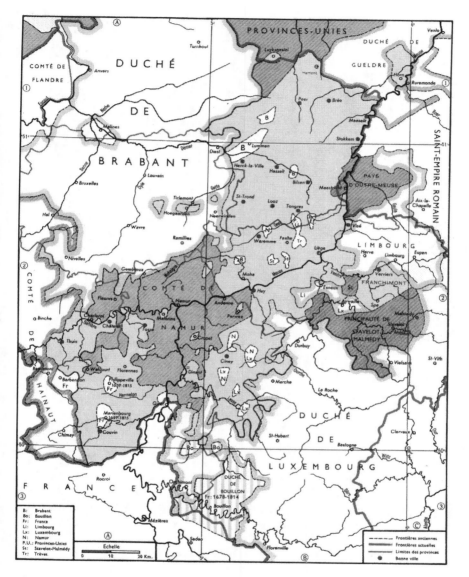

Plate 1 Map of the Principality of Liège and of the territories of Ernest of Bavaria.
© Centre d'Histoire des Sciences et des Techniques, Université de Liège.

Plate 2 Map of the itinerary in the city, right-hand side, Julius Milheuser, *Legia sive Leodium vulgo*, Liège, 1649.

© Centre d'Histoire des Sciences et des Techniques, Université de Liège.

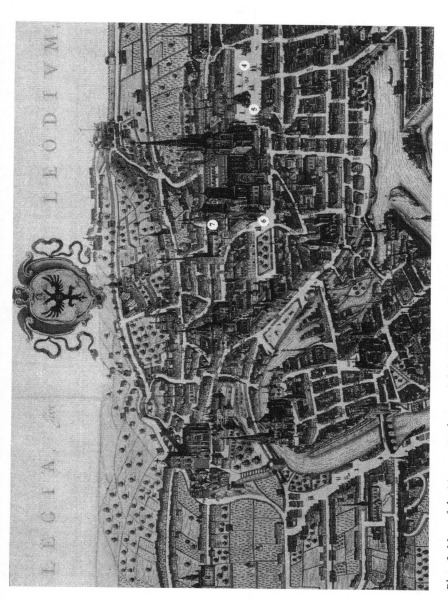

Plate 3 *Map of the itinerary in the city*, left-hand side, Julius Milheuser, *Legia sive Leodium vulgo*, Liège, 1649.

© Centre d'Histoire des Sciences et des Techniques, Université de Liège.

Plate 4 Felipe Gil de Mena, *Fiestas en Plaza Mayor de Valladolid: Dia Primero* (1656). (*Celebrations in the Plaza Mayor, Valladolid: First day*).

Photographs by Carlos Barrena. Courtesy of and property of the City Council of Valladolid.

Plate 5 Felipe Gil de Mena, *Fiestas en Plaza Mayor de Valladolid: Dia Quarto* (1656). (*Celebrations in the Plaza Mayor, Valladolid: Fourth day*).

Photographs by Carlos Barrena. Courtesy of and property of the City Council of Valladolid.

Plate 6 Mascarades at Binche, 1549. Water-coloured pen drawing, 398 by 397 millimetres, with elements picked out in gold.

© Koninklijke Bibliotheek van België, Cabinet des Dessins. F 12930, plano C.

Plate 7 Bal de Henri III.
© RMN-Grand Palais (musée du Louvre)/Thierry Le Mage.

Plate 8a Leandro Bassano, *Portrait of Doge Marino Grimani.*

© Gemäldegalerie Alte Meister, Staatliche Kunstsammlungen Dresden, Gal. Nr. 281.

Plate 8b Leandro Bassano, *Portrait of Dogaressa Morosina Morosini Grimani.*

© Gemäldegalerie Alte Meister, Staatliche Kunstsammlungen Dresden, Gal. Nr. 282.

Plate 9 Dogaressa Morosina Morosini Grimani leaving Palazzo Grimani in the *Bucintoro*.
© Museo Correr, Venezia, Inv. Cl. I n. 0285.

Plate 10 Claudia Felicitas of Tyrol's suite of twelve rooms in the North Wing of Schloss Eggenberg's *piano nobile*, as they currently appear.
© Schloss Eggenberg/UMJ Graz/P. Gradischnigg.

Plate 11 Archduchess Anna's suite in the South Wing of Schloss Eggenberg.
© Schloss Eggenberg/UMJ Graz/P. Gradischnigg.

Plate 12 Anthoni Schoonjans, *Emperor Leopold I, after 1680.*
© Schloss Eggenberg/UMJ Graz/N. Lackner.

Plate 13 Unknown artist, Empress Claudia Felicitas in her bridal gown, Oberöster-
reichisches Landesmuseum Linz.

© Schloss Eggenberg/UMJ Graz/F. Kryza-Gersch.

Plate 14 The welcome inscription above the main entrance of Schloss Eggenberg today.

© Schloss Eggenberg/UMJ Graz/P. Schuster.

Plate 15 Filippo Lauri and Filippo Gagliardi, *Carousel in the courtyard of Palazzo Barberini for Queen Christina of Sweden*, oil on canvas, 1656, Museo di Roma.

© 2014. Photo Scala, Florence – courtesy of Sovrintendenza di Roma Capitale.

Plate 16 The 'Wheelbarrowers': Parisians going to the Champ de Mars. 1792 (gouache on card), Lesueur Brothers.

© Musée de la Ville de Paris, Musée Carnavalet, Paris, France/Bridgeman Images.

7 *Les Réjouissances de la Paix*, 20–23 March 1660

The allegorical transformation of Lyon into a city of peace for the celebration of the Pyrenees Peace Treaty

Nikola Piperkov

The Pyrenees Peace Treaty was signed on 7 November 1659. A consequence of the Thirty Years War, it ended the conflict which had made opponents of the Bourbon and Habsburg dynasties since 1635. The Treaty's clauses entailed not only territorial changes but also the formation of a political alliance through the marriage of Louis XIV with the Spanish Infanta, Maria Theresa. From the time of its proclamation, the Treaty was celebrated throughout France and Europe. One of the celebrations was conducted in Lyon on 20–23 March 1660,[1] several months after the official signature. On the day when peace was proclaimed, the city authorities chose a simple *cavalcade* and a *Te Deum* in the Cathedral Church of Saint John.[2] The delay[3] was a matter of not only organisation and logistics but also symbolic decorum. November was the month leading up to winter, the harshest of seasons, as well as the end of the year. In its place, the new year was chosen, and within it the month of March, the first month of the republican Roman calendar.[4] As a symbol of a new era, this new dating marked the passage between a time of conflict and a time of peace.

---

1 This was a matter of political choice, as Lyon had never been directly involved in the war. According to Claude-François Ménestrier, *Les Réjoüissances de la Paix [. . .]* (Lyon: Chez Benoist Coral, 1660), pp. 3–4, Louis XIV, seeing the prosperity of Lyon, still living in peace, was inspired by the city and prompted to stop the hostilities. To celebrate this choice, the city prepared a celebration and tried to claim an important role in the political outcome. The magnificence of the decorations was intended to represent the magnificence of Lyon, one of the kingdom's most important cities during the sixteenth century. The Religious Wars, however, not only reduced its population but also significantly lessened its political importance. This former glory was intended to be recollected by a series of ephemeral and permanent decorations created for different occasions from 1655 to 1680, which include this particular celebration.

2 Ménestrier, *Les Réjoüissances de la Paix*, p. 7.

3 Ibid., p. 6. The reason for the delay was the absence of Camille de Neufville, count-archbishop of Lyon.

4 See Macrobius, *Saturnalia*, I, 12–13 in *Macrobius Aurelius [opera]* (Badium Ascensium, 1519).

The official or public festival

The main allegorical feature of the official festival, a triumphal arch (Figure 7.1), was commissioned by the city's government, and was presumably realised by the Jesuit friar, Claude-François Ménestrier.[5]

His *ekphrasis* (account and interpretation) of the triumphal arch is the only document attesting to its meaning and even its existence. It was made public on 20 March, the first day of the festival, with the explicit intention of explaining the delay of the celebration and its symbolism. The painter Thomas Blanchet[6] provided the *modello* for the arch and his collaboration with the Jesuit friar was a choice led by a pursuit of prestige: the same two personnel were engaged simultaneously on the decoration of the City Hall,[7] and their involvement in the festival celebration was intended to demonstrate the importance of the occasion.

The arch was constructed on the *pont de la Saône*. Since this bridge was the only link between the river banks, and since it made an important contribution to the commercial road between Paris and Italy, Ménestrier's device transformed it into the symbolic 'heart' of the city. Moreover, the road was connected with yet another bridge, this time on the river Rhône, the *pont de la Guillotière*.[8] In medieval times, this used to mark the border between the Holy Roman Empire and the Kingdom of France. It is therefore likely that the choice of the *pont de la Saône* was a matter of political significance, and that the choice was invested with a highly symbolic meaning: a bridge on the road from the Habsburgs' to the Bourbons' domains as a metaphor for a new alliance between France and Spain.[9]

---

5 *Attribution:* The invention of this ephemeral decoration can be attributed to Ménestrier, even though his name does not appear in the textual or graphical sources: see Ménestrier's reference to 'nostre dessein', *Les Rejouissances de la Paix*, p. 3; and Ménestrier, *Factum justificatif . . . relatif à la publication de l'Histoire de règne de Louis le Grand* (Paris: n.p., 1694), in which he claims to have invented this device. Lucie Galactéros de Boissier, *La vie et l'œuvre de Thomas Blanchet* (s.n.,* 1982), attributes the invention to Ménestrier and the pictorial design to Thomas Blanchet. Details: *Invention:* Ménestrier, by order of the city magistrature. *Conduct:* Ménestrier [?]. *Drawing:* Thomas Blanchet. *Engraving:* Nicolas Auroux. *Execution:* Thomas Blanchet and others. **s.n.* = *sine nomine* (i.e. no publisher's name or place of publication).

6 Appointed city painter, probably shortly after he was commissioned to decorate the City Hall in 1655.

7 See Lucie Galactéros de Boissier, 'Thomas Blanchet: La Grande Salle de l'Hôtel de Ville de Lyon', *Revue de l'art* 47 (1980), 29–42 and Nikola Piperkov, *Ecrire les images: Claude-François Ménestrier et son invention d'un langage allégorique au Grand Siècle français, Mémoire de Master II, sous la direction de Mme Colette Nativel* (s.n., 2010), pp. 86–93.

8 See J. Burnouf *et al.*, *Le Pont de la Guillotière. Franchir le Rhône à Lyon* (Lyon: DARA, 1991).

9 It is interesting to compare this design with the one Ménestrier created in 1664, only four years later, for the visit of the papal legate Flavio Chigi. This time it was the *pont du Rhône (pont de la Guillotière)* that was explicitly chosen in order to convey the idea of consensus between the Pope and the French King, who had argued on religious matters. See Ménestrier, *Description de l'arc de triomphe dressé à la porte du Pont du Rhône. . .* (Lyon: Chez Antoine Iullieron, 1664).

Figure 7.1 Nicolas Auroux, after Thomas Blanchet, *Triumphal arch on the bridge over the river Saône,* copper engraving, 1660, fol. 15, in Claude-François Ménestrier, *Les Rejouissances de la Paix* (Lyon, 1660).

The ephemeral arch was dedicated to the element of Fire.[10] A 'fire of joy' (a fireworks display) was supposed to counter the flames of war, as a metaphorical parallel for the phoenix eternally rising from its ashes.[11] This metaphor was also a deliberate rhetorical allusion to memory or reputation, as further developed in Ménestrier's *ekphrasis*, where he stresses that it is not war but peace that makes a monarch worthy of honour. Ménestrier compares the miraculously wise negotiation of peace by the young prince Louis with the achievements of Charlemagne and Saint Louis and insists that '*les marbres le diront à la postérité*'.[12] The ephemeral fireworks were thus paradoxically viewed as an eternal celebration, a canonisation that would inscribe in letters of fire the name of Louis XIV in the memory of mankind.

The historical subject was carefully chosen. Adapted from Ovid's *Fasti*, it referred to the *Closing of the Temple of Janus* (see Figure 7.2).

As the pagan God of doors, whose altar stood on the Capitol in Rome, Janus came to be associated with the state of peace. The Temple gates were closed when peace came to the Empire; its gates were opened when war was announced[13] – which, during the Roman Republic, was usually done in the month of March. So, instead of choosing war, Louis XIV chose peace in the month of Mars – a right-minded decision worthy of allegorical celebration.[14]

The same subject was also developed as a rhetorical device, since Janus gave his name to January, the first month of the year in the new calendar. With January (Janus) being the new March (Mars), Ménestrier imagined the fireworks display as representing the beginning of a new era, when peace would reign over war and where the gates of the temple of Janus would be closed forever.[15] This abstract concept was conveyed by the first order of the triumphal arch: a *quadrifrons*, presumably derived from and recalling Pamphilio Totti's description of what was erroneously considered at the time the actual temple of Janus in Rome, a 'four-fronted' structure near the meat

---

10 The four elements were evoked and Fire chosen as the most important. Ménestrier insists that it was with the help of the elements (representing nature itself) that Louis XIV had won the war. Therefore, victory in battle came accompanied by the victory of nature: the Earth gave flowers for his triumph; the Air transported the sound of his glory; the Water allowed his warships to be victorious; and the Fire gave him its flame. As Fire, Louis XIV was able to rule over all other elements: to dry the Earth, evaporate the Water and penetrate the Air. Moreover, fire is coloured red like the cape of Mars, whose month was chosen for the occasion; like the blood that was spilt during the war; and like the new bloodline that was to be created by the political alliance of France and Spain.

11 Symbol of eternity and a recognised emblem of power. See Piero Valeriano, *Les hiéroglyphiques de Jan Pierre Valerian, vulgairement nommé Pierius [. . .]* (Lyon, 1615), pp. 246–8.

12 Ménestrier, *Les Rejouissances de la Paix*, p. 5, 'the [very] marbles will tell it to future generations'; and Ibid., p. 3, 'the goal of the *pompa* is to conserve the flames of joy for eternity'.

13 Ovid, *Fasti*, I, 89–293 in *Les Fastes.I – III* (Paris, 1992 edn).

14 The two-headed pagan god was seen as presiding over the New Year.

15 In the year preceding the autonomous reign of Louis XIV, the idea of the New Year (or new era) had a strong political implication. Louis XIV had closed the gates of Janus's temple which his father Louis XIII had opened, thus steering foreign policy on to a new course.

Figure 7.2 The Temple of Janus, detail of Nicolas Auroux, after Thomas Blanchet, *Triumphal arch on the bridge over the river Saône*, copper engraving, 1660, fol. 15, in Claude-François Ménestrier, *Les Rejouissances de la Paix* (Lyon, 1660).

© Bibliothèque municipale de Lyon, Rés 373716. Photo: Nikola Piperkov.

market.[16] At its centre, the statue of Janus held the keys of the year, personified by the four seasons as figured on the tympani. On the statue's pedestal was painted an Ouroboros (a serpent devouring its own tail),[17] indicating symbolically that this particular new year or new era would last eternally.[18]

The inscriptions on the entablatures further clarified this association. Four inscriptions in Latin convey a general understanding of the Peace.[19] Two others, one opposite Saint Nizier Church and the other opposite the Stock Exchange, were in French; their easy intelligibility may be taken as a sign that they introduced a message meaningful to the citizens.[20]

Opposite Saint Nizier Church, the inscription ran as follows:

> *Si jadis un César ferma l'Auguste temple,*
> *Du démon de la guerre, et fit naistre la Paix*
> *Du flambeau de l'amour un prince sans exemple*
> *Le brvle maintenant pour ne l'ouvvrir iamais.*
> [If once Caesar closed the great temple

16 See Pamphilio Totti, *Rittrato di Roma moderna* (Rome: Appresso V. Mascardi, 1638). During the early modern period, the *Ianus Quadrifrons* was thought to be the temple of Janus. This attribution is, however, false. It is in fact a triumphal arch built in 356 for Emperor Constantinus II.

17 The figure of a serpent devouring its own tail was regarded as a symbol of the Egyptian year. See Servius, *In tria Virgilii opera expositio*, note to *Æneid*, V, 85: Servius, *In tria Virgilii opera expositio* (Trykkeren af Servius, 1475) . . . *annus secundum Ægyptios indicabatur ante inventas litteras picto dracone caudam suam mordente, quia in se recurrit*'.

18 The Ouroboros was interpreted as a symbol of eternal regeneration. See Horapollon, *Degli segni hieroglyphici* (Venice, 1547) n°2: '*Come si discriuano il mundo: Quando uogliono scriuere il Mondo, pingono un Serpente che diuora la sua coda, figurato di uarie squamme, per le quali figurano le Stelle del Mondo. Certamente questo animale è molto graue per la grandezza, si come la terra, è anchora sdruccioloso, perilche è simile all'acqua: e muta ogn' anno insieme con la uecchiezza la pelle. Per laqual cosa il tempo faccendo ogn'anno mutamento nel mondo, diuiene giouane. Ma perche adopra il suo corpo per il cibo, questo significa tutte le cose, le quali per diuina prouidenza son generate nel Mondo, douere ritornare in quel medesimo*'.

19 I. *Sedatis tandem bellorum incendiis / Festivos ignes excita Gallia, / Ut illuceat orbi quies. / Noca effice sidera felicitatis tuae / Horoscopo / Et Missilibus ignum linguistique / Publica gauda populus gratulare.* II. *Sperate fausta Pacis auguria: / Ex quo coepit felicitatis annus / Reliquis esse productior. / Malorum damna / Compensante publicis gaudiis; / Dies fastis addita / Pacis nomine conservatur. / Et lapillo notanda candido, UNIONE signetur.* III. *Martis haec Pyra fax hymenaei est, / Quam e Ludodivi pectore / Vicax amoris favilla accendit. / Insignite pacifico Regis nomine / Mensem alias martium nunc Augustum / Ver auspicamini non arietis facibus / Sed amoris. / Sic meliori nomine Lugdunum erit / Civitas lucis non luctus.* IV. *Cineribus nuper diem sacram fecerit / Metanora (?) / Hanc totam festis ignibus consecrant / Lugdunensium vota / Date ventis cineres populi, / ne felici e busto / Bellorum hydra repullulet.*

20 The city is physically divided in two parts by the river Saône. From the Middle Ages onwards, the treaty of Verdun used the river as a boundary between Lotarigia and Western Francia. Ménestrier holds to this administrative division later in his *ekphrasis* of private decorations.

Of the demon of War and thus brought Peace,
By the fire of love a prince like no other
Burns it to ashes and will never open it again.]

Opposite the Stock Exchange the inscription ran:

> *Quittons le souvenir de nos travaux soufferts,*
> *Et pres d'un feu si beau sechons toutes nos larmes:*
> *Vulcan arreste Mars, il le tient dans ses fers*
> *Et ne travaille plus a luy faire des armes.*
> *Louys brule son Temple, et ce Roy glorieux*
> *Ne veut plus pour Autels que nos coeurs et nos yeux.*
> [Let us put aside the memory of our painful enterprises,
> And let us dry our tears next to so beautiful a fire as this:
> Vulcan arrests Mars, holds him prisoner
> And no longer forges weapons for him.
> Louis burns his Temple and thus this glorious King
> Instead of an altar desires no more than our hearts and our eyes.]

In fact, during the seventeenth century, Saint Nizier Church was used as an assembly hall for the city governors, known as *échevins* (magistrates). Its façade had been rebuilt appropriately for a secular building by 1581. We can plausibly suggest that the political message of the first inscription was intended not for the general population but rather the city authorities whose houses and administrative buildings were on the same side of the river. On the other hand, a sentimental ode such as the second inscription was addressed to the city's main market, the domain of free citizens, who were in this way given a model of how they should 'read' the peace treaty.

The second level of the triumphal arch (Figure 7.3) showed Mercury descending from the skies, bearing an order to close the Temple's doors.[21]

As a messenger of Jupiter, Mercury represents the legate of Louis XIV, the new Jupiter. In a strictly French context, Mercury personified the foreign relations of the Kingdom: at a slightly later date he was depicted on the ceiling of the *Galerie des Glaces* in Versailles fulfilling this role – he stands in the middle of the design so that we are unable to tell if he is flying to the Hall of War, at one end, or to the Hall of Peace, at the opposite end.[22] Also,

---

21 Mercury and Janus already shared a common iconographical tradition; see Sebastian Münster, *Cosmographia* (Basel, 1544–1552).

22 This use is probably related to Piero Valeriano, *Les hiéroglyphiques de Jan Pierre Valerian, vulgairement nommé Pierius. . .* (Lyon, 1615); Menaces et paix. Chapitre XLIII. *Quelques non-mesprisables auteurs estiment que ces Serpents empestrez par mutuels entrelancements, signifient les menaces & la paix tout-ensemble. Lequel simulacre on dit que les Gephyreens firent porter deuant eux lors qu'Eumolpe deffit les Athéniens. Car à la monstre du Caducée l'on fit estat qu'ils voulussent donner la paix aux paisibles, & des menace, aux assaillants.*

Figure 7.3 Mercury carrying the order to close the Temple of Janus and Amalthea as an allegory of the Benefits of Peace, detail of Nicolas Auroux, after Thomas Blanchet, *Triumphal arch on the bridge over the river Saône*, copper engraving, 1660, fol. 15, in Claude-François Ménestrier, *Les Rejouissances de la Paix* (Lyon, 1660).

Mercury probably personified the Peace itself. According to Piero Valeriano, the bringers of peace are called *caduceatores* (caduceus bearers), so the god's caduceus (the staff with entwined snakes carried by Mercury as a messenger of the gods) should be hieroglyphically interpreted as an instrument and emblem of peace.[23] As its embodiment, Mercury is also opposed to Mars in the famous *quadro riportato* (easel or ceiling painting) of Gianfrancesco Romanelli's *The Pyrenees Peace Treaty*, painted in 1659 for the Queen's Chambers in the Louvre.

Lastly, on top of the construction, Amalthea, holding a Cornucopia and an olive branch, personified the benefits of peace.[24] At times of peace, as the Latin writers explain, arms were melted down and from them instruments of agriculture were forged. A very popular theme in Dutch engravings from the sixteenth century onwards, this topic was used to oppose the destructive forces of war to the benefits of agriculture, development and industry, brought about by political alliances.

The arch with its elaborate allegories was burnt to ashes following one hour of fireworks. According to Ménestrier, the event bore close resemblance to a theatrical performance. Starting with a great roar, symbolising war, a flying Mercury enveloped in flames arrived at the device and, upon his approach, the temple's gates collapsed. Fireworks were then progressively set on fire from top to bottom of the device.

Private festivals

After the official celebrations, another two days were dedicated to a series of private festivities. On Monday 22 March and Tuesday 23rd,[25] there were no fewer than twenty-six of these, some nearly as elaborate and expensive as the public event. There were all kinds of schemes, from triumphal arches to statues, from simple banners to *pegmata* (stages). Also, lanterns were suspended from the windows of houses and the windows themselves were

23 Piero Valeriano, *Les hiéroglyphiques: Paix. Chapitre XLVI. Tel entrelaccement & fructueuse concorde de Serpents, semble estre cause (ce dit Pline) que les estrangers ayent entourrlé de Serpents la hante du Caducée pour signifier la paix, car ce n'est point la coustume d'y mettre des Serpents crestez. Dauantage, tant de medalles embellies de Caducées portent l'inscription & la deuise de paix . . . on void vne petite figure qui porte vn Caducée & vne branche d'oliuier auec ceste inscription PAX AVGVST La paix d'Auguste.*

24 She stood on a pedestal adorned with the following emblems: *fusée* ('a rocket') with the Italian inscription *Chel che m'auuiua m'affoga* ('What fires me, destroys me'); a fire consuming the ephemeral construction and the temple of Janus; a phoenix with the Spanish inscription *D'unas llamas a otras* ('One fire leads to another'), intended to indicate that the fires of love and joy would replace the fires of war; a lightning bolt with the Latin inscription *Terret sed non diu* ('it terrifies but not for long').

25 There is a gap from Saturday, 20 March to Monday, 22 March. We can explain this as a matter of observing decorum: Sunday is the day of the Lord, and it would have been inappropriate to celebrate secular power on that day.

decorated with flowers, crowns, coats of arms and other *insignia* of power and peace. The cathedral's *Westwerk* and the City Hall's façade were illuminated by candles arranged so as to compose various figures. In addition, Ménestrier indicates that there were day-time activities including banquets, a competition on horseback (*course de la Bague*) and a liturgy.

Ménestrier's detailed account of the various celebrations on 22 and 23 March may be summarised as follows:

Monday, 22 March 1660, the Saint John river bank:[26]

1. Location: Quartier de rue Tramassac (Quartier du Bœuf); Commissioned by the Prévôt des Marchands (Provost); Subject: The power of the provost; Source: Inspired by Virgil's *Georgics*, 4. 453–527. The shepherd Aristaeus (the provost) loses his bees (citizens), which return to him after the sacrifice of an ox (the name of the neighbourhood); **2.** Location: Quartier du Change; Subject: A personification of the Sweetness and Abundance of Peace holding fruits and flowers;[27] **3.** Location: Quartier des trois Maries; Subject: The benefits of peace; Description: A pyramid on the top of which is shown a dove holding an olive branch.[28] On its base Flora, Cerera and Minerva symbolized sweetness, utility and honesty; **4.** Location: Quartier du Gourguillon; Subject: The political alliance of France and Spain; Description: Two figures holding hands as the symbol of *concordia* in front of a giant heart (*cor*);[29] **5.** Location: Quartier de porte Froc; Subject: The temple of Peace; **6.** Location: Quartier de la boucherie Saint Paul; Subject: Mars chained by Amor; **7.** Location: Quartier de la Juiverie; Subject: *Discordia*;[30] **8.** Location: Quartier de rue de Flandres, in front of the customs post (douane); Subject: Bellona chained to the Pillars of Hercules (Spain vanquished by France); **9.** Location: Quartier du port Saint Paul; Subject: Personification of Peace enveloped by the personification of Fury. Once the fire had consumed the enveloped figure, Peace became visible; **10.** Location: Quartier du grenier à sel; Subject: Fireworks with the coats of arms of Lyon and France; **11.** Location: Quartier Saint Georges; Subject: Peace triumphs over War; Description: Triangular machine with inscriptions glorifying the king and the victory.

---

26 See Ménestrier, *Réjouissances de la paix*, pp. 47–75.
27 See Cesare Ripa, *Iconologia* (Rome, 1593), p. 189.
28 Genesis, 8:11.
29 See Andrea Alciati, *Toutes les emblèmes* (Lyon: Guillaume Rouille, 1558), p. 63: '*Au sang civil ardent de toutes pars / Quand par soy cheut / Romme, terre de Mars, / Coustume estoit les bandes ensemble estre, / Et assembler l'une à l'autre la dextre / Concorde, & foy ha celluy signe humain, / Que ceulx que joinct la foy, touchent la main. / C'est le commun signe de la foy civile que /toucher la main dextre l'un à l'aultre.*'
30 See Ripa, *Iconologia*, pp. 60–61.

Tuesday, 23 March 1660, Saint Nizier River bank celebrations:

12. Location: Quartier de la fontaine Saint Marcel (the new Town Hall); Commission: The Grolier family; Subject: The Golden Age; Description: A cave decorated with *cornucopiae* and trophies, in the middle of which a beehive was depicted;[31] **13.** Location: Quartier Saint Vincent; Subject: The fire of peace; Description: A quadrangular *pegma* (stage), symbol of stability, with the Latin inscription *Ignis iste est Symbolum Pacis* (this flame is the symbol of peace);[32] **14.** Location: Quartier de la Lanterne; Subject: Cupid, representing political alliance, stands victorious on the tomb of Mars; **15.** Location: Quartier Saint Vincent; Subject: Cupid holding the emblems of the four elements, signifying *harmonia mundi* (world peace); **16.** Location: Quartier Saint Pierre; Subject: Hercules, representing peace and France, is triumphant over the Hydra, representing war and Spain; **17.** Location: Quartier Saint Nizier; Subject: A quadrangular machine with emblems on each side invented for the occasion: Peace victorious over a dragon; Peace victorious over Mars and Bellona; Peace hears the voice of the people; Peace gives its riches to the populace; **18.** Location: Quartier de l'Herberie; Subject: Arch with a pyramid on the top;[33] inscription: *Deliciae regnant, Diem regnat Pax* (delights rule when Peace rules the day); **19.** Location: Quartier de la croisette; Subject: Peace disarming Mars; **20.** Location: Rue Mercière (Via Mercatoria); Subject: Alexander the Great cuts the Gordian knot; **21.** Location: Quartier du port du Temple; Description: a personification of Controversy, draped in white and black, holding water and fire. Below her are the two wheels of worldly sorrows, representing inconstancy and fortune;[34] **22.** Location: Quartier du Bouchanin (place Bellecour); Subject: Triumphal arch dedicated to peace and inspired by the good government of the Biblical David;[35] **23.** Location: Quartier du Paradis; Subject: *Renomée* (Fame, Renown); **24.** Location: Quartier de l'Hôpital; Subject: Temple of Mars; **25.** Location: Quartier de la Haute Grenette; Subject: The Peace of Lyon; Description: Arch consumed by fireworks. In the middle a lion (Lyon), and on top of it a personification

31 See below.
32 Decorations 13 and 14 develop Ménestrier's design in a such a way that we can suggest that the description of the fireworks was made public before the actual celebration.
33 The pyramid and the triangular form are a recurrent motif in all these decorations. Ménestrier was a great admirer of Egyptian antiquity and wrote about hieroglyphs. He was also in charge of the *Cabinet des Medailles* in the Jesuit College in Lyon. According to Dominique de Colonia, *Antiquités de la ville de Lyon. . .* (Lyon, 1701), the *Cabinet* contained many Egyptian artefacts. We may suggest that the pyramid motif was relevant to mid-sixteenth-century Lyon's preoccupation with egyptomania.
34 See below.
35 Jeremiah, 33:17–21.

of Peace;[36] **26.** Location: Quartier de la Grande Rue; Subject: The Golden Age returns to France.[37]

As this detailed enumeration shows, the role of private contributions is less clear than in the case of the public celebrations. Only some of the private devices have identifiable commissioners or patrons and none of them has an indentifiable designer. Their overall significance is closely related to the topic of peace and all of the chosen subjects are to a considerable degree relevant to the general themes of Ménestrier's official design, either by means of variation (e.g. 2. Sweetness of Peace; 3. Benefits of Peace), political interpretation (4. *Concordia* as metaphor for political alliance), opposed meanings (6. and 19. Mars vanquished) or mythological associations (16. Hercules killing the Hydra; 20. Alexander the Great cutting the Gordian knot). Their design is not only proof that the city's people felt concerned over political changes but that, above all, they are also a sign that the complex allegorical language of the official programme was part of a widely diffused visual culture understandable to most of the population.

It is highly likely that the different neighbourhoods of Lyon, probably financing their decorations by private contributions, were in competition with each other, and that the political occasion was a pretext for contested prestige. Each *quartier* emulated another in an intellectual tussle in which wit played as important a role as financial investment. Ménestrier thus judged the Quartier du port du Temple's invention as one of the most effective (21) (see Figure 7.4).

Comparing its ephemeral decoration to others which incorporated triumphal aches, temples and even caves, Ménestrier's judgement was not based on size or magnificence but on subject matter: the personification of Controversy (*Contrariété*)[38] draped in white and black, holding water and fire, stood on a pedestal on which were shown two wheels of worldly sorrows, signifying inconstancy and fortune. The subject stood out by virtue of its originality and contributed a certain philosophical aspect to the overall topic of peace: peace is forged by harmonising contraries; fortune is irrelevant as only a wise consensus can restore balance. Thus, a particular political alliance became a pretext for a general discourse on harmony, connecting issues of politics to natural processes.

It also appears that several ephemeral decorations served individual interests. The device commissioned by the city provost had very little to do with the Pyrenees Peace Treaty but a great deal to do with a demonstration of his own authority (1.). (See Figure 7.5.)

---

36 Adapted from Ripa, *Iconologia*, pp. 189–90.
37 Adapted from Ovid, *Metamorphosis*, I, 89–124; see Ovid, *Les Métamorphoses d'Ovide, traduites en prose françoise par N. Renouard*. . . (Paris: Chez Pierre Billaine, 1637).
38 A personification absent from Ripa's 1593 *Iconologia*, and from its 1636 French translation by Jean Baudoin.

Figure 7.4 Nicolas Auroux, after Thomas Blanchet, *Personnification of Contro-*
versy, copper engraving, 1660, fol. 68, in Claude-François Ménestrier,
Les Rejouissances de la Paix.

Figure 7.5 Nicolas Auroux, after Thomas Blanchet, *The shepheard Aristaeus loses his bees. Allegory of the provost's power*, copper engraving, 1660, fol. 47, in Claude-François Ménestrier, *Les Rejouissances de la Paix*.

© Bibliothèque municipale de Lyon, Rés 373716. Photo: Nikola Piperkov.

The chosen subject was inspired by Virgil's *Georgics*: the shepherd Aristaeus (the Prévôt), as noted above, loses his bees (citizens), which return to him after the sacrifice of an ox, a logogram of the neighbourhood (Quartier du Boeuf) where the device was situated. Summarised as his first item by Ménestrier, who seems to have arranged his *ekphrasis* by order of precedence rather than by geographical logic, this design can be interpreted as the submission of the Saint John river bank to the power of the provost.

The same logic applies to the first device described on the Saint Nizier river bank, on Terreaux square (12.). Commissioned by the Groliers – a rich and influential family which took an active part in the city magistrature – this ephemeral decoration stood where the new Town Hall was constructed only ten years previously (see Figure 7.6).

The device featured a beehive, an emblem that Andrea Alciati had used in order to signify peace: *De guerre paix* (peace out of war).[39] Ménestrier's interpretation conveniently derives from this iconographical inheritance and evokes Pliny the Elder's *Natural History*, where bees are described as hard workers and a metaphor for society.[40] In that respect, the beehive featured as an emblem of good government, and a glorification therefore of the governors who ruled over the Saint Nizier river bank.

On the topic of bees, a comparison can be made between the provost's and the Groliers' devices. While the provost represented the French king, the council of the magistrature (*les échevins*) had very recently relocated from Saint Nizier Church to the new Town Hall and were governed by privileges originally bestowed on them in the thirteenth century. Their respective devices stood on opposite sides of the city, divided in two – physically, by the river, and administratively by the scope of their executive power.

With a total of twenty-seven *représentations*, the Joys of Peace theme animated the entire city of Lyon and was clearly also an occasion for the celebration of power. Every *Quartier* and every personality contributed to a three-day festival where public and private devices played an equally important role. Thus, Lyon itself was metamorphosed into the city of Peace, with Ménestrier's design and the temple of *Pax* as the jewel in the crown.

The transformation of the city was so successful that it gained popularity and momentum. On the eve of 24 June, when Saint John the Baptist, the city's patron, was celebrated according to the liturgical calendar of

---

39 Alciati, *Toutes les emblèmes*, p. 213: 'Voy, Que le heaulme en guerre souvent mis / Tant de fois tinct du sang des ennemis. / En temps de Paix sert de rusche, à la mousche / Contenant cire, & miel doulx à la bouche.'

40 Pliny the Elder, *Historia naturalis*, XI, 4§11: See Pliny the Elder, *L'Histoire du Monde de C. Pline Second. . .* (Lyon, 1581) 'Sed inter omnia ea principatus apibus et iure praecipua admiratio, solis ex eo genere hominum causa genitis. Mella contrahunt sucumque dulcissimum atque subtilissimum ac saluberrimum, fauos confingunt et ceras mille ad usus uitae, laborem tolerant, opera conficiunt, rem publicam habent, consilia priuatim quoque, at duces gregatim et, quod maxime mirum site, mores habent praeter cetera, cum sint neque mansueti generis neque feri.'

Figure 7.6 Nicolas Auroux, after Thomas Blanchet, *'De guerre paix'. Allegory of the Golden Age*, copper engraving, 1660, fol. 58, in Claude-François Ménestrier, *Les Rejouissances de la Paix*.

the Roman church, another *ioye publicque* was installed on the *pont de la Saône*. Dedicated once again to the subject of peace, it was regarded as a recollection of the original festival and a synthesis of all the political ideas, administrative discourses and even theological concepts transmitted during the festal Joys of Peace:

> *Le souvenir des malheurs passez à des douceurs si charmantes que l'on prend plaisir de l'entretenir. Les images des travaux que nous avons essuyez . . . se présentent à nos yeux, flatent agréablement nos esprits, & dans la tranquillité du repos nous touuons de la douceur à nous remettre en mémoire les disgraces de la fortune, & les agitations de nostre vie.*
>
> *Il ne faut pas donc s'estonner qu'apres avoir satisfait au devoir public avec tant de pompe & magificence, nous dressions de nouueaux trophées à la paix des depoüilles de la guerre. Cette furie a trop causé de malheurs en Europe. . . ; il faut multiplier les supplices pour accroistre nostre ioye, & lui dresser autant de buchers qu'elle a désolé des Prouinces . . .*[41]

[The memory of sorrows was transformed into such delight that we took pleasure in recollecting them. The remembrance of our work . . . was still vivid, flattering our spirits, and in the tranquility of our resting moments we found enough delight to recall in memory the injuries of fortune and the agitations of our worldly lives. Hence, you will not be surprised to find that, after satisfying our public duty with such magnificent display, we created once again trophies to peace from the remnants of war. That fury had already caused too much sorrow in Europe. . . ; we have to emphasise its injuries in order to increase our joy, and create as many achievements as the provinces it had destroyed]

In addition to his *ekphrasis* of the festivities, Ménestrier published a short treaty on fireworks, entitled *Advis nécessaire pour la conduite des feux d'artifice*. This work cannot be dated with certainty, but we may suggest that it was finished shortly after the end of the festival and that the festival served as inspiration and model for its conception. Dedicated to the element of fire, all devices were associated in one way or another with pyrotechnics. The profusion of fireworks provided a three-day display of continuous 'fire', a burgeoning interest in the subject and, we may imagine, an occasion for emulation between the assembled specialists in pyrotechnics, discussing the matter and competing with each other.

Ménestrier theorises fireworks as the flame of love, which ignites the heart by visual pleasure in order to convey an Idea to the mind.[42] He also suggests

---

41 Ménestrier, *Les Rejoüissances de la Paix*, p. 75.
42 Ménestrier, *Advis*, p. 4: '*La Ioye n'est pas seulement magnifique dans ses profusions, elle y paroît ingenieuse . . . En épanouissant le Coeur, elle donne passage aux estincelles du sang, qui servent à la formation des belles Idées; & le Feu qu'elle allume, ne passe pas seulement dans les yeux pour les rendre plus vifs; il donne encore de la vigueur à l'imagination, & semble la rendre feconde. Elle a cela de commun auec l'Amour. . .*'

that ephemeral decorations have the greatest impact only when associated with fireworks, because in the hours of darkness the viewer's attention is attracted to the sole bright object. [43] Moreover, he defines a fireworks display as a composite work of art where engineering, pyrotechnics, design and painting are all brought to bear by the inventor's conception, a role equivalent to that of a theatre director. As such, the inventor should have in mind all the rules of dramaturgy: decorum, subject, text and ornament.

Decorum is intended to render the subject convincing. Location and setting should naturally bring meaning to the subject, so a subject must never be adapted to a location or an event.[44] For example, it is impossible to render the Ship of Argos in a place where there is no river, but even if there is, it should in some way be symbolically relevant to the location. Ménestrier states that in regard to Paris, this subject is only meaningful because there is a ship in the city's coat of arms.

Fireworks are equivalent to role-play. They should be well-timed and carefully designed, as the different kinds of fire signify different kinds of emotions and ideas. According to Ménestrier, fire itself had a rhetorical meaning and should be adapted with decorum to the device. Burning figures and emblems are highly symbolic actions and Ménestrier advises against staging effigies of saints, monarchs and virtues in a fireworks display, which is not only 'ridiculous' in itself but also politically dangerous.[45]

Concerning ornament: all figures should have a meaning and are composed by images that require interpretation, either hieroglyphics, emblems, inscriptions or personifications. The inventor must choose carefully when designing these ornaments because they do not have the same value. Inscriptions are there to explain the occasion and emblems to moralise it. Hieroglyphics and personifications serve to convey abstract ideas that are the true meaning of the poetical invention.

This short treatise, even though insignificant among Ménestrier's vast corpus of printed work, is of capital importance for the understanding of his theoretical ideas. It was published shortly after his thesis on visual rhetoric and can be regarded as the *modello* for the 1662 *Art des emblèmes*, where several of the devices of the Joys of Peace are used as examples. Some of its ideas can also be traced as far into the future as the famous *Philosophie des images énigmatiques*, published in 1684.

The official fireworks and ephemeral devices of the *pont de la Saône* can be identified as Ménestrier's first festival commission. We can judge its

---

43 Ibid., pp. 5–6: '*Elle l'allume [le feu] au milieu des tenebres de la nuit pour en rendre l'éclat plus sensible.*'
44 The subject can also be relevant to the occasion by its nature: historic or emblematic (Ménestrier, *Advis*, pp. 8–17), natural (ibid., p. 18) or mixed (ibid., p. 18).
45 Ménestrier, *Advis*, p. 21: '*L'une des principales observation qu'il faut faire en la conduite de ces Feux, est de n'y mettre aucune figure dont on puisse trouuer l'occasion de railler; & que comme on les fait ordinairement brûler, on puisse faire la plainte...*'

success by its notable outcomes. In 1661, the guild of publishers and engravers passed another commission to Ménestrier to celebrate the birth of the dauphin.[46] Then, in 1664, Ménestrier devised two triumphal arches for the visit of the papal legate Flavio Chigi to Lyon.[47] In 1663, the marriage of the duke of Savoy, Charles-Emmanuel, to the French princess Françoise d'Orléans Valois was the occasion for Ménestrier to extend his scope from Lyon to Chambéry.[48] He later designed ephemeral decorations in Annecy, Grenoble and Paris, and exercised the profession of iconographer for over forty years, until his death in 1705.

Bibliography

Manuscript sources

Bibliothèque municipale, Lyon, Ms 942, Lyon.
Bibliothèque municipale, Lyon, Ms 943, Lyon.

Printed primary sources

Alciati, Andrea, *Toutes les emblèmes* (Lyon: Guillaume Rouille, 1558).

Horapollon, *Degli segni hieroglyphici* (Venice, 1547).

Macrobius, *Macrobius Aurelius [opera]* (Badium Ascensium, 1519).

Ménestrier, Claude-François (attr.), *Advis necessaire pour la conduite des feux d'artifice* (Lyon: Benoist Coral [?], 1660).

Ménestrier, Claude-François, *Les Réjoüissances de la Paix avec un Recueil de diuerses pièces sur ce sujet* (Lyon: Benoist Coral, 1660).

Ménestrier, Claude-François, *Les Rejouissances de la Paix, faites dans la Ville de Lyon le 20 Mars 1660* (Lyon: Guillaume Barbier, 1660).

Ménestrier, Claude-François, *L'Art des Emblèmes* (Lyon: Benoist Coral, 1662).

Ménestrier, Claude-François, *Eloge historique de la ville de Lyon* (Lyon: Benoît Coral, 1669).

Ménestrier, Claude-François, *Histoire du Roy Louis le Grand par les Medailles [. . .]* (Paris: Jean-Baptiste Nolin, 1694; Amsterdam: P. Mortier, 1694).

Münster, Sebastian, *Cosmographia* (Basel, 1544–1552).

Ovid, *Fastes*, newly translated and edited by Anne-Marie Boxus and Jacques Poucet (Louvain: University Ed., 2004).

Ovid, *Les Métamorphoses d'Ovide, traduites en prose françoise par N. Renouard. . .* (Paris: Pierre Billaine, 1637).

Pliny the Elder, *L'Histoire du Monde de C. Pline Second. . .* (Lyon, 1581).

Ripa, Cesare, *Iconologia* (Rome, 1593).

---

46 Ménestrier, *Description de la machine du feu d'artifice, dressé pour la naissance de Monseigneur le Dauphin . . . le 20 Nouembre 1661* (Lyon, 1661).

47 Ménestrier, *Relation de l'entrée de Monseigneur l'Eminentissime cardinal Flavio Chigi [. . .]* (Lyon: Chez Antoine Iullieron, 1664).

48 Ménestrier, *Dessein de l'appareil des noces . . . de . . . Françoise d'Orléans Valois, à Chambéry* (Lyon: Chez Pierre Guillimin, 1663).

Servius, *In tria Virgilii opera expositi* (Trykkeren af Servius, 1475).
Valeriano, Piero, *Les hiéroglyphiques de Jan Pierre Valerian, vulgairement nommé Pierius . . .* (Lyon, 1615).

Secondary sources

*s.n. = *sine nomine* (no publisher's name or place of publication)
Allut, Paul, *Recherches sur la vie et sur les œuvres du P. Claude-François Ménestrier de la Compagnie de Jésus [. . .]* (Lyon: N. Scheuring, 1856).
Burnouf, J., *et al.*, *Le Pont de la Guillotière. Franchir le Rhône à Lyon* (Lyon: DARA, 1991).
Caille, Christine, *Entrées solennelles et cérémonies dans l'œuvre du père Claude-François Ménestrier. Mémoire soutenu à l'Université Paris-Est Créteil-Val de Marne* (s.n.*, 1996).
Colonia, Dominique de, *Antiquités de la ville de Lyon. . .* (Lyon: Thomas Amaulry, 1701).
Galactéros de Boissier, Lucie, 'Thomas Blanchet: La Grande Salle de l'Hôtel de Ville de Lyon', *Revue de l'art* 47 (1980), 29–42.
Galacteros de Boissier, Lucie, *La vie et l'œuvre de Thomas Blanchet (1614 – ?1689). Thèse soutenue à l'Université Lyon II* (s.n.*, 1982).
Martin, Henri-Jean (ed.), *Entrées royales et fêtes populaires à Lyon du XVe au XVIIe siècle. Catalogue* (Lyon: Bibliothéque municipale, 1970).
Piperkov, Nikola, *Ecrire les images: Claude-François Ménestrier et son invention d'un langage allégorique au Grand Siècle français, Mémoire de Master II, sous la direction de Mme Colette Nativel* (s.n.*, 2010).
Sabatier, Gérard (ed.), *Claude-François Ménestrier: les jésuites et le monde des images* (Saint-Martin-d'Hères: PUG, 2010).
Ternois, Daniel (ed.), *L'Art baroque à Lyon. Actes du Colloque, 27–29 octobre 1972, Université Lyon II* (Lyon: Institut d'Histoire de l'art, 1972).

Part II

Space and occasional performance

8 Space for dancing

Accommodating performer and spectator in Renaissance France

Margaret M. McGowan

An image taken from emperor Maximilian I's *Freydal* illustrates dancing at court about 1500 (see Figure 8.1).[1]

The emperor and two ladies look out from a raised platform onto six figures performing a round dance to the sound of drum and pipe, lit by a single torch bearer. Male dancers are masked while ladies wear formal court dress with trains. This represents danced spectacle in its most simplified form: space and dress virtually unchanged from everyday use.

Such routine danced entertainment after dinner spread across Europe in the following decades. It could attain the splendour of the mascarades danced in the Great Hall of the newly constructed palace at Binche in 1549 when Emperor Charles V visited his sister, Mary of Hungary, Regent of the Low Countries.[2] In a drawing of the event (see Plate 6), the emperor is shown at the far end of the hall, seated between his two sisters, with his son Philip and a few courtiers. They are looking at groups of disguised figures dancing. The space, framed by the beams of the high ceiling and adorned with tapestries, seems immense, as does the distance between performers and royal spectators. The hall was 100 feet in length and 45 feet wide, and the artist provides a composite view of episodes from the mascarades.[3] To

---

1 See Maximilian I, *Freydal des Kaisers Maximilien I. Turniere und Mummereien*, ed. Quirin von Leitner (Vienna: A. Holzhausen, 1880–82).

2 The principal contemporary source for the elaborate *fêtes* at Binche is J.C. Calvete de Estrella, *El felicissimo viaje d'el . . . Principe Don Philippe . . . desde España* (Antwerp: Nucio, 1552). For a critical account of the days of festivity, consult Léon Marquet and Samuel Glotz, 'Une relation allemande méconnue (1550) des fêtes données par Marie de Hongroie à Binche et à Mariemont en août 1549', *Société des Bibliophiles belges séant à Mons, Cahiers Binchois* 50 (March 1991), 89–148, where (in addition to the text) thirty-six illustrations are provided.

3 The upper hall of Binche (destroyed by the French in 1554) measured approximately 108 by 50 (Spanish?) ft, according to Vicente Álvarez, *Relación des camino y buen viaje que hizo el Príncipe de España D. Phelipe. . .* (s.l. [Medina del Campo], 1551), while the lower one, erected on the foundations of the twelfth-century castle on the site, measured 100 by 45 Hainaut ft or 29.3 x 13.2 metres (1 Hainaut masonry foot of 10 inches corresponds to 29.34 centimetres), as confirmed by the excavations of the year 2000. Details of the decoration can be found in the washed drawing conserved in the Royal Library of Belgium, Brussels, Prints and drawings, F12930, plano C. See Albert Van de Put, 'Two Drawings of the Fêtes at

Figure 8.1 After-dinner entertainment *c.*1500 at the Court of Maximilian I, from
Freydal des Kaisers Maximilien I. Turniere und Mummereien, II, 112.

Photo: Margaret M. McGowan.

the left, a group of four knights and four ladies have just completed their
dance; in the foreground, two pairs of disguised elderly dancers who had

Binche for Charles V and Philip II, 1549', *Journal of the Warburg and Courtauld Institutes* 3
(1939–40), 49–57; and *Maria van Hongarije. Koningin tussen keizers en kunstenaars 1505–
1558*, eds Bob C. van den Boogert and Jacqueline Kerkhoff (Utrecht and 's-Hertogenbosch:
Rijksmuseum Het Catharijneconvent and Noordbrabants Museum, 1993), p. 311, cat. no.
213. On the architecture of Jacques Du Broeucq, see Krista De Jonge, 'Antiquity Assimilated: Court Architecture 1530–1560', in Krista De Jonge and Konrad Ottenheym (eds),
*Unity and Discontinuity: Architectural Relations between the Southern and Northern
Low Countries 1530–1700* (Architectura Moderna 5) (Turnhout: Brepols, 2007),
pp. 55–78.

performed a German dance; and the larger group to the right – the centre-piece of the show – a danced combat between knights and savages.[4] Thus, danced episodes which had been performed in sequence are depicted as happening simultaneously.

Creating space for dancing presented few practical difficulties at Binche; however, in smaller halls, organisers' ingenuity was taxed to the full, a fact recognised by dancing masters themselves, as Guglielmo Ebreo da Pesaro explained in a chapter on partitioning the ground in his treatise on the *Art of Dancing*:

> This [partitioning] is supremely necessary to the perfect art of dancing, where there is need of keen discernment and unfaltering judgement in taking account of the place and room for dancing, and carefully apportioning it and measuring it in one's mind.[5]

At Bordeaux, in 1575, Pierre de Brach (lawyer, poet, member of the Parlement and friend of Michel de Montaigne) put on a danced spectacle in his house, a *Mascarade du triomphe de Diane*,[6] in honour of Diane de Foix, madame de Candale. This performance was given after dinner when the tables had been removed and the space prepared for dancing. Brach explains how three or four rows of benches were set along the length of the hall for the company, with ladies having reserved places. When Diane de Foix took her seat, she could observe a small altar installed in front of the chimney and musicians upon a raised platform in the corner of the hall.[7] The mascarade told a simple story: the triumph of Chastity over Love. Performers and machines (such as the chariot of Diana) entered either through the long windows from the garden or through doors hidden in the panelling.[8] They came in and made an entire circuit of the place, to show off their costumes and their dancing ability before playing out their little drama. The whole

---

4 For an analysis of the types of dancing performed at this festival, see Daniel Heartz, 'Un Divertissement de palais pour Charles Quint à Binche', in Jean Jacquot (ed.), *Fêtes de la Renaissance*, II (Paris: CNRS, 1960), pp. 329–42.

5 Guglielmo Ebreo da Pesaro, *De Pratica seu arte tripudii* (*On the Practice or Art of Dancing*), ed. Barbara Sparti (Oxford: Oxford University Press, 1993), p. 95; see also, Antonio Cornazano, *Libro dell'arte di danzare* [1455], trans. M. Inglehearn and P. Forsyth, *The Book on the Art of Dancing* (London: Dance Books, 1981), p. 18.

6 Pierre de Brach published a detailed account of his mascarade in *Poëmes* (Bordeaux: S. Millanges, 1576), ff. 177–201. Concetta Cavallini's recent assessment of Brach's mascarade sets into relief the important role given to music, 'Pierre de Brach et le spectacle "privé" à Bordeaux au XVIe siècle', in Marie-Bernadette Dufourest, Charles Mazouer and Anne Surgères (eds), *Spectacles et pouvoirs dans L'Europe de l'Ancien Régime (XVIe – XVIIIe siècles)*, Actes du colloque, Université Michel de Montaigne, Bordeaux III, 17–19 Nov., 2009 (Tübingen: Verlag, 2011), pp. 13–27.

7 Brach, *Mascarade*, f. 178: '*des haut-bois logés sur un eschaffaut volant en un recoin de la salle*'.

8 Ibid., f. 183, Brach describes the pilgrims who entered the hall by a hidden door: '*quatre Pelerins d'Amour entrans dans la salle par une porte desrobée*'.

area was used, the varied dance steps being fitted into the space available: Cupid demonstrated his power through a prancing style taking him from one end of the hall to the other; love-lorn pilgrims aroused sympathy with their dancing imitative of despair; and Diana and her nymphs performed dances of triumph built from complex figures emphasising both individual skills and the capacity to combine in complicated group movements.[9]

The size of the hall meant that performers and spectators were in close proximity. So intimate, in fact, was their relationship that during the action spectators rose from their seats to inspect Cupid's altar; they tried to avoid the birds released by the pilgrims which flew about the hall (f. 186v); they engaged in dialogue with Diana and Cupid as each sought to triumph; they expressed aloud their feelings of amazement at the action, their 'ravishment' at the sweet singing of Apollo, and their extreme pleasure in the pilgrims' show of feeling and despair.[10] Ladies received with enthusiasm the gifts which Diana's nymphs offered (ff. 199v–199); while Diane de Foix, moved by the supplications to her, graciously granted the pilgrims freedom (ff. 199v–201). Finally, the spectators mingled with the maskers during the ball which ended the entertainment lasting most of the night.

Similar patterns of creating space for dancing could be found in towns all over France at this period. It was the most popular form of entertainment at carnival and at other festive times in wealthy households and at court, as Felix Platter's *Journal* records: 'The rich bourgeois give balls to which young ladies may be taken. After dinner, in the light of torches, they dance the *branle*, the *galliard*, the *volte*, the *tire-chaîne* and others, and go on until the morning'.[11] Marguerite de Valois, on her journey through Flanders in 1577, observed the same phenomenon, expressing astonishment that inhabitants whom she thought of as uncultured '*ne participent nullement à cette naturelle rusticité qui sembloit estre propre aux Flamands*'.[12] Every day she was offered banquets and balls. At Cambray, the bishop gave a dinner and a ball to which he invited all the ladies from the town; at Mons, the comte de Lalain offered the same *divertissement*, and Marguerite underlines the beauty and spaciousness of that dining hall: '*les tables levées, le bal*

---

9 For an analysis of the dances performed in this mascarade, see my article, 'Recollections of Dancing Forms from sixteenth-century France', *Dance Research* 21.1 (2003), 10–26.

10 How far Brach's comments provide an accurate impression of spectators' views is difficult to assess as his hyperbole is frequent; he described Diane de Foix, for instance, as a new goddess descended from Heaven (*Mascarade*, f. 177v), and her triumph as greater than those of Scipio or Pompey (ibid., f. 195v).

11 Felix Platter, *Beloved Son Felix: The Journal of Felix Platter*, trans. Sean Jeannett (London: F. Muller, 1961), p. 48, [reporting from Montpellier]. 'After dinner, in the light of torches, they dance the *branle*, the *gaillard*, the *volte*, the *tire-chaîne* and others, and go on until the morning'.

12 Marguerite de Valois, *Mémoires*, eds Michaud and Poujoulat, Iere série, vol. 10, *Mémoires pour servir à l'histoire de France* (Paris: 1838), pp. 392–453, p. 427: '[the inhabitants] have none of that natural rusticity which seemed natural to the Flemish'.

commença en la salle mesme que nous estions, qui estoit grande et belle;[13] and again, at Namur, Don Juan of Austria celebrated Marguerite's arrival with a banquet in the great hall of the castle; when the tables had been removed, there was a ball which, again, lasted most of the night.

The surviving evidence for such occasions is fragmentary, scattered and not always easy to interpret. However, references are abundant and point to the importance attached by princes to the careful creation of dedicated space for dancing from a very early period. One of the earliest records of such space involved Leonardo da Vinci, who built the stage and organised the hall for the *Festa del Paradiso* (performed in Milan in 1490). The central area between the ducal dais and the stage built on two levels above the hall was reserved for dancing. It was surrounded on two sides by benches for the ladies, and a third set of benches at the foot of the stage accommodated the masked dancers as they waited to perform.[14]

For more ambitious projects of international import, larger spaces had to be constructed. These were frequently erected in the inner courtyards of royal palaces. André Chastel was the first to underline the ambitious nature of these temporary spaces, at once familiar and yet transformed.[15] Awareness of this dual character would have doubled the excitement for spectators and performers, who, as is seen in their memoirs where they comment on the beauty of the decorations, were both curious and knowledgeable about the detail of the metamorphosis and measured the splendour of each occasion against the experience of earlier magnificences where similar transformations had been enacted. The familiar, metamorphosed and recognised as such, was essential to the success of a performance.

In April 1518, at Amboise, the celebrations for the wedding of Madeleine de la Tour d'Auvergne to Lorenzo, duke of Urbino, lasted ten days. They took place in the tented hall which had transformed the inner courtyard of the royal palace. The ceiling of this temporary space represented the Heavens.[16] Around the perimeter, scaffolding had been erected for ladies wearing diverse national dress. They had come to see and to participate in an

13 Marguerite de Valois, *Mémoires*, p. 438: 'Once the tables were removed the dancing began in the hall where we were, which was large and beautiful'. On occasion, the company moved from the place where they had dined to a hall next door which had been set aside for dancing; see Carmelo Occhipinti, *Carteggio d'Arte degli Ambasciatori estensi in Francia (1536–1553)* (Pisa: Scuola Normale Superiore, 2001), Paris, 4 January, 1546, p. 122.

14 The disposition of the hall is discussed in detail by Elena Povoledo, 'Origins and Aspects of Italian scenography', in Nico Pirrotta and Elena Povoledo (eds), *Music and Theatre from Poliziano to Monteverdi*, trans. K. Edles (Cambridge: Cambridge University Press, 1982), pp. 293 ff.

15 André Chastel, 'Le lieu de la fête', in Jean Jacquot (ed.), *Fêtes de la Renaissance* I (Paris: CNRS, 1958), pp. 419–23.

16 The space had first been used to celebrate the baptism of the Dauphin three days earlier (25 April, 1518), as recorded by Stazio Gadio whose letter is given in Monique Chatenet, *La cour de France au XVIe siècle* (Paris: Picard, 2002), pp. 229–30.

enormous danced spectacle involving seventy-two performers divided into six groups, performing alternately Spanish, German and Italian dances. Interrupted by an elaborate banquet, the ballets continued until 6 o'clock in the morning.[17]

In the same year (28 December) a similar solution was found at the Bastille in Paris, this time to celebrate the engagement of the 10-month-old Dauphin of France to Princess Mary of England, aged 3. The vast space of the courtyard (600 feet long), was covered with cloth, supported by ropes, on which the sky was again painted with signs of the zodiac so calculated as to indicate felicity and concord, and was scattered with mirrors to reflect the light of thirty large chandeliers.[18] The fête, organised by Galeazzo Visconti, was an elaborate affair involving dancing, feasting, mascarades and processions, and took place in a temporary hall 270 feet long. Anne-Marie Lecoq has attempted a reconstruction of this festival space divided into an *orchestra* – the main hall flanked by two terraces on three levels for spectators (seating capacity two hundred and fifty persons), and a raised platform representing the king's space transformed into Paradise with trees, fruits and flowers.[19] The king and his entourage entered the hall at 4.30 p.m., and participated in two hours of dancing (chiefly stately pavanes), before enjoying a magnificent banquet followed by more dancing which, this time, included mascarades with large numbers entering the performing area in waves. Variously disguised, they danced to Italian music[20] and performed Italian dances as well as those of other nations. Sources are vague and do not agree about the nature of these figures: Rincio has twelve dancers dressed in Spanish style, twelve in French costume, while others are disguised as prophets, Sybils, cardinals or Greeks.[21] These characters danced round and round, then in line formation, jumping and performing *moresques* so expertly that spectators applauded spontaneously.[22] No scenery was provided beyond the rich decoration of the hall and the profusion of lights, and the spectators were at some distance from the dancing on raised seats at the side of the hall. Admiration for the performers, for the combinations of figures and steps of the groups of dancers, and for the magnificence of the costumes,

---

17 See descriptions in Pierre de Vaissière, *Le château d'Amboise* (Paris: Perrin, 1935), p. 132; and in Ivan Cloulas, *Catherine de Médicis* (Paris: Fayard, 1979), pp. 30–31.

18 The principal source for the study of this fête is the report of the milanese Bernardino Rincio (in the entourage of cardinal Du Prat), who published French and Latin versions of his account: *Sylva* and *Le Livre et Forest de messire Bernardin Rince* (Paris: Jean de Gourmont, 1519); these formed the basis of an important analysis by Anne-Marie Lecoq, 'Une fête italienne à la Bastille en 1518', in Jean Guillaume (ed.), *Il se rendit en Italie. Etudes offertes à André Chastel* (Paris: Flammarion, 1987), pp. 149–69. See also R.J. Knecht, 'The Bastille Banquet, 22 December 1518' in this volume, pp. 41–53.

19 Lecoq, 'Une fête', p. 168.

20 Ibid., p. 156.

21 Rincio, *Silva*, B iv (cited by Lecoq, 'Une fête', p. 164).

22 Rincio, *Le Livre et Forest*, p. 106.

was what was called for to impress the English visitors. Yet, the flow of the spectacle was interrupted when – after a flurry of mascarades – ladies stepped down from the galleries to dance another pavane. Ballet triumphed at the end when fifty masked dancers came in groups into the spectacle-space, and their danced figures lasted until midnight.

The care and ingenuity employed in such temporary constructions was also evident at Fontainebleau in July 1546 when the *cour ovale* was covered over for the festivities designed to celebrate the baptism of Princess Elizabeth, future Queen of Spain. According to Guillaume Paradin, the theatre was made of wood,[23] and most observers described the hall as an enormous marquee. A central mast secured the many ropes which held in place, above, a huge silk frame, again made to resemble the heavens.[24] The hall had five arcades, in the centre of which was the king's golden dais; below the platform, in the highest part of the courtyard, was the space reserved for feasting and dancing.[25] A special parquet floor had been laid down for the dancing, and this wooden floor was covered with a cloth so designed that it could be danced upon without danger. We know little about the actual dancing, except for the presence of strange, masked animals of prodigious size and fierceness,[26] but the closeness of the spectators is made clear from the fact that when the time for dancing came, the new cloth-covered floor was so crowded with people that François I seized an 'hallebarde' to chase them off.[27]

Henri II and Catherine de Medici were not content to make do with arrangements that merely modified palace courtyards; they sought new buildings even if they were only temporary. In 1549, ambassador Alvarotti reported to the duke of Ferrara news of a beautiful wooden hall, wonderfully

23 Guillaume Paradin, *Histoire de nostre temps* (Lyon: Jean de Tournes and Guillaume Gazeau, 1550), p. 144.
24 T. and D. Godefroy, *Le Cérémonial françois*, 2 vols (Paris: Sebastien Cramoisy, 1649), II, pp. 146–8: '*un grand voile de soye bleüe, en guise d'un ciel, où estoient attachées quantité d'estoilles d'or, lesquelles rendoient dans cette Cour un éclat parfaitement agréable*' ('a wide sheet of blue silk, resembling a sky, on which were attached a profusion of golden stars which illuminated the courtyard with perfectly delightful light').
25 The most detailed description of this temporary space was given by Bertano, the pope's representative at the French court; he wrote back to Rome, on 4 July, see Chatenet, *La cour de France*, pp. 225–6. See also Anne-Marie Lecoq, 'Les résidences royales à l'épreuve des fêtes', in Jean Guillaume (ed.), *Architecture et vie sociale: L'organisation intérieure des grandes demeures au XVe et au XVIe siècles* (Paris: Picard, 1984), pp. 83–96. Similar structures were erected at Châtellerault in 1541 for the marriage of the duc de Clèves to the princess of Navarre, although the Italian reporters claimed that the courtyard here was much smaller than that at home; see *Lodovico da Thiene* (20 June, 1541) to the duke of Ferrara in Occhipinti, *Carteggio*, pp. 63–5; see also Sacrati in Occhipinti, ibid., p. 62, and Sebastien Piccoté, *Cronique du roy François Ier de ce nom*, ed. G. Guiffrey (Paris: Bibliothèque nationale, 1860), pp. 366–7.
26 Paradin, *Histoire*, p. 145.
27 Reported in Chatenet, *La cour de France*, p. 140.

adorned, in which many fine mascarades were danced.[28] The king, for his accession celebrations, had indeed commissioned his architect Philibert de l'Orme to design a suitable structure for his *fêtes*. Philibert conceived a huge entrance, a triumphal arch with three openings onto a great hall (40 metres long) with twenty tall windows affording plenty of light; the walls were lavishly decorated for banquets and ballets.[29] Ten years later, the king's secretary Jules Gassot referred in his *Memoirs* to the extraordinary festivities put on for the double weddings of the king's sister to the duke of Savoy and of his daughter Elizabeth to the king of Spain.[30] For this occasion, Philibert built a new temporary hall, somewhat larger, with pavilions placed at each corner (see Figure 8.2).[31]

The architect gives a full account of the possibilities of this structure, boasting of its flexibility and explaining how the galleries gave access to the pavilions, how these could be used as dressing rooms for changing for ballets, or as retiring places, or even as space where a prince might eat. From his comments and from the instructions he gives to carpenters and decorators,[32] it is easy to see that his designs were eminently practical, capable of change and adaptation. Such space was relatively inexpensive, not requiring continual maintenance and easy to dismantle when no longer needed. However, the hall built in 1559 for dance and celebration was never used for that purpose; it served for the lying in state of the dead king, Henri II, killed in a tournament.

In 1565, at Bayonne, in order to alleviate the strains of ceremony and the difficult negotiations with emissaries from the Spanish king, Philip II, Catherine organised a country outing on 23 June. Frenchmen and Spaniards, to the sound of music, rode together in boats along the river Adour to the island of

28 Alvarotti, 1 July, 1549, Occhipinti, *Carteggio*, p. 230: '*bellissima sala fatta di legname e tutta belle apparate . . . gran quantità di bellissime mascarate*'. Earlier temporary structures had been fashioned at Marseilles in 1533 for the marriage of the future Henri II to Catherine de Medici. This involved a prolonged interview between François I and the pope, who had come to bless the marriage of his niece. Corridors and rooms above ground joined buildings together for the festivities; details of their work and of the fêtes can be found in Honoré de Valbelle's *Journal* (BnF, ms.fr. 5072), published by A. Hamy, *Entrevue de François Ier avec Clement VII à Marseille, 1533 – Reception, cérémonies, d'après le journal d'Honoré de Valbelle* (Paris: Bibliothèque nationale, 1900).
29 Philibert de l'Orme, *Premier tome de l'architecture* (Paris: Federic Morel, 1567) details the elements of the triumphal entrance, f. 244ᵛ, and depicts the frontage opposite f. 245. Catherine Grodecki has published all the documents relating to this commission, giving payments to Guillaume Rondel and Baptiste Pellerin (painters) and to Scibec de Carpi. She also provides detailed dimensions, *Les travaux de Philibert de l'Orme pour Henri II et son entourage, 1547–1566* (Paris: Librairie des Arts et Métiers, 2000), document 10, pp. 31–2.
30 Jules Gassot, *Sommaire mémorial*, Société de l'histoire de France (Paris: Champion, 1934), p. 14.
31 Philibert de l'Orme, *Nouvelles inventions pour bien bastir à petits fraiz* (Paris: Federic Morel, 1561), f. 31.
32 Philibert de l'Orme, *Nouvelles inventions*, ff. 21–31; the formal agreements relating to the building of the hall were published by Grodecki, *Les travaux*, document 11, pp. 32–3.

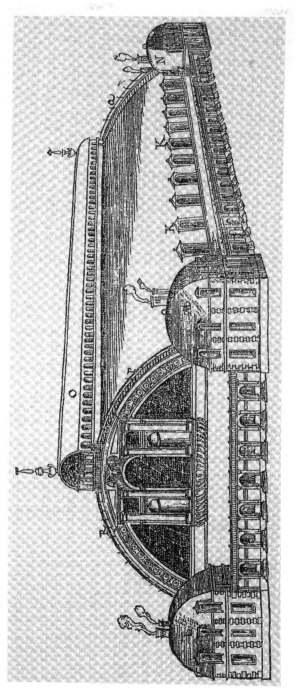

Figure 8.2 A temporary palace for banquets and ballets, designed by Philibert de l'Orme for Henri II, king of France, 1559. Photo: Margaret M. McGowan.

Aigueneau where chosen members of the court, dressed as elegant shepherds and nymphs, performed country dances to greet the company. The dancing stressed freshness and informality, strikingly original and much admired by the Spanish.[33] Then came a banquet followed by ballets; these took place in a specially constructed arbour, octagonal in shape with tables set into its niches around a fountain; the whole structure cost 100,000 *livres tournois*. The dancing went on until midnight, and would have gone on longer had it not been for the rain which poured down in torrents and destroyed everything.

It is interesting that the dancing space here was created from scratch, away from the palace – an imaginative, if risky, innovation. However, for the ballet which Catherine commissioned to honour the Polish ambassadors' visit to Paris in 1573, she had at her disposal the superb gardens of the Tuileries palace, just coming into being through the genius of Philibert de l'Orme.[34] Several witnesses have recorded their impressions of the hall: the memorialist Brantôme, while commenting on the size of the space, was drawn to the striking originality of the ballet danced by sixteen nymphs representing the provinces of France.[35] D'Aubigné also praised the complex dancing of the nymphs who, he wrote, danced twice – first with masks, and then without; he, too, stressed the dimensions of the place, calling it *'un pavillon d'excessive grandeur'*.[36] For his part, Jacques-Auguste de Thou who, in his *Histoire* rarely commented on festivities, was intrigued by the effect of the dancing, whose figures – however disordered they seemed to the eye – never broke out of the harmony they created. The steps, de Thou observed, had been especially invented for the occasion.[37]

The engraving published in Jean Dorat's account of the *fête* (Figure 8.3) illustrates the difficulty of securing accurate visual evidence of such occasions.

From it, one would have to question the alleged size of the dancing space which one ambassador described as a *teatrum*.[38] Nor, from the engraving,

33 The description of this dancing and of the island is given in two accounts published by Victor E. Graham and William McAllister Johnson, *The Royal Tour of France by Charles IX and Catherine de' Medici, Festivals and Entries 1564–66* (Toronto: Toronto University Press, 1979), Appendix xiii, p. 289 and Appendix xviii, p. 310. Marguerite de Valois, *Mémoires*, p. 403, remembers the occasion differently. For an analysis of her testimony, see my *Dance in the Renaissance: European Fashion, French Obsession* (New Haven and London: Yale University Press, 2008), pp. 161–5.

34 De l'Orme refers several times to the work he was doing for the Queen Mother's palace of the Tuileries, *Premier Tome*, ff. 244v, 251 and 267.

35 Pierre de Bourdeille, seigneur de Brantôme, *Oeuvres complètes*, ed. Jules Renouard, 8 vols (Paris: Auguste Desprez, 1822–26), vol. 7, p. 371.

36 Agrippa d'Aubigné, *Histoire universelle*, ed. Baron A. de Ruble, 10 vols (Paris: Société de l'Histoire de France, 1886–1909), vol 4, p. 178.

37 Jacques-Auguste de Thou, *Histoire universelle*, 11 vols (London: [n.p.], 1734), vol. 7, pp. 11–12.

38 For this description from a diary written by ambassador Andrzej Górka (c. 1534–83), see Ewa Kociszewska, 'War and Seduction in Cybele's Garden: Contextualising the *Ballet des Polonais*', *Renaissance Quarterly* 65 (2012), pp. 809–63, Appendix I.

Figure 8.3 Depiction of the opening scene from the *Ballet des Polonais*, 1573, from Jean Dorat, *Magnificentissimi Spectaculi*.

Photo: Margaret M. McGowan.

can we appreciate the intricate movements of the dancers (shown in first position at the beginning of their performance); nor can we see the many lights which apparently lit up the hall. We can glimpse the inner disposition of the pavilion space; the overall wooden structure, decorated with colours, greenery and heraldic devices; the balustrades down the sides of the structure which cut off male spectators from immediate contact with the dancers. Yet, according to ambassador Górka, an immense crowd of people filled the galleries, and sat on the benches and even on the ground.[39] The benches and the crowd are not shown in the engraving, which simply depicts the raised platform under a domed ceiling where Catherine, the king and chief invitees can just be picked out, and the line of court ladies seated on the steps at each side. These ladies appear close to the dancers and, certainly, a greater intimacy was created at the end of the ballet when each of the sixteen dancers offered plaques of gold to the royal spectators and their chief guests. From these records we can even divine the concentration of those eyewitnesses who described the movement of the dancers so precisely: they could follow the complex pattern of the figures, since the choreography left spaces between each movement so that the onlooker could absorb its intricacies before the next sequence began.[40]

Creating a new temporary building for danced spectacle was still relatively rare at this time; large palace halls were generally adapted for such need, as the court continued to be somewhat nomadic. Philibert de l'Orme insisted that doorways of what he called '*Salle Royale que nous appelons Salle de bal*' must be sufficiently large to permit easy access for large mobile floats.[41] In Paris, apart from the Louvre, the archbishop's palace and the City Hall were regularly transformed for royal weddings and *fêtes*. The former was emptied of its furniture for the wedding of Mary Queen of Scots to the

39 Ibid., pp. 850–54.
40 Jean Dorat informs us that the choreographer was Beaujoyeulx, *Magnificentissimi spectaculi in Henrici regis Poloniae gratulationem descriptio* (Paris: Federic Morel, 1573). For a discussion of the precise nature of this dancing and the role of the spectator, see my *Dance in the Renaissance*, pp. 111–114, and Florence Vuillemier-Laurens and Pierre Laurens, 'Le bal des Polonais (1573) anatomie d'une description', in Christine de Buzon and Jules-Eudes Girot (eds), *Jean Dorat, poète et humaniste de la Renaissance* (Geneva: Droz, 2007), pp. 131–65.
41 ('Royal Hall which we call Ball Room'), De l'Orme, *Premier Tome*, pp. 236v – 237. Had the doors of the Hôtel de Ville been wide enough in 1558, Etienne Jodelle would not have experienced the disasters which he detailed in *Le Recueil des Inscriptions* (1558), when his machines were too large to enter the hall, *Oeuvres complètes*, ed. E. Balmas, 2 vols (Paris: Gallimard, 1965–68). For an analysis of this work, see my 'Apology, Justification and Monuments to Posterity', in Benoît Bolduc (ed.), *Texte: Texte et Représentation. Les arts du spectacle (XVIe–XVIIIe siècles)* (Toronto: Toronto University Press, 2004), pp. 83–104. For the generalised use of the 'grande salle' or 'sala grande', see the essays of Sophie Pickford, 'Music in the French Domestic Interior', and Laura Moretti, 'Spaces for Musical Performance in the Este Court in Ferrara (c. 1440–1540)', in Deborah Howard and Laura Moretti (eds), *The Music Room in Early Modern France and Italy* (Oxford: Oxford University Press and British Academy, 2012), pp. 79–83 and pp. 213–36.

Dauphin in April 1558,[42] and the ceiling decorated with jewels – emeralds, sapphires and other precious stones.[43] There, after a sumptuous banquet, the royal party and members of the court danced for several hours before going to the Hôtel de Ville where more banquets, mascarades and ballets awaited. From benches built the length of the hall, spectators were surprised by seven musicians dressed as planets who glided in playing and singing praises.[44] Then, through the double doors of the Audience Chamber, came a large troop of horses (twenty-five of them, all artificial and made from willow) bearing princes and their servants; then a triumphal car with musicians; after came a dozen unicorns ridden by princes wonderfully garbed, with another triumphal car with nine muses, and more handsome 'horses'. The parade and the mascarades lasted two hours, then maskers and princesses danced together. Finally, six beautiful ships slipped in as though gliding on calm water; they were guided by masked princes who had come to carry the ladies off to bed. The dances and mascarades were performed within the circle left by the mechanical floats which, after their entry, were arranged around the perimeter of the hall.

The following year, the same locations were used to celebrate the double weddings of Elizabeth of France to Philip II and the king's sister Marguerite to the duke of Savoy. This time, however, the city aldermen complained: although invited to the banquet in the archbishop's palace, they could not gain access as the confusion was so great.[45] Monies had been spent in vain: Charles le Conte, builder, had been paid 4,250 *livres tournois* for transforming the space; carpenters inserted thirty-two niches around the walls for the convenience of spectators, while Christophle de Leras supplied, among many other things, thirty-six huge chandeliers.[46] Contemporary sources described

---

42 Claude Haton, *Mémoires (1553–1582)*, ed. Laurent Bourquin (Paris: Comité des travaux historiques et scientifiques, 2001), p. 111.

43 Ibid., p. 111. For a detailed description of the Salle du Palais, see Arnold van Buchel, whose *Journal* was translated by Alexandre Vidier, published in the *Mémoires de la société de l'Histoire de Paris et de l'île de France*, vol. 26 (Paris, 1900), pp. 59–195; the salle is described, pp. 85–6, and was destroyed by fire in 1618.

44 Details about the floats and the dancing are given in *Discours du grand et magnifique triomphe faict au mariage de tres noble et magnifique Prince François de Valois, Roy-Dauphin . . . et très haulte et vertueuse Princesse Madame Marie d'Estrevart, Roine d'Escosse* (Paris: Annet Briere, 1558); Ivan Cloulas, *Henri II* (Paris: Fayard, 1985) provides an analysis of the mascarades, pp. 488–9. A painting of the wedding hung on the walls of the great hall at Meudon and was praised by Van Buchel, *Journal*, p. 94.

45 Haton tells us that all the furniture was again taken to the convent of St Augustine to make way for the festivities, *Mémoires*, p. 136; the complaints from the aldermen are recorded in the *Mémoires* of François de Lorraine, duc de Guise in Michaud and Poujoulat (eds), Iere série VI (Paris, 1838), p. 445, and Godefroy, *Le Cérémonial*, vol. 2, p. 20.

46 Details recorded at the end of Guise's *Mémoires*, p. 449: 'A Josse Queldron, 65 *livres 50 sols* pour l'enrichissement de 32 loges dans la grande salle du palais, garnies de cartouches . . . A Christophle de Leras, menuisier, 70 livres pour 36 chandeliers et des tables pour servir au palais le jour des noces'.

the magnificence and the dancing, evoking the splendours of the hall and the excitement of the coordinated movements of the ballets;[47] details of the machines and of the performances seem, however, to have been lost in the aftermath of Henri II's death.

Fortunately, we have abundant records for the '*noces Joyeuse*', the marriage of the duc de Joyeuse to the Queen's sister in 1581 when, during four weeks, twenty-three different festival events were put on, of which a high point was the *Balet Comique de la Reyne*, performed on Sunday, 15 October.[48] This is the only ballet for which we have a detailed printed account prepared by the author and choreographer Balthasar de Beaujoyeulx.[49] The ballet was performed in the Salle du Petit Bourbon, situated in an hôtel adjacent to the Louvre, still admired by Henri Sauval at the end of the seventeenth century for its spaciousness and incredible height.[50] Built by Thibaud Métézeau about 1570, the hall, 70 metres long and 27 metres wide[51] – the largest in Paris – could hold 2,500 persons.[52] It had first seen the performance of a ballet to celebrate the marriage of the future Henri IV to Marguerite de Valois in 1572,[53] and it was transformed again in 1581.

An engraving from the text by Beaujoyeulx (Figure 8.4) shows the audience orientation with two focal points; royal spectators at one end and gardens of delight at the other, with the bulk of the spectators in wooden galleries built down each side.

Lelio Ruggieri, writing to his master, the duke of Ferrara, interpreted the form of the hall as an amphitheatre.[54] Within this space, the décor was

47 The most impressive evocation was provided by Marc Claude de Buttet, 'Epithalame aux nosses', in P. Lacroix (ed.), *Oeuvres poétiques*, 2 vols (Paris: Bibliothèque nationale, 1880), vol. 1, pp. 135–60; see discussion below.

48 For the ambitious scale of this festival, see Monique Chatenet and Luisa Capodieci, 'Les triomphes des noces de Joyeuse (17 septembre–19 octobre, 1581) à travers la correspondance diplomatique italienne et *L'Epithalame* de Jean Dorat', *Bulletin de la Société de l'Histoire de l'Art français* (Paris: Société de l'Histoire de l'Art français, 2007), pp. 9–54. In addition, see Beaujoyeulx's printed account (note 49 below).

49 A facsimile edition of the original text (Paris, Adrian le Roy, Robert Ballard and Mamert Patisson, 1582) was published with an introduction by Margaret M. McGowan, *Le Balet Comique de la Reyne*, Medieval and Renaissance Texts and Studies (New York: Binghamton, 1982).

50 Henri Sauval, *Histoire et recherches des antiquités de la ville de Paris*, 2 vols (Paris: Charles Moette and Jacques Chardon, 1724), vol. 2, p. 210.

51 Dimensions calculated by Germaine Prudhommeau, 'A propos du Ballet Comique de la Reine', *La Recherche en Danse* 3 (1984), 15–24.

52 J-M Pérouse de Montclos, 'La grande salle de l'hôtel du Petit Bourbon, à côté du Louvre, oeuvre inédite de Thibaud Métézeau des années 1570', *Bulletin de la Société de l'Histoire de l'Art français* (1995), 15–21.

53 An account of these festivities, where the disposition of the machines in the hall was very similar, can be found in Simon Goulart, *Relation du massacre de la Saint-Barthélemy*, from *Mémoires de l'Estat de France sous Charles IX* (Middelburg: n.p., 1578), printed in Cimber, *Archives curieuses de l'Histoire de France* (Beauvais: n.p., 1835), vol. 7, pp. 77–165.

54 Chatenet and Capodieci, 'Les triomphes des noces de Joyeuse', document 13, p. 44.

Figure 8.4 The opening scene from the *Balet Comique de la Reyne* (1581) by Balthazar de Beaujoyeulx.

Photo: Margaret M. McGowan.

dispersed, with mobile machines installed along the length of the hall as well as at the upper end. Cloud machines were used for the descent of gods, while mobile floats came in and went out from under the arches at the upper end of the hall. The entertainment mingled speech, song, contest and dancing. In 1572, the monarch had taken an active role in the performance; in 1581, Henri III's part was very different. Fronting the action, he witnessed a more integrated conception of machines, singers and dancers. Static elements of the décor included the *voûte dorée*, Pan's wood and Circé's garden. Both Pan's wood and the golden vault were sizeable structures; both were 18 feet long; and the wood was 12 feet wide, the vault 9 feet. Circé's garden, which had two alleys and four flower beds, was 12 feet across with an extra 30 feet allowed for the two trellises on either side, making the hall at least 45 feet wide. The trellisses were 24 feet high[55] and functioned as places for music making to accompany the eight mobile chariots which swept through the trellised archways (15 feet wide) on either side of Circé's garden. Each machine made at least one full circuit before depositing dancers or musical performers, and then disappeared beneath the archway to the left of the garden. It was fortunate that the mobile machines cleared the dancing area since they were quite substantial. The fountain that brought in the twelve naiads, for instance, was 12 feet wide and 7 feet high; the wood that carried the four dryads was also 12 feet wide; while Minerva's chariot reached 18 feet at its apex.

As Beaujoyeulx made clear, dancing was the central activity. When the first ballet of the twelve naiads was abruptly interrupted, Circé visibly displayed her power. The nymphs had got down from their fountain and had made their appearance on the floor, accompanied by twelve pages and ten violins taking up their position in a triangular formation in the middle of the hall, facing the king. From there, their dancing evolved into twelve different geometric figures ending on a well-known dance tune (*La Clochette*),[56] which brought them in a crescent formation up to the king's dais. There, in close proximity to that being of power on earth, Circé immobilised them. Their lengthy dance had taken them from one end of the hall to the other, and their many geometric-patterned movements explored the entire territory between Pan's wood and the golden vault. For a moment, Mercury animated them, but Circé's power cut in again and turned them into statues a second time. Then, the enchantress drew the unwilling dancers in a subdued procession back into her domain – as captives.

At the end of the entertainment, the same use of the full expanse of the available space came when Circé's power had been broken by the combined force of Jupiter, Minerva and Henri III. Four dryads emerged from the back

---

55 Both Pan's wood and the golden vault were sizeable structures; both were 18 feet long, and the wood was 12 feet wide, the vault, 9 feet.

56 The music for this dance, *La Clochette*, is given in the livret, sigs. Hiiv–Hiiiv.

of the hall and danced their way to its centre, to be joined there by the twelve naiads released from captivity who made their way two by two. Across this central space, they performed fifteen measures so skilfully that, at the end, each dancer faced the king. In a group, they then advanced towards the monarch's seat and danced the *grand ballet*, made up of forty geometric figures. The ballet was so devised that individual movements exploited all the space; there was alternating activity between naiads and dryads, involving chain movements with four circles interlaced and then unravelling, and a great variety of figures representing every geometric shape. Music had helped to define the dancing space.[57] In addition to the flutes and pipes that sounded from Pan's wood and the harmonies issuing forth from the golden vault, two groups of five violins, initially positioned at the end of the hall, moved forward as the dancing progressed, so that powerful effects were achieved with musical sounds coming from different parts of the hall simultaneously, or alternating to underline the changes in the character of the ballet. Machines and performers (dancers and musicians) shared the same space, not as rivals but as mutually supporting each other's individual performances.

This remarkable occasion constituted a pinnacle of danced spectacle in France in the sixteenth century. More permanent, dedicated space in royal palaces was required to accommodate the increased size of the spectacle and the ambitions of architect, artist, poet and choreographer to produce works which would give full rein to harmonised performance and match the political designs of princes. The construction of large halls for festivities had in fact begun before the end of François I's reign, and architectural historians have carefully studied their inception and growth in France. It suffices, therefore, simply to note that Henri II in 1549 ordered the completion of the *salle de bal* in his palace at St Germain, begun about 1539;[58] commissioned from Philibert de l'Orme the transformation of the loggia at Fontainebleau into a *salle des fêtes* in 1548;[59] and commanded Jean Goujon to begin the

57 Anne Daye has provided an interesting interpretation of the dancing in the *Balet Comique*, based on Beaujoyeulx's use of the number 3; see 'Honneur à la Dance: A Choreographic Analysis of the Ballet Entries of the *Balet Comique de la Reyne*', in Barbara Ravelhofer (ed.), *Terpsichore 1450–1900*, International Dance Conference, Ghent: Belgium, 11–18 April 2000 (Ghent: The Institute for Historical Dance Practice, 2000), pp. 71–84.

58 For details on the completion of the ballroom at St Germain, see Chatenet, *La cour de France*, pp. 23–7, and Léon de Laborde, *Les comptes des bâtiments du roi, 1528–1571*, 2 vols (Paris: J. Baur, 1867–1880), vol 1, p. 32.

59 Information on the gradual construction and decoration of the *salle de bal* at Fontainebleau can be found in Chatenet, *La cour de France*, pp. 233–7, Laborde, *Les comptes*, vol. 1, pp. 283, 374, and from the chronology of the architect's works established by J-M Pérouse de Montclos in his facsimile edition of Philibert de l'Orme's *Traités d'architecture* (Paris: Léonce Legat, 1988), pp. 24–8; see also Van Buchel's admiring account, *Journal*, pp. 160–64.

huge reception room in the Louvre (1549–1550)[60] which was to receive many later additions and enrichments such that, in 1600, Thomas Platter could write that he saw there an immense hall, destined for dancing, with a golden ceiling and tapestry-covered walls, together with a special place (the Tribune) reserved for the king.[61]

Although such great halls were frequently transformed to accommodate space for dancing, since choreography had become much more complex and its setting more theatrical, what was required was not more large reception rooms but specially built theatres such as those which were being fashioned in Italy. France needed Italian engineers and scenographers. A kind of half-way house was attempted during Louis XIII's reign, when stages were erected at the end of great reception rooms and when the audience began to be seated on raised seats often arranged in a semi-circle. Such was the accommodation for the large *ballets de cour* mounted in Paris from 1610. Yet, the dancing took place not on the temporary stage but in the hall linked to the stage by a double staircase. While cloud machines increasingly invaded the theatre space, spectators were still in the same area as the dancers.[62] All this was to change when the proscenium arch was introduced, bringing about a transformation in dancing technique. There was, now, the possibility of individual, more-than-human performances within the frame of the stage, performances supported by the whole body of dancers with group routines executed around a single performer.

There was still, however, even in the new conditions of marked separation, a desire for spectators and performers to mingle in social dancing at the end of a performance. This sometimes meant that the cast descended from the stage into the hall and chose partners from the audience. It could also mean the movement of spectators onto the stage to do the dancing. By some secret mechanism, at the end of the ballet *La Prospérité des armes de la France* (1641), danced in the theatre which Cardinal de Richelieu had constructed in his palace, a bridge came forth from the stage into the hall, allowing the principal members of the court (including the monarch) to pass onto the stage where they participated in *branles* and *gaillardes*.[63] Thus, the

---

60 See Chatenet, *La cour de France*, pp. 238–44. Other *salles de bal* were planned for Diane de Poitiers (Limours, 1555), see Grodecki, *Les travaux*, documents 25–30, pp. 64–9, and for Anet, see Occhipinti, *Carteggio*, p. clxv. For other projects in the Tuileries, at Charleval and at Verneuil, see Jacques Androuet Du Cerceau, *Les plus excellents bastiments de France*, presented by David Thomson (Paris: Sand and Corti, 1988).

61 Thomas Platter, *Description de Paris*, ed. J.R. Lejeune (Paris: Société de l'Histoire de Paris, 1896), pp. 189–91.

62 This relationship between steps and hall can be exemplified by a reading of the *ballets livrets* published during the reign of Louis XIII, now available in Marie-Claude Canova-Green, *Ballets pour Louis XIII. Danse et politique à la cour de France (1610–1643)* (Toulouse: Société des littératures classiques, 2010).

63 The elaborate décor and stage machines were the work of an Italian, Gian Maria Mariani, temporarily resident in France. For a *mise au point*, see Anne Le Pas de Sécheval, 'Le Cardinal de Richelieu, le Théâtre et les décorateurs italiens; nouveaux documents sur *Mirame* et

ball is transferred from the hall to the stage, becoming a spectacle in its own right, enhanced by being framed within the proscenium arch.

This development was a long way off. For the sixteenth century in France, I have argued that dancing space was notable for its diversity, for the pragmatic solutions and ingenious discoveries which inspired organisers of danced spectacle, and for the continuing development of interplay between spectator and performer. The evidence, as always at this date, is sketchy and incomplete: drawings and engravings tend to summarise several events or to provide a mere snapshot of a moment's performance. Eyewitnesses are generally interested in the gorgeous costumes and in the quality and diversity of the dancing, taking performance space for granted.

Poets and artists have also left their record of such spectacles, and their visions provide a fitting conclusion to this exploration of dancing space. One of the three well-known paintings of dancing at the court of Henri III represents a ball given in the upper hall of the Louvre during the celebrations for the 'noces Joyeuse' in 1581 (see Plate 7).[64] Only the bride and groom dance, while the royal party (easily identifiable) look on from a slightly raised dais, surrounded by members of the court. The artist has given only an approximate and highly selective view of the hall – no musicians' gallery, no royal tribune, no ornate ceiling. Rather, it is a crowded place with most spectators static, standing and looking out at us. The only movement is suggested by the couple at the centre of the picture – poised to dance – and by the four musicians, three lutenists and a violinist.

To obtain a heightened sense of such an occasion, one must resort to poetry. Pierre de Ronsard's *La Charite*, published in 1578, evokes another dancing couple: Charles IX and his sister Marguerite:

> *Il estoit nuit, et les humides voiles,*
> *L'air espoissi de toutes parts avoyent,*
> *Quand pour le ballet les dames arrivoyent,*
> *Qui de clairté, paroissoient des estoiles.*
> *Robes d'argent et d'or laborieuses*
> *Comme à l'envy flambantes esclattoyent;*
> *Vives en l'air les lumières montoyent*
> *A traits brillans de pierres precieuses.*[65]

[It was night, and its damp veils and the thick air of dusk had invaded all parts, when the ladies arrived for the ball, so radiant that they seemed like stars. Their frocks were worked with gold and silver as if

Le Ballet de la Prospérité des armes de la France (1641)', *XVIIe siècle* 186, 47e année 1 (1995), 135–45.

64 Attributed to Hermann van der Mast, according to Michael Lowe, 'The Lute: An Instrument for All Seasons', in Deborah Howard and Laura Moretti (eds), *The Music Room in Early Modern France and Italy* (Oxford: Oxford University Press and British Academy, 2012), pp. 144–56.

65 Pierre de Ronsard, *Les Amours*, ed. H. and C. Weber (Paris: Garnier, 1963), pp. 363–8, lines 109–116.

their sparkle rivalled that of flames; high into the air, the light of their precious jewels leapt with brilliant rays.]

Ronsard captures the excitement of anticipation, which he makes startlingly visual and sensual, and conjures up the fast steps of the *volta* focusing on the princess, lifted high into the air, whirled around the room by her brother.

Some years earlier, the poet Marc-Claude de Buttet celebrated the union of Savoy and France in 1559 with a poetic vision of that great dancing space, the episcopal palace next to Notre Dame in Paris, where banquets for royal weddings were traditionally enjoyed.[66] First, he evokes the empty space which emphasises the hall's admirable length and mighty height:

> Toute vide on la void d'un cours fort spacieux,
> Grande, longue, admirable et où les vieux aïeux
> Des bons peres Gaulois et des rois plus antiques
> Toujours ont celebré les triomphes publiques.[67]

The banquet comes next with its sugar delicacies and the greedy fingers of hungry princes; then, finally, the ball begins. Buttet shows the manner of the social dancing, its elegance and control, and the complex movements unfailingly performed in keeping with the measures of the music. Then, suddenly, he shatters this serenity, as professional masquers attired in sumptuous clothes invade the hall, taking over all the space to perform their rapid, virtuoso figures. For a moment, princes and their ladies are absorbed together in tight intimacy with the masquers but, as the latter begin their ballet, court performers stand aside to look on. 'Who does not admire the dazzling garments and the movement', exclaims the poet,

> see how they manage their steps with such an even stride that it verily seems as though this whole is but a single movement! Who does not marvel to see the rhythm that worthy baladins keep when they dance so skilfully.[68]

Here we are made to feel present, drawn in alongside the courtiers in the swirl of the dancing, privileged to be in a great hall, witnesses to a thrilling spectacle.

66 For an analysis of other poets' contribution to the celebration of the marriage of princess Marguerite, sister of Henri II, to the duke of Savoy, see Margaret M. McGowan, 'Réjouissances de Mariage: 1559. France-Savoie', in Marie-Thérèse Bouquet-Boyer and Pierre Bonniffet (eds), *Claude le Jeune et son temps en France et dans les Etats de Savoie, 1530–1600* (New York: Peter Lang, 1996), pp. 177–89.
67 ('[One sees it – the hall] completely empty, its spacious sweep wide, long and admirable where venerable ancestors of our gaulois fathers, and where ancient kings have always celebrated their public triumphs'), Buttet, *Epithalame*, vol. 1, p. 151.
68 Ibid., p. 151.

Bibliography

Primary Sources

Aubigné, Agrippa d', *Histoire universelle*, ed. Baron A. de Ruble, 10 vols (Paris: Société de l'Histoire de France, 1886–1909).

Beaujoyeulx, Balthasar de, *Le Balet Comique de la Reyne* (Paris: Adrian le Roy, Robert Ballard and Mamert Patisson, 1582), facsimile with introduction by Margaret M. McGowan, Medieval and Renaissance Texts and Studies (New York: Binghamton, 1982).

Bourdeille, Pierre de, seigneur de Brantôme, *Oeuvres complètes*, ed. Jules Renouard, 8 vols (Paris: Auguste Desprez, 1822–26).

Brach, Pierre de, *Mascarade*, in *Poëmes* (Bordeaux: S. Millanges, 1576).

Brach, Pierre de, *Poëmes* (Bordeaux: S. Millanges, 1576).

Buchel, Arnold van, *Journal*, trans. Alexandre Vidier, in *Mémoires de la société de l'Histoire de Paris et de l'île de France*, vol. 26 (Paris, 1900), pp. 59–195.

Buttet, Marc Claude de, *Epithalame aux nosses*, in *Oeuvres poétiques* ed. P. Lacroix, 2 vols (Paris: Bibliothèque nationale, 1880).

Cornazano, Antonio, *Libro dell'arte de danzare [1455]*, trans M. Inglehearn and P. Forsyth, *The Book of the Art of Dancing* (London: Dance Books, 1981).

Discours du grand et magnifique triomphe faict au mariage de tres noble et magnifique Prince François de Valois, Roy-Dauphin . . . et très haulte et vertueuse Princesse Madame Marie d'Estrevart, Roine d'Escosse (Paris: Annet Briere, 1558).

Dorat, Jean, *Magnificentissimi spectaculi in Henrici regis Poloniae gratulationem descriptio* (Paris: Federic Morel, 1573).

Du Cerceau, Jacques Androuet, *Les plus excellents bastiments de France*, presented by David Thomson (Paris: Sand and Corti, 1988).

Ebreo da Pesaro, Guglielmo, *De pratica seu arte tripudii [1463]*, trans. Barbara Sparti, *On the Practice or Art of Dancing* (Oxford: Oxford University Press, 1993).

Estrella, J.C. Calvete de, *El felicissimo viaje d'el . . . Principe Don Philippe . . . desde España* (Antwerp: Nucio, 1552).

Gassot, Jules, *Sommaire mémorial*, Société de l'Histoire de France (Paris: Champion, 1934).

Godefroy, T. and D., *Le Cérémonial françois*, 2 vols (Paris: Sebastien Cramoisy, 1649).

Goulart, Simon, *Relation du massacre de la Saint-Barthélemy*, in *Mémoires de l'Estat de France sous Charles IX* (Middelburg: n.p., 1578), printed in Cimber, *Archives curieuses de l'Histoire de France* (Beauvais: n.p., 1835), vol. 7, pp. 77–165.

Haton, Claude, *Mémoires (1553–1582)*, ed. Laurent Bourquin (Paris: Comité des travaux historiques et scientifiques, 2001).

Jodelle, Etienne, *Le Recueil des Inscriptions* (1558), in *Oeuvres complètes*, ed. E. Balmas, 2 vols (Paris: Gallimard, 1965–68).

Lorraine, François de, duc de Guise *Mémoires*, in Michaud and Poujoulat (eds), Iere série VI (Paris: 1838).

Maximilian I, *Freydal des Kaisers Maximilien I: Turniere und Mummereien*, ed. Quirin von Leitner (Vienna: A. Holzhausen, 1880–2).

Orme, Philibert de l', *Nouvelles inventions pour bien bastir à petits fraiz* (Paris: Federic Morel, 1561).

Orme, Philibert de l', *Premier tome de l'architecture* (Paris: Federic Morel, 1567).

Orme, Philibert de l', *Traités d'architecture*, facsimile, ed. by J-M Pérouse de Montclos (Paris: Léonce Legat, 1988).

Paradin, Guillaume, *Histoire de nostre temps* (Lyon: Jean de Tournes and Guillaume Gazeau, 1550).

Piccoté, Sebastien, *Cronique du roy François Ier de ce nom*, ed. G. Guiffrey (Paris: Bibliothèque nationale, 1860).

Platter, Felix, *Beloved Son Felix: The Journal of Felix Platter*, trans. Sean Jeannett (London: F. Muller, 1961).

Platter, Thomas, *Description de Paris*, ed. J.R. Lejeune (Paris: Société de l'Histoire de Paris, 1896).

Rincio, Bernardino, *Le Livre et Forest de messire Bernardin Rince* (Paris: Jean de Gourmont, 1519).

Rincio, Bernardino, *Sylva* (Paris: Jean de Gourmont, 1519).

Ronsard, Pierre de, *Les Amours*, ed. H. and C. Weber (Paris: Garnier, 1963).

Sauval, Henri, *Histoire et recherches des antiquités de la ville de Paris*, 2 vols (Paris: Charles Moette and Jacques Chardon, 1724).

Thou, Jacques-Auguste de, *Histoire universelle*, 11 vols (London: n.p., 1734).

Valbelle, Honoré de, *Journal*, pub. by A. Hamy. *Entrevue de François Ier avec Clement VII à Marseille, 1533 – Reception, cérémonies, d'après le journal d'Honoré de Valbelle* (Paris: Bibliothèque nationale, 1900).

Valois, Marguerite de, *Mémoires*, eds Michaud and Poujoulat, Iere série, vol. 10, *Mémoires pour servir à l'histoire de France* (Paris: 1838).

Secondary Sources

Bolduc, Benoît (ed.), *Texte et Représentation. Les arts du spectacle (XVIe–XVIIIe siècles)* (Toronto: Toronto University Press, 2004).

Boogert, Bob C. van den and Jacqueline Kerkhoff (eds), *Maria van Hongarije: Koningin tussen keizers en kunstenaars 1505–1558* (Utrecht and 's-Hertogenbosch: Rijksmuseum Het Catharijneconvent and Noordbrabants Museum, 1993).

Bouquet-Boyer, Marie-Thérèse and Pierre Bonniffet (eds), *Claude le Jeune et son temps en France et dans les Etats de Savoie, 1530–1600* (New York: Peter Lang, 1996).

Buzon, Christine de and Jules-Eudes Girot (eds), *Jean Dorat, poète et humaniste de la Renaissance* (Geneva: Droz, 2007).

Canova-Green, Marie-Claude, *Ballets pour Louis XIII: Danse et politique à la cour de France (1610–1643)* (Toulouse: Société des littératures classiques, 2010).

Cavallini, Concetta, 'Pierre de Brach et le spectacle "privé" à Bordeaux au XVIe siècle', in Marie-Bernadette Dufourest, Charles Mazouer and Anne Surgères (eds), *Spectacles et pouvoirs dans L'Europe de l'Ancien Régime (XVIe-XVIIIe siècles)*, Actes du colloque, Université Michel de Montaigne, Bordeaux III, 17–19 November, 2009 (Tübingen: Verlag, 2011), pp. 13–27.

Chastel, André, 'Le lieu de la fête', in Jean Jacquot (ed.), *Fêtes de la Renaissance* I (Paris: CNRS, 1958), pp. 419–23.

Chatenet, Monique, *La cour de France au XVIe siècle* (Paris: Picard, 2002).

Chatenet, Monique and Luisa Capodieci, 'Les triomphes des noces de Joyeuse (17 septembre–19 octobre, 1581) à travers la correspondance diplomatique italienne et *L'Epithalame* de Jean Dorat', *Bulletin de la Société de l'Histoire de l'Art français* (Paris: Société de l'Histoire de l'Art français, 2007), pp. 9–54.

Cloulas, Ivan, *Catherine de Médicis* (Paris: Fayard, 1979).

Cloulas, Ivan, *Henri II* (Paris: Fayard, 1985).

Daye, Anne, 'Honneur à la Dance: A Choreographic Analysis of the Ballet Entries of the *Balet Comique de la Reyne*', in Barbara Ravelhofer (ed.), *Terpsichore 1450–1900*, International Dance Conference, Ghent: Belgium, 11–18 April, 2000 (Ghent: The Institute for Historical Dance Practice, 2000), pp. 71–84.

De Jonge, Krista, 'Antiquity Assimilated: Court Architecture 1530–1560', in Krista De Jonge and Konrad Ottenheym (eds), *Unity and Discontinuity: Architectural Relations Between the Southern and Northern Low Countries 1530–1700* (Architectura Moderna 5) (Turnhout: Brepols, 2007), pp. 55–78.

Dufourest, Marie-Bernadette, Charles Mazouer and Anne Surgères (eds), *Spectacles et pouvoirs dans l'Europe de l'Ancien Régime (XVIe–XVIIIe siècles)*, Actes du Colloque Université Michel de Montaigne, Bordeaux III, 17–19 November, 2009 (Tübingen: Verlag, 2011).

Górka, Andrzej, *Diary*, in Ewa Kociszewska, 'War and Seduction in Cybele's Garden: Contextualising the *Ballet des Polonais*', *Renaissance Quarterly* 65 (2012), Appendix 1.

Graham, Victor E. and William McAllister Johnson, *The Royal Tour of France by Charles IX and Catherine de' Medici, Festivals and Entries 1564–66* (Toronto: Toronto University Press, 1979).

Grodecki, Catherine, *Les travaux de Philibert de l'Orme pour Henri II et son entourage, 1547–1566* (Paris: Librairie des Arts et Métiers, 2000).

Guillaume, Jean (ed.), *Architecture et vie sociale. L'organisation intérieure des grndes demeures au XVe et au XVIe siècles* (Paris: Picard, 1984).

Guillaume, Jean (ed.), *Il se rendit en Italie. Etudes offertes à André Chastel* (Paris: Flammarion, 1987).

Heartz, Daniel, 'Un Divertissement de palais pour Charles Quint à Binche', in Jean Jacquot (ed.), *Fêtes de la Renaissance*, II (Paris: CNRS, 1960), pp. 329–42.

Howard, Deborah and Laura Moretti (eds), *The Music Room in Early Modern France and Italy* (Oxford: Oxford University Press and British Academy, 2012).

Jacquot, Jean (ed.), *Les Fêtes de la Renaissance*, vols 1 and 2 (Paris: CNRS, 1958 and 1960).

Knecht, R.J., 'The Bastille banquet, 22 December 1518', in J.R. Mulryne, Krista De Jonge, R.L.M. Morris and Pieter Martens (eds), *Occasions of State: Early Modern European Festivals and the negotiation of Power* (Abingdon, UK and New York: Routledge, 2019), pp. 41–53.

Kocsiszewska, Ewa, 'War and Seduction in Cybele's Garden: Contextualising the *Ballet des Polonais*', *Renaissance Quarterly* 65 (2012), 809–63.

Laborde, Léon de, *Les comptes des bâtiments du roi, 1528–1571*, 2 vols (Paris: J. Baur, 1867–1880).

Le Pas de Sécheval, Anne, 'Le Cardinal de Richelieu, le Théâtre et les décorateurs italiens; nouveaux documents sur *Mirame* et *Le Ballet de la Prospérité des armes de la France* (1641)', *XVIIe siècle*, no. 186, 47e année (1995), 135–45.

Lecoq, Anne-Marie, 'Les résidences royales à l'épreuve des fêtes', in Jean Guillaume (ed.), *Architecture et vie sociale. L'organisation intérieure des grandes demeures au XVe et au XVIe siècles* (Paris: Picard, 1984), pp. 83–96.

Lecoq, Anne-Marie, 'Une fête italienne à la Bastille en 1518', in Jean Guillaume (ed.), *Il se rendit en Italie: Etudes offertes à André Chastel* (Paris: Flammarion, 1987).

Lowe, Michael, 'The lute: An Instrument for All Seasons', in Deborah Howard and Laura Moretti (eds), *The Music Room in Early Modern France and Italy* (Oxford: Oxford University Press/British Academy, 2012), pp. 144–56.

Marquet, Léon and Samuel Glotz, 'Une relation allemande méconnue (1550) des fêtes données par Marie de Hongrie à Binche et à Mariemont en août 1549', *Société des Bibliophiles belges séant à Mons, Cahiers Binchois* 50 (March 1991), 89–148.

Moretti, Laura, 'Spaces for Musical Performance in the Este Court in Ferrara (c. 1440–1540)', in Deborah Howard and Laura Moretti (eds), *The Music Room in Early Modern France and Italy* (Oxford: Oxford University Press and British Academy, 2012), pp. 213–36.

McGowan, Margaret M., 'Réjouissances de Mariage: 1559. France-Savoie', in Marie-Thérèse Bouquet-Boyer and Pierre Bonniffet (eds), *Claude le Jeune et son temps en France et dans les Etats de Savoie, 1530–1600* (New York: Peter Lang, 1996), pp. 177–189.

McGowan, Margaret M., 'Recollections of Dancing Forms from Sixteenth-Century France', *Dance Research* 21.1 (2003), 10–26.

McGowan, Margaret M., 'Apology, Justification and Monuments to Posterity', in Benoît Bolduc (ed.), *Texte: Texte et Représentation. Les arts du spectacle (XVIe-XVIIIe siècles)* (Toronto: Toronto University Press, 2004), pp. 83–104.

McGowan, Margaret M., *Dance in the Renaissance: European Fashion, French Obsession* (New Haven and London: Yale University Press, 2008).

Occhipinti, Carmelo, *Carteggio d'Arte degli Ambasciatori estensi in Francia (1536–1553)* (Pisa: Scuola Normale Superiore, 2001).

Pérouse de Montclos, J-M., 'La grande salle de l'hôtel du Petit Bourbon, à côté du Louvre, oeuvre inédite de Thibaud Métézeau des années 1570', *Bulletin de la Société de l'Histoire de l'art français* (1995), 15–21.

Pickford, Sophie, 'Music in the French Domestic Interior', in Deborah Howard and Laura Moretti (eds), *The Music Room in Early Modern France and Italy* (Oxford: Oxford University Press/British Academy, 2012), pp. 79–83.

Povoledo, Elena, 'Origins and Aspects of Italian scenography', in Nico Pirrotta and Elena Povoledo (eds), *Music and Theatre from Poliziano to Monteverdi*, trans. K. Edles (Cambridge: Cambridge University Press, 1982).

Prudhommeau, Germaine, 'A propos du Ballet Comique de la Reine', *La Recherche en Danse* 3 (1984), 15–24.

Ravelhofer, Barbara (ed.), *Terpsichore 1440–1900*, International Dance Conference, Ghent, 11–18 April, 2000 (Ghent: The Institute for Historical Dance Practice, 2000).

Vaissière, Pierre de, *Le château d'Amboise* (Paris: Perrin, 1935).

Van de Put, 'Two Drawings of the Fêtes at Binche for Charles V and Philip II, 1549', *Journal of the Warburg and Courtauld Institutes* 3 (1939–1940), 49–57.

Vuillemier-Laurens, Florence and Pierre Laurens, 'Le bal des Polonais (1573) anatomie d'une description', in Christine de Buzon and Jules-Eudes Girot (eds), *Jean Dorat, poète et humaniste de la Renaissance* (Geneva: Droz, 2007), pp. 131–65.

Ducal display and the
contested use of space in late
sixteenth-century Venetian
coronation festivals

Maartje van Gelder

In April 1597, the Ducal Palace in Venice was turned completely inside out. The palace functioned as both the seat of government and the residence of the doge. Under ordinary circumstances, its offices were the domain of members of the patriciate or political elite as well as secretaries, notaries and other bureaucrats – essentially a secondary elite – drawn from the ranks of the *cittadini* (citizens). Yet on Monday, 28 April 1597, patricians and *cittadini* had to make way for ordinary Venetians, or *popolani*, a category that included everyone who had no formal political role other than that of subject.[1] That Monday, patrician magistrates handed the keys to their offices over to members of the guilds; two days later, eighty patrician judges abandoned their law courts, fleeing the noise and disturbance produced by the guilds carrying out benches that normally provided seating for more than one thousand members of the patrician Great Council. Other councils had to relocate from one end of the palace to the other so that their rooms could be used as storage space for silverware, tapestries and other furnishings.[2] The guilds had a week to prepare their festivities surrounding the ceremonial coronation of Dogaressa Morosina Morosini (1545–1614), wife of Doge Marino Grimani (1532–1605). (See Plates 7 and 8.)

Venice has often been described as an urban theatre, with the waters of the canals and the lagoon lending a special theatrical quality to its striking festivals and ceremonies.[3] Perhaps no other festival has attracted as much

1 At the end of the sixteenth century, Venice had circa 170,000 inhabitants. The percentage of patricians was roughly 8 per cent, but the boundaries of the *cittadini* class are less clear. The vast majority of Venetians belonged to the category of the *popolani*. On the social categories in Venetian society, see Anna Bellavitis, 'Family and Society', in Eric R. Dursteler (ed.), *A Companion to Venetian History, 1400–1797* (Leiden and Boston: Brill, 2013), pp. 317–51.
2 Giovanni Rota, *Lettera nella quale si descrive l'ingresso della Serenissima Morosina Morosini Grimani Prencipessa di Vinetia: co' la cerimonia della Rosa benedetta, mandatala à donare dalla Santità del Nostro Signore* (Venice: Gio. Anto. Rampazetto, 1597), fol. A3v.
3 *Venice, cità excelentissima: Selections from the Renaissance Diaries of Marin Sanudo*, eds Patricia H. Labalme and Laura Sanguineti White; trans. Linda L. Carroll (Baltimore: Johns

attention as that organised for Morosina Morosini's coronation on 4, 5 and 6 May 1597.[4] It was an exceptionally extravagant affair that in many ways jarred with Venetian republican civic culture. The ducal couple used the festival's architecture and decorative programme to present what was effectively a regal image.[5] The event impressed many thousands of spectators from Venice and beyond, while the doge made sure that printed festival books, paintings, engravings and other material objects kept its memory alive long afterwards.[6] Both the unique character of the festival and the abundance of sources have aroused significant scholarly interest. The rich descriptions by Giovanni Rota, Dario Tuzio and Giovanni Stringa, especially, have been mined by those interested in Venetian ceremonial culture or in the figure of the dogaressa, a rare female presence in the realm of Venetian political culture.[7] Edward Muir focused on the festival's message of ducal ambition, which clashed with the notion of the doge as an elected *primus inter pares* rather than a dynastic ruler. To Muir, the ceremony was

---

Hopkins University Press, 2008), p. 487; Bronwen Wilson, 'Venice, Print, and the Early Modern Icon', *Urban History* 33/1 (2006), 39. On Venetian festivals, see, for example, Margherita Azzi Visentini, 'Festival of State: The Scenography of Power in Late Renaissance and Baroque Venice', in Sarah Bonnemaison and Christine Macy (eds), *Festival Architecture* (London and New York: Routledge, 2008), pp. 74–128; Iain Fenlon, *The Ceremonial City: History, Memory and Myth in Renaissance Venice* (New Haven and London: Yale University Press, 2007); Matteo Casini, *I gesti del principe: La festa politica a Firenze e Venezia in età rinascimentale* (Venice: Marsilio, 1996); Patricia Fortini Brown, 'Measured Friendship, Calculated Pomp: The Ceremonial Welcomes of the Venetian Republic', in Barbara Wisch and Susan Scott Munshower (eds), *"All the World's a Stage. . .": Art and Pageantry in the Renaissance and Early Baroque*. Vol.1 *Triumphal Celebrations and the Rituals of Statecraft* (Pennsylvania, PA: Pennsylvania State University, 1990), pp. 136–86; Edward Muir, *Civic Ritual in Renaissance Venice* (Princeton: Princeton University Press, 1981); Lina Padoan Urban, 'Apparati scenografici nelle feste veneziane cinquecentesche', *Arte Veneta* 23 (1969), 145–55.

4 See, for instance, Pompeo Molmenti, *La Dogaressa di Venezia* (Turin: Roux e Favale, 1884), pp. 305–25; Muir, *Civic Ritual*, pp. 293–6; Bronwen Wilson, 'Il bel sesso e l'austero Senat: The Coronation of Dogaressa Morosina Morosini Grimani', *Renaissance Quarterly* 52/1 (1999), 73–139; Maximilian Tondro, 'Memory and Tradition: The Ephemeral Architecture for the Triumphal Entries of the Dogaresse of Venice in 1557 and 1597' (Ph.D thesis, University of Cambridge, 2002). On the dogaressa as a political figure, Holly Hurlburt, *The Dogaressa of Venice, 1200–1500: Wife and Icon* (New York: Palgrave Macmillan, 2006).

5 Muir, 'Images of Power: Art and Pageantry in Renaissance Venice', *The American Historical Review* 84/1 (1979), 47–8.

6 An overview of relevant sources and images can be found in Lina Padoan Urban, 'Feste ufficiali e trattenimenti privati', in Girolamo Arnaldi and Manlio Pastore Stocchi (eds), *Storia della cultura veneta. Il Seicento*, 2 vols (Vicenza: Neri Pozza, 1983), vol. 1, pp. 576–7.

7 Rota, *Lettera*; Dario Tuzio, *Ordine et modo tenuto nell'incoronatione della Serenissima Moresina Grimani Dogaressa di Venetia l'anno MDXCVII. adi 4 di Maggio. Con le feste, e giochi fatti, etc* (Venice: Nicolò Peri, 1597); and *Venetia città nobilissima, et singolare, descritta in XIIII. libri da M. Francesco Sansovino et hora con molta diligenza corretta, emendata, e più d'un terzo di cose nuove ampliata dal M.R.D. Giovanni Stringa* (Venice: A. Salicato, 1604), fols 280r–90r and 431v–2v. For the role of the dogaressa in Venetian political ceremony, Wilson, 'Il bel sesso'.

also proof of the increasingly elitist character of Venetian sixteenth-century ritual: no fishmonger or gondolier could have understood the classical epigrams and highbrow allegories embedded in the decorative programme.[8] In this interpretation, the main active involvement of guild members and other *popolani* was in the festival's preparations; their role as spectators during the event itself was of less importance.

Undoubtedly the doge and his wife used the festival to flaunt their ambitions with an audience of fellow patricians in mind. This chapter argues, however, that through its strategic use of space the festival also projected a message explicitly aimed at the thousands of spectators who were not part of Venice's political or cultural elite. The top-down model of festivals, ceremonies and rituals produced by an elite for a mute and largely passive audience consisting of – in Muir's words – the 'disenfranchised masses', has been replaced by one in which such events are seen as acts of communication, often conveying multiple messages, open to multiple interpretations, to multiple audiences.[9] It is difficult, often impossible, to understand how spectators, both educated and uneducated, experienced and interpreted festivals.[10] The 1597 coronation festival for Dogaressa Morosina Morosini, however, can be read as not just a statement of patrician ambition but also an *explicit* commentary on pressing social and political issues that involved the broader Venetian population.[11]

In contrast to earlier discussions of the festival, I will focus less on the dogaressa and more on the doge. This is not to say that Morosina Morosini did not have an exceptional role in the festival and probably also in its planning. By all accounts, Marino Grimani wanted to organise a feast that would do justice to his beloved wife of almost forty years, and she was its dazzling central figure.[12] The doge, by contrast, was in visual terms almost

---

8 Muir, 'Images of Power', 51. Similarly: Padoan Urban, 'Apparati', 145, 154.

9 See, for instance, Peter Burke, *Historical Anthropology of Early Modern Italy: Essays on Perception and Communication* (Cambridge: Cambridge University Press, 1987) and the introduction to Melissa Calaresu, Filippo de Vivo and Joan-Pau Rubiés (eds), *Exploring Cultural History: Essays in Honour of Peter Burke* (Farnham and Burlington, VT: Ashgate, 2010).

10 Henry Zerner, 'Looking for the Unknowable: The Visual Experience of Renaissance Festivals', in J.R. Mulryne, Helen Watanabe-O'Kelly and Margaret Shewring (eds), *Europa Triumphans: Court and Civic Festivals in Early Modern Europe*, 2 vols (Aldershot and Burlington, VT: Ashgate, 2004), vol. 1, pp. 93–5. For an attempt at understanding the audience's reception of rituals, see Maria José del Rio Barredo, 'Rituals of the Viaticum: Dynasty and Community in Habsburg Madrid', in Melissa Calaresu, Filippo de Vivo and Joan-Pau Rubiés (eds), *Exploring Cultural History: Essays in Honour of Peter Burke* (Farnham and Burlington, VT: Ashgate, 2010), pp. 55–76.

11 For festivals as implicit commentaries on social and economic assumptions and practices, see J.R. Mulryne, 'Introduction', in J.R. Mulryne and Elizabeth Goldring (eds), *Court Festivals of the European Renaissance: Art, Politics and Performance* (Aldershot and Burlington, VT: Ashgate, 2002), p. 1.

12 According to the letters of papal nuncio Antonio Maria Gratiani, Biblioteca Museo Correr – Venezia (hereafter: BMC), Codice Morosini Grimani 358, c. 247.

completely absent: in a (failed) attempt to prevent dynastic posturing, strict regulations forbade the couple from appearing side by side during the festivities. To understand fully the social and political implications of the modifications, ephemeral and permanent, made to Venetian urban space – outside and inside the Ducal Palace, on land and on water – Doge Marino Grimani deserves a more prominent role in the analysis.[13]

Although numerous scholars have examined the decorative and iconographic character of the 1597 festival, they have not looked behind the scenes. Yet the private archive of the Grimani–Morosini family holds a rich cache of financial records and cashbooks, which allows us to do just that.[14] Meticulously kept by the doge himself, the many pages of expenses throw light on the planning and construction of the festival and hence on Grimani's agenda. The goal here, though, is not merely to point out a lacuna in the source material, but to argue that neglecting the financial records is symptomatic of a tendency to study the 1597 festival as an isolated event: the coronation of Morosina Morosini has become unmoored from its Venetian ceremonial counterpart, the ducal *incoronazione* of 1595 and the social and political context of the last decades of the sixteenth century. By incorporating an analysis of the family's financial records and by recontextualising the dogaressa's coronation, this chapter shows how the festival's ephemeral architecture, decorative programme and popular entertainment temporarily altered the social and political meaning of Venice's central urban and ceremonial space. The change was not uncontested, yet Grimani was able to sidestep patrician opposition by choosing an alternative, but equally central, location for one of the most spectacular elements of the festival.

Doge Grimani's coronation, 1595: chaos in place of order

Giovanni Rota wrote the most detailed and authoritative account of Dogaressa Morosina's coronation festival. He probably had access to the organisers or might have been one of the event's planners himself.[15] Before starting to describe the 1597 coronation, however, Rota first takes the readers of his festival book back to the election of Doge Marino Grimani two years earlier, in April 1595. After Doge Pasquale Cicogna's death at the start of that

13 Giuseppe Gullino, 'Marino Grimani', *Dizionario Biografico degli Italiani* 59 (2003). (www. treccani.it/enciclopedia/marino-grimani_(Dizionario-Biografico)/).

14 Art historians have used the cashbooks to reconstruct Grimani's art patronage; see Michel Hochmann, 'Le mécénat de Marino Grimani. Tintoret, Palma le Jeune, Jacopo Bassano, Giulio le Moro et le décor du Palais Grimani; Vèronése et Vittoria à San Giuseppe', *Revue de l'Art* 95 (1992), 41–51; Wladimir Timofiewitsch, 'Quellen und Forschungen zum Prunkgrab des Dogen Marino Grimani in San Giuseppe di Castello zu Venedig', *Mitteilungen des Kunsthistorischen Institutes in Florenz* 11/1 (1963), 33–54.

15 Rota, *Lettera*, fol. [H4r]. Rota finished his description a mere ten days after the event, on 16 May 1597. On the differences between the contemporary descriptions, see Tondro, 'Memory and Tradition', pp. 68–72.

month, Rota tells us, the ensuing ducal election lasted a record-breaking four weeks. Among the ducal candidates was Marino Grimani, a patrician known for his charitable nature and donations of bread to the hungry. The Venetian sixteenth century was characterised by cyclical scarcity and epidemics, and in 1595 the city–state was in the grip of a famine that had started almost a decade earlier.[16] Unsurprisingly, the generous Grimani was the most popular candidate among the majority of Venetians, a majority that had no formal say in the election. When finally, on 26 April, Grimani became the new doge, popular enthusiasm was overwhelming.

While ordinary Venetians hoped that Grimani would use his powers to guarantee a stable bread supply, many of his patrician peers suspected the new doge of demagoguery. In theory, Venetian doges exercised very little power in the Venetian Republic: laws and regulations circumscribed their role, reducing the dogeship to a mostly representative office. Each new doge had to take the ducal oath or *promissione*, which was adjusted and expanded before every ducal election. The *promissione* dictated, for example, that the doge was not allowed to open his own correspondence. All his verbal and written communications were closely supervised, he could not receive foreign visitors unattended or leave the city without permission and his sons could not hold office. Yet, at the same time, the doge was the symbolic representative of the Venetian state and deeply involved in the daily business of government, which meant that a strong doge did have ways to influence the political direction of the Republic.[17] Grimani's fellow patricians were apprehensive of how he might employ his popularity.

What disturbed them even more was that Grimani's election was followed by an exceptional outburst of collective euphoria among ordinary Venetians, which came close to rebellious disorder. According to Rota, a pro-Grimani author, the celebrations were the biggest and most enthusiastic in Venetian history.[18] The city exploded with joy: people 'as if moved to rapture by ecstasy and out of control with happiness, abandoned their homes, shops, squares and their own businesses', converging on the Ducal Palace, singing and shouting in praise of the new doge. The continuous ringing of church bells created a deafening noise, fireworks exploded and people lit bonfires on the Grand Canal and in every square and street, 'so that it seemed as if Venice was going up in flames'. A large crowd wanted to congratulate Grimani in the Ducal Palace, but its doors were kept shut as a precaution. What Rota fails to mention, but what other evidence shows, is that at that

---

16 Brian Pullan, *Rich and Poor in Renaissance Venice: The Social Institutions of a Catholic State to 1620* (Cambridge, MA: Harvard University Press, 1971), especially pp. 356–67, 544–5.

17 Robert Finlay, *Politics in Renaissance Venice* (New Brunswick: Rutgers University Press, 1980), pp. 109–23.

18 Rota, *Lettera*, fol. [B1v]: ' . . . *li maggiori, et li più affetuosi, che in alcun tempo si dimostrassero mai per altro Prencipe*'.

point joy at Grimani's election turned to frustration and vandalism. Market stalls and government property at Rialto and San Marco were smashed to pieces, and the debris was used to feed two enormous bonfires.[19] All night people continued to shout and sing in the streets, lighting fires and setting off fireworks, in a festive frenzy that bordered on the riotous.[20]

Destructive and unchecked revelry is not usually associated with Venice: contemporaries praised the *Serenissima* ('the most serene one') for its political and social stability, while historians have argued that Venetian feasts and rituals played an important part in the popular acceptance of patrician rule.[21] Yet patricians seem to have been conscious of, and also frequently worried about, outbursts of popular disorder.[22] The day after Grimani's election, however, *popolani* fervour was brought under control by the traditional and structured ceremonies of the ducal coronation.[23] The first of three coronation stages took place in the Basilica di San Marco, where the doge was presented to the community of Venetians. The Basilica had a dual function as both the doge's private chapel and the city's most prominent church, home to the body of its patron saint. The Piazza di San Marco formed the background to the coronation's second stage, which consisted of the doge tossing coins to the crowds, a ritual known as the *sparsio*. Grimani and his male relatives threw some 1,400 ducats to the assembled people, while his wife and daughters threw another 200 ducats from the windows of the Ducal Palace. These sums went well beyond what was customary on such occasions; Grimani's own *promissione* had stipulated the distribution of only one hundred ducats.[24] The third and final part of the coronation took place on the *Scala dei Giganti* (Stairway of the Giants) in the courtyard of the Ducal Palace, where the doge was crowned first with the *camauro*, the white skullcap, and then with the *corno*, his embroidered crown.[25] (See Figure 9.1.)

---

19 BMC, Codice Cicogna 2479; Archivio di Stato di Venezia (hereafter: ASV), Deliberazioni, Terra, filza 135, c. 211–12.
20 According to the report by Juan de Zornoza, ambassador for Parma, Archivio di Stato di Parma, busta 615 (1579–1599) Venezia, 29 April 1595.
21 This is one of the main arguments of Muir, *Civic Ritual*. See also Robert C. Davis, *The War of the Fists: Popular Culture and Public Violence in Late Renaissance Venice* (Oxford: Oxford University Press, 1994) and Florence Alazard, *Art vocal, art de gouverner: la musique, le prince et la cité en Italie du Nord 1560–1610* (Paris: Minerve, 2002).
22 Finlay, *Politics*, p. 55.
23 Andrea da Mosto, *I dogi di Venezia nella vita pubblica e vita privata* (Florence: A. Martello, 1977), pp. XXII–XXXI; Padoan Urban, 'Feste ufficiali', p. 575; Muir, *Civic Ritual*, pp. 281–2. The Gabrieli Consort & Players have reconstructed and recorded the music for Grimani's coronation mass celebrated in San Marco a day later, on 28 April 1595.
24 On *promissioni*, see Muir, *Civic Ritual*, p. 286 and Da Mosto, *I dogi*, p. XXV. For Grimani's *promissione*, see BMC, F.2409, Promissione Marino Grimani 1595.
25 Over the centuries it was the *camauro*, not the crown, that took on a sacred significance, Muir, *Civic Ritual*, pp. 281–2.

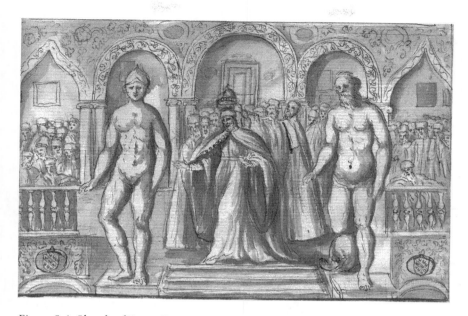

Figure 9.1 Sketch of Doge Grimani's coronation.
© Museo Correr, Venezia, Cod. Morosini-Grimani, Origine della famiglia Morosina, 270, c.65.

Traditionally, the coronation was followed by festivities that could be more or less lavish, depending on each doge's personal preferences. Grimani went all out. He spent a staggering seven thousand ducats in total, paying for the *sparsio*, but also for celebratory banquets, musicians, decorations for his family palace and, of course, charitable donations.[26] To put these amounts into perspective: a skilled craftsman working in the Arsenal shipyard in this period was paid the equivalent of fifty ducats per year.[27] The sum of roughly five hundred ducats the new doge spent on distributing bread and wine throughout the entire city was what impressed ordinary Venetians most. Their hopes for a generous head of state were fulfilled, and shouts of '*Viva, viva*' greeted Grimani for months afterwards.[28] Yet

26 ASV, Archivio Privato Grimani-Barbarigo (hereafter: APGB), busta 33, c. 343v-6v. Also G. Giomo, 'Le spese del nobil uomo Marino Grimani nella sua elezione a doge di Venezia', *Archivio veneto* XXXIII (1887), 443–54, which is based on another version of the expenses from a separate, now lost, register.

27 Frederic C. Lane, *Venice: A Maritime Republic* (Baltimore: Johns Hopkins University Press, 1973), p. 333. Also Brian Pullan, 'Wage-Earners and the Venetian Economy, 1550–1630', *The Economic History Review* 16/3 (1964), 407–26.

28 British Library, Add. 8581, 'Chronicle of Venice', c. 736r.

in a city–state where ducal charity was supposed to be altruistic and in conformity with traditional restrictions, such actions did not put his peers at ease.

Organising the 1597 festival

The Venetian populace fully expected the dogaressa's coronation to take place shortly after Grimani's own election; instead, the event was delayed for two years. Most scholars have attributed the delay to his patrician opponents, who were afraid that Grimani's spending power would turn the dogaressa's coronation into an unprecedented glorification of his family.[29] Whereas the ducal coronation was strictly circumscribed, there were hardly any regulations concerning the *incoronazione* of a dogaressa, primarily because of its rarity. The only other coronation of a dogaressa in the sixteenth century had taken place forty years earlier, in 1557, to honour Zilia Dandolo, while another hundred years separated the Dandolo coronation from the previous one.[30] The Republic's official ceremony books (*cerimoniali*) contained no information on dogaressa coronations, which caused the organisers in 1557 to wonder what the ceremony should actually entail.[31] The lack of regulations allowed for a great deal of freedom, which would explain patrician nervousness about leaving the event in the hands of a popular doge, whose penchant for ostentation was matched by his spending power. Instead of consolidating Venetian social relations, the festival might have just the opposite effect.

The delay, however, seems to have been the doge's own decision. Both Rota and Tuzio stress that it was Grimani himself who kept postponing the event. His concern for the 'public good' forced him to wait until the availability of food supplies could feed not just the city itself, but also all the Italian and foreign visitors.[32] Finally, in the spring of 1597, the urban warehouses were sufficiently full. Whereas the festivities organised by Grimani in 1595 had been primarily an improvised reaction to the outcome of an uncertain election, marred by unprecedented spontaneous celebrations on the streets, this time the ducal couple had had two years to plan.

---

29 Da Mosto, *I dogi*, p. 315, suggests it was part of Grimani's *promissione*. Although the *promissione* contains no such condition, most scholars have followed Da Mosto, see Muir, *Civic Ritual*, p. 293; Hochmann, 'Le mécénat', p. 42; Casini *I gesti*, p. 302; Wilson, 'Il bel sesso', p. 83.

30 Many, but not all, sixteenth-century doges were unmarried or widowers. War and outbreaks of the plague had also prevented dogaressa coronations from taking place; see Casini, *I gesti*, pp. 290–303; Molmenti, *La Dogaressa*, pp. 278–9 and Hurlburt, *The Dogaressa*.

31 Tondro, 'Memory and Tradition', p. 66; *Venetia città nobilissima*, fols 275r–8v; Muir, *Civic Ritual*, p. 292.

32 Rota, *Lettera*, fol. [A2r–v]; Tuzio, *Ordine et modo*, p. 4.

On the one hand, the 1597 coronation of the dogaressa would consist of elements that echoed the ducal coronation – the dogaressa, for instance, would be presented with the *promissione*, which she would swear to uphold. On the other hand, it would incorporate elements already present in the Dandolo festival: the guilds would decorate the Ducal Palace, the dogaressa would make the symbolic *translatio* from the family palace to the Ducal Palace in the *Bucintoro* and she would entertain hundreds of patrician and *cittadini* women. But most importantly it would be an occasion of unprecedented lavishness and a demonstration of the ducal couple's political agenda.

One potentially inflammatory element was the presentation of the Golden Rose, a personal gift from Pope Clement VIII to Morosina Morosini. In the final decades of the sixteenth century, Venetian–papal relations were increasingly strained, and an important contingent of Venetian patricians was highly suspicious of Rome. Eventually these tensions would develop into the open conflict known as the Interdict (1606–1607). Marino Grimani had always been known as an advocate of a pro-papal course.[33] Despite protests from Leonardo Donà (1536–1612), a patrician who belonged to the anti-Habsburg and anti-papal camp, and the most vocal of Grimani's opponents, a special representative of the pope presented the Rose to the dogaressa on the third day of the festival in the Basilica.[34]

The donation of the Golden Rose was a highlight of the Grimani–Morosini festival, but the entire event was filled with numerous other ceremonies, processions and banquets.[35] When examining the festival's organisation, most attention has been devoted to the forty young patricians in charge of the entertainment for the nobility or to the efforts of the guilds. Traditionally, the dogaressa was the patroness of Venice's artisanal guilds, which is why they were given the task of decorating the Ducal Palace, building festival structures on the Piazza San Marco and organising a fleet of decorated boats to accompany the *Bucintoro*, the state galley transporting Morosina Morosini.[36] (See Plate 9.) When Grimani met with the guilds before the festival, he stressed that they should do what they could while spending as little as possible, given the difficult economic times.[37] Although several poorer

---

33 Molmenti, *La dogaressa*, p. 322. BMC, Codice Morosini Grimani 358, c.243–7.
34 BMC, *Codice Morosini Grimani 358*, c. 248. For a recent and brief description of political tensions within the patriciate, Alfredo Viggiano, 'Politics and Constitution', in Eric R. Dursteler (ed.), *A Companion to Venetian History, 1400–1797* (Leiden and Boston: Brill, 2013), p. 59. As a starting point for the historiography on Donà, see Gaetano Cozzi, 'Leonardo Donà (Donati, Donato)', *Dizionario Biografico degli Italiani* 40 (1991). (www.treccani.it/enciclopedia/leonardo-dona_(Dizionario-Biografico)/).
35 For more details, see Rota, *Lettera* and Tuzio, *Ordine*.
36 Muir, *Civic Ritual*, pp. 293–4. For the role of the guilds, see especially George McClure, *The Culture of Profession in Late Renaissance Italy* (Toronto: University of Toronto Press, 2004), pp. 163–72.
37 *Venetia, città nobilissima*, fol. 280v.

guilds asked to be released from their obligations, guilds overall spent a considerable amount of money.[38]

The lion's share of the festival's costs, however, was borne by the doge himself, who spent close to 6,000 ducats in the process, almost matching the cost of his own coronation. The Grimani–Morosini cashbooks show payments to Venetian retailers who provided Morosina Morosini's festive clothing, including three ducal crowns (probably one for each day) as well as clothes for her female retinue and for her two dwarfs. Grimani also paid for musicians and a series of regattas, and for the food, drink, cooks and other staff for the various banquets. He hired hundreds of additional chairs, stools and beds, while other expenses included commemorative medals with Morosina's image, gifts of money and luxury goods, fireworks and decorations.[39]

Grimani's control was not, however, just financial. His own *cavaliere* or master of ceremonies, Salustio Gnecchi, was in charge of overseeing the entire event. It was Gnecchi, for instance, who allocated the rooms in the Ducal Palace to the various guilds.[40] His primary task, it emerges, was to supervise the adornment of the architectural cluster formed by the Palace, the Piazza San Marco, the Piazzetta and the Basilica di San Marco. Civic and liturgical rituals had tied these spaces together since the earliest centuries of the Venetian Republic, amalgamating them into the centre of Venice's 'devotional and political geography'.[41] It was over the use of this highly charged space that the ducal couple clashed harshly with their patrician peers.

Jousting in the piazza

The dogaressa and the doge drew up plans for a grandiose jousting tournament in the Piazza San Marco, something for which they initially received permission.[42] For centuries, tournaments had been an occasion for Europe's ruling dynasties to shine. By the late sixteenth century, tournaments had evolved from a military sport into the theatrical enactment of a joust, while continuing to form part of royal entries, coronations and weddings.[43] In Venice, jousts had been a standard part of festivities in the thirteenth and

---

38 Tuzio, *Ordine et modo*, p. 4. The wealthy guild of the grocers (*marzeri*) spent close to five hundred ducats. On the *marzeri* and their expenses, see Tondro, 'Memory and Tradition', p. 9. See also Muir, *Civic Ritual*, p. 294.

39 ASV, APGB, busta 33, cc. 353v–8v.

40 Rota, *Lettera*, fol. [A3r]. On 11 April 1597, Gnecchi began declaring expenses made for the organization of the coronation, ASV, APGB, busta 33, c. 352v.

41 Iain Fenlon, *Piazza San Marco* (London: Profile Books, 2009), p. xvi. Sanudo, *Venice, città excelentissima*, pp. 495 and 487.

42 BMC, *Codice Morosini Grimani 358*, c.284.

43 Richard Barber and Juliet Barker, *Tournaments: Jousts, Chivalry and Pageants in the Middle Ages* (New York: Boydell Press, 1989), pp. 83–9; 167–9. See also Gregory Hanlon,

fourteenth centuries. In 1253, for instance, a jousting tournament was organised in the Piazza for a ducal coronation. In contrast to jousts in dynastic states, these jousts were mostly an exercise for Venice's military forces instead of an opportunity for the local elite to show off. Although nobles of other states often ridiculed Venetian patricians for their poor horsemanship, the republican ideal will have been the main reason for their lack of engagement in equestrian pursuits.[44] The jousts' popularity with Venetian spectators and their potential for inciting rowdy behaviour, however, caused the authorities to impose stricter control at the end of the fourteenth century.[45] The last serious joust was held in Venice around 1500, but the practice continued in the cities on the *Terraferma*, which were close to Venetian military encampments.[46] Perhaps Grimani, who had served as governor of the main *Terraferma* cities, had witnessed a few of these tournaments himself.

By the time of Morosina's coronation, no joust had been held in the Piazza for almost a century. To revitalise this tradition, with its clear link to dynastic rule and military leadership, the ducal couple sought the assistance of the captain-general of Venice's infantry, the noble mercenary Giovanni Battista Bourbon del Monte (1541–1614). At the start of April 1597, Grimani sent a courier to the *Terraferma* to tell Del Monte that he was invited to take care of the joust. A patrician messenger followed in order to 'discuss the joust that is going to take place on the day of the coronation'.[47] Del Monte, as the city-state's principal commander, was to use his military expertise to organise the tournament, recruit participants and oversee the logistics, which involved importing a considerable number of horses.

'Glorifying War in a Peaceful City: Festive Representations of Combat in Baroque Siena (1590–1740)', *War in History* 11/3 (2004), 249–77 and Strong, *Art and Power*, pp. 55–6.

44 There were, however, horses and stables in the city right up to the nineteenth century; see Elizabeth Horodowich, *A Brief History of Venice: A New History of the City and Its People* (Philadelphia, PA and London: Running Press, 2009), p. 82. Also Finlay, *Politics*, 19.

45 Barber and Barker, *Tournaments*, p. 78. In 1367, it was decided that no joust or any kind of tournament could be organized without formal permission. Davis, *The War of the Fists*, p. 15. The plebeian game of the *pugni* (mock combat between *popolani*) became increasingly popular at this time, possibly as a more controllable alternative.

46 The Venetians organized a final tournament to celebrate the end of the War of Ferrara in 1482, see M.E. Mallett and J.R. Hale, *The Military Organization of a Renaissance State: Venice, c. 1400 to 1617* (Cambridge: Cambridge University Press, 1984), pp. 209–10. Marino Sanudo mentions preparations for a joust to be held in 1502 by Hungarian nobles during the visit of the future queen of Hungary to Venice, *Venice, città excelentissima*, p. 70.

47 On 7 April Grimani paid a courier forty-eight ducats to ask Del Monte to return to Venice ('per andare à ritrovar il signore da Monte per farli intendere di nostro [messaggio et] venir à Venetia'), ASV, APGB, busta 33, c.354r. Grimani also paid the expenses (155 ducats) for the patrician Nicolò Corner to find Del Monte and 'trattar dela giostra si avra da far per il zorno dela ditta incoronatione', ASV, APGB, busta 33, 355v. For the involvement of Da Monte, see also BMC, *Codice Morosini Grimani 358*, c.248.

The ducal couple also engaged Venice's foremost architect, Vincenzo Scamozzi, to design a setting for 'regal' entertainment in the Piazza.[48] For years Scamozzi had worked on the renovation of the San Marco area, but his project had encountered intense opposition from certain factions within the patriciate, among them Leonardo Donà, and ended in compromise. Scamozzi knew that adapting the Piazza, the architectural space that was supposed to mirror the Republic's constitutional continuity and fundamental values, would be highly controversial.[49] Perhaps eager to mould the space at least temporarily to his vision, Scamozzi proposed to design new and innovative constructions, including a hippodrome in 'imitation of the Ancients'.[50] It could be used for Del Monte's jousting tournament, for wagon and horse races, but also for more plebeian forms of entertainment, such as the popular *caccia dei tori* (bull-baiting).[51]

All these plans for games in the Piazza came to nothing. Donà took steps to hinder the festivities in several ways. He first argued that the city's food supplies were simply not adequate to support the festival.[52] When this strategy did not work, Donà claimed that attracting great numbers of people carried the risk of unseemly chaos right in the heart of the city. Popular entertainment in the Piazza could, he said, incite spectators and destabilise the social order. This last argument must have evoked memories of the riot-like scenes in the Piazza two years earlier, and those who previously had supported the plans for the joust now began to waver. The doge decided to put the matter before the Council of Ten, the college responsible for maintaining the public peace. Once he recognised that the Ten were swayed by Donà's arguments, Grimani withdrew his proposal and called off both Del Monte and the architect Scamozzi, who subsequently devoted his attention to designing the most impressively decorated boat of the festival, the *Teatro detto Il Mondo*. The doge, however, was left without a suitably impressive form of popular entertainment only days before the start of the festival.

---

48 *Venetia, città nobilissima*, fol. 431v: 'Poco dopo per l'Incoronatione della Dogaressa Morosina Grimana mentre si pensava di fare del publico molte cose regie, fu dato carico al sudetto Scamozzi Architetto'.

49 For the plans for the *renovatio* of Piazza San Marco, Manfredo Tafuri, *Venice and the Renaissance* (Cambridge, MA: Harvard University Press, 1989), pp. 164–96; Deborah Howard, *Venice Disputed: Marc'Antonio Barbaro and Venetian Architecture* (New Haven and London: Yale University Press, 2011), pp. 171–91.

50 Scamozzi proposed to construct 'fra l'altre cose (novissime a nostri tempi) un' Hippo-dromo, overo carro nella Piazza maggiore di San Marco, nel quale si potessero far giuochi di carrette, & altre corsi di cavalli, ammaestrati intorno akke Mete, ad imitatione de gli Antichi, & parimente giostre, tornei, e simiglianti cose', *Venetia, città nobilissima*, fol. 431v. See also Lina Padoan Urban, 'Teatri e "Teatri del mondo" nella Venezia del Cinquecento', *Arte Veneta* 20 (1966), 137–46.

51 During the 1557 dogaressa coronation, bull-baiting had taken place in the Piazza and in the Ducal Palace's courtyard; see Gregorio Marcello, *Ordine et progreesso* [sic] *del trionfo fatto l'anno MCMLVII, all 19 di settembrio per l'incoronatione della Serenissima Dogaressa Priola* (Venice: Marco Claseri, 1597), fol. A4r.

52 BMC, *Codice Morosini Grimani 358*, c. 248.

Playing to the crowds

In the week before the festival, workers constructed stands and tribunes and placed numerous rows of benches and chairs in the San Marco area to accommodate the spectators. Yet despite these preparations, every seat and all available standing room was already filled by the early hours of 4 May. Piazza San Marco became overcrowded with masses of people, who produced a deafening noise.[53] Those who had been fortunate enough to find a position at the windows of the Ducal Palace or other buildings on the Piazza quickly found themselves crushed together so tightly that they could not move. Others, in search of an unobstructed view, started to climb columns, pillars, beams, ledges, rooftops and even chimneys, while daredevils clung to the bare metal fixtures in the walls or hung from the *merli*, the rooftop crenellations.[54] The painting of Morosina Morosini leaving the Grimani Palace at San Luca gives an impression of the massive audience: people are spilling from windows, balconies, *altane* (wooden terraces) and rooftops (see Plate 9). In such a *mêlée* it was easy for social distinctions to become blurred, perhaps even for disorder to get the upper hand.

Yet despite the city centre being filled to bursting, no untoward incidents occurred. Rota started his festival book with the chaotic scenes after Grimani's election, but he ended it with passages that underlined how order had prevailed during the 1597 dogaressa coronation. Although, according to him, every Venetian and an infinite number of foreigners filled the city's streets and canals, no offensive action or word created disturbances 'in the public or private places of the city'.[55] Tuzio added that the 'multitude [was] so calm and peaceful, that not a minimum of disorder took place, even if, so they say, the number of foreign people exceeded more than forty thousand'.[56]

Rota ascribed the crowd's orderliness in part to God's favour but then went on to give a more mundane reason: while most of Europe suffered from dearth and shortage of food, Venice alone remained unaffected. Strategically forgetting that a decade of famine had only just ended, Rota continued, stating that in 'this month of May, especially, Venice has found herself with a great abundance of grains, which have come from far away regions', testifying to the 'singular prudence and charity of the Most Serene Republic

---

53 Rota, *Lettera*, fol. [A3v–A4v].
54 Rota, *Lettera*, fol. [A4r–v] and [C2r]; Tuzio, *Ordine*, pp. 15–6.
55 Rota, *Lettera*, fols [H3v–H4r]: 'con tanta frequenza di gente di varie nationi, sono passate di giorno, & di notte, le cose tutte con incredibil quiete, senza che sia seguito pur minimo mottivo, non dirò de' fatti, mà nè anco di parole offensive ne' publici, ò ne'privati luoghi della Città'.
56 Tuzio, *Ordine*, pp. 20–1: 'ma quel ch' io stimo forse più, è il vedere l'istessa numerosa gente talmente quieta, & pacifica che non successe mai pur uno minimo disordine, con tutto, che si dica, che il numero della gente forastiera ascendesse à piu di quarantmille'.

towards her subjects'.[57] This was a reference to the arrival of ships carrying Northern European grain, made possible by the relaxation, under Grimani's dogeship, of some of the protectionist Venetian laws against foreign shipping. Tuzio chimed in, pointing out that during the festival 'the *piazze* were continuously abundant not just with bread, but every other type of food, such as meat, poultry and fish'.[58] By describing a city filled with orderly spectators, both Rota and Tuzio counterbalanced the images of upheaval surrounding Grimani's own coronation and, predictably, stressed Venice's reputation as the *Serenissima*. Yet it is their emphasis on the abundance of food that provides a crucial clue to an alternative reading of the festival's iconographic programme, a reading that brings to the fore the visual and spectacular message the organisers aimed at the crowds of non-elite spectators.

An iconographically literate spectator might have understood all or at least most of the allegorical references, perhaps filling in certain blanks with his or her imagination, but a far broader group must have been able to grasp recurrent visual motifs.[59] Arguably, the festival's most prominent ephemeral construction was the butchers' guild's triumphal arch on the Piazzetta.

Giacomo Franco's engraving (see Figure 9.2) captures the aquatic procession of the dogaressa and her cortege just before she entered the San Marco area through the arch.

Triumphal arches were essentially a foreign custom, something that was at odds with the Venetian egalitarian use of public space. Although self-images of prominent Venetians filled private palaces and the façades and interiors of churches, monuments of individuals did not have a place in public squares or the Piazza.[60] The first temporary arch within the Venetian urban structure had been constructed for the coronation of the dogaressa in

---

57 Rota, *Lettera*, fols [H3v–H4r]: 'non è certo punto inferiore, anzi degno d'eterna memoria, il considerare che, essendosi fin da principio dell' anno passato fatta sentire in molte parti d'Europa, la penuria, & la sterilità d'ogni sorte di biade, Vinetia, frà tante città, & provincie, sia stata, si può dir, sola senza patimento alcuno, & più tosto in questo mese di Maggio si sia ritrovata copia grandissima de' grani, fatti venire dall'estreme regioni, con essempio di songolar prudenza, & carità, di questa Serenissima Republica, verso li suoi sudditi, & che, nel tempo di questa solennità, vi sia stata, oltre la quantità grande di bello, & buonissimo pane, ch'era in molti luoghi publicamente venduto, abondanza grandissima di carne, di pesce, & di ogn' altra sorte di vettovaglie'.

58 Tuzio, *Ordine*, p. 21: 'resta à dire che quello che più parmi di maggior consideratione, & degno di essemplare memoria, fù questo che in tal tempo un popolo d'infinito numero, con notabile quantità di diversi forastieri di più nationi, havesse le piazze continuamente abondanti non solamente di pane, ma di ogni altra sorte di vettovaglia, cosi di carni, & pollami, come di pesce.'

59 For an example of a contemporary iconographic reading of the permanent decorations in Piazza San Marco in the mid-sixteenth century, see David Rosand, *Myths of Venice: The Figuration of a State* (Chapel Hill: University of North Carolina Press, 2001), pp. 126–8.

60 The equestrian statue of mercenary Bartolomeo Colleoni on the Campo S. Giovanni e Paolo is the exception to this rule.

Figure 9.2 Giacomo Franco, *Arrival of the* Bucintoro *at the Molo.*

1557.[61] It was no surprise that the planners of the 1597 event adopted the arch and then turned it into a much more sumptuous construction, filled with allegories and mottoes on every level and all sides. The designers of the arch probably consulted the first edition of Cesare Ripa's *Iconologia* (1593).[62] As a structure, the arch recalled the triumphal arch designed by Andrea Palladio for the entry of Henry III, king of France, in 1574, which had, however, been situated on the peripheral site of the Lido.[63]

61 On the first arch constructed in Venice, also by the butchers' guild, for the 1557 coronation, see Maximilian L.S. Tondro, 'The First Temporary Triumphal Arch in Venice (1557)', in J.R. Mulryne and Elizabeth Goldring (eds), *Court Festivals of the European Renaissance: Art, Politics and Performance* (Aldershot and Burlington, VT: Ashgate, 2002), pp. 335–62.
62 Bernardo Fogari, a miniaturist, had designed the arch after consulting with the lawyer Attilio Facio, see Rota, *Lettera*, fol. C4v; *Venetia, città nobilissima*, fols 281–2. Also Muir, 'Images of Power', p. 48; McClure, *The Culture of Profession*, p. 162. For the use of Ripa's *Iconologia*, see Tondro, 'Memory and Tradition', p. 68. The use of emblem books and mythological encyclopaedias was common practice in designing European court festivals; see Strong, *Art and Power*, p. 26.
63 Wilson, 'Il bel sesso', p. 76.

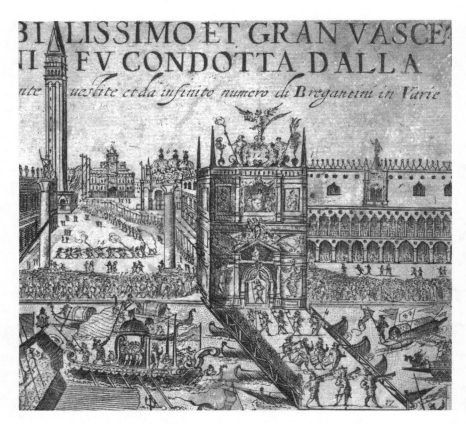

Figure 9.3 The triumphal arch on the Piazzetta. Detail of Giacomo Franco, *Arrival of the* Bucintoro *at the Molo.*

None of the depictions of the arch correspond with the detailed descriptions by Rota and Stringa, but Franco's engraving (see Figure 9.3) seems to come closest.[64] On the side facing the waterfront, the 1597 arch was decorated with two large paintings depicting classical deities. One was Neptune, a familiar figure in Venice's iconographic programme. On the Palace's *Scala dei Giganti* he was paired with Mars, the god of war (see Figure 9.1), but on the arch the designers chose a lesser-known deity:

---

64 For the description of the arch, see *Venetia, città nobilissima*, fol. 281 and Rota, *Lettera*, fols C4r–D4v. The arch also figures in Andrea Vicentino's painting of Morosina's arrival at San Marco, but since he painted quickly and from memory, the representation is not very clear or detailed, Padoan Urban, 'Apparati scenografici', 152–4.

Ops, Roman goddess of abundance and fertility. Mottoes explained to the literate viewer that Neptune and Ops represented the Venetian overseas dominions and the *Terraferma*, together with the Grimani and Morosini families.[65] With her hands filled with edible plants, fruits and cereals, Ops visually represented abundance and food, a forceful message given the recent hunger years.

At the top of the arch stood a female representation of Venice, holding ears of grain in her hand; she was flanked by depictions of the virtues Justice, Clemency, Equity and Munificence. This last virtue was echoed on the other side of the arch, which looked into the Piazzetta and was dedicated primarily to the doge and his political career. Among the many personifications and symbols was a painting of a richly dressed woman distributing money with both hands to a crowd of people. She represented Grimani's work as a Procurator of Saint Mark, the second-most prestigious office in the Republic and closely linked to acts of charity, but she could also be interpreted as a reference to Grimani's personal reputation for generosity and even to his *sparsio* two years earlier.[66]

During the festival, the doors of the Ducal Palace stood wide open, allowing the public to visit the offices decorated by the guilds.[67] The artisans' contributions were a combination of their own input and that of people like Gnecchi, responsible for the sophisticated Latin inscriptions and thematic continuity.[68] Inside the Palace, visual and textual references to abundance cropped up throughout the decorative programme. The painters' guild, for instance, contributed a display that represented the doge's virtues, which included both Liberality and *Abbondanza*. The message of plenty, however, was nowhere as prominent as in the decorated rooms of the Grain Office. This space, which under normal circumstances housed the surveyors of Venice's provisioning programme, had been assigned to the German bakers. They celebrated the Republic's ample supplies of grain in both a highbrow and lowbrow idiom, combining quotations from Horace and other classical authors with baked decorations, such as large roses of bread.

The bakers had given pride of place to a painting of Ceres, the daughter of Ops and goddess of agriculture and crops. Ceres, according to the description by Giovanni Stringa, was depicted as the Goddess of Grain, crowned with a garland made out of ears of wheat. In her left hand she held a horn

---

65 On the importance of (written and spoken) mottoes, see Stephen Orgel, *The Illusion of Power: Political Theater in the English Renaissance* (Berkeley: University of California Press, 1975), pp. 25–6. On the *Scala dei Giganti* Mars and Neptune symbolized Venice's authority over land and sea.

66 Rota, *Lettera*, fol. [D3v]. The Procurators managed the execution of wills and bequests made by Venice's inhabitants to the *Procuratoria di San Marco*, distributing alms and allocating cheap housing.

67 McClure, *The Culture of Profession*, p. 160.

68 Tondro, 'Memory and Tradition', p. 128.

of plenty, filled with sheaves of wheat, while her right hand carried more sheaves. His depiction of Ceres and her attributes followed to the letter Cesare Ripa's description of Abundance '*in forma di Matrona*'.[69] Ripa, for whom Ceres symbolised a Golden Age immune from scarcity, in turn based his description on representations of Annona, the Roman personification of the grain supply.[70] A motto under the Venetian painting read '*Hilarius flavescent*' ('More cheerfully they become golden'), a reference to the flourishing of the crops under the goddess's, and by extension the ducal couple's, protection.[71] These classical references would have been deciphered by only a select few, perhaps even only by those familiar with Ripa's recent publication. But for those not versed in Latin, mythology or iconography, the entire display still carried a clear visual message of abundance.[72]

That same message of plenty was broadcast by the alternative entertainment the doge and his event planners had scrambled to put together for the festival's final day after Donà's intervention had led to the cancellation of the tournament in the Piazza. The cashbooks show that on 1 May, just three days before the festival started, Grimani engaged a group of Dutch sailors to perform a *naumachia* or mock naval battle. These sailors had arrived a couple of days before with a convoy of ships from the Dutch provinces of Holland and Zeeland, carrying grain to feed the Venetians.[73] Amid all the other preparations, Grimani ordered silk liveries and matching hats for the sailors, in the colours of the Grimani family (pink and white). He had wood sent to the Dutch ships to modify the sloops for the *naumachia*, and he ordered painters to paint the boats in a suitable colour for the games.[74]

Giacomo Franco has depicted the aquatic joust or '*giochi navali*' behind Scamozzi's floating *Teatro detto Il Mondo* (see Figure 9.4). In his engraving, the boats carry flags with heraldic lilies, which were part of the Morosini family's coat of arms.[75]

On 6 May, the doge and dogaressa, seated separately on two different balconies of the Palace, got ready to watch the aquatic games. It was one of the festival's biggest attractions, drawing throngs of spectators. People

69 Cesare Ripa, *Iconologia, ovvero descrittioni dell'imagini universali: cavate dall'antichita et da altri luoghi* (Rome: per gli eredi di Gio. Gigliotti, 1593), fols A1v–2v.
70 Barbette Stanley Spaeth, *The Roman Goddess of Ceres* (Austin: University of Texas Press, 1996), p. 26.
71 Rota, *Lettera*, fol. F4v; Tuzio, *Ordine*, pp. 9–10. According to McClure, this motto does not have a classical origin; McClure, *The Culture of Profession*, p. 326.
72 See Zerner, 'Looking for the Unknowable', for a similar argument.
73 Van Gelder, *Trading Places: The Netherlandish Merchants in Early Modern Venice* (Leiden and Boston: Brill, 2009), pp. 41–66.
74 On the colours, see Giovanni Nicolò Doglioni, *Historia venetiana scritta brevemente* (Venice: Damiano Zenaro, 1598), p. 1032. The *naumachia* cost Grimani between 100 and 150 ducats, ASV, APGB, busta 33, cc. 354r, 354v, 355r.
75 A few Dutch sloops are also present in Franco's engraving of the *Bucintoro* arriving at the arch (see Figure 9.2).

IL NOBILISS. TEATRO DETO IL MONDO FATO FARE DALLI 40
Gentilhomeni eletti da sua Ser.tà nell' entrata della Ser.ma Dogaressa Moresina Grimani
Prima forma: 1597.

Figure 9.4 Giacomo Franco, *Il nobilissimo teatro.*
© Museo Correr, Venezia, Cod. Moresini-Grimani, Origine della famiglia Moresina, 270, c. 65.

watched from the waterfront, others from aboard the innumerable boats. The Dutch – '*huomini pratichi, & arditi nel mare*', according to Rota[76] – came rowing in from the island of Giudecca, opposite the San Marco area, and saluted the ducal couple with a deafening volley of cannon shots. They then performed their *naumachia* with some twenty sloops: four men rowed each sloop, while a fifth stood on a platform with a long *bastone* (lance), as Franco's engraving shows. Two boats fought duels in tournament-style until only one man was left standing, to the amusement and applause of the crowd.[77] All the chroniclers commented on the *naumachia*, praising the quality of the boats, the skill of the northern sailors and the foreignness of their games, which also included two men on different boats pulling apart live eels and geese. The doge personally handed out prizes to the sailors,

---

76 Rota, *Lettera*, fol. [H1v].
77 Tuzio, *Ordine*, pp. 19–20. Such games were a standard part of Dutch festivals; see J. ter Gouw, *De volksvermaken* (Haarlem: Bohn, 1871). See for instance those organized for Maria de Medici's visit to the Dutch Republic in 1638, J. Puget de la Serre, *Histoire de l'entrée de la reyne mère du roy tres-chrestien dans les Provences Unies des Pays-Bas* (London: Jean Raworth, George Thomason and Octavian Pullen, 1639), fols Q2r–3v.

amid loud applause of the spectators.[78] Yet folded into the amusement was a clear message: the sailors of the foreign grain ships, dressed in the ducal couple's colours, pledged their services to the doge, thus guaranteeing the Venetian people a well-provisioned city during his reign.

From ephemeral to permanent

The day after the festival, a satisfied Doge Grimani walked the short distance from his residence to the council chambers on the other side of the Ducal Palace to thank the guilds for their efforts. After he left, guild members started dismantling all the ephemeral decorations and other temporary structures.[79] With the Palace back in order again, the doge undertook an additional step to consolidate the memory of both his wife's and his own coronation, commissioning paintings and probably also Rota's festival booklet. Two years later, in 1599, he ordered the construction of a funerary monument for himself and the dogaressa in the peripheral church of San Giuseppe in Castello.[80] At first glance his choice of San Giuseppe makes little sense: it was quite a distance from the Grimani Palace and an out-of-the-way place for a doge to be buried. Most doges preferred the imposing church of San Giovanni and Paolo, which became the *locus* for increasingly personalised ducal funeral monuments.[81] San Giuseppe, by contrast, attracted little patrician patronage.[82] Charitable initiatives, however, had long linked the Grimani family to this particular part of Castello. Also, the church had been the site of frequent papal visits and appears to have been associated with popular religious devotion.[83] All these aspects fit into Grimani's political profile.

With no other families vying for its space, Grimani set out to turn San Giuseppe into the most personalised church interior in the whole of Venice. Already in the 1580s he had dedicated the chapel of the high altar to his deceased father.[84] But it was the funerary tomb for himself and his wife that radically changed the inside of the church: to accommodate the construction

---

78 Tuzio, *Ordine*, p. 20.

79 Rota, *Lettera*, fol. [H3r].

80 Timofiewitsch, 'Quellen und Forschungen', p. 54. Jan Simane, *Grabmonumente der Dogen. Venezianische Sepulkralkunst im Cinquecento* (Sigmaringen: J. Thorbecke, 1993), especially pp. 107–39.

81 On medieval ducal funeral monuments, see Debra Pincus, *The Tombs of the Doges* (Cambridge: Cambridge University Press, 2000).

82 Stephen Holt, 'Paolo Veronese and his Patrons' (PhD thesis, University of St Andrews, 1991), pp. 153–4. The San Giuseppe belonged to the convent of Augustinian nuns.

83 On the Grimani family's ties to Castello, see Antonio Foscari and Manfredo Tafuri, 'Sebastiano da Lugano, i Grimani e Jacopo Sansovino, artisti e committenti nella chiesa di Sant'Antonio di Castello', *Arte Veneta* (1982), 100–23; Holt, 'Paolo Veronese', p. 154.

84 Thomas Martin, 'Grimani Patronage in S. Giuseppe di Castello: Veronese, Vittoria and Smeraldi', *The Burlington Magazine* 133/1065 (1991), 831.

of the wall-filling monument, which dwarfs all other memorials, the northern doorway had to be moved (Figure 9.5).[85]

The doge himself closely supervised the design and building, and the monument was finished within his lifetime, which was highly unusual. Once again, the costs were enormous: the entire structure, finished in 1604, cost 5,865 ducats.[86] It effectively turned San Giuseppe into a Grimani pantheon.

The monument was shaped like a triumphal arch, and although this was a fashionable form, its shape, proportions and symbolisms recall the ephemeral arch of 1597.[87] Each level of the monument celebrates the doge's glory, from the sculpture group representing the theological virtues Charity, Hope and Love on the pediment, the octagonal relief of the kneeling doge and dogaressa before the Virgin Mary, to the reclining images of the doge and dogaressa on their sarcophagi and other, smaller elements. The funerary monument's iconographic suggestion that Grimani was divinely elected as doge as a reward for his virtues is exceptional within the Venetian context.[88]

The doge made sure that representations of the coronations formed a conspicuous part of the impressive monument, at an easily visible height. On 18 November 1601, he ordered two bronze depictions of 'the coronations of his Serenity and the Most Serene Dogaressa' with the sculptor Cesare Groppo, indicating the precise measurements of the reliefs and the figures in them.

The two reliefs, seen here in Figures 9.6 and 9.7, represent Grimani's own crowning and Morosina receiving the Golden Rose in the Basilica. One and a half years later the reliefs were finished and transported to San Giuseppe, to be installed directly below the doge's and dogaressa's sarcophagi and thus perpetually link one coronation to the other, clearly visible to parishioners and other visitors to the church. A satisfied Grimani paid 460 ducats for the bronze reliefs, donating additional sums of drinking money (three ducats *per beverazo*) to the sculptor and his workers.[89] By the time the entire monument in San Giuseppe was finished, there was little left of the Grimani–Morosini fortunes. Having no male heirs, the couple had felt no need to

---

85 For the specifics on the monument's construction, see Timofiewitsch, 'Quellen und Forschungen'.

86 Andrea da Mosto, *I dogi di Venezia con particolare riguardo alle loro tombe* (Venice: Ferd. Ongania, 1939), pp. 201–6.

87 Wilson, 'Il bel sesso', pp. 85–6; Muir, *Civic Ritual*, p. 295. On the arch as a fashionable choice for funerary monuments, see Kathryn B. Hiesinger, 'The Fregoso Monument: A Study in Sixteenth-Century Tomb Monuments and Catholic Reform', *The Burlington Magazine* 118/878 (1976), 287. Holt, 'Paolo Veronese', pp. 161–2.

88 Simane suggests a closer connection to the papal tombs of Sixtus V and Pius V in the Sistine chapel, Simane, *Grabmonumente*, pp. 115–6. A similar theme, of Grimani being divinely elected by Saint Mark instead of by his patrician peers, was one of the themes in Morosina's coronation festival, Muir, 'Images of Power', 47–8.

89 See Timofiewitsch, 'Quellen und Forschungen', p. 44.

Figure 9.5 Funeral monument for Doge Marino Grimani and Dogaressa Morosina Morosini Grimani in San Giuseppe di Castello.

© Francesco Turio Bohm, Fotografo, Venezia.

Figure 9.6 Cesare Groppo, *Doge Marino Grimani's coronation*, bronze relief on the Grimani funeral monument in San Giuseppe di Castello, below the doge's sarcophagus.

© Francesco Turio Bohm, Fotografo, Venezia.

preserve the family fortune, investing instead in munificence, feasts, art and architecture, both ephemeral and permanent.[90] The dynastic ambition projected through the 1597 coronation's imagery was always more rhetorical than actual.

90 ASV, Notarile – Testamenti, b.1249/I, c.181r – v. The costs of the dowries for the couple's daughters had been significant, but a major expense had also been the construction of the Grimani family palace.

Figure 9.7 Cesare Groppo, *Dogaressa Morosina Morosini Grimani receives the Golden Rose*, bronze relief on the Grimani funeral monument in San Giuseppe di Castello, below the dogaressa's sarcophagus.

© Francesco Turio Bohm, Fotografo, Venezia.

Conclusion

For most spectators, the festival for the dogaressa's coronation had been the feast of a lifetime. The celebrations in 1595 had already demonstrated both Grimani's spending power and the extent of his popular support, and despite patrician opposition, the 1597 festival only confirmed his ambitions. The display of personal power took full advantage of Venice's terrestrial and aquatic space, something most prominently displayed in Grimani's decision to organise the alternative joust on the *Bacino*, in defiance of

Donà's successful efforts to cancel the tournament in the Piazza. The 1597 coronation transmitted different messages to different audiences: it gave patrician women an uncommonly central role in state ritual, and it flaunted Grimani's political ambitions by celebrating the ducal couple in an almost regal style, a theme effectively continued on the funerary monument in San Giuseppe. But the festival also carried a message intended for a much broader public, namely that in a period of frequent famines the city and its people were in the safe hands of a 'father of the poor', the generous and benevolent doge.

Instead of the collective responsibility of the ruling elite, the festival communicated that Grimani himself was in charge of the steady supply of bread and grain. This contentious message was transmitted through the use of symbols of abundance woven into the festival architecture and the decorations in the palace, later repeated on the funerary monument. The display by the German bakers – including the fact that after years of empty bread shops there was sufficient grain and bread to spare for decorative purposes – recalled the Venetians' hopes at Grimani's election and emphasised the contrast between the previous decade of dearth and the abundance of the present. This was forcefully underlined by the Dutch sailors' participation in the event. One unforeseen outcome was that patrician irritation resulted in the formal prohibition of future dogaressa coronations.[91] Ironically, this only further emphasised the singular character of the 1597 coronation festival.

Although it is impossible to reconstruct exactly how the public experienced the festival, the memory of the two coronations proved persistent. Grimani adroitly shaped that memory by engaging authors and artists to produce a range of festival books, paintings, coins and engravings, which recorded the iconic elements of his wife's coronation in their urban setting, such as the triumphal arch on the Piazzetta, the aquatic games on the *Bacino* and the ceremony of the Golden Rose in the Basilica. In an additional challenge to Venetian ideas about the use of public space, Grimani turned the peripheral church of San Giuseppe in Castello into a family memorial, accessible to all and with the two coronations forming the central theme of the oversized funerary monument. Again, it is not possible to determine to what extent these objects, artefacts and narratives shaped and mediated the memory of these events. It is clear, however, that ordinary Venetians remembered and passed on the memory of Grimani munificence. In 1612, six years after Grimani's death, a crowd of Venetians taunted his successor, the parsimonious Leonardo Donà, by hailing him with shouts of 'Viva, viva Doge Grimani, *padre dei poveri*'.[92]

---

91 Molmenti, *La Dogaressa*, pp. 340–41. Despite this decision, Doge Silvestro Valier organized a coronation for his wife Elisabetta in 1694.

92 Biblioteca Nazionale Marciana, Ms. It VII, 1818 (9436), c.88v: 'li fanciulli, et anco quasi tutto il populo li dettero una ramanzina gagliarda, gridando ad alta voce "Viva, viva il Doge Grimani, Padre dei Poveri".'

Bibliography

Printed primary sources

Doglioni, Giovanni Nicolò, *Historia venetiana scritta brevemente* (Venice: Damiano Zenaro, 1598).

Marcello, Gregorio, *Ordine et progreesso* [sic] *del trionfo fatto l'anno MCMLVII, all 19 di settembrio per l'incoronatione della Serenissima Dogaressa Priola* (Venice: Marco Claseri, 1597).

Puget de la Serre, J., *Histoire de l'entrée de la reyne mère du roy tres-chrestien dans les Provences Unies des Pays-Bas* (London: Jean Raworth, George Thomason and Octavian Pullen, 1639).

Ripa, Cesare, *Iconologia, ovvero descrittioni dell'imagini universali: cavate dall'antichita et da altri luoghi* (Rome: per gli eredi di Gio. Gigliotti, 1593).

Rota, Giovanni, *Lettera nella quale si descrive l'ingresso della Serenissima Morosina Morosini Grimani Prencipessa di Vinetia: co' la cerimonia della Rosa benedetta, mandatala à donare dalla Santità del Nostro Signore* (Venice: Gio. Anto. Rampazetto, 1597).

Tuzio, Dario, *Ordine et modo tenuto nell'incoronatione della Serenissima Moresina Grimani Dogaressa di Venetia l'anno MDXCVII. adi 4 di Maggio. Con le feste, e giochi fatti, etc* (Venice: Nicolò Peri, 1597).

Venetia città nobilissima, et singolare, descritta in XIIII. libri da M. Francesco Sansovino et hora con molta diligenza corretta, emendata, e più d'un terzo di cose nuove ampliata dal M.R.D. Giovanni Stringa (Venice: A. Salicato, 1604).

Secondary sources

Alazard, Florence, *Art vocal, art de gouverner: la musique, le prince et la cité en Italie du Nord 1560–1610* (Paris: Minerve, 2002).

Barber, Richard and Juliet Barker, *Tournaments. Jousts, Chivalry and Pageants in the Middle Ages* (New York: Boydell Press, 1989).

Barredo, Maria José del Rio, 'Rituals of the Viaticum: Dynasty and Community in Habsburg Madrid', in Melissa Calaresu, Filippo de Vivo and Joan-Pau Rubiés (eds), *Exploring Cultural History: Essays in Honour of Peter Burke* (Farnham and Burlington, VT: Ashgate, 2010), pp. 55–75.

Bellavitis, Anna, 'Family and Society', in Eric R. Dursteler (ed.), *A Companion to Venetian History, 1400–1797* (Leiden and Boston: Brill, 2013), pp. 317–51.

Brown, Patricia Fortini, 'Measured Friendship, Calculated Pomp: The Ceremonial Welcomes of the Venetian Republic', in Barbara Wisch and Susan Scott Munshower (eds), *"All the World's a Stage . . .": Art and Pageantry in the Renaissance and Early Baroque*. Vol. 1, *Triumphal Celebrations and the Rituals of Statecraft* (Philadelphia, PA: University of Pennsylvania Press, 1990), pp. 136–87.

Burke, Peter, *Historical Anthropology of Early Modern Italy. Essays on Perception and Communication* (Cambridge: Cambridge University Press, 1987).

Calaresu, Melissa, Filippo de Vivo and Joan-Pau Rubiés (eds), *Exploring Cultural History: Essays in Honour of Peter Burke* (Farnham and Burlington, VT: Ashgate, 2010).

Casini, Matteo, *I gesti del principe. La festa politica a Firenze e Venezia in età rinascimentale* (Venice: Marsilio, 1996).

Cozzi, Gaetano, 'Leonardo Donà (Donati, Donato)', *Dizionario Biografico degli Italiani* 40 (1991). (www.treccani.it/enciclopedia/leonardo-dona_(Dizionario-Biografico)/).

Da Mosto, Andrea, *I dogi di Venezia con particolare riguardo alle loro tombe* (Venice: Ferd. Ongania, 1939).

Da Mosto, Andrea, *I dogi di Venezia nella vita pubblica e vita privata* (Florence: A. Martello-Giunti editore, 1977).

Davis, Robert C., *The War of the Fists: Popular Culture and Public Violence in Late Renaissance Venice* (Oxford: Oxford University Press, 1994).

Fenlon, Iain, *The Ceremonial City: History, Memory and Myth in Renaissance Venice* (New Haven and London: Yale University Press, 2007).

Fenlon, Iain, *Piazza San Marco* (London: Profile Books, 2010).

Finlay, Robert, *Politics in Renaissance Venice* (New Brunswick: Rutgers University Press, 1980).

Foscari, Antonio and Manfredo Tafuri, 'Sebastiano da Lugano, i Grimani e Jacopo Sansovino, artisti e committenti nella chiesa di Sant' Antonio di Castello', *Arte Veneta* (1982), 100–23.

Gelder, Maartje van, *Trading Places: The Netherlandish Merchants in Early Modern Venice* (Leiden and Boston: Brill, 2009).

Giomo, G., 'Le spese del nobil uomo Marino Grimani nella sua elezione a doge di Venezia', *Archivio Veneto* XXXIII (1887), pp. 443–54.

Gouw, J. ter, *De volksvermaken* (Haarlem: Bohn, 1871).

Gullino, Giuseppe, 'Marino Grimani', *Dizionario Biografico degli Italiani* 59 (2003). (www.treccani.it/enciclopedia/marino-grimani_(Dizionario-Biografico)/).

Hanlon, Gregory, 'Glorifying War in a Peaceful City: Festive Representations of Combat in Baroque Siena (1590–1740)', *War in History* 11/3 (2004), 249–77.

Hiesinger, Kathryn B., 'The Fregoso Monument: A Study in Sixteenth-Century Tomb Monuments and Catholic Reform', *The Burlington Magazine* 133/1065 (1976), 283–93.

Hochmann, Michel, 'Le mécénat de Marino Grimani. Tintoret, Palma le Jeune, Jacopo Bassano, Giulio le Moro et le décor du Palais Grimani; Vèronése et Vittoria à San Giuseppe', *Revue de l'Art* 95 (1992), 41–51.

Holt, Stephen, 'Paolo Veronese and his Patrons' (Ph.D. thesis, University of St Andrews, 1991).

Horodowich, Elizabeth, *A Brief History of Venice. A New History of the City and Its People* (Philadelphia, PA and London: Running Press, 2009).

Howard, Deborah, *Venice Disputed. Marc'Antonio Barbaro and Venetian Architecture* (New Haven and London: Yale University Press, 2011).

Hurlburt, Holly, *The Dogaressa of Venice, 1200–1500: Wife and Icon* (New York: Palgrave Macmillan, 2006).

Labalme, Patricia H. and Laura Sanguineti White (eds), *Venice, città excelentissima: Selections from the Renaissance Diaries of Marin Sanudo*, trans. Linda L. Carroll (Baltimore: Johns Hopkins University Press, 2008).

Lane, Frederic C., *Venice. A Maritime Republic* (Baltimore: Johns Hopkins University Press, 1973).

Mallett, M.E. and J.R. Hale, *The Military Organization of a Renaissance State: Venice, c.1400 to 1617* (Cambridge: Cambridge University Press, 1984).

Martin, Thomas, 'Grimani Patronage in S. Giuseppe di Castello: Veronese, Vittoria and Smeraldi', *The Burlington Magazine* 133/1065 (1991), 825–33.

McClure, George, *The Culture of Profession in Late Renaissance Italy* (Toronto: Toronto University Press, 2004).

Molmenti, Pompeo, *La Dogaressa di Venezia* (Turin: Roux e Favale, 1884).

Muir, Edward, *Civic Ritual in Renaissance Venice* (Princeton: Princeton University Press, 1981).

Muir, Edward, 'Images of Power: Art and Pageantry in Renaissance Venice', *The American Historical Review* 84/1 (1979), 16–52.

Mulryne, J.R., 'Introduction', in J.R. Mulryne and Elizabeth Goldring (eds), *Court Festivals of the European Renaissance. Art, Politics and Performance* (Aldershot and Burlington, VT: Ashgate, 2002), pp. 1–14.

Orgel, Stephen, *The Illusion of Power: Political Theater in the English Renaissance* (Berkeley: University of California Press, 1975).

Pincus, Debra, *The Tombs of the Doges* (Cambridge: Cambridge University Press, 2000).

Pullan, Brian, 'Wage-Earners and the Venetian Economy, 1550–1630', *The Economic History Review* 16/3 (1964), 407–27.

Pullan, Brian, *Rich and Poor in Renaissance Venice. The Social Institutions of a Catholic State, to 1620* (Cambridge, MA: Harvard University Press, 1971).

Rosand, David, *Myths of Venice: The Figuration of a State* (Chapel Hill: University of North Carolina Press, 2001).

Simane, Jan, *Grabmonumente der Dogen: Venezianische Sepulkralkunst im Cinquecento* (Sigmaringen: J. Thorbecke, 1993).

Stanley Spaeth, Barbette, *The Roman Goddess of Ceres* (Austin: University of Texas Press, 1996).

Strong, Roy, *Art and Power; Renaissance Festivals 1450–1650* (Woodbridge: Boydell, 1984).

Tafuri, Manfredo, *Venice and the Renaissance* (Cambridge, MA: MIT Press, 1989).

Timofiewitsch, Wladimir, 'Quellen und Forschungen zum Prunkgrab des Dogen Marino Grimani in San Giuseppe di Castello zu Venedig', *Mitteilungen des Kunsthistorischen Institutes in Florenz* 11/1 (1963), 33–54.

Tondro, Maximilian, 'The First Temporary Triumphal Arch in Venice (1557)', in J.R. Mulryne and Elizabeth Goldring (eds), *Court Festivals of the European Renaissance: Art, Politics and Performance* (Aldershot and Burlington, VT: Ashgate, 2002), pp. 335–62.

Tondro, Maximilian, 'Memory and Tradition: The Ephemeral Architecture for the Triumphal Entries of the Dogaresse of Venice in 1557 and 1597' (Ph.D. thesis, University of Cambridge, 2002).

Urban, Lina Padoan, 'Teatri e "Teatri del mondo" nella Venezia del Cinquecento', *Arte Veneta* 20 (1966), 137–46.

Urban, Lina Padoan, 'Apparati scenografici nelle feste veneziane cinquecentesche', *Arte Veneta* 23 (1969), 145–55.

Urban, Lina Padoan, 'Feste ufficiali e trattenimenti privati', in Girolamo Arnaldi and Manlio Pastore Stocchi (eds), *Storia della cultura veneta. Il Seicento*, 2 vols (Vicenza: Pozza, 1983), vol. 1, pp. 575–600.

Viggiano, Alfredo, 'Politics and Constitution', in Eric R. Dursteler (ed.), *A Companion to Venetian History, 1400–1797* (Leiden and Boston: Brill, 2013).

Visentini, Margherita Azzi, 'Festival of State: The Scenography of Power in Late Renaissance and Baroque Venice', in Sarah Bonnemaison and Christine Macy (eds), *Festival Architecture* (London and New York: Routledge, 2008), pp. 74–112.

Wilson, Bronwen, ' "Il bel sesso e l'austero Senato": The Coronation of Dogaressa Morosina Morosini Grimani', *Renaissance Quarterly* 52/1 (1999), 73–139.

Wilson, Bronwen, 'Venice, Print, and the Early Modern Icon', *Urban History* 33/1 (2006), 39–64.

Zerner, Henry, 'Looking for the Unknowable: The Visual Experience of Renaissance Festivals', in J.R. Mulryne, Helen Watanabe-O'Kelly and Margaret Shewring (eds), *Europa Triumphans. Court and Civic Festivals in Early Modern Europe*, 2 vols (Aldershot and Burlington, VT: Ashgate, 2004), vol. 1, pp. 74–98.

10 *Con grandissima maraviglia*

The role of theatrical spaces in the festivals of seventeenth-century Milan

Francesca Barbieri

The historical and cultural context of seventeenth-century Milan was highly favourable to the development of theatrical performance; indeed, the demand for and hosting of performance underwent great intensification, and the events themselves became ever more spectacular. It is known that theatricality in Milan during the Baroque period acted as 'a powerful unifier of the different systems of artistic, religious and political representation'.[1] In fact, theatre and theatricality constituted the most important communicative mode during the Baroque era. Accordingly, the iconographic and rhetorical programmes devised for Milanese public events and festivals placed noteworthy emphasis on theatrical elements. It may be added that although different types of theatrical performances were taking place in seventeenth-century Milan,[2] this city and this moment in history also witnessed the birth of the theatrical genre now known as opera.[3] Opera was performed on the

---

1 The quoted definition of theatricality as '*potente aggregante dei diversi sistemi di rappresentazione*' comes from Annamaria Cascetta, 'Introduzione', in Annamaria Cascetta and Roberta Carpani (eds), *La scena della gloria: Drammaturgia e spettacolo a Milano in età spagnola* (Milan: Vita & Pensiero, 1995), p. 6.

2 For example, the presence of the companies of the *Commedia dell'Arte* was usual and much appreciated by the Spanish governors of Lombardy. Milan hosted some of the most famous troupes of actors of the time, such as the *Gelosi, Confidenti, Uniti, Accesi* and *Fedeli*; see Roberta Giovanna Arcaini, 'I comici dell'Arte a Milano: accoglienza, sospetti, riconoscimenti', in *La scena della gloria: Drammaturgia e spettacolo a Milano in età spagnola* (Milan: Vita & Pensiero, 1995), pp. 329–78 and more recently Elena Tamburini, *Culture ermetiche e commedia dell'arte: Tra Giulio Camillo e Flaminio Scala* (Rome: Aracne, 2016), chapters IV–VI. In addition, Jesuit school drama played a key role in seventeenth-century Milan; see Giovanna Zanlonghi, *Teatri di formazione: actio, parola e immagine nella scena gesuitica del Sei-Settecento a Milano* (Milan: Vita & Pensiero, 2002).

3 Milan, as Davide Daolmi suggests, was a very important centre for the origins of opera, but it was highly influenced by Venice. For an overview, see Davide Daolmi, *Le origini dell'opera a Milano 1598–1649* (Turnhout: Brepols, 1998). In connection with the introduction of Baroque art, the dramatic rules of Aristotle's *Poetics* were attacked in Venice by a number of authors who refused the classical principle of the three unities (place, time and action). As a consequence, many dramatic texts of that period were disrespectful towards the unity of place and, in this way, they could legitimise frequent and very spectacular

occasion of both dynastic and political events; thus, theatrical performances and dynastic festivals should be studied in parallel with opera.

The most important ceremonies of the seventeenth century, such as royal entries and funerals as well as religious events, have been the focus of considerable research attention.[4] In addition, the activities of the Jesuits and their use of theatre for didactic purposes have been widely investigated, and a great deal of attention has also been devoted to the origins of opera. The present chapter adds to the literature by investigating how the role of theatrical space in royal ceremonies in Milan developed over the course of the seventeenth century. More specifically, it focuses on the key role played by theatre in two specific royal events: the passage of Margherita of Austria through Milan in 1598–1599 and the passage of Maria Anna of Austria in 1649. In addition, some insights are provided into the wedding festival that took place in 1672, when Gaspar Téllez-Girón de Osuna, the Spanish Governor of Milan, married the noblewoman Anna Antonia de Benavides.

In order to analyse the increasing importance of theatrical representation, it is first of all necessary to consider the origin and location of the different theatrical spaces in Milan. Indeed, the location of the theatres was in itself meaningful because they were situated within the Palazzo Regio Ducale – the residence of the Spanish governor ruling Milan.[5] The Palazzo Regio Ducale was located in the centre of Milan, more precisely in the Piazza del Duomo (Cathedral Square). Being home to both the royal palace and the cathedral, the square was the political and religious heart of the city. Due to the many structural modifications made to the palace over the centuries, it has been difficult to study how the theatrical spaces in this location changed over time. However, we know that during the seventeenth century, a series of palace courtyards and rooms were being used as theatrical spaces,[6] although the first permanent theatre in the palace dates to 1598. Through an analysis

---

changes of scene. The visual aspect became a basic element in Venetian performances: as a consequence, in the second half of the seventeenth-century, Venice became the most important centre in Europe as regards opera and stage design. See Per Bjurström, *Giacomo Torelli and Baroque Stage Design* (Stockholm: Almqvist & Wiksell, 1961).

4 The Baroque age has been the subject of much study over recent decades by various scholars of the Università Cattolica of Milan under the direction of Annamaria Cascetta; see Cascetta and Carpani (eds), *La scena della gloria*; Annamaria Cascetta (ed.), *Forme della scena barocca*, monographic issue of *Comunicazioni sociali* 15/2–3 (1993); Annamaria Cascetta (ed.), *Aspetti della teatralità a Milano nell'età barocca*, monographic issue of *Comunicazioni sociali* 16/1–2 (1994).

5 Milan was under Spanish dominion from 1535 to 1706. For further details about the Palazzo Regio Ducale, see Enrico Colle and Fernando Mazzocca (eds), *Palazzo Reale di Milano* (Milan: Skira, 2001).

6 For a recent hypothesis of the distribution of theatrical spaces in Palazzo Reale, see Daolmi, *Le origini*, in particular pp. 54–5 and 428–9. See also Paolo Mezzanotte, 'Costruzione e vicende del Teatro di Corte in Milano', *Atti del Collegio degli Ingegneri ed Architetti* 2 (1915), 1–24.

of the above-mentioned royal festivals, this chapter investigates the functions of the first permanent theatre – the so-called Salone Margherita – and the development of an additional new theatre in the seventeenth century.

The entry of Margherita of Austria

In 1598, Margherita of Austria (Graz 1584 – El Escorial 1611) travelled to Madrid to marry Philip of Spain,[7] son of King Philip II and heir to the Spanish throne. *En route* to the Spanish court, Margherita visited many Italian cities, including Ferrara, Mantua and Cremona, and spent two months in Milan.[8] The entry of the royal bride to Milan is of historic relevance because Milan was the major city within the Spanish dominions in northern Italy. In cooperation with the local authorities, the Spanish Governor, Juan Fernandez de Velasco, began his diligent preparations in July 1598. Besides the ephemeral *apparati*, the passage of the royal bride also motivated the construction of various permanent structures in the streets of Milan, as well as in the theatre within the Palazzo Regio Ducale. In particular, decorative elements in the triumphal arches and in the theatre erected for Margherita were related. Everything was magnificently prepared. However, Philip II of Spain, father-in-law of the bride, died just before Margherita's entry.[9] As a consequence, the programme of festivities was modified because Margherita became queen, as wife of Philip III, and the theatrical performances were reduced in scale because she was in mourning.

Nevertheless, Margherita made her entrance into Milan through the gate of Porta Romana (the Roman Gate) on the last day of November. Porta Romana, as its name suggests, has ancient origins dating back to the Roman

---

7 A festival book exists of the ceremonies which took place in Milan; see Guido Mazenta, *Apparato fatto dalla città di Milano per riceuere la serenissima regina D. Margarita d'Austria* (Milan, 1598). Some items of this dynastic event have already been investigated: see Elena Cenzato and Luisa Rovaris, ' "Comparvero finalmente gl'aspettati soli dell'austriaco cielo". Ingressi solenni per nozze reali', *Comunicazioni sociali* 16/2 (1994), 71–112; Paola Venturelli, 'La solemne entrada en Milan de Margherita d'Austria, esposa de Felipe III', in Maria Luisa Lobato and Bernardo José García (eds), *La fiesta cortesana en la época de los Austrias* (Valladolid: Junta de Castilla y Leòn, 2003), pp. 233–47; Stefano Della Torre, 'Gli apparati trionfali del 1598', *Studia Borromaica* 22 (2008), 81–100; and Franca Varallo, 'Margaret of Austria's Travel in the State of Milan Between 1598 and 1599', in Fernando Checa Cremades and Laura Fernández Gonzáles (eds), *Festival Culture in the World of the Spanish Habsburgs* (London and New York: Routledge, 2015), pp. 135–54.

In 2006, a conference entitled *Il viaggio attraverso l'Italia di Margherita d'Austria regina di Spagna 1598–1599. Ingressi Feste Cerimonie* focused on Margherita's trip within Italy (the proceedings, edited by Maria Ines Aliverti, are forthcoming). See http://mdaustria.arte. unipi.it/margheritaprogramma.html, most recent access July 2017.

8 Margherita arrived in Milan on 30 November 1598 and left for Pavia on 3 February 1599; see Cenzato and Rovaris, p. 95. For details about Margherita's stay in Pavia, see Fabrizio Fiaschini, *Margherita, Alberto e Isabella. Ingressi trionfali a Pavia nel 1599* (Novara: Interlinea, 2012).

9 Philip II died on 13 September 1598.

era. However, the gate that can be seen today was specifically constructed for the occasion of Margherita's visit. The Roman Emperors made their entries into Milan through the original Porta Romana, and the monarchs of the modern age followed the Roman tradition, making their entries through the new gate, standing in roughly the same location, and then followed a similar route into the city centre. In 1541, Charles V was the first monarch to make his entry into Milan through the 'new' Porta Romana; and from that time on, the Corso di Porta Romana became the standard route of royal entries into Milan.[10] Margherita's royal entry through Porta Romana accommodated the procession conducting the bride into the city, where she was greeted and paid appropriate homage by the civic and political authorities. Seven triumphal arches had been erected at various stations along the route between the Porta Romana and Piazza del Duomo. Once the procession arrived in the Piazza del Duomo, the queen-designate entered the cathedral, where a *Te Deum* was sung. After the religious ceremony, she made her entrance into Palazzo Regio Ducale.

The festival book of the event provides a detailed description of the arches and their decorations. The first arch, the Arco di Porta Romana, was built of stone and conceived as permanent. As noted, it is still visible today, and was recently restored.[11] For the occasion of the royal procession, it was dedicated to the bride and richly decorated, including allegorical figures and inscriptions. In particular, it was adorned with inscriptions and *imprese* alluding to the name 'Margherita' (or *margarita*), the Latin word for pearl, considered a symbol of female virtue. The *apparati* and the *imprese* repeatedly recalled this allusion; the visual pun relating to Margherita's name permeated the decorative scheme. The dedication of the arch, placed in a niche over the central archway, introduced for the first time the idea that Margherita was indeed a precious *margarita*:

INGREDERE LAETA SERENISSIMA
MARGARITA AVSTRIACA
MAXIMA PIA FELIX AVGVSTA
AMPLISSIMAM ITALIAE VRBEM
FREQVENTISSIMO EXVLTANTE POPVLO
MAIESTATISQ[UE] TVAE PRAESENTIA
TANQVAM EXPECTATISSIMO TRIVMPHO GESTIENTE

10 Before Charles V, monarchs entered Milan through Porta Ticinese, which was also the route used by religious authorities. Subsequently, the route via Porta Ticinese became a sacred way given over to the archbishops' entries. See Maria Luisa Gatti Perer (ed.), *Milano ritrovata: l'asse via Torino* (Milan: Il Vaglio Cultura Arte, 1986).
11 Porta Romana is located at the centre of a city square called Piazza Medaglie d'Oro. See www.milanoneicantieridellarte.it/arco-di-porta-romana, most recent access July 2017. On the recent restoration of the Arch see Rebecca Fant, 'Le Mura Spagnole di Milano: gli interventi conservativi (2006–2009) e la loro negazione', *Istituto Lombardo (Rend. Scienze)* 146 (2012), 37–64.

VNA ENIM OMNIVM VOCE VIRTVS IPSA LOQVITVR
ET PRAEDICAT
TE ILLAM ESSE PRETIOSAM MARGARITAM
QVAE PHILIPPI III POTENTISS[IMI] REGIS IMPERIVM
MAGNITVDINE AEQVAT
PONDERE FIRMAT
CANDOREQ[UE] VNIVERSVM ORBEM ILLVSTRAT.[12]

[Proceed, happy, most Serene Margherita of Austria, great, most pious, fortunate, august, into this most spacious of Italian cities, while crowds exult in and celebrate your majestic presence as if at a long-awaited triumph, while virtue herself speaks with one voice and proclaims that you are that precious *margarita*, which the rule of the most powerful Philip III strengthens in greatness, makes weighty in significance and for brightness illuminates the universal world.]

In the intercolumns, at the sides of the central archway, two allegorical statues were positioned, as well as two *imprese* that are still visible today (see Figure 10.1). On the right-hand side was the statue of *Salus publica* (in Roman religion, the Goddess of safety and welfare). The related *impresa* depicted a pearl in an open oyster floating on waves, accompanied by the motto *De coelo cibus et candor* ('food and radiance from heaven'). In fact, according to an ancient legend, oysters rise to the sea-surface in the morning to receive the morning dew as food, which then forms the pearl.[13] By analogy, Margherita derives her qualities from heaven, like the pearl, and she can thus transmit her virtues to the world. The *impresa* on the left-hand side exhibited the same image of the oyster with the motto *Nitentes ut spargat radios* ('thus it spreads bright rays'), making it associated with the statue of *Felicitas publica* (the Roman Goddess of prosperity and happiness). The concept of the queen as a source of happiness or radiance on the basis of her virtue was suggested at the beginning of her triumphal entry by the pearl analogy and was repeated in the *apparati* with the symbolism clearly explained.

The remaining six triumphal arches were dedicated to various members of the royal family, and were gathered in the Piazza del Duomo, the arrival point of the procession.[14] The cathedral itself hosted religious ceremonies for the occasion. In particular, the sixth arch was applied as a temporary façade to the Duomo, and dedicated to Margherita's wedding and her virtues. The arch was decorated with seven allegorical statues related to

12 Mazenta, *Apparato*, A4r.
13 See Filippo Picinelli, *Mondo simbolico formato d'imprese scelte, spiegate, ed illustrate con sentenze, ed erudizioni . . . in questa impressione da mille, e mille parti ampliato* (Venice, 1678), chapter XXIV, pp. 430–35.
14 See Mazenta, *Apparato*, C3v–D2v.

Figure 10.1 Milan, Arch of Porta Romana: *imprese* and decorations (detail).
© Photo: Rebecca Fant.

the Sacrament of Marriage[15] and carried six *imprese* with subjects alluding to marriage. The visual pun on the queen's name was again present,
and the arch was decorated with six *imprese*, each of which included a
pearl and a different motto.[16] The images and their mottos recalled the
idea expressed in the *imprese* of the first arch in the Porta Romana, but,
in this case, the pearl received its radiance and food from heaven and bore
more specific religious meanings, underlined by the context in which the
arch was placed, in front of the cathedral. The Piazza del Duomo was the
arrival point for the procession, being home to both the cathedral and
the Palazzo Regio Ducale, the latter of which hosted the event's political
ceremonies and, significantly, the festivities in its theatre specifically built
for the occasion.

15 The statues represented a series of personifications: Chiesa, Sacramento del Matrimonio,
   Castità, Fede, Concordia, Fecondità and Educazione (the Church, the Sacrament of Marriage, Chastity, Faith, Concord, Fertility and Education).
16 See Mazenta, *Apparato*, D2r.

The theatre was constructed by order of the Spanish Governor Velasco in a very short time; the festival book testifies that it was built '*con grandissima maraviglia*'[17] (to the great amazement) of the Milanese citizenry.[18] This first permanent theatre in Milan was a square room with two rows of parallel columns, and was named the Salone Margherita, in honour of the queen.[19] The Salone was enriched with decorations, paintings and frescos representing mythological subjects; facing the stage was a loggia with a canopy for the queen.

It is known that only one tragicomedy was performed in the theatre due to the state of mourning for Philip II's death. No further details regarding an opera known to have been performed have come down to us. The festival book nevertheless reveals important details about the theatre's decorations. In particular, it describes eighteen *imprese* with different images and mottoes.[20] Once again, the *imprese* alluded to the name of Margherita and, interestingly, the last of them presented the coat of arms of Milan, namely the Biscione (a large grass snake).[21] This heraldic device shows a serpent in the act of consuming a human being, but in this case, with a pearl also depicted. The result was a circular composition, with the last *impresa* clearly showing that the city was deeply transformed by the presence of the queen. Thus, the decorations within the theatre continued themes present in the triumphal arches. In essence, the decorations within the Salone Margherita completed the ephemeral *apparati* erected in outdoor locations.

The entry of Maria Anna of Austria

Fifty years later, Milan was involved in another royal entry related to a princely marriage: Maria Anna of Austria (Vienna 1634 – Madrid 1696) was on her way to Madrid to marry Philip IV of Spain. The political and civic authorities of Milan decided to follow the same ceremonial order adopted for Margherita of Austria in 1598. It therefore became necessary to erect *apparati* throughout the city streets to accompany the sovereign to Palazzo Regio Ducale, and to arrange adequate festivities for her two-month stay in Milan. The event has been widely studied; therefore, this chapter will focus exclusively on the relationship between the urban *apparati* and the

17 Ibid., E2v.
18 The author of the festival book calls him a '*prudentissimo architetto*' ('very wise architect') to emphasise his commitment to the construction of the theatre; see ibid., E3r.
19 We have no iconographic sources regarding the Salone, but a drawing exists which probably refers to the Salone in 1598 – this drawing was reproduced in Daolmi, *Le origini*, p. 141. An engraving by Melchiorre Gherardini, dating to 1633, also provides us with an image of the theatre when it was used for a banquet for the visit of the Cardinal-Infante Ferdinando, see ibid., p. 355.
20 See Mazenta, *Apparato*, E3v–E4r.
21 The Biscione was the ancient emblem of the House of Visconti from the eleventh century.

performances staged for the occasion.[22] Worthy of note is the prominence of the pictorial and scenographic elements within the spaces used for the festivities, with all their allegorical and encomiastic meanings.

On 17 June 1649, Maria Anna of Austria made her entry through the Porta Romana with a traditional procession accompanying her to the cathedral. Four triumphal arches were erected at stations along the route from the Porta Romana to the Piazza del Duomo. The creators of the iconographic scheme of the arches were the Jesuits – one of the most important religious orders of the time in Milan.[23] In addition, the Jesuits were commissioned to stage a Latin drama, entitled *Il Teseo*,[24] which was performed once again in the Salone Margherita inside the Palazzo Regio Ducale.[25] The visual and rhetorical themes presented in the arches were echoed in the theatrical performance, since the Jesuits generally focused their attention on the political and moral qualities of members of the relevant royal family. Thus, the ephemeral *apparati* of the triumphal arches and *Il Teseo* combined historical, mythical and religious episodes related to the idea of *magnificentia*. This Latin term (literally 'grandeur' or 'greatness') alludes to the greatness of mind and soul ideally typical of monarchs.[26] Accordingly, the triumphal arches celebrated Maria Anna's virtues and the deeds of her family members.

In particular, the first arch – the Porta Romana, built of stone for Margherita as described above – was now dedicated to Maria Anna, with its new ephemeral decorations based on the themes of marriage and maternity (see Figure 10.2).[27] A pair of paintings by Gian Cristoforo Storer extended the decorations with representations of two Biblical scenes.[28] The protagonist of the first of these (see Figure 10.3) was the Queen of Sheba, represented

22 Three festival books provide numerous details: *La pompa della solenne entrata fatta dalla serenissima Maria Anna austriaca figlia dell'inuittissimo imperante Ferdinando Terzo et sposa del potentissimo Filippo Quarto . . . nella città di Milano: Con la descrittione de gli apparati, & feste* (Milan, 1651); *Real solenne entrata in Milano delle maestà della regina Maria Anna moglie del re cattolico n.s. Filippo IV, e del re d'Ungaria, e Boemia Ferdinando Francesco suo fratello. . .* (Milan, 1649); *Festa fatta in Milano nel Regio Ducal Palazzo, il giouedì 15 luglio 1649, alla maestà della regina n.s. Maria Anna d'Austria. . .* (Milan, 1649). Several studies have focused on the event; see Cenzato and Rovaris; Daolmi, *Le origini*, pp. 241–60; Luisa Rovaris, 'La festa barocca: la real solenne entrata di Maria Anna d'Austria a Milano nel 1649', *Archivio Storico Lombardo* 113 (1987), 48–80; Zanlonghi, *Teatri*, pp. 131–73.
23 See ibid.
24 See *Argomento, allegoria, et idea del Teseo da rappresentarsi nel Regio Ducal Teatro da' scolari dell'Università di Brera della Compagnia di Gesù . . .* (Milan, 1649).
25 The Salone was not only a space dedicated to theatrical performances, but above all it was used for banquets and other ceremonies during festivals; see Daolmi, *Le origini*, p. 120 ff.
26 See Zanlonghi, *Teatri*, pp. 139–41.
27 The festival book describes a series of allegorical statues: Hymen (god of marriage ceremonies), Religion, Prudence, Grace and Beneficence. See *La Pompa*, pp. 11–12.
28 For details about the German painter Storer, see Giulio Bora, 'Note sull'attività milanese di Gian Cristoforo Storer', *Arte lombarda* 98–99 (1991), 29–40.

Figure 10.2 Girolamo Quadrio, Arch of Porta Romana, 40.2 x 29 cm, etching, in *La pompa . . . della solenne entrata fatta dalla serenissima Maria Anna austriaca* (Milan, [1651]). ZCC.05.0001/01.

Figure 10.3 Giacomo Cotta, Salomon and the Queen of Sheba, 22 x 30 cm, etching, in *La pompa . . . della solenne entrata fatta dalla serenissima Maria Anna austriaca* (Milan, [1651]). ZCC.05.0001/01.

© Milan, Biblioteca Nazionale Braidense. Courtesy of the Ministero dei beni e delle attività culturali e del turismo. Further reproduction or duplication by any means is prohibited.

kneeling while offering gifts to the wise Solomon.[29] In this way, an analogy was created between Maria Anna and the ancient Queen. As the future bride of Philip IV, Maria Anna would have brought a large dowry to her husband-to-be, who for wisdom was widely likened to King Solomon. The female protagonist of the second picture (see Figure 10.4) was Rachel, wife of Jacob, who was depicted in the act of greeting her future husband by staging a rich parade.[30] The Biblical figure of Rachel was also significant because she received the gift of fertility from God. The theme of marriage and maternity was only present in the first arch, dedicated to the bride. It was not repeated in the following three arches. Nevertheless, it is worth noticing similar motifs within the Salone Margherita.

In the theatre, *Il Teseo* was performed on 20 June, a few days after Maria Anna's arrival. The performance can be considered tragicomedy, and the

29 The episode is narrated in the Bible, 1 Revelations, 10.
30 The story of the marriage of Rachel is described in the Bible, Genesis, chs. 29–30.

Figure 10.4 Giacomo Cotta, Rachel meets Jacob, 21.7 x 30 cm, etching, in *La pompa . . . della solenne entrata fatta dalla serenissima Maria Anna austriaca* (Milan, [1651]). ZCC.05.0001/01.

plot, based on a mythological subject, points towards several allegorical interpretations. Furthermore, the dramatic script reveals that a great deal of attention was paid to scenery.[31] For example, some noteworthy stage props and machinery were used at the beginning of the performance; indeed, the opening scene revolved around the use of a traditional theatre device, namely cloud chariots, with company of gods – Jupiter, Pallas and Juno – making their descent on a cloud. Jupiter gives the introduction and Juno begins her prologue.[32] She introduces themes of royalty and maternity, being the patroness of marriage and childbirth, celebrates the royal marriage and prophesies the birth of a royal heir:

> *Itene, gran Reina, a gran Monarca,*
> *ite e date l'erede a tanto impero.*

31 Many of the most important artists of the time were commissioned to stage *Il Teseo*, even if their names are not mentioned in the festival books; see *La pompa*, p. 48.
32 The scene is set in a garden; see *Argomento*, p. 10.

Io, che pronuba oro sono,
sarò Lucina al fortunato parto.
Parto! Ah, parto! Non devo
tacer ciò che ne' fati
internata la mente
della futura età presaga sente.[33]

[Great queen, go to the great king, go and give an heir to this great empire. Now I am *pronuba* (one who presides over marriage) and will be *Lucina* (goddess of childbirth) at the time of your happy giving of birth. Childbirth, oh childbirth! I do not have to hide what my mind, able to reveal fate, sees in the future age].

While the play's script echoes the themes displayed in the first arch, we must also consider the theatre itself. The ceiling, for example, was decorated with a painting by Camillo Landriani.[34] This decoration dated back to 1598, and showed a young girl sleeping among flowers while three goddesses – Juno, Minerva and Venus – offered her a series of symbolic gifts. These gifts exemplified the desired qualities of a royal bride. The young girl served as an *alter ego* for Queen Margherita, as suggested by the festival book of 1598.[35] In 1649, the same allegorical meanings could equally be attached to Maria Anna but, in addition, the *incipit* of the play and the above-mentioned opening scene with the three gods depicted in a garden clearly mirrored Landriani's painting. However, the link between the outdoor *apparati* and the stage design was not limited to the beginning of the drama. Once again, the Salone Margherita formed a pivotal space where the themes presented by the ephemeral *apparati*, the decorations and the drama were echoed and combined, providing a harmonic and all-encompassing display of the values celebrated in the Royal Entry.

The second arch along the route to Piazza del Duomo was placed near the Rocchetta of Porta Romana, and was dedicated to Maria Anna's brother, Ferdinand IV, son of the Emperor Ferdinand III.[36] Its decorations included five oil paintings aimed at celebrating the glorious origins of the Empire; thus, they paid homage not only to Ferdinand IV, but to the Empire as a whole by displaying the deeds of various celebrated past emperors. It is also noteworthy that the first picture focused on the figure of Roman Emperor Constantine, shown sailing for Nicaea where he convened the first Christian Council. The scene (see Figure 10.5) portrayed Constantine and his army in combat on a stormy sea, an image which has allegorical meaning in that it alludes to the obstacles Constantine had to face in defence of the Christian faith.

---

33 *Allegoria*, Prologo, vv. 109–116.
34 See Mazenta, *Apparato*, E3v.
35 See Zanlonghi, *Teatri*, pp. 148–9.
36 See *La Pompa*, p. 15. La Rocchetta was an ancient fortification located on the route of the medieval walls of Milan. It was demolished in the eighteenth century.

Figure 10.5 Giacomo Cotta, Constantine sails for Nicaea, 22.3 x 30.4 cm, etching, in *La pompa . . . della solenne entrata fatta dalla serenissima Maria Anna austriaca* (Milan, [1651]). ZCC.05.0001/01.

The allegorical meanings set out in the oil paintings of the arch near the Rocchetta of Porta Romana were also recalled in some scenes of *Il Teseo*. Indeed, the obstacles which confronted Theseus are described in the libretto using an allegoric image: the *Argomento* summarises the plot and narrates the story of Theseus at the time of his arrival in Athens.[37] Before being recognised by his father King Aegeus, he had to struggle against the intrigues of Medea, who wanted her son Medus to become heir to Theseus. What's more, he had to defeat a conspiracy plotted by Pallante, who was trying to take the throne with the help of his fifty sons. In the *Idea dell'Atto Quarto* (the theme of act 4), the personification of Deception illustrates the destiny of Theseus through a metaphorical image:

> *L'Inganno . . . gli fa vedere come in figura la tempesta, che sono per suscitare contro dell'innocente Teseo. Compare dunque una nave, i cui passeggeri, navigando con bonaccia van cantando, ma alteratosi*

37 *Allegoria*, pp. 6–7.

d'improvviso il mare raccolgono prima le vele, crescendo poi la tempesta, fan getto: infine dando la nave a traverso, et urtando in scoglio coperto van tutti in acqua.[38]

[Deception . . . shows them the storm as a figure which will rise against the innocent Theseus. A ship appears and its passengers, sailing calm seas, are singing, but suddenly, as the seas rise, they at first fold the sails, then, as the storm grows further, they jettison the cargo. Finally, as the ship lists and runs aground upon a submerged rock, they are all thrown into the water].

Deception explains that the ship is a metaphor representing Theseus's situation, as he too would have to face a storm of suspicion and intrigue. Parallels to the oil painting representing Constantine and his army in stormy seas most likely played a part in the scenery. The scene, therefore, as well as being a tribute to the sovereigns, featured as a celebration of the power of virtue to overcome any obstacle.

The Jesuits had evidently paid special attention to the development of a performance in line with the themes expressed in the ephemeral *apparati*. The analysis offered here is too brief to provide a comprehensive interpretation of all the parallels; however, a last example referring to the second arch may be mentioned. The protagonist of the final oil painting of the second arch was Otto the Great, the supposed founder of the Holy Roman Empire.[39] The scene represented his coronation in Milan in 961. The event took place in the Basilica of Sant'Ambrogio, a crucial location for Milan's historical and cultural identity.[40] Once again, the scene offered dynastic homage contextualised within Milanese local identity. Moreover, the final scene of *Il Teseo* also developed the same theme. The scene is set in a royal courtyard where Theseus is recognised as the legitimate heir by his father Aegeus, receives the regalia, and begins to rule Athens.[41] There are no scenographic sources, so we cannot reconstruct the stage set; nevertheless, we might imagine that parallel depictions were most likely evident. Moreover, it is probable that the set may have recalled the Palazzo Regio Ducale, where the performance took place. In one fashion or another, the legitimisation of power continued to be celebrated within the seat of ducal authority in Milan.

The Palazzo Regio Ducale, we know, hosted a second theatrical spectacle, the musical comedy *Il Giasone*. It was performed by a troupe named Comici Febiarmonici '*nel solito luogo delle Comedie*'[42] ('in the usual place of comedies') and featured beautiful stage sets. Although no further information exists about the drama, we can infer that a clear contrast was created with both *Il*

---

38 Ibid., p. 27.
39 See *La Pompa*, p. 15.
40 The Basilica was built by St Ambrose in AD 379–386; see Maria Luisa Gatti Perer, *La Basilica di S. Ambrogio. Il tempio ininterrotto* (Milan: Vita & Pensiero, 1995).
41 *Allegoria*, pp. 35–6.
42 *La Pompa*, pp. 48–9.

Teseo, which had been performed in the official and noble space of the Salone Margherita, and *Il Giasone*, performed in the new theatre which was open to the public during the theatre season. So, although the two dramas shared a similar mythological theme, as their titles suggest, they were addressed to a different public. Although the theatres offered separate developments of the themes presented in the outdoor *apparati*, they nonetheless took advantage of the visual medium to illustrate the concept of *magnificentia*, the source of inspiration for the whole festival. *Apparati* and performances cooperated in showing not only the virtues of the royal guests present in Milan and their Houses, but also the virtues looked for in sovereigns in general.

The wedding of the Spanish Governor of Milan in 1672

From the two dynastic events considered in this chapter, we can hypothesise that the theatrical spaces inside the Palazzo Regio Ducale increased in importance during the festivals of the seventeenth century. This hypothesis leads us to consider the final event we shall address here.[43] In 1672, Gaspar Téllez-Girón de Osuna, the Spanish Governor of Milan, married Anna Antonia de Benavides. The marriage was celebrated by proxy in Madrid, after which the bride left for Milan to join her husband. In this case, Anna Antonia entered through the Porta Ticinese, thus following the route usually taken by governors making their entrance into Milan. For the purposes of civic pageantry, the situation in Milan was complicated by the military and political presence of Spanish foreign powers. The civic authorities, and in particular the *Senato* of Milan, did not approve the order set for the procession, and so did not take part in the ceremony.[44] The outdoor *apparati* were low key and, as Anna Antonia was not a royal bride like Margherita and Maria Anna, the traditional *Te Deum* at the end of the procession was sung in the church of S. Celso.

The event in Milan took place during Carnival season, with the festival full of entertainments, such as masquerades, parades of triumphal chariots

---

43 The event has been widely investigated by Roberta Carpani, 'La storia sanata. Il libretto di "Il trionfo d'Augusto in Egitto" di Carlo Maria Maggi', in Cascetta and Carpani (eds), *La scena della gloria*, pp. 329–77; Roberta Carpani, *Drammaturgia del comico: i libretti per musica di Carlo Maria Maggi nei "theatri di Lombardia"* (Milan: Vita & Pensiero, 1998). It should also be added that a third event occurred in the seventeenth century, similar to the ones considered in the present chapter, the passage of royal bride Margherita Teresa of Austria in 1666, thus confirming the key role of the theatre, and of opera in particular, in such events: for more details, see Cenzato and Rovaris; Carpani, *Drammaturgia*, pp. 38–47. Relevant observations by the author of this chapter concerning the Governors of Milan, festivities and theatre can be found in the virtual exhibition *Exchanging views. The Viceroys of Naples and the Spanish Monarchy's Image in the Baroque* (www.ub.edu/ enbach/?idioma=en, most recent access, July 2017). For the printed version see Francesca Barbieri, 'Milan, una corte "indirecta"', in Ida Mauro. Milena Vicecontre and Joan-Lluis Palos (eds), *Visiones cruzadas. Los virreyes de Nápoles y la imagen de la Monarquía de España en el Barroco* (Barcelona: Universitat de Barcelona Edicions, 2018), pp. 32–4.

44 See Carpani, *La storia sanata*, pp. 332–36.

and fireworks.[45] Of special interest, some operas and plays were performed in the Palazzo Regio Ducale. We have no information on the Spanish comedies performed during the festival, but we do know that the governor paid particular attention to the two operas staged for the occasion, *Il trionfo d'Augusto in Egitto* and *Amor tra l'armi*.[46] Carlo Maria Maggi,[47] the major Milanese literary figure of the time, was commissioned to write the libretto of *Il trionfo d'Augusto*. The plot of the drama deals with the themes of power and marriage: Augusto served as an *alter ego* for the governor, whose virtue was celebrated. The happy ending staged a fictional wedding between Augusto and Cleopatra. Beyond the encomiastic plot, *Il trionfo* differed from the above-mentioned performances of 1598 and 1649 in that the opera, being performed during Carnival, was simultaneously a ceremonial event reserved for nobles and an opera open to the public.[48]

The performance probably mirrored the tastes of the time. No printed festival book exists for the event, but the libretto was printed, including a series of eight elegant engravings. These represent the various stage sets: *il giardino della bellezza* (the garden of beauty); a *foresta* (forest); a *stanza* (room); a series of *padiglioni* (pavilions); *la reggia di Plutone* (Pluto's Royal Palace); an *arsenale con le statue dei Tolomei* (an arsenal with the statues of the Ptolemies); a *città* (city view).[49] We can recognise these typologies as being typical of Baroque stage design. As a matter of fact, Milan had become an important operatic centre during the seventeenth century, and the attention paid to scenic design may be interpreted in a more general context.[50] The magnificent visual aspects of the performance contributed to celebrating the greatness of the governor, while the engravings served as reminders of the magnificent stage sets.

Conclusion

The events considered in this chapter reveal the growing importance of theatrical performance within dynastic Milanese festivals. In particular, the spaces dedicated to theatre within the Palazzo Regio Ducale multiplied and

---

45 Anna Antonia made her entry on 21 December 1672.

46 See the relevant librettos: *Il trionfo d'Augusto in Egitto, opera in musica dedicata e cantata all'Ecc.ma Sig.ra D. Anna Antonia Di Benavides . . . nelle sue nozze coll'Ecc.mo Sig.r D. Gaspar Tellez Girone . . . Nel Regio Teatro di Milano l'anno 1672* (Milan, [1672]); *Amor tra l'armi overo Corbulone in Armenia opera in musica. Dedicata all'eccellentissima signora D. Catterina Ponze de Leon, . . . cantata nelle nozze tra l'eccel.mo sig.r d. Gaspar Tellez Giron, Gomez di Sandovale, . . . e l'eccell.ma sig.ra D. Anna Antonia di Benavides, . . . Nel Regio Teatro di Milano l'anno 1673* (Milan, [1673]).

47 Carlo Maria Maggi (Milan 1630 – Milan 1699), writer and poet, is considered to be the father of Milanese literature. For details of his theatrical works, see note 43.

48 See Carpani, *La storia sanata*, pp. 339–41.

49 The engravings are published in Cascetta and Carpani (eds), *La scena della gloria*, figures 47–54.

50 See Cesare Molinari, *Le nozze degli dei: un saggio sul grande spettacolo italiano nel Seicento* (Rome: Bulzoni, 1968).

diversified over the course of the century. On the one hand, this was due to the birth of commercial opera, but on the other, the location of the theatres inside the palace made them the ideal place for the exaltation of power. Thus, the theatre became the place where festivals reached their climax, and where the issues presented in the urban *apparati* were merged and inter-related. For Margherita's entrance in 1598, the theatre was significant for its construction and its decoration, while in 1649 the script and the scen-ery of the drama acquired great importance. The theatrical aspects became even more prominent in 1672, when the entire rhetorical programme was entrusted to the festival performances.

Over the course of the seventeenth century, urban *apparati* and theatrical performance became increasingly related. The themes and the stage sets of these events reflected the general rhetorical and iconographical programmes created for the festivals. In particular, both urban *apparati* and theatre sets became gradually more and more focused on visual effects. This evolution is also demonstrated by the increasing attention paid to images in the festival books, which increasingly contained iconographic documentation concern-ing the *apparati*. Furthermore, in the printed librettos, engravings depicting the sets of the drama were often included. All of these strategies combined to make for lasting memories of the celebration of power developed in the ceremonies and festivals. The importance attached to the preparation of appropriate *apparati* and performances is also demonstrated by the involve-ment of important literary, artistic and religious personalities of the time, as well as the significant financial commitments entailed.

The entries of royal brides in 1598 and 1649 provided a model for cer-emonies in Milan throughout the seventeenth century, while the following century witnessed significant changes in format for royal festivals. Elisabetta Cristina of Brunswick, betrothed to King Charles III of Spain, visited Milan in 1708, and the festival format adopted for the entry of a royal bride changed for the first time since the entry of Margherita of Austria. She was honoured with the traditional procession, but no triumphal arches were erected along the route.[51] Maria Teresa of Austria received a similar ceremony in 1739, when she visited Milan. Although the *apparati* became generally less remark-able in the eighteenth century compared to the previous century, the theatre maintained its centrality and the Regio Ducale Theatre, erected in place of the Salone Margherita, became the centrepiece of dynastic celebration.[52]

51 See Giovanna D'Amia, 'La città fatta teatro: apparati effimeri ed "embellissement" urbano nella Milano del Settecento', in Annamaria Cascetta and Giovanna Zanlonghi (eds), *Il tea-tro a Milano nel Settecento* (Milan: Vita & Pensiero, 2008), pp. 97–124.

52 The second half of the eighteenth century was a crucial period for Milan. Archduke Fer-dinand of Habsburg, son of Maria Teresa of Austria, married Maria Beatrice d'Este and established his court in Milan in 1771. This saw the beginning of a series of changes to the format of political ceremonies, festivals and public events. The Regio Ducale Teatro of Milan played a key role during the wedding festival in 1771. It was an old theatre and needed some restoration work, but it held significant importance with regard to its stage design

Bibliography

Printed primary sources

Amor tra l'armi overo Corbulone in Armenia opera in musica. Dedicata all'eccellentissima signora D. Catterina Ponze de Leon, . . . cantata nelle nozze tra l'eccel.mo sig.r d. Gaspar Tellez Giron, Gomez di Sandovale, . . . e l'eccell.ma sig. ra D. Anna Antonia di Benavides, . . . Nel Regio Teatro di Milano l'anno 1673 (Milan, [1673]).

Argomento, allegoria, et idea del Teseo da rappresentarsi nel Regio Ducal Teatro da' scolari dell'Università di Brera della Compagnia di Gesù . . . (Milan, 1649).

Festa fatta in Milano nel Regio Ducal Palazzo, il giouedì 15 luglio 1649, alla maestà della regina n.s. Maria Anna d'Austria . . . (Milan, 1649).

Il trionfo d'Augusto in Egitto, opera in musica dedicata e cantata all'Ecc.ma Sig.ra D. Anna Antonia Di Benavides . . . nelle sue nozze coll'Ecc.mo Sig.r D. Gaspar Tellez Girone . . . Nel Regio Teatro di Milano l'anno 1672 (Milan, [1672]).

La pompa della solenne entrata fatta dalla serenissima Maria Anna austriaca figlia dell'inuittissimo imperante Ferdinando Terzo et sposa del potentissimo Filippo Quarto . . . nella città di Milano. Con la descrittione de gli apparati, et feste (Milan, [1651]).

Mazenta, Guido, *Apparato fatto dalla città di Milano per riceuere la serenissima regina D. Margarita d'Austria* (Milan, 1598).

Picinelli, Filippo, *Mondo simbolico formato d'imprese scelte, spiegate, ed illustrate con sentenze, ed erudizioni . . . in questa impressione da mille, e mille parti ampliato* (Venice, 1678).

Real solenne entrata in Milano delle maestà della regina Maria Anna moglie del re cattolico n.s. Filippo IV, e del re d'Ungaria, e Boemia Ferdinando Francesco suo fratello . . . (Milan, 1649).

Secondary sources

Arcaini, Roberta Giovanna, 'I comici dell'Arte a Milano: accoglienza, sospetti, riconoscimenti', in *La scena della gloria: Drammaturgia e spettacolo a Milano in età spagnola* (Milan: Vita & Pensiero, 1995), pp. 329–78.

---

because of the presence of the brothers Fabrizio and Bernardino Galliari. The archduke was very interested in festivals and theatre: two new theatres were built in Milan under his reign, namely La Scala (1778) and La Canobbiana (1779). For an overview, see Francesca Barbieri, Roberta Carpani and Alessandra Mignatti (eds), 'Festa, rito e teatro nella "gran città di Milano" nel Settecento', *Studia Borromaica* 24 (2010), 889–1090 and Alessandra Mignatti, *Scenari della città: ritualità e cerimoniali nella Milano del Settecento* (Pisa and Rome: Serra, 2013). Recent studies focus in particular on the relationship between stage design and justice: Francesca Barbieri, 'Giustizia e ingiustizia nella scenografia milanese al tempo di Beccaria', in Annamaria Cascetta and Danilo Zardin (eds), *Giustizia e ingiustizia a Milano tra Cinque e Settecento, Studia Borromaica* 29 (2016), pp. 561–606; Alessandra Mignatti, 'La giustizia in scena fra città e teatro nella Milano di metà Settecento: Dal rito pubblico nelle piazze al rito ludico del Regio Ducale Teatro con le scenografie dei Fratelli Galliari', ibid., 515–60; see also the exhibition catalogue, Francesca Barbieri and Alessandra Mignatti (eds), 'Virtù, scene, supplizi. Rappresentazioni della Giustizia nella Milano del Settecento', ibid., pp. 617–773. See also Francesca Barbieri, *I significati dell' apparenza. La scenografia teatrale a Milano nel secondo Settecento (1765–1792)*, forthcoming.

Barbieri, Francesca, Roberta Carpani and Alessandra Mignatti (eds), 'Festa, rito e teatro nella "gran città di Milano" nel Settecento', *Studia Borromaica* 24 (2010), vol. II, 889–1090.

Barbieri, Francesca, 'Giustizia e ingiustizia nella scenografia milanese al tempo di Beccaria', in Annamaria Cascetta and Danilo Zardin (eds), *Giustizia e ingiustizia a Milano tra Cinque e Settecento*, *Studia Borromaica* 29 (2016), 561–606.

Barbieri, Francesca and Alessandra Mignatti (eds), 'Virtù, scene, supplizi: Rappresentazioni della Giustizia nella Milano del Settecento', in Annamaria Cascetta and Danilo Zardin (eds), *Giustizia e ingiustizia a Milano tra Cinque e Settecento*, *Studia Borromaica* 29 (2016), 617–773.

Barbieri, Francesca, 'Milan, una corte "indirecta"', in Ida Mauro. Milena Viceconte and Joan-Lluis Palos (eds), *Visiones cruzadas. Los virreyes de Nápoles y la imagen de la Monarquía de España en el Barroco* (Barcelona: Universitat de Barcelona Edicions, 2018), pp. 32–4.

Barigozzi Brini, Amalia and Cecilia Bocciarelli, 'Temi e tipologie dell'effimero', in Marcello Fagiolo (ed.), *Le capitali della festa. Italia settentrionale*, 2 vols (Rome: De Luca, 2007), vol. 1, pp. 210–46.

Bora, Giulio, 'Note sull'attività milanese di Gian Cristoforo Storer', *Arte lombarda* 98–99 (1991), 29–40.

Bjurström, Per, *Giacomo Torelli and Baroque Stage Design* (Stockholm: Almqvist & Wiksell, 1961).

Carpani, Roberta, *Drammaturgia del comico: i libretti per musica di Carlo Maria Maggi nei "theatri di Lombardia"* (Milan: Vita & Pensiero, 1998).

Carpani, Roberta, 'La storia sanata: Il libretto di "Il trionfo d'Augusto in Egitto" di Carlo Maria Maggi', in Cascetta and Carpani (eds), *La scena della gloria*, pp. 329–77.

Cascetta, Annamaria (ed.), *Forme della scena barocca*, monographic issue of *Comunicazioni sociali*, 15/2–3 (1993).

Cascetta, Annamaria (ed.), *Aspetti della teatralità a Milano nell'età barocca*, monographic issue of *Comunicazioni sociali*, 16/1–2 (1994).

Cascetta, Annamaria and Roberta Carpani (eds), *La scena della gloria. Drammaturgia e spettacolo a Milano in età spagnola* (Milan: Vita & Pensiero, 1995).

Cenzato, Elena and Luisa Rovaris, ' "Comparvero finalmente gl'aspettati soli dell'austriaco cielo". Ingressi solenni per nozze reali', *Comunicazioni sociali* 16/2 (1994), 71–112.

Colle, Enrico and Fernando Mazzocca (eds), *Palazzo Reale di Milano* (Milan: Skira, 2001).

D'Amia, Giovanna, 'La città fatta teatro: apparati effimeri ed "embellissement" urbano nella Milano del Settecento', in Annamaria Cascetta and Giovanna Zanlonghi (eds), *Il teatro a Milano nel Settecento* (Milan: Vita & Pensiero, 2008), pp. 97–124.

Daolmi, Davide, *Le origini dell'opera a Milano 1598–1649* (Turnhout: Brepols, 1998).

Della Torre, Stefano, 'Gli apparati trionfali del 1598', *Studia Borromaica* 22 (2008), 81–100.

Fant, Rebecca, 'Le Mura Spagnole di Milano: gli interventi conservativi (2006–2009) e la loro negazione', *Istituto Lombardo (Rend. Scienze)* 146 (2012), 37–64.

Fiaschini, Fabrizio, *Margherita, Alberto e Isabella: Ingressi trionfali a Pavia nel 1599* (Novara: Interlinea, 2012).

Gatti Perer, Maria Luisa, *La Basilica di S. Ambrogio. Il tempio ininterrotto* (Milan: Vita & Pensiero, 1995).

Gatti Perer, Maria Luisa (ed.), *Milano ritrovata: l'asse via Torino* (Milan: Il Vaglio Cultura Arte, 1986).

Gatti Perer, Maria Luisa, 'La sostanza dell'effimero', in Marcello Fagiolo (ed.), *Le capitali della festa. Italia settentrionale*, 2 vols (Rome: De Luca, 2007), vol. 1, pp. 188–209.

Mezzanotte, Paolo, 'Costruzione e vicende del Teatro di Corte in Milano', *Atti del Collegio degli Ingegneri ed Architetti* 2 (1915), 1–24.

Mignatti, Alessandra, *Scenari della città: ritualità e cerimoniali nella Milano del Settecento* (Pisa and Rome: Serra, 2013).

Mignatti, Alessandra, 'La giustizia in scena fra città e teatro nella Milano di metà Settecento. Dal rito pubblico nelle piazze al rito ludico del Regio Ducal Teatro con le scenografie dei Fratelli Galliari', in Annamaria Cascetta and Danilo Zardin (eds), *Giustizia e ingiustizia a Milano tra Cinque e Settecento*, Studia Borromaica 29 (2016), pp. 515–60.

Molinari, Cesare, *Le nozze degli dei: un saggio sul grande spettacolo italiano nel Seicento* (Rome: Bulzoni, 1968).

Rovaris, Luisa, 'La festa barocca: la real solenne entrata di Maria Anna d'Austria a Milano nel 1649', *Archivio Storico Lombardo* 113 (1987), 48–80.

Tamburini, Elena, *Culture ermetiche e commedia dell'arte. Tra Giulio Camillo e Flaminio Scala* (Rome: Aracne, 2016).

Varallo, Franca, 'Margaret of Austria's Travel in the State of Milan Between 1598 and 1599', in Fernando Checa Cremades and Laura Fernández Gonzáles (eds), *Festival Culture in the World of the Spanish Habsburgs* (London and New York: Routledge, 2015), pp. 135–54.

Venturelli, Paola, 'La solemne entrada en Milan de Margherita d'Austria, esposa de Felipe III', in Maria Luisa Lobato and Bernardo José García (eds), *La fiesta cortesana en la época de los Austrias* (Valladolid: Junta de Castilla y Leòn, 2003), pp. 233–47.

Zanlonghi, Giovanna, *Teatri di formazione: actio, parola e immagine nella scena gesuitica del Sei-Settecento a Milano* (Milan: Vita & Pensiero, 2002).

11 *Palazzo eguale alle Reggie più superbe*

Schloss Eggenberg in Graz and the imperial wedding of 1673

Paul Schuster

restavano all' arrivo di S. M., la qual gionse ancor quella sera, salutata dall' Artigleria del Castello di Graz, ad Eggenberg palazzo mezz' hora distante del Princip: Giov: Sigifredo di questo nome, che la vastita, l' ordine, e gl' ornamenti dell' Architettura lo costituiscono eguale alle Reggie più superbe, e gl' addobbi de i quali l' havea interiormente tutto ricoperto, con aggionger in quest' occasione, senza risparmio di spesa, alle sue ricche suppellettili quanto di più vago, e prezioso si può tesser in auree tele, o effigiar al vivo con le sete, e con gl' ori, lo rendevano per così gran Principessa un alloggio ben degno, nel quale per quei due giorni trattò il Principe tutta la Corte con indicibile, ma sua hereditaria splendidezza.[1]

[they awaited the arrival of Her Imperial Majesty, who reached the Palace of Eggenberg that same evening after being welcomed by the Artillery of the Castle of Graz. The palace of Prince Johann Seyfried is located half an hour away from the town. In its architectural vastness, style and embellishments it is on a par with the most superb of royal palaces. Without sparing any cost, Prince Eggenberg had all the interior rooms redecorated especially for this occasion. Countless precious items, as well as textiles fashioned in gold and silver, which were virtually able to breathe life into the subjects there depicted, adorned accommodation worthy of a noble princess. Prince Eggenberg hosted her and her entire court retinue with his inexpressible and hereditary splendour.]

Only once during the seventeenth century was Schloss Eggenberg centre-stage for an outstanding event of truly international dimensions.[2] A mere seven months after the death of his first wife, Margarita Teresa of Spain, in March 1673, Emperor Leopold I (1640–1705) married for a second time.

---

1 *Breve Descrizzione del Viaggio, et Arrivo in Gratz della Maestà dell'Imperatrice Claudia Felice nata Arciduchessa d'Austria &c. Delle Augustissime Nozze celebrate con la medesima dalle Maestà Cesarea dell'Imperator Leopoldo* (Graz: Heredi Widmannstetter, 1673).
2 I would like to express my gratitude to Dr Barbara Kaiser for her support, guidance through the sources and the knowledge she passed on to me for this article.

Figure 11.1 Entry of the Imperial Bride into Graz on 15 October 1673. Engraving by Cornelis Meyssens and Johann Martin Lerch, 1673. Styrian State Archive, Graz.

© Schloss Eggenberg/UMJ Graz.

His wedding to Claudia Felicitas of Austria-Tyrol (1653–1676) was held in Graz in October of the same year. Schloss Eggenberg was chosen as a residence for the imperial bride and her mother, Archduchess Anna, née Medici. In the search for an appropriate wedding location and a suitable residence for the imperial bride, Graz and the nearby Eggenberg Palace seemed to comply almost perfectly with every single requirement. Moreover, this event provided Prince Johann Seyfried of Eggenberg (1644–1713) with a unique opportunity to present himself as a bountiful host on a par with the first families of the realm, and to exhibit his splendid new palace.[3]

Johann Seyfried's grandfather, Prince Hans Ulrich, diplomat and chief minister to Emperor Ferdinand II, commissioned his new family seat to be built to the west of Graz in 1625. The residence of the imperial governor

3 Friedrich Kryza-Gersch and Barbara Ruck, *Ave Claudia Imperatrix: Die Hochzeit Kaiser Leopolds I. mit Claudia Felicitas von Tirol in Graz 1673*, Ausstellungskatalog (Graz: Abteilung Schloss Eggenberg, 1983).

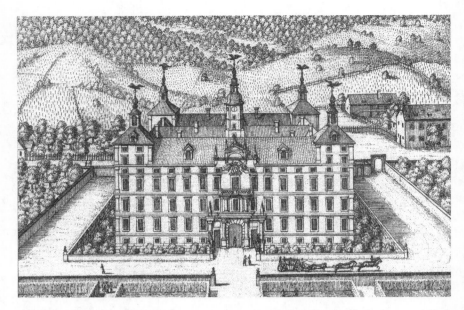

Figure 11.2 Perspective rendering of Schloss Eggenberg. Illustration from P. Johannes
Macher's GRAECIUM, Andreas Trost, before 1700.

© Schloss Eggenberg/UMJ Graz.

Hans Ulrich von Eggenberg served both as an example of political architecture and as a sophisticated way of legitimising his family's rule. Architectur-
ally, it drew its inspiration from comparable residences within the Habsburg
dominions in Spain and the Spanish Netherlands.[4]

In 1665, one year before his wedding to Eleonora Princess of Liech-
tenstein, Johann Seyfried came into his inheritance and continued building work on Schloss Eggenberg, which was still unfinished at the time.[5] In
accordance with his status, the entire second floor was magnificently furnished to serve him and his wife as a prestigious suite of rooms. Although
the valuable furnishings on the *piano nobile* were lost by no later than the
mid-eighteenth century, the huge cycle of over five hundred ceiling paintings

4 For the Eggenberg Family and Schloss Eggenberg see: Gerhard Bernd Marauschek, 'Die
   Fürsten zu Eggenberg: Unter besonderer Berücksichtigung ihres Kunstmäzenatentums'
   (Dissertation, Karl-Franzens-Universität, Graz, 1968); Barbara Kaiser, *Schloss Eggen-
   berg* (Wien: Christian Branstätter Verlag, 2006); Hannes P. Naschenweng, 'Eggenberg', in
   Werner Paravicini (ed.), *Höfe und Residenzen im spätmittelalterlichen Reich. Grafen und
   Herren*, Residenzen-Kommission der Akademie der Wissenschaften zu Göttingen, *Residen-
   zforschung*, vol. 15, IV, 1 (Ostfildern: Jan Thorbecke Verlag, 2012), 353–371.
5 Kaiser, *Schloss Eggenberg*.

in their lavish stucco frames has survived until today. Equally, the great hall in the middle of the enfilade has remained virtually unchanged with its cycle of allegorical paintings celebrating the Eggenberg rule.[6] Later refurbishment of the rooms in a Rococo style was restricted to the furniture, stoves and wall decorations.

Historical sources document the stay of the imperial bride Claudia Felicitas, Archduchess of Austria, in Schloss Eggenberg in late 1673.[7] They provide the first account of the just-finished furnishings, and the use and function of the building, which would be in full operation for the first time two days before the wedding. We don't know when precisely Graz and Schloss Eggenberg were selected as venues for the wedding, but it was not before August 1673 that a final decision on Claudia Felicitas as the new empress was taken. Vienna was ruled out as a site for the celebrations because the imperial court was officially still in mourning following the death of Margarita Teresa in March. Leopold, too, expressly wanted his wedding to Claudia Felicitas to be a restrained affair – '*sin mucho ruydo*'[8] – because the court was still deep in mourning.[9] His wishes were respected. Compared to his first wedding to the Infanta of Spain in 1666, the celebrations in Graz would be staged along far more modest lines.

Doubtless, Johann Seyfried's family connections also played a significant role in the Viennese Court's search for a suitable place to host the wedding. After all, Johann Seyfried's brother-in-law Prince Ferdinand von Dietrichstein was a confidant of the emperor, who had also just appointed him '*Obersthofmeister*'[10] to the future empress.

Prince Eggenberg therefore had only about two or three months to get everything ready and turn his palace into an imperial residence. It was a race against time. The twenty-four rooms on the second floor which had been lavishly furnished for himself and his wife were turned into two magnificent guest apartments to host the bride and her mother during the last days before the wedding. The painters and carpenters were required to work

---

6 Barbara Ruck, 'Hans Adam Weissenkircher: Fürstlich Eggenbergischer Hofmaler. Mit einem Versuch zur Rekonstruktion des Programms für seinen allegorischen Gemäldezyklus im Eggenberger Planetensaal' (Dissertation, Universität, Graz, 1982).

7 Michael Franckenberger, *Prächtiger Einzug zu den Kayserli: Beylager Der Allerdurchleuchtigsten Großmächtigsten Fürstin und Frauen, Frauen Claudia Felice Römische Kayserin* (Graz: Wittmannstätterische Erben, 1673); *Breve Descrizzione del Viaggio, et Arrivo in Gratz della Maestà dell'Imperatrice Claudia Felice nata Arciduchessa d'Austria &c. Delle Augustissime Nozze celebrate con la medesima dalle Maestà Cesarea dell'Imperator Leopoldo* (Graz: Heredi Widmanstetter, 1673); *Entrée de sa Maiesté Imperiale a Gratz. Et la suitte de son Mariage avec la Serenissime Princesse d'Innspruch, le 15. Octobre 1673* (1673); Haus- Hofund Staatsarchiv (HHStA), Wien, Habsburg-Lothringen, Familienarchiv, Familienakten-Vermählungen, Karton 32, 33. HHStA, Zeremonialprotokolle (Z2, 1660–1674).

8 'without much fuss'.

9 Kryza-Gersch and Ruck, *Ave Claudia Imperatrix*, p. 28.

10 Head of the Court Household.

extra shifts and night shifts, for which additional candle rations were also issued.[11] By 30 September, the painters were still busy trying to complete the ceiling paintings, even though Claudia and her mother had long left their residence in Innsbruck and set off on the arduous twenty-two-day journey to Graz. On 13 October, the huge travelling party with more than three hundred and fifty participants entered Schloss Eggenberg through the rear gate, 'preceded by the sight of several thousand flickering torches in the evening'. The empress-to-be was welcomed in front of the palace *'bei der senfften'*[12] by Johann Seyfried, his older brother Johann Christian, their wives and their sister Maria Elisabeth, princess Dietrichstein. To greet his guests, Prince Eggenberg had had an inscription in the form of a chronogram mounted above the portal. After the obligatory kissing of hands, the guests were led to their rooms.

In addition to the three printed descriptions of the celebrations, the court protocol,[13] together with letters written by Prince Ferdinand von Dietrichstein,[14] add further to our knowledge of the events in October 1673.

Claudia had a suite of twelve adjoining rooms in the North Wing placed at her disposal (see Figure 11.3: rooms 24–13).[15]

The walls were decorated with precious textiles embroidered in gold and silver, alongside Flemish Gobelin tapestries with depictions of mythological scenes. In one of the rooms the walls were decorated with two mirrors and forty-eight paintings in gold and silver frames instead of the usual *'Prunkthuecher'*.[16] The floors were covered with further textiles and carpets. The spectacular ceilings with their huge cycle of over 500 individual scenes of history- and landscape-paintings, emblems and mythological and allegorical depictions in lavish stucco frames are praised by all commentators. A further room contained Claudia's canopy bed, which was also magnificently decorated and supported by four black twisted columns. Both the bed curtains and the coverings were golden in colour and embroidered with silver flowers. The suite set aside for the archduchess Anna was located directly opposite in the South Wing (see Figure 11.3; rooms 1–12).[17] This apartment also contained twelve rooms, set out exactly as in the North Wing. And according to the descriptions, it was no less magnificently furnished. The one difference was that the textile decoration was in blue and *'duncklen wittiblichen farben'*.[18] Both apartments included a

11 Steiermärkisches Landesarchiv (StLA), Graz, Familienarchiv Herberstein, Abteilung Eggenberg (E), Rentamtsrechnungsbücher der Herrschaft Eggenberg, E 149/2.
12 'in her sedan chair'. (HHStA), Habsburg-Lothringen, Familienarchiv, Familienakten-Vermählungen, Karton 32, 33.
13 HHStA, Zeremonialprotokolle (Z2).
14 HHStA, Habsburg-Lothringen, Familienarchiv, Familienakten-Vermählungen, Karton 32, 33.
15 Franckenberger, *Prächtiger Einzug*, fol. 5v.
16 'splendid tapestries'. Franckenberger, *Prächtiger Einzug*, fol. 5v.
17 Franckenberger, *Prächtiger Einzug*, fol. 5v.
18 'subdued colours appropriate to a widow'. Franckenberger, *Prächtiger Einzug*, fol. 5v.

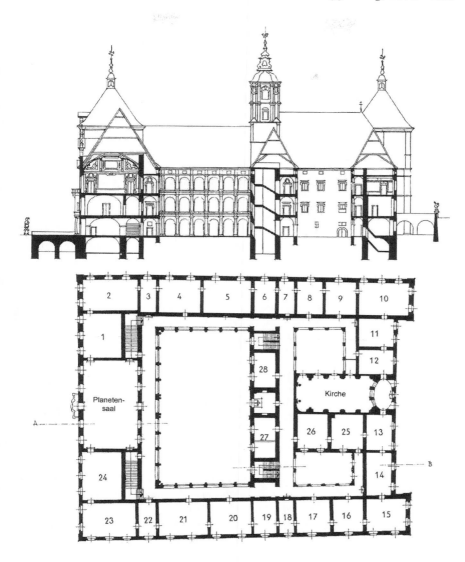

Figure 11.3 Schloss Eggenberg, layout of the second floor (*piano nobile*).
© Schloss Eggenberg/UMJ Graz.

'*grosser Saal*'[19] where the guards were accommodated. This central and largest room in Schloss Eggenberg only came to be decorated with paintings years later. As the '*Planetensaal*',[20] it became the high point of the

19 Great Hall (later room of the planets). Franckenberger, *Prächtiger Einzug*, fol. 5v.
20 Room of the planets.

Eggenberg *piano nobile*. In 1673, the ceiling and wall spaces had been (partly) stuccoed but were still empty. Even so, this state of incompletion evidently did not prevent Johann Seyfried from considering the Schloss worthy to accommodate high-ranking guests.

As the Italian description quoted at the start of this chapter mentions, the decision to choose Schloss Eggenberg was taken not only because of its splendour and precious furnishings. In 1673, no other residence in the hereditary lands could compete with it.[21] The size and arrangement of the rooms also met the requirements which court ceremony stipulated for a future empress. The structural layout in Schloss Eggenberg probably dates back to the original design of 1625, which had been created for the first prince as the imperial governor. Its use as a temporary imperial residence indicates just how much the building met imperial standards in terms of dimensions and distribution of space. Moreover, state apartments comprising twelve uncommonly well-spaced adjoining rooms are rare at that time.[22] The second floor could easily accommodate two guest apartments consisting of a joint guard room, three preceding rooms and an audience chamber. The audience chamber was connected to a further succession of eight rooms for individual use (state or private). (See Plates 10 and 11.)

However grand, Eggenberg was not designed for an event of this scale. It is not clear where the two Eggenberg brothers and their households, as well as the bride's entourage, were accommodated at the same time. Johann Seyfried left his new apartments on the second floor to his two illustrious guests. His brother and sister-in-law were also due to arrive from Bohemia and would have to be put up in accordance with their status. One possible idea was for the two princes and their wives to occupy apartments in the suite on the first floor. Yet that would already have taken up two-thirds of

21 'eguale alle Reggie più superbe', *Breve Descrizzione*.
22 For room sequences, imperial state apartments and ceremony in Habsburg residences, see Herbert Karner, 'The Habsburg Country Residences Around Vienna in the Seventeenth Century and Their Relationship to the Hofburg Palace', in Barbara Arciszewska (ed.), *The baroque villa: suburban and Country Residences c. 1600–1800* (Wilanów: Wilanów Palace Museum, 2009), pp. 187–96; Herbert Karner, 'Raumordnung und Identität – Spanisches in Wien?' in Werner Paravicini and Jörg Wettlaufer (eds), *Vorbild – Austausch – Konkurrenz* (Ostfildern: Thorbecke, 2010), pp. 275–88; Krista De Jonge, 'Ceremonial Space. Exchanges Between the Burgundian Low Countries and Spain in Early Modern Palace Architecture (1520–1620)', published in Spanish translation as: 'Espacio ceremonial. Intercambios en la arquitectura palaciega entre los Países Bajos borgoñones y España en la Alta Edad Moderna (1520–1620)', in Krista De Jonge, B.J. García and A. Esteban Estríngana (eds), *El Legado de Borgoña. Fiesta y Ceremonia cortesana en la época de los Austrias (1454–1648)* (Madrid: Fundación Carlos de Amberes y Marcial Pons Historia, 2010), pp. 61–90; Krista De Jonge, 'Introduction. Court Residences as Places of Exchange in Late Medieval and Early Modern Europe (1400–1700)', in B.J. García (ed.), *Felix Austria: Lazos familiars, cultura política y mecenazgo artistic entre las cortes de los Habsburgo / Family Ties, Political Culture and Artistic Patronage between the Habsburg Court Networks* (Madrid: Fundación Carlos de Amberes y PALATIUM – European Science Foundation – RNP, 2013).

all the available space in the palace, and indeed exhausted the entire supply of prestigious rooms in the building. Admittedly, kitchens and storerooms were also accommodated in the vaulted rooms on the ground floor. But where could room be found for the members of the imperial household? Claudia and her mother alone were about to arrive with their entourage of more than 350 people.[23] Naturally, there was always recourse to the city's townhouse. We do not know for certain whether one of the two brothers stood down and agreed to stay there. What we do know is that space was at a premium for two days in Eggenberg.

The example of Schloss Eggenberg clearly shows how rapidly space could be freed up for extraordinary occasions and how impressed contemporaries were by the result. In contrast, far more extensive manipulation was presumably required to prepare the imperial castle of the *Grazer Burg* as the residence for the emperor. None of the chroniclers, however, provides any descriptive details of the rooms in the antiquated city castle. Consequently, the measures undertaken for the emperor's brief stay may well have produced less than impressive results. No-one had lived in the Habsburg residence since 1619, most of which had been completed in the late Gothic period. The final extensions to the complex had been made under Archduke Karl and his wife in the second half of the sixteenth century.

All descriptions, in contrast, unanimously praise the splendour of the residence occupied by Claudia Felicitas. She did not leave the palace during her two-day stay at Eggenberg. On the morning after her arrival, promptly at 9 o'clock, the representatives of the Styrian estates reached Eggenberg with over thirty carriages in tow. The audience with the imperial bride took place in her '*Verhörsaal*'[24] on the second floor, the walls of which were decorated with purple velvet with golden trimmings. On the same morning Leopold also dispatched his '*Oberstkämmerer*'[25] to Schloss Eggenberg to kiss Claudia's hand. At 4 o'clock in the afternoon a column of fifty carriages drove up in front of the house: the emperor had arrived in Eggenberg accompanied by several members of the court household. To welcome him, Claudia went to meet her bridegroom at the foot of the staircase. After the visit – the historical record does not tell us what was said or how the visit went – she accompanied him 'as far as the first room'.[26] The final day before the wedding ended with the visit of the Papal Nuncio.

For Claudia, the actual day of the wedding on 15 October began with her receiving the Venetian ambassador. This was followed by the arrival of her new ladies-in-waiting from Vienna. The Emperor Leopold also paid her another courtesy visit before the wedding. This time, however, Claudia and her mother waited for him 'at the last door of the hall leading to the

---

23 Kryza-Gersch and Ruck, *Ave Claudia Imperatrix*, p. 35.
24 Audience Chamber. Franckenberger, *Prächtiger Einzug*, fol. 6r.
25 Head of the Imperial Chamber.
26 HHStA, Zeremonialprotokolle (Z2).

corridor'[27] – in other words, no longer on the stairs but on the second floor. The three of them then spent an hour together in the '*retirata*' (private apartment) until Leopold set off back to the city.[28] (See Plate 12.) This was probably the starting signal for the wedding celebrations. In the afternoon, the court's period of mourning was finally lifted and all the guests changed from black mourning-dress into lavish wedding-attire. Slowly, the participants of the wedding procession began to assemble in front of the house. Meanwhile, Claudia had donned her magnificent bridal gown. (See Plate 13.) In the absence of a male member of the dynasty who could fetch the bride on behalf of the emperor, Leopold entrusted his '*Oberststallmeister*',[29] Count Dietrichstein, with this duty. The '*Unterhofmarschall*',[30] Count Oetting, was given the less enviable task of arranging the entrance into the city; over ninety coaches, each drawn by six horses, had to be marshalled for this purpose.

The surroundings of the Schloss must also have been up to these exceptional requirements. Leading the carriages in a column over one mile in length along the principal axis of the formal garden to the forecourt – still walled at the time – and then channelling it back towards the city in the correct order, as required by protocol, would not have been practical. As Claudia's arrival had shown, it must also have been usual to enter the grounds from the rear. Probably the only way to regulate this high volume of traffic would have been to set up a one-way system which would guide the procession from the park's rear gate (the site of the court stables), alongside the palace, across the forecourt and finally along the principal axis towards the city.

At 5 o'clock in the afternoon, the huge procession set off. The coaches were preceded by small military detachments and accompanied by mounted escorts, the '*arcieri*' guards,[31] the city councillors, servants, musicians, drummers, trumpeters and countless other people. Johann Seyfried and his brother rode in Count Dietrichstein's carriage. An avenue of chestnut trees, which had been hastily planted to mark this special occasion, lined the approximately four kilometre–long route from Schloss Eggenberg to the edge of the city. This thoroughfare was to survive for the following two hundred years; its final section still exists today.

Dusk had already fallen when the procession approached the city. The festive illumination of the walls, the firing of cannons from the bastions and the pealing of all the church bells must have created an atmosphere as noisy as it was impressive. On her arrival at the city boundary, the imperial bride was

27 Ibid.
28 HHStA, Habsburg-Lothringen, Familienarchiv, Familienakten-Vermählungen, Karton 32,33.
29 Grand Equerry.
30 Deputy Steward of the Household.
31 'ceremonial unit'.

WAHRE ABBILDUNG DER KAYSERLICH UND LANDS FÜRSTLICHEN HAUBT STADT GRAZ WIE SELBE VON AUF GEGEN DEN UNTERGANG ZU SEHEN IST

Figure 11.4 View of the City and Fortress of Graz, Andreas Trost, 1703. In the background, Schloss Eggenberg with the connecting avenue of chestnut trees.

© Schloss Eggenberg/UMJ Graz.

welcomed by the city council, which continued to accompany her through lanes and squares lined with a rejoicing population to the '*Hofkirche*',[32] where the wedding was held.

The conclusion of the ceremony was signalled to the crowd outside by volleys of gunfire, after which the wedding party walked along a connecting passage to the imperial *Burg* which was situated next to the *Hofkirche*. The empress went to her rooms to grant the assembled ladies of the city the honour of kissing her hand. At 9 o'clock in the evening, the guests who had been invited to the banquet gathered in the '*Ritterstube*'.[33] The high table of the imperial couple was set up below a golden canopy, and the buffet arranged underneath a red canopy. Next to it there were also side tables for drinks as well as a stage for the musicians. At 11 o'clock in the evening the imperial couple, accompanied by the Papal Nuncio, retired to their bedchamber. Only then was the whole of the court household permitted to take its place at table. The celebratory mood also persisted in the city. On this and on the following nights, the townspeople put colourful lanterns in the windows of their houses, bathing the entire city in a festive glow.

For the remainder of her stay in Graz, Claudia resided at the side of her husband in the *Grazer Burg* where she granted audiences and where evening concerts took place. Visits to several abbeys and churches, hunting trips to the outskirts of the city and minor music events had been meticulously planned for the coming eighteen days. The Jesuit College treated the imperial pair to a two-day performance of Niccolò Avancini's play *Cyrus*.[34] On 3 November, when the court set off back to Vienna, the bride's mother also departed on her journey home. This marked the end of an extraordinary event which had once again placed Graz at the centre of international interest after a very long time.

Prince Eggenberg could also look back with satisfaction on his role as host. After all, the whole of Europe's attention had been fixed on Eggenberg for a few days. Furthermore, several printed descriptions of the imperial wedding, in German, Italian and French, made him and his resplendent new residence famous far beyond the borders of the hereditary lands, even though it took him years of struggle to cope with the financial burdens imposed by his hospitality. Only a few descriptions or reports referring to Schloss Eggenberg which appeared in subsequent centuries neglect to mention this extraordinary event in the building's history. Even today, the chronogram above the palace portal still recalls the residence of Claudia Felicitas and the prince, and their stay on this extraordinary occasion. (See Plate 14.)

32 Court Church (today's Graz Cathedral). Franckenberger, *Prächtiger Einzug*, fol. 10r.
33 Knights' Hall. HHStA, Zeremonialprotokolle (Z2).
34 *Cyrus zu Hochzeitlichen Ehren-Spihl Ihro Kayserlichen Majestätten Leopoldo I. und Claudiae Felici, von Der Academischen Jugend deß Erz-Herzog-lichen Collegij, und der Universitet der Societet Jesu zu Grätz / auff offentlicher Schau-Bühn vorgestellt. Im Jahr 1673* (Graz: Widmanstädterischen Erben, 1673).

Bibliography

Manuscript sources

Haus-, Hof- und Staatsarchiv (HHStA), Wien.
HHStA, Habsburg-Lothringen, Familienarchiv, Familienakten-Vermählungen, Karton 32, 33 (Prince Ferdinand von Dietrichstein's letters to Emperor Leopold I).
HHStA, Zeremonialprotokolle (Z2, 1660–1674).
Steiermärkisches Landesarchiv, Graz (StLA).
StLA, Familienarchiv Herberstein, Abteilung Eggenberg (E), Rentamtsrechnungsbücher der Herrschaft Eggenberg.

Printed Primary Sources

Breve Descrizzione del Viaggio, et Arrivo in Gratz della Maestà dell'Imperatrice Claudia Felice nata Arciduchessa d'Austria &c. Delle Augustissime Nozze celebrate con la medesima dalle Maestà Cesarea dell'Imperator Leopoldo (Graz: Heredi Widmanstetter, 1673).
Cyrus zu Hochzeitlichen Ehren-Spihl Ihro Kayserlichen Majestätten Leopoldo I. und Claudiae Felici, von Der Academischen Jugend deß Erz-Herzog-lichen Collegij, und der Universitet der Societet Jesu zu Grätz/auff offentlicher Schau-Bühn vorgestellt. Im Jahr 1673 (Graz: Widmanstädterischen Erben, 1673).
Entrée de sa Maiesté Imperiale a Gratz. Et la suitte de son Mariage avec la Serenissime Princesse d'Innspruch, le 15. Octobre 1673 (1673).
Michael Franckenberger, *Prächtiger Einzug zu den Kayserli. Beylager Der Allerdurchleuchtigsten Großmächtigsten Fürstin und Frauen, Frauen Claudia Felice Römische Kayserin* (Graz: Wittmannstätterische Erben, 1673).

Secondary sources

De Jonge, Krista, 'Ceremonial Space: Exchanges Between the Burgundian Low Countries and Spain in Early Modern Palace Architecture (1520–1620)', published in Spanish translation as: 'Espacio ceremonial. Intercambios en la arquitectura palaciega entre los Países Bajos borgoñones y España en la Alta Edad Moderna (1520–1620)', in Krista De Jonge, B.J. García and A. Esteban Estríngana (eds), *El Legado de Borgoña. Fiesta y Ceremonia cortesana en la época de los Austrias (1454–1648)* (Madrid: Fundación Carlos de Amberes y Marcial Pons Historia, 2010), pp. 61–90.
De Jonge, Krista, 'Introduction. Court Residences as Places of Exchange in Late Medieval and Early Modern Europe (1400–1700)', in B.J. García (ed.), *Felix Austria: Lazos familiars, cultura política y mecenazgo artistic entre las cortes de los Habsburgo/Family Ties, Political Culture and Artistic Patronage between the Habsburg Courts Networks* (Madrid: Fundación Carlos de Amberes y PALATIUM – European Science Foundation – RNP, 2013).
Kaiser, Barbara, *Schloss Eggenberg* (Wien: Christian Brandstätter Verlag, 2006).
Karner, Herbert, 'The Habsburg Country Residences around Vienna in the Seventeeth Century and Their Relationship to the Hofburg Palace', in Barbara Arciszewska (ed.), *The baroque villa: Suburban and Country Residences c. 1600–1800* (Wilanów: Wilanów Palace Museum, 2009), pp. 187–96.

Karner, Herbert, 'Raumordnung und Identität – Spanischen in Wien?' in Werner Paravicini and Jörg Wettlaufer (eds), *Vorbild – Austausch – Konkurrenz* (Ostfildern: Thorbecke, 2010), pp. 275–88.

Kryza-Gersch, Friedrich and Barbara Ruck, *Ave Claudia Imperatrix: Die Hochzeit Kaiser Leopolds I. mit Claudia Felicitas von Tirol in Graz 1673*, Ausstellungskatalog (Graz: Abteilung Schloss Eggenberg,1983).

Marauschek, Gerhard Bernd, 'Die Fürsten zu Eggenberg: Unter besonderer Berücksichtigung ihres Kunstmäzenatentums' (Dissertation, Karl-Franzens-Universität Graz, Graz, 1968).

Naschenweng, Hannes P., 'Eggenberg', in Werner Paravicini (ed.), *Höfe und Residenzen im spätmittelalterlichen Reich. Grafen und Herren*, Residenzen-Kommission der Akademie der Wissenschaften zu Göttingen, *Residenzforschung*, vol. 15, IV, 1 (Ostfildern: Jan Thorbecke Verlag, 2012), pp. 353–71.

Ruck, Barbara, 'Hans Adam Weissenkircher: Fürstlich Eggenbergischer Hofmaler: Mit einem Versuch zur Rekonstruktion des Programms für seinen allegorischen Gemäldezyklus im Eggenberger Planetensaal' (Dissertation, Universität Graz, Graz, 1982).

Vocelka, Karl, *Habsburgische Hochzeiten 1550–1600: kulturgeschichtliche Studien zum manieristischen Repräsentationsfest* (Vienna: Böhlaus, 1976).

12 In public and in private

A study of festival in seventeenth-century Rome

Joanna Norman

On 28 February 1656, a magnificent *giostra* (tournament) was held in a temporary arena built on the north side of the Barberini family palace at the Quattro Fontane in Rome[1] (see Plate 15). At the third hour (about 9 o'clock at night), a procession of Roman knights, dressed in blue and silver costumes, entered the arena followed by the Three Graces, drawing a triumphal car representing Roma – Amor ('Roma' reversed). The procession continued with the arrival of the opposing side: a troupe of Amazons, dressed in red and gold and led by Prince Maffeo Barberini wearing an extraordinary plumed headdress. They in turn were followed by the Furies, pulling another triumphal car, this one representing Disdain. Accompanied by musicians and one hundred and twenty grooms, the two troupes paraded around the *teatro* before engaging in combat, firing pistols as they advanced towards each other. Their combat was interrupted by Hercules, arriving astride *'un mostruoso Dragone, il quale vomitava ardenti fiamme'* which both teams had to fight with sword and shield.[2] An end to the combat, with victory for neither side, came with the entrance of the Chariot of the Sun (the hit of Carnival two years previously[3]) bearing the sun god Apollo and accompanied by the Four Seasons and the Twenty Four Hours, at which point the performers left the field to the accompaniment of music.[4]

This mock-battle, commemorated in a contemporary painting by Filippo Lauri and Filippo Gagliardi (and now in the Museo di Roma), is a particularly spectacular example of the entertainments that enlivened the palaces,

---

1 Georgina Masson, 'Papal Gifts and Roman Entertainments in Honour of Queen Christina's Arrival', in Magnus von Platen (ed.), *Queen Christina of Sweden: Documents and Studies, Analecta Reginensia*, I (Stockholm, 1966), pp. 244–61, p. 258.

2 'A monstrous dragon, which vomited glowing flames'. Quoted in Maurizio Fagiolo dell'Arco, *La Festa barocca* (Rome: De Luca, 1997), p. 386.

3 Frederick Hammond, 'Creation of a Roman Festival: Barberini Celebrations for Christina of Sweden', in Stefanie Walker and Frederick Hammond (eds), *Life and the Arts in the Baroque Palaces of Rome: Ambiente Barocco* (New Haven and London: Yale University Press, 1999), pp. 53–69, p. 66.

4 Fagiolo dell'Arco, *Festa*, p. 386.

streets and piazzas of Rome during the course of the year, especially during the annual festive period of Carnival. Like most such events, it was motivated by reasons more serious than pure entertainment. It was held in honour of Queen Christina of Sweden, who had converted to Catholicism and abdicated the Swedish throne in the previous year, subsequently travelling to Rome. Queen Christina's arrival in Rome in December 1655 was a highly significant event for the city. As the daughter of King Gustavus Adolphus, the Swedish monarch who had died for the sake of the Protestant cause during the Thirty Years War, her conversion represented an extraordinary victory for the Catholic Church over the continuing threat of Protestantism. As such, her arrival in the city provided a particularly strong motivation for celebration during the carnival of 1656. The interest her visit occasioned is encapsulated in the contemporary comment of a French diplomat, Hugues de Lionne, who wrote, '*toute l'occupation de cette court n'est presentement qu'a la Reyne de Suede*'.[5]

This preoccupation with Queen Christina manifested itself in a series of magnificent spectacles which offered the city and its inhabitants the opportunity to celebrate the first year of the pontificate of Pope Alexander VII, as well as the victory of Christina's conversion to the Catholic Church.[6] At the same time, it also offered the opportunity for the leading families of Rome to compete with each other in their expression of honour to pope and queen through the events they each financed and staged. The Farnese decorated the façade of their palace with temporary decorations which celebrated Christina's conversion, while Prince Camillo Pamphilj, keen to ensure his family retained a prominent position following the death of the Pamphilj pope, Innocent X, had a balcony built in front of his palace on the via del Corso, so that the queen could watch the masquerades and *palio* races that took place in the street during the day.[7] Most extravagant of all, however, was the contribution of the Barberini, principally Prince Maffeo and his uncle Cardinal Francesco. Not only did they stage three splendid operas in their palace theatre, which was embellished with a royal box furnished with a crowned *baldacchino* for the purpose, but their magnificent *giostra* provided a culmination for the whole city's carnival celebrations for the queen.[8]

This event was particularly important for the Barberini family, since only a few years previously they had been living in exile in France. After the death of Pope Urban VIII, an investigation into their finances – following their bankrupting of the papal treasury for their own ends – had led them

5 'This court is currently preoccupied only with the Queen of Sweden'. Quoted in Masson, 'Papal Gifts', p. 244.
6 Fagiolo dell'Arco, *Festa*, p. 384.
7 Fagiolo dell'Arco, *Festa*, p. 384.
8 Hammond, 'Creation of a Roman Festival', p. 59.

to flee to France and their Roman properties to be confiscated.[9] However, by 1656 all the key members of the Barberini family had returned from exile and their properties had been restored to them. Their political fortunes were already beginning to revive, in large part thanks to the marriage in 1653 of Maffeo Barberini to Olimpia Giustiniani, great-niece of Innocent X, which brought a reconciliation of sorts with the Pamphilj family. By staging the most complex, splendid and lavish of all the festivities performed for the queen in Rome during this period, they therefore saw a means of re-establishing their pre-eminence as the leading cultural players on the Roman stage, in the hope of thereby increasing their political importance. That they were chosen to do so (under the supervision of the secretary of state, Giulio Rospigliosi), by the new pope, Alexander VII, represented a return to favour and a vote of confidence in their wealth and their ability to produce a magnificent event worthy of the occasion. The Barberini seized this opportunity, creating a spectacle that not only honoured the queen and pope but also served to remind Rome of the glories of the reign of their family pope, Urban VIII, and show that they were once again at the heart of the new administration.[10]

In keeping with the splendour of all aspects of the festivities for Queen Christina, the costs involved were immense. In addition to the special effects, such as the fire-breathing dragon, the performers were elaborately costumed with tall headdresses of feathers, described as '*cimeri di penne cosi ampli, e pomposi, che non si sà come tra l'ondeggiamento dell'aria potessero sostenere in capo una machina si spatiosa, e grave*'.[11] Although these costs were partly shared, since participants were expected to contribute to the costs of their own costumes through an account set up at the Monte di Pietà, the Barberini provided much of the financing themselves. Maffeo Barberini is documented as having spent 1,429.50 *scudi* on associated expenses ranging from the construction of the temporary arena and the provision of lighting, seating and transport to the supply of music, decorative materials and the printing and binding of programmes. In total, the Barberini family spent 3,966.50 *scudi* on '*comedie e feste fatte p[er] la venuta della Regina di Suetia*' in a period when the salary of the *maggiordomo* of Palazzo Barberini was a mere 200 *scudi* a year.[12]

Like other festivities held in Rome, the Barberini festivities for Queen Christina served particular political purposes that resulted from the unique

9 Patricia Waddy, *Seventeenth-Century Roman Palaces: Use and the Art of the Plan* (New York and Cambridge: Architectural History Foundation and MIT Press, 1990), p. 170.
10 Hammond, 'Creation of a Roman Festival', pp. 53–4.
11 'Crests of feathers, so broad and magnificent, that nobody knows how with the movement of the air they can keep on their heads such a large and heavy device'. Quoted in Hammond, 'Creation of a Roman Festival', p. 66.
12 'Comedies and entertainments created for the arrival of the Queen of Sweden'. See Hammond, 'Creation of a Roman Festival', p. 60.

character and make-up of the city. As the spiritual and administrative heart of the Catholic Church, Rome was home to numerous religious orders and welcomed pilgrims in their droves, particularly during the Jubilee or Holy Years celebrated every quarter century, when numbers reached the hundreds of thousands.[13] Increasingly in the seventeenth century it was also a tourist city, filled with visitors keen to see the ancient and modern marvels of Rome. Although Italy would not be unified for another two centuries, the decline of previously powerful city–states meant that even in the seventeenth century Rome was starting to take on the nature of a capital city, wealthy and international in its foreign residents and temporary visitors.[14]

From a political perspective, Rome's governance by a non-hereditary, elected ruler with both sacred and secular power led to instability and tension. Since such a system essentially entailed a transition from one family dynasty to another every few years (and sometimes more often), it is hardly surprising that each pope, elected by an elite from within its own heavily politicised ranks, appointed members of his own family and circle to the most important positions of government, in order to guarantee himself some basis of support. Since some of these positions were for life, they often created conflict after his death, with whichever family succeeded next to the pontificate keen to establish its own status and power base in the same way.[15]

In addition, Rome was a significant diplomatic centre in Europe in the seventeenth century. Although its power was beginning to wane, it still held enough sway to warrant the permanent presence at the papal court of ambassadors and cardinal-protectors from each Catholic nation in Europe. These representatives sought to influence papal policy and secure support for their various national interests, both in Rome and beyond, particularly those threatened by conflicts that were taking place on the European stage.[16] In this period, it was those between France and Spain that dominated Rome, with each nation's protectors and supporters seeking to gain favour and financial assistance from the pope, as Thomas Dandelet has extensively explored in writing of Rome as a 'contested locus of power' in the seventeenth century.[17]

---

13 Laurie Nussdorfer, 'The Politics of Space in Early Modern Rome', *Memoirs of the American Academy in Rome* 42 (1997), 161–86, 169.

14 Francis Haskell, *Patrons and Painters: A Study in the Relations Between Italian Art and Society in the Age of the Baroque* (New Haven and London: Yale University Press, 1980), p. 14.

15 Frederick Hammond, *Music and Spectacle in Baroque Rome: Barberini patronage under Urban VIII* (New Haven and London: Yale University Press, 1994), p. 5. While some functions ceased automatically with a pope's death, others were tenured for life.

16 See Nussdorfer, 'Politics of Space', pp. 168–9.

17 Thomas Dandelet, 'Setting the Noble Stage in Baroque Rome: Roman Palaces, Political Context, and Social Theatre, 1600–1700', in Stefanie Walker and Frederick Hammond (eds), *Life and the Arts in the Baroque Palaces of Rome: Ambiente Barocco* (New Haven and London: Yale University Press, 1999), pp. 39–51, p. 49.

For all these competing parties, festivities served as an important component in an overall programme of political and cultural negotiation and persuasion that was enacted in the streets, piazzas, palaces and churches of the city. Religious festivities such as canonisations were celebrated in St Peter's and in other churches, but also with processions from one church to another, as in 1622, when the joint canonisation in St Peter's of six saints was followed by a procession carrying the standards of the new saints through the city, leaving each one in a different Roman church like a triumphal victory parade. When a new pope was elected he began his pontificate with the *possesso*, a ritual procession from the Vatican through the city, culminating at the church of St John Lateran, where he was handed the keys to the city, thus taking symbolic possession of it. The visits of distinguished ambassadors or royal guests occasioned similar processions and entries, akin to classical triumphs. When Queen Christina made her official entrance into Rome on 23 December 1655, she was treated to a banquet outside the city and presented with diplomatic gifts by Monsignor Farnese on behalf of the pope. When she then entered the city through its official entrance, the Porta del Popolo, she was met by Prince Pamphilj and Prince Barberini and journeyed to St Peter's, which was adorned with tapestries, velvets and brocades embroidered with her arms and crown.[18] Similarly, individual realms – most notably France, Spain and the Holy Roman Empire – held public celebrations for significant national events such as the birth of an heir. On such occasions, fireworks were organised by that nation's ambassadors and cardinal-protectors, often complex affairs that took months to build and a night to destroy, such as those designed by Gianlorenzo Bernini for the birth of a dauphin of France in 1662. Banquets and theatrical entertainments also often formed part of the celebrations for these events – performances of dramas, *intermezzi* and operas, and the staging of carousels and other equestrian events such as that performed for Queen Christina, all intended as demonstrations of prestige.

In all such events, public or private spaces were mobilised and temporarily transformed for the occasion. A close look at the painting of the carousel for Queen Christina shows that the brightly coloured performers and theatrical machines at the centre of the *campo* are framed – as is the painting itself – by the temporary theatre in which it was performed. This structure was built specifically for the event to the designs of Giovanni Francesco Grimaldi, as described in a contemporary account: '*L'industria ingegnosa haveva ridotto quel cortile in un vaghissimo teatro*'.[19]

This '*vaghissimo teatro*' used the permanent architecture of the palace, built by Urban VIII's Barberini nephews from 1626, as the starting point for its design. The north side of the palace served as one long side of the arena and the palace theatre (positioned by the east wall) as one short side,

---

18 Fagiolo dell'Arco, *Festa*, p. 378.
19 'Ingenious industry had turned that courtyard into a most beautiful theatre'. Quoted in Fagiolo dell'Arco, *Festa*, p. 386.

both covered with a temporary two-story balcony structure that continued the line of the *piano nobile* around the space to form the uppermost limit of the theatre, surmounted with flaming urns to light the nocturnal event.[20] Despite its ephemeral nature, the temporary theatre required several buildings to be knocked down in the courtyard to the north side of the palace, while the usual entrance to the palace's north wing was covered by the temporary structure.[21] Facing the palace, directly opposite the central loggias which housed the Barberini, Queen Christina and cardinals and other eminent guests, was a triumphal arch decorated with scenes of the Labours of Hercules – a reference to fortitude and power – with musicians seated on its top.[22] On this side of the arena, less important audience members were accommodated not only in the two-story balconies that continued in an unbroken line from the palace, but also in seven tiers of open seating. As shown in Gagliardi and Lauri's painting, the effect is of a structure that seems entirely solid but that transforms this whole side of the palace from a secondary façade into both theatrical backdrop and auditorium, its boxes bedecked in the papal and royal Swedish colours and with rented tapestries hanging from the windows to adorn the bare walls.

This creation of a temporary arena for a seventeenth-century Roman festivity is less common than one might suppose. The only other significant example is that organised, twenty years previously, by the older generation of the Barberini family (the nephews of Urban VIII) for a *giostra del saracino* (a 'Saracen' joust or tournament) held in 1634 in honour of Prince Alexander Vasa of Poland (see Figure 12.1).

This event differed in two key respects from that for Queen Christina in 1656. Firstly, the dedicatee of the festival was not actually present: because of a dispute over precedence, the prince left Rome prematurely, with the spectacle continuing regardless. Although the official printed account of the event stated that Cardinal Antonio Barberini had desired to think of '*qualche festa degna d'un tanto Prencipe, à fine di tenerlo divertito in quei giorni d'allegrezza con qualche nobile passatempo*', other accounts seem to contradict this.[23] The Ferrarese poet Fulvio Testi, resident in Rome, wrote to Francesco I d'Este in Modena, implying that the prince was not the driving force behind the event:

> *Publicano di farla per lo fratello del Re di Polonia ch'è qui ma il fine reale è di tenere allegro il Papa, il quale si trova assai malenconico, e di fargli credere che, nonostante la mala soddisfazione che pretendono*

20 Hammond, 'Creation of a Roman Festival', p. 65.
21 Ibid., p. 65. See also Patricia Waddy, 'The Design and Designers of Palazzo Barberini', *Journal of the Society of Architectural Historians* 35.3 (1976), 151–85, 177.
22 Fagiolo dell'Arco, *Festa*, p. 386.
23 'Some kind of celebration worthy of such a great prince, so as to keep him diverted in those days of merriment with some kind of noble diversion'. See *Festa fatta in Roma, alli 25. di Febraio MDCXXXIV e data in luce da Vitale Mascardi* (Rome, 1634), p. 1.

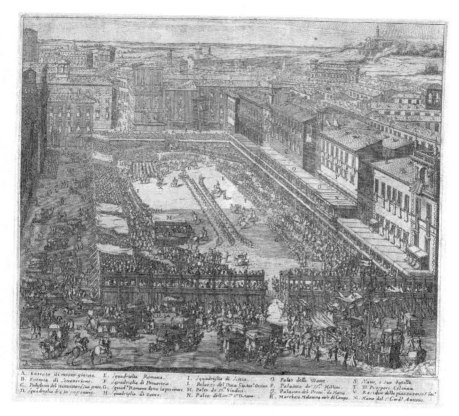

Figure 12.1 François Collignon after Andrea Sacchi, *Temporary theatre for the giostra in Piazza Navona for Prince Alexander of Poland*, etching and engraving, 1634.

gli Spagnoli, tutta Roma gioisce et applaude alla diuturnità del suo pontificato.

[They claim to do it for the brother of the king of Poland who is here, but the real aim is to maintain the spirits of the pope, who is rather melancholy, and to convince him that, despite the dissatisfaction of the Spanish, that all Rome rejoices and applauds the perpetuity of his pontificate.][24]

The second difference was that rather than the environs of the Barberini palace, this time it was the public space of Piazza Navona that was used.

24 Fagiolo dell'Arco, *Festa*, p. 285.

A temporary theatre was constructed at the southern end of the piazza. Banks of seating were built on all four sides, with openings at the two short ends for twenty-four horsemen, divided into six quadrilles, to enter and display their skills by running at the quintain (a post serving as the goal of a tilting exercise). The quintain took the form of a Saracen, as a reference to the enduring threat of the Ottoman Empire.[25] As a somewhat old-fashioned demonstration of courtly skills, the *giostra del saracino* evoked the princely tournaments of the Middle Ages and medieval notions of chivalry and courtly love. Beginning at the sixteenth hour, it lasted for five hours, watched by the '*Principali Personaggi, Ambasciatori de' Prencipi, Dame Titolate et Signori*' seated in the stands, houses and palaces facing the arena.[26] At nightfall, after the running at the quintain was over, a banquet was held by Donna Anna Colonna Barberini, the wife of Taddeo, the secular head of the family. At the same time, a spectacular triumphal car in the form of a ship was paraded through the streets of Rome to entertain the people, illuminated by over one thousand lights and carrying Bacchus and the Bacchantes, and with a smaller boat carrying musicians following in its wake.[27]

The long, narrow arena designed for the 1634 *giostra* was recorded in a painting by Andrea Sacchi, commissioned by the Barberini to mark the occasion, and also in a printed festival book with engravings by François Collignon after Sacchi's designs. This book includes a fold-out engraving of the *teatro* with details of the location of significant figures and buildings and of the ship of Bacchus. Unlike the painting of the carousel for Queen Christina, the temporary nature of the arena in Piazza Navona is absolutely clear in the images that record it. The viewpoint taken is completely different. Rather than the lower perspective employed by Filippo Lauri and Gagliardi, which places the viewer within the seemingly solid arena, Andrea Sacchi's painting and François Collignon's engraving after it place the viewer high above Piazza Navona, looking down on the action as if from a great height. This gives a very clear impression of how the arena fits into the space of the public piazza and shows very clearly the temporary nature of its construction.[28]

It seems worthy of comment that one family would use two very different spaces for the staging of two similar events, albeit twenty years apart, and begs the question as to why this is the case. In attempting some meaningful answers, one might say that the choice of venue seems to be bound up with the notion of public and private space in Rome, and the fluidity characterising it in this period. The use of public spaces for essentially private events was relatively common practice in Rome, particularly by foreign ambassadors

25 Martine Boiteux, 'Carnaval annexé: Essai de lecture fête romaine', *Annales. Histoire, Sciences socials* 32.2 (1977), 356–80, 374.

26 'Elite people, ambassadors of princes, titled ladies and noblemen'. From the *Avvisi di Roma*, quoted in Fagiolo dell'Arco, *Festa*, p. 286.

27 The full account is given in the official publication: see *Festa fatta. . .*, 1634.

28 Hammond, *Music*, p. 214.

and representatives. In 1637, the election of Ferdinand III as the 'King of the Romans' – the heir to the Habsburg Empire – was celebrated by Spanish ambassadors and sympathisers with a series of fireworks-machines over the course of several nights. Extolling the victories of the Holy Roman Empire, these fireworks took place in the piazzas outside particular palaces, such as those organised by the Spanish ambassador, the marchese di Castel Rodrigo, which took place in the Piazza di Spagna.[29] Through a number of different structures, the fireworks represented the triumph of the Empire over heresy, rebellious states and the Ottoman threat. These messages culminated on the last night with a fireworks-machine in the form of a castle that exploded to reveal a statue of the king of the Romans on horseback (see Figure 12.2).

This statue was then pulled through the piazza and into the palace of the Spanish ambassador, an action that was likened in official accounts to the story of the Trojan horse, although with the clear difference that this represented '*un Cavallo, in cui sedeva il nuovo Rè, non per la destruttione, mà per la difesa de' popoli à lui felicemente soggetti*'. (See Figure 12.3.)[30]

The following year, the French retaliated in similar fashion when an heir to the throne was born: the future Louis XIV. This occasioned both a *cavalcata* (cavalcade) from Ponte Sisto to Piazza Navona and fireworks in front of the French national church of S. Luigi dei Francesci.

Such events, organised by national ambassadors in order to celebrate nationally significant occasions, represented a temporary colonisation of what was theoretically public, neutral space. By appropriating these public arenas, they were temporarily able to claim the space for their nation in order to proclaim its power. Since this was common practice, it would be surprising if the Barberini had not been motivated by similar concerns in their decision to use Piazza Navona for the 1634 *giostra* for Prince Alexander. By this time, the new Palazzo Barberini alle Quattro Fontane had been built, and could have hosted the event.[31] However, Piazza Navona carried with it certain political and cultural associations that were particularly useful to the Barberini at this time. Piazza Navona had long associations with the ludic history of Rome, its oval form recalling its ancient origins as the Stadium of Domitian, used for games and gladiatorial combat, and thereby placing the *giostra* within the festive heritage of Rome. Moreover, since the

---

29 Laurie Nussdorfer, 'Print and Pageantry in Baroque Rome', *Sixteenth Century Journal* 29.2 (1998), 454.

30 'A horse, on which sat the new king, not for the destruction, but for the defence of the peoples happily subject to him'. *Relatione delle feste fatte in Roma dall'Eccelentiss. Sig. Marchese di Castel Rodrigo Ambasciatore della Maestà Cat. nella Elettione di Ferdinando III Rê de' Romani* (Milan: Dionisio Gariboldi, 1637), p. 7.

31 Waddy, *Seventeenth-Century Roman Palaces*, pp. 194–9. Taddeo and Anna Colonna Barberini had moved into the palace in 1632 with their two young sons. Although the central block of the palace had not yet been decorated and the south wing was not complete at this time, the north wing was ready.

Figure 12.2 Claude Lorrain, *Fireworks revealing the statue of the King of the Romans*, etching, 1637.

piazza was the location of the Spanish national church, S. Giacomo degli Spagnoli, it may also have represented a temporary rupture of Spanish control by the Francophile Barberini family. During the seventeenth century, Piazza Navona was one of the principal battlegrounds on which the Spanish and French fought their wars of cultural one-upmanship, a reflection of very real conflicts fought on battlefields far from Rome.[32] Since Urban VIII Barberini was the first Francophile pope to be elected for sixty-five years, it is not inconceivable that this may have played into the family's decision-making.[33] It is possible that this theory may be supported by the printed and painted records of the 1634 *giostra*. Sacchi's viewpoint is deliberately partial, only showing the southern part of the piazza and giving the impression that the temporary theatre dominated far more space than it actually did. It also results in the church of St Giacomo, seen in the shadows to the left, seeming entirely side-lined by the scale and splendour of the arena.

Linked to the political resonances of the space, there was an additional factor. The urban environment of central Rome was so built-up in the seventeenth century that space was at a premium and politically charged, as Laurie Nussdorfer has suggested in writing of the 'eloquence of voids', particularly within the Tiber bend.[34] A temporary private use of supposedly 'public' space can be compared to the competitive palace-building in which papal and powerful families participated at the time: an expression of status, wealth and power. Just as the Barberini were engaged over a number of years in buying up a series of properties in order to expand the cramped site of their central-Roman palace in via dei Giubbonari, here perhaps they made a conscious decision to use a large public space imbued with certain resonances.[35] Piazza Navona provided the Barberini with a theatre in the centre of the city through which they could make a claim for the personal power of their family. Through the enactment of the carousel and its financing – at 60,000 *scudi*, this was the most expensive of all seventeenth-century festivities[36] – the Barberini made an explicit show of their cultural and economic standing in the city, and did so in a place where it could be seen by everybody. By closing off an area of Piazza Navona and building on it a structure to which access was controlled, they created a temporary Barberini stronghold in the centre of one of the most politicised spaces in the city.

Although access to the quintain arena was controlled, one particular aspect of the event was deliberately open to the public. The triumphal car, the ship of Bacchus, was considered such a draw that *'fu risoluto di non negare questa sodisfattione al popolo, di farla condurre per la Città, e spetialmente per la strada del corso'*.[37] (See Figure 12.4.) This ship was decorated profusely with the emblems of the Barberini family – bees, sun and

32 Dandelet, 'Setting the Noble Stage', p. 46.
33 Ibid., pp. 39–42.
34 Nussdorfer, 'Politics of Space', p. 166.
35 For the 'Casa Grande' in via dei Giubbonari see Waddy, *Seventeenth-Century Roman Palaces*, pp. 132–72.
36 Boiteux, 'Carnaval annexé', p. 367.
37 'It was decided not to deny this satisfaction to the people, to parade it through the city, and especially along the via del Corso'. See *Festa fatta in Roma*, pp. 129–30.

Figure 12.3 Claude Lorrain, *Statue of the King of the Romans*, etching, 1637.

laurel – and with the column and siren of the Colonna family, representing the alliance of these two families through the marriage of Donna Anna Colonna and Taddeo Barberini.

The reasons for focusing on this alliance were significant. As relative newcomers in Rome, the Barberini needed their relationship with one of the oldest Roman noble families: it granted them legitimacy and give their family

Figure 12.4 François Collignon after Andrea Sacchi, *Ship of Bacchus, from the giostra for prince Alexander of Poland*, etching and engraving, 1634.

the illusion of longevity.[38] It was particularly important because in Rome, the closest female relative to the Pope effectively played the role of his consort. As the wife of the secular head of Urban VIII's family, Anna Colonna Barberini played this role, her status contributing to the importance of a family pope in raising the profile and standing of the Barberini.[39] Parading the ship, with its prominent Barberini–Colonna decoration, reinforced to all of Rome the importance of an alliance already expressed within the confines of the family palace. In 1629–1631, Andrea Sacchi had been commissioned to paint a ceiling fresco on the subject of Divine Wisdom in the new Palazzo Barberini alle Quattro Fontane. Adorning the ceiling of Anna Colonna Barberini's anteroom, Sacchi's fresco included Barberini and Colonna motifs as a permanent celebration of the alliance.[40] Since this fresco would only have been visible to visitors to the palace, the use of the same imagery on the triumphal car, drawn through the most important streets of Rome, served to transmit this message to a much wider public.

38 Boiteux, 'Carnaval annexé', p. 370.
39 Waddy, *Seventeenth-Century Roman Palaces*, p. 193.
40 Hammond, 'Creation of a Roman Festival', p. 49.

That it was desirable to annex the public space of the piazza as the Barberini did for the 1634 *giostra* is reinforced by the events of the 1644 *possesso* of Innocent X, the hispanophile Pamphilj pope elected following the death of Urban VIII. As usual, Innocent's *possesso* took place from the Vatican to the Lateran, along routes adorned by important Roman families with triumphal arches and other ephemeral decorations that depicted events from Innocent's clerical life, or recalled the ancient history of Rome or proclaimed the universal power of the church. In the evening, however, the fireworks-machines to celebrate his *possesso* took place in Piazza Navona, directly in front of Palazzo Pamphilj, the family palace that the new pope had recently remodelled as a cardinal in 1636–1638. The fireworks he organised took the form of a mountain representing Mount Ararat, with Noah's ark resting on top of it. Noah opened his arms to receive the dove which descended on a rope from Palazzo Pamphilj to light the touchpaper of the fireworks, sending the ark up in flames. This was described in a printed account by Bonelli de' Rasori as follows:

> *nella Fontana incontro il Palazzo dell'Eminentiss. Panfilio, fu fatto similmente il Monte, come sopra, & da basso in modo d'antri, ove erano aggiustati quelli stessi Tritoni di marmo della Fontana, in cima al Monte ci era l'Arca scoperta di sopra, & Noè affacciato mezo fuori, con le braccia aperte per ricever la Palomba, quale stava vicino al tetto dell'Eminentiss. & havea da scender per una corda, e dar fuoco à l'Arca.*[41]
>
> [in the fountain opposite the palace of the Most Eminent Pamphilj, another mountain was created, as above, and the base was like caverns, where those same marble tritons of the fountain had been adopted, and at the mountain's peak was the ark, open-topped, and with Noah leaning half out, with his arms open to receive the dove, which stood near His Eminence's roof. And it had to descend on a cord, and set fire to the ark.]

Like the Barberini, the Pamphilj were not an old Roman family by origin, and so Innocent X's election first to the cardinalate and subsequently to the papacy was of special significance. This was expressed in Innocent's *possesso* fireworks. By way of the dove, the emblem of the Pamphilj family, the fireworks made a direct claim for the Pamphilj and their role in the city and its governance, given physical expression in the presence of their family palace in Piazza Navona. The significance attributed to the event is supported by an unusually high number of pamphlets published to commemorate it,

---

41 *Copioso e Compito Racconto della Cavalcata e Cerimonie fatte nell'andare à prendere il possesso in S. Giovanni Laterano N. S. Innocentio X . . . descritta da Giorgio Maria Bonelli de Rasori* (Rome: Lodovico Grignani, 1644), p. 11.

which focused above all on the climactic events in the piazza rather than the procession.[42]

If the political benefits of employing public spaces for such events were so significant, one might question why, in 1656, the Barberini chose to enact their most lavish spectacle for twenty years within the confines of their own palace rather than in one of the city's largest, most famous and evocative public spaces. Firstly, it is not necessarily the case that by enclosing such a spectacle within the confines of a palace it became more private than one staged in a public square but within a temporary theatre closed to those not invited to enter it.[43] The fact that in 1634 the ship of Bacchus was stated as being drawn through the streets specifically '*di non negare questa sodisfattione al popolo*' indicates strongly that the '*popolo*' were not part of the audience present in the temporary arena where the actual *giostra* was staged.[44]

Secondly, it may be a result of other papal initiatives that made Piazza Navona no longer as enticing a location in 1656 as it had been twenty years earlier. During his own cardinalate and papacy, Innocent X had created a Pamphilj architectural pocket in Piazza Navona through the commission of the Fountain of the Four Rivers and the redevelopment of the Pamphilj palace and the church of Sant'Agnese. As such, the Barberini may have been disinclined to use a space now associated with a rival family – indeed, one of their greatest enemies. However, since by this time the enforced reconciliation by marriage between the Pamphilj and the Barberini had already taken place, this seems perhaps unlikely.

Thirdly, the choice of location seems to be bound up with the status of the Barberini in Rome at this time, and the focus which they wanted to place on the event. As a family in Rome, the standing of the Barberini was very different in 1656 – only recently returned from exile – from its status in 1634 – as relatively new arrivals but the family of the ruling pope. In the 1634 *giostra*, the most important element was the association with the Colonna family and the status this bestowed on the Barberini. In 1656, it was more important to display their association with the new pope and Queen Christina, in order to reclaim something of their cultural supremacy and demonstrate their reintegration into Roman society.

The choice, however, of Palazzo Barberini alle Quattro Fontane seems to represent a change in the means chosen to express status and, in particular, longevity, an exceptionally important consideration in this fluid environment of constantly shifting politics and alliances. Rather than focusing on building a notion of longevity through heredity, embodied in a marriage alliance with ancient Roman nobility (as with the Colonna emblems on the ship in 1634),

---

42 Rose Marie San Juan, *Rome: A City Out of Print* (Minneapolis, London: University of Minnesota Press, 2001), p. 166.
43 Boiteux, 'Carnaval annexé', pp. 370–71.
44 Ibid., p. 376.

or through the link to Rome's classical past by using the ancient space of Piazza Navona, there seems to be a shift of focus in 1656 towards the family palace as the embodiment of permanence in the city. By foregrounding their palace – one of the most extraordinary constructions in seventeenth-century Rome – they could reassert themselves as a family able to stand alongside a new pope and a queen, this status made manifest both through the magnificence of the spectacle and the permanent structure of their palace. This was reinforced by the use of the permanent palace in other Carnival festivities for Queen Christina. Three operas were staged in the palace theatre in her honour, with sets by Grimaldi and spectacular stage effects, including real fountains playing on stage with water piped from the palace gardens.[45] The use of the palace as both a permanent and temporary theatre seems to represent a consolidation of Barberini cultural activity rooted in the palace, and thereby a reassertion of its status as the nucleus of artistic life in Rome.[46] Since the position of the palace on the Quirinal hill was also designed to look across the city to St Peter's, such a focus on the palace also reminded the Roman elite of the source of Barberini power in the pontificate of Urban VIII, expressed within the palace through Pietro da Cortona's fresco on the ceiling of the *salone*, from which this view could be seen.[47]

Finally, it is important to say something about the audience beyond those actually present at these spectacles. Whether we work from printed images or accounts of spectacles, letters or paintings, each brings its own complications. Paintings were often commissioned by patrons as records, and in order to show the full magnificence of an event, depicted all its different moments as simultaneous episodes on a single canvas, as can be seen in Gagliardi and Lauri's painting. Letters often reflected national or regional prejudices.[48] Printed accounts were published well in advance of the events and described ideal scenarios rather than relaying what actually took place, as Giacinto Gigli complained in his *Diario di Roma* of the 'accounts' of Innocent X's *possesso*.[49] However, even if their reliability as sources is flawed, these publications represent significant audiences. Laurie Nussdorfer's analyses of one hundred printed texts of Roman *feste* produced from 1623 to 1655 have shown that printed accounts were used by foreign powers to augment the effect of such events in raising their prestige with the papacy, such as the twelve different publications issued to celebrate the festivities for the election of the King of the Romans in 1637.[50]

However, Nussdorfer's research has also shown that although unillustrated pamphlets were relatively quick and cheap to produce, and thus

45 Hammond, 'Creation of a Roman Festival', p. 61.
46 Fagiolo dell'Arco, *Festa*, p. 384.
47 Waddy, 'Design and Designers', pp. 218–19.
48 Hammond, *Music*, p. 128.
49 Nussdorfer, 'Print and Pageantry', p. 462.
50 Ibid., pp. 453–7.

available to many, a festival book such as the *relatione* produced to com-memorate the 1634 *giostra*, nearly one hundred pages long and including thirteen engravings, was a rare and lavish object, costing six hundred *scudi* to produce, the annual rent of a Roman palace.[51] As such, it is important to evaluate the claims to wide dissemination of these events with caution. If such an extravagant festival book could only have been available to the wealthiest, it suggests that the patrons of these events were, for all their references to the '*popolo*', clearly intent on directing their efforts as much in print as in actuality at a self-selected elite audience.

As with expensive printed publications, so the audiences for paintings were restricted. Andrea Sacchi's painting of the 1634 *giostra* was recorded in a 1644 inventory of Palazzo Barberini as being hung '*nella sala accanto [al salone] dove si facevano le Comedie*' – an anteroom, where plays were performed and everyone who sought an audience had to wait.[52] Similarly, when the Swedish architect Nicodemus Tessin the Younger visited Palazzo Barberini in 1687–1688, he commented on seeing '*ein sehr grosses undt artiges carousel gemahlet vom Ph. Lavori, so noch lebet, dieses carousel ist der Konigin Christina zu ehren gehalten worden, auf der erhobenen terrassen vor dem grossen platz, undt ist sehr magnifique gewesen*'.[53] By commissioning paintings of the festivities they had organised and hanging these paintings in the public rooms of their palace, the Barberini may be seen to have drawn together the different strands of their cultural activity and centred it at the Quattro Fontane. In contrast to the fluidity and potential tension of public space, the palace and its environs represented uncontested Barberini territory, to which only a select few could gain access. In this space, the Barberini could remind visitors, through the architecture and frescoed ceilings of the palace, its paintings collections and theatrical activity, of their revived cultural supremacy in the city. At the same time, the location of the palace and its view towards St Peter's conveyed an even more important message, reminding visitors of the source of Barberini power and status in the papacy of Urban VIII. By bringing these two messages together, consolidating different aspects of Barberini patronage within the site of the palace, Palazzo Barberini alle Quattro Fontane became the embodiment of the family's permanent presence and cultural and political status in Rome.

51 Ibid., p. 446. The authorship of the festival book was credited to Cardinal Guido Bentivoglio, a Ferrarese aristocrat and brother of the marchese Enzo Bentivoglio, who planned the tournament.

52 Marilyn Aronberg Lavin, *Seventeenth-Century Barberini Documents and Inventories of Art* (New York: New York University Press, 1975), p. 158.

53 'A very large and beautiful carousel painted by Ph. Lavori, who still lives. This carousel was held in honour of Queen Christina, on the upper terrace in front of the large piazza and was very magnificent'. See Merit Laine and Börje Magnusson (eds), *Nicodemus Tessin the Younger: Travel Notes, 1673–77 and 1687–88* (Stockholm: Nationalmuseum, 2002), p. 302.

Bibliography

Primary Sources

Copioso e Compito Racconto della Cavalcata e Cerimonie fatte nell'andare à prendere il possesso in S. Giovanni Laterano N. S. Innocentio X . . . descritta da Giorgio Maria Bonelli de Rasori (Rome: Lodovico Grignani, 1644).

Festa fatta in Roma, alli 25. di Febraio MDCXXXIV e data in luce da Vitale Mascardi (Rome, 1634).

Relatione delle feste fatte in Roma dall'Eccelentiss. Sig. Marchese di Castel Rodrigo Ambasciatore della Maestà Cat. nella Elettione di Ferdinando III Rê de' Romani (Milan: Dionisio Gariboldi, 1637).

Secondary Sources

Boiteux, Martine, 'Carnaval annexé: Essai de lecture fête romaine', *Annales. Histoire, Sciences socials* 32.2 (March–April 1977), 356–80.

Dandelet, Thomas, 'Setting the Noble Stage in Baroque Rome: Roman Palaces, Political Context, and Social Theatre, 1600–1700', in Stefanie Walker and Frederick Hammond (eds), *Life and the Arts in the Baroque Palaces of Rome: Ambiente Barocco* (New Haven and London: Yale University Press, 1999), pp. 39–51.

Fagiolo dell'Arco, Maurizio, *La Festa barocca* (Rome: De Luca, 1997).

Hammond, Frederick, *Music and Spectacle in Baroque Rome: Barberini Patronage Under Urban VIII* (New Haven and London: Yale University Press, 1994).

Hammond, Frederick, 'Creation of a Roman Festival: Barberini Celebrations for Christina of Sweden', in Stefanie Walker and Frederick Hammond (eds), *Life and the Arts in the Baroque Palaces of Rome: Ambiente Barocco* (New Haven and London: Yale University Press, 1999), pp. 53–69.

Haskell, Francis, *Patrons and Painters: A Study in the Relations Between Italian Art and Society in the Age of the Baroque* (New Haven and London: Yale University Press, 1980).

Laine, Merit and Börje Magnusson (eds), *Nicodemus Tessin the Younger: Travel Notes, 1673–77 and 1687–88* (Stockholm: Nationalmuseum, 2002).

Lavin, Marilyn Aronberg, *Seventeenth-Century Barberini Documents and Inventories of Art* (New York: New York University Press, 1975).

Masson, Georgina, 'Papal Gifts and Roman Entertainments in Honour of Queen Christina's Arrival', in Magnus von Platen (ed.), *Queen Christina of Sweden: Documents and Studies*, Analecta Reginensia, I (Stockholm: P.A. Norstedt & Söner, for the Nationalmuseum in Sweden, 1966), pp. 244–61.

Nussdorfer, Laurie, 'The Politics of Space in Early Modern Rome', *Memoirs of the American Academy in Rome* 42 (1997), 161–86.

Nussdorfer, Laurie, 'Print and Pageantry in Baroque Rome', *Sixteenth Century Journal* 29.2 (Summer 1998), 439–64.

San Juan, Rose Marie, *Rome: A City Out of Print* (Minneapolis and London: University of Minnesota Press, 2001).

Waddy, Patricia, 'The Design and Designers of Palazzo Barberini', *Journal of the Society of Architectural Historians* 35.3 (October 1976), 151–85.

Waddy, Patricia, *Seventeenth-Century Roman Palaces: Use and the Art of the Plan* (New York and Cambridge: Architectural History Foundation and MIT Press, 1990).

Epilogue

Turning tables

From elite to egalitarian banquets in late eighteenth- and early nineteenth-century Paris

Tim White

> *Since the Revolution, there has not been a political event in France that was not both organised at, and celebrated with, a banquet.*[1]

Food is central to festivity,[2] from the grandeur of the dining hall and the extravagance of the food, to the precise ordering of who may sit at table and where their seat should be or was positioned.[3] Many early modern festival books include accounts of banquets and those invited and the often-symbolic significance of their clothes and jewellery. They also comment on the foods themselves and the magnificence of their presentation and service, particularly noting the inclusion of newly discovered delicacies and culinary marvels. The skills of those managing the events are celebrated, as are the grand settings in which the celebrations take place. Such occasions had, and maintain to this day, a significant place in personal and state ostentation and the display of power, connoting influence and largesse, with those attending being regarded as persons of political influence.

In late eighteenth- and early nineteenth-century France, public and private banquets were both celebrated and condemned, with both celebration and condemnation reflecting an overt assessment of a political and social order at crisis point. The need to eat does not fluctuate according to the system of government in place, but the desire to eat well, and to be seen to do so, may straddle politically significant shifts between monarchy, empire and republic. The fellowship of the table remained steadfast in this period as an ideal, albeit not without challenge from the newly revolutionary politics of

---

1 Armand Lebault, *La table et le repas à travers les siècles* (Paris: Laveur, 1910), p. 683.
2 The first known appearance of the word 'festival' in the English language is to be found in the *Gawain* poet's *Cleanness* (*c.* 1400), where it is employed adjectively as that 'pertaining to a feast, befitting a feast-day'. See 'festival, adj. and n.', *OED Online.* Oxford University Press, June 2017. Web. 31 July 2017.
3 See Roy Strong, *Feast: A History of Grand Eating* (London: Pimlico, 2003).

egalitarianism. Rebecca Spang, referring to events surrounding the French
Revolution of 1789, concludes:

> people needed both food, clothes, shelter, and some sort of coherent
> belief system. [. . .] The table refused to be simply theorized – whenever
> an attempt was made, there was always a critic to the Left or Right
> (usually Left) to ask who was providing the food and who was washing
> the dishes. And yet, concurrently, the shared meal proved too powerful
> an icon and too important a dream for the French to reject it as merely
> one of despotism's hollow superstitions.[4]

****

This short epilogue to *Occasions of State*, chronologically subsequent to the
book's other chapters, focuses on three Parisian banquet occasions spanning
a period of more than one hundred years. The first, a Funeral Supper staged
in the pre-revolutionary Paris of 1783, pays tribute to the enduring capacity
of satire to target with precision an oppressive regime; the second, a fervent,
idealistic celebration of communal meals, accompanied the Feast of the Federation in 1790 for the first anniversary of the Storming of the Bastille; and,
lastly, the third, a banquet in 1900 which tested the limits of representative
civic and municipal democracy.

The Funeral Supper, 1783: Grimod's satiric re-staging of the *grand couvert*

Browsing the long list of characteristics usually ascribed to Alexandre Balthazar Laurent Grimod de la Reynière, one would search in vain for lack of
self-esteem. Lawyer turned theatre critic, renowned *gourmand* and now best
remembered as the author of the first restaurant guide,[5] Grimod's inherited
wealth was much diminished by his enthusiasm for hosting dinner parties,
none more notorious than that staged in 1783.

For the event, three hundred black-bordered invitations to the funeral and
last rites of 'M. Balthazar Grimod de la Reynière, Esquire, Advocate to Parliament and drama critic', were dispatched, inviting attendance at 9 p.m. –
corresponding with the usual time of an evening meal – on the first day of
Lent, 1 February 1783. On arrival, guests had their invitations scrutinised.
The twenty-two chosen to dine proceeded onward. The rest were ushered
to a gallery above. Guests selected as diners had to negotiate a checkpoint

4 Rebecca L. Spang, *The Invention of the Restaurant: Paris and Modern Gastronomic Culture*, Harvard Historical Studies (Cambridge, MA: Harvard University Press, 2001), p. 95.
5 Alexandre Grimod de la Reynière, *Almanach des gourmands* (Paris: Maradan, 1803). The
first of eight annual volumes, much of this first volume has been translated into English.
(www.almanachdesgourmands.com/?page_id=40).

Figure E.1 Funeral Supper given by Grimod de la Reynière the Younger at his Hôtel in the Champs Elysées, Paris, 1 February 1783.

Illustration for *The XVIIIth Century* by Paul Lacroix (Bickers and Son, *c.*1880).

© Look and Learn, image M137087.

where, as a first interrogation, they were required to align themselves either with M. de la Reynière (père), 'oppressor of the people', or M. de la Reynière, 'defender of the people'. Correctly choosing the latter, the twenty-two diners were led first to a guard room occupied by men dressed as medieval heralds, thence to a further interrogation by a figure sheathed in chain mail, before finally proceeding to the inner sanctum, the dining room, perfumed with incense wafted by two choir boys. Here they took their seats. Taking pride of place at the centre of the table sat a catafalque, an elevated platform upon which a dead body might rest, while every place at the table was assigned not just a chair but also, alongside each, an upright coffin.[6]

Confirming that widely circulating rumours of his death were indeed much exaggerated, Grimod appeared before his guests in a role which seems to have hovered between high priest and master of ceremonies. Following an initial course composed entirely of *charcuterie*, Grimod declared that all the products served as ingredients of this course originated from the butcher's shop owned by his father's cousin, and encouraged guests to patronise the business. Similarly, the inclusion of a course prepared in olive oil was explained as evidence of Grimod's humble origins, since the oil was supplied by another relative, on this occasion in the grocery trade.[7]

Viewing, in contrast to dining, guests were ushered in groups into the gallery above to watch some sections of the meal as the twenty-course supper proceeded. By the conclusion of the meal at three in the morning, with all the viewing spectators departed, the dining guests attempted to leave but found the doors locked. They were required to remain in the dining room until a pair of Swiss guards unlocked the door four hours later.

News of this remarkable event spread by word of mouth and was preserved in a range of conflicting accounts written by diners, spectators and those who reconstructed proceedings from the accounts of others. For some, the event offered further confirmation of Grimod's unsteady command of his mental faculties. For others, the funereal aspects aligned the occasion with the mortuary banquets of the distant past, most obviously the Hell Banquet of the Roman Emperor Domitian.[8] Yet neither reading addresses the significance of mounting such an occasion, or the experience of the guests in attending it. No-one who became aware of the banquet would have missed its satiric allusion to the *grand couvert*, a public meal

---

6 Phyllis P. Bober, 'The Black or Hell Banquet', in Harlan Walker (ed.), *Oxford Symposium on Food and Cookery, 1990: Feasting and Fasting: Proceedings* (London: Prospect Books, 1990), p. 55. The upright coffins do not appear in Figure E1.

7 Spang, *The Invention of the Restaurant*, p. 88.

8 Bober, 'The Black or Hell Banquet', p. 57. Domitian (Roman emperor AD 81–96), famed for his cruelty, was reputed to have invited his friends to a banquet, subsequently known as the Hell Banquet, mounted in a blacked-out room and served by black-faced, black-clad (or naked but painted black) servants amid terrifying sounds. Beside each guest was set a small black column looking like a monument, with the guest's name inscribed. The guests feared for their lives, even as they were carried home on litters. In the event, they were unharmed.

consumed by the royal family in the Salon of the Grand Couvert at Versailles. The many thousands who crowded the royal palace in hope of patronage dutifully performed their allotted roles at the *grand couvert*. As Esther Aresty spells out, Louis XIV's unquestioned, central brilliance as the 'Sun King' was reflected in the orbits of lesser bodies forever in circulation around the monarch at table:

> each move of a dish in the direction of royalty was governed by some rule, and the honour of tendering the dish or object was reserved for men of noble birth. The king's napkin reposed on a cushion like a holy relic. The cushion, in turn, was placed in an elaborate piece, a nef, fashioned in the form of a galleon complete with sails, and presented by the appointed noble when the king signaled. [. . .] In the absence of the ranking profferer, royalty would endure thirst rather than violate the rules of precedence.[9]

These rigid, hierarchically configured arrangements flow from the monarch downwards to courtiers, to their retainers and provisioners and, beyond the confines of Versailles, to regional and local centres of governance, where the performance of legitimacy utilised similar rules of precedence.

By contrast, Grimod's feast is devoid of such time-honoured etiquette. There are those performing the act of eating on a stage and those spectating from above. The self-perpetuating logic of the *grand couvert*, deriving its rationale from the complicity of all involved, is here revealed as a perverse, arbitrary division between those who are permitted to eat and those who are not. In one of his many pieces of theatre criticism, Grimod insists that the performer should not be seen to derive satisfaction from performing his role, lest it infuriate the audience:

> An actor is pleased with his work, which is excusable, even welcome; but the art of the actor is in concealing that perfect contentment with oneself; otherwise the public will be angry and, not without justification will say:
>
> > This is usurping our rights; the pleasure of the actor provokes jealousy and sadness in the audience.[10]

Despite this assertion, the Funeral Supper materialises the pleasure of the performers, invited to dine in an excessive manner while their fellow citizens above are not only subjected to the obvious delight the diners display, but

---

9 Esther B. Aresty, *The Exquisite Table: A History of French Cuisine* (Indianapolis: The Bobbs-Merrill Company, Inc., 1980), p. 22.

10 Alexandre Grimod de la Reynière, *Revue des comédiens: ou, Critique raisonnée de tous les acteurs, danseurs et mimes de la capitale* (Paris: Favre, 1808), vol. II, p. 45.

cannot do other than salivate in response to the odours that waft upwards. Jacques Rancière, writing in the early twenty-first century, declares that spectators are poorly served by a spectacle that begets the stupor from which Brecht and Artaud have (by different means) sought to rouse them.[11] At Grimod's banquet, spectators in the gallery were not served at all, and their lack of food was explained not as deference but as a manifest injustice, belligerently teasing their unsated appetites. Rancière describes 'the idea of the theatre as a specifically communitarian place', subsequently arguing that, as a presupposition, what distinguishes theatre spectators from those watching on television is that

> theater is communitarian in and of itself. That presupposition of what 'theater' means always runs ahead of the performance and predates its actual effects. But in a theater, or in front of a performance, just as in a museum, at a school, or on the street, there are only individuals, weaving their own way through the forest of words, acts, and things that stand in front of them or around them.[12]

Grimod's audience in the gallery are deprived of any sense of *communitas*, given that they are separated at the outset from those of their original number who are fed and fêted below. Rancière's audience members are nourished with materials that are appropriated and assembled in such a way that he or she becomes part of an 'emancipated community . . . of storytellers and translators'.[13] The seemingly irreconcilable difference between those who watch and those who eat is only resolved after the event when accounts of the diners' experiences emerge, their eventual involuntary incarceration being a privation calculated to complement those who have been unfed but also unfettered.

Grimod's re-staging of the *grand couvert*, celebrating his humble origins in trade and having scant regard for the basic needs of his guests, is fittingly dressed in funereal garb, a portent of the eclipsing of the monarchy that was soon to follow. Grimod himself was prescient enough to take an extended sojourn in the South of France and returned, disinherited[14] and hungry, to promote attention to food in a Paris that, far from distancing itself from the culinary excesses of the past, found a growing public all too eager to surpass them.[15]

---

11 Jacques Rancière, 'The Emancipated Spectator', *Artforum* (March 2007), 274.

12 Ibid., p. 278.

13 Ibid., p. 280.

14 His loss of wealth was the consequence of a subsequent dinner-party that mercilessly mocked his father, including having his father's vacant seat occupied by a live pig. See Aresty, p. 80.

15 See Priscilla Parkhurst Ferguson, 'Writing out of the Kitchen: Carême and the Invention of French Cuisine', *Gastronomica* 3.3 (2003), 40–51.

The Feast of the Federation, 1790: a celebration to mark the first anniversary of the storming of the Bastille

Epicurean philosopher Jean Anthelme Brillat-Savarin, writing in 1825 of the significant changes since the storming of the Bastille, restricts his remarks to the culinary domain, although he cannot ignore the connection between food and politics:

> We have, also, created political banquets, which have recurred incessantly during the past thirty years whenever it has been necessary to exercise a particular influence over a great number of individuals. It is a type of meal which demands great lavishness, to which no one pays any heed, and the enjoyment of which is only felt in retrospect.[16]

A mere four days after the Bastille was taken, Charles, Marquis de Villette, declared euphorically that *fraternité* might be realised through the holding of a 'national festival' on the anniversary of the event.[17] He went further:

> the rich and the poor would be united and all ranks would mix . . . The capital, from one end to the other, would be one immense family, and you would see a million people all seated at the same table; toasts would be drunk to the ringing of church bells and to the sound of a hundred cannon blasts. On that day, the nation will hold its *grand couvert*.[18]

Although the ambition for what was to become the Festival of the Federation saw no diminution over the coming months, the time available to bring about these aspirations steadily decreased until at the beginning of June, just six weeks prior to the anniversary, the National Assembly agreed to the event being staged in Paris. Richard Etlin's reflections on preparations for the event focus on deliberations relating to the location and arrangement of the site, mindful as they always were to avoid structures or scenography that would re-inscribe the privileges of the *ancien régime*. The amphitheatre at the Champs de Mars was to be a realisation of Rousseau's dissolving of the distinction between actor and spectator.[19] The labour required to create

---

16 Jean Anthelme Brillat-Savarin, *The Physiology of Taste: Or, Meditations on Transcendental Gastronomy*, trans. M.F.K. Fisher (New York, London and Toronto: Alfred A. Knopf, 1971), p. 306.
17 Richard A. Etlin, 'Architecture and the Festival of Federation, Paris, 1790', *Architectural History* 18 (1975), 23.
18 Quoted in Spang, *The Invention of the Restaurant*, p. 96.
19 'Plant a pole with a wreath of flowers in the middle of the square, invite the people, and you have a party. Better still, give the audience a show by making them the actors themselves; make everyone see and appreciate each other so that they may be better unified', Jean-Jacques Rousseau, *Lettre à d'Alembert sur les spectacles* [1758] (Paris: Garnier Frères, 1889), p. 268.

an amphitheatre capable of holding 400,000 people, even one of modest elevation, was significant. Even though the earthworks were not created in a day, the name used to commemorate the amphitheatre's construction, the Day of the Wheelbarrows (*Journée des brouettes*), testifies both to the extent of the mobilisation and the haste with which the project was realised. In implying this mobilisation and haste, the building work anticipated the fusing of actor and spectator during the ceremony itself. All and sundry worked with, and could be seen to be working by, their fellow labourers, all of them drawn from every walk of life, as both written and visual records insist. (See Plate 16.)

Even unrelenting rain failed to dampen the egalitarian ardour characteristic of the festivities at the Champs de Mars and the ensuing feast for five thousand guests.[20] For the vast proportion of those excluded from the meal because of the overwhelming numbers of would-be guests, the organisers had no response. 'They had not', Mona Ozouf writes, 'foreseen that collective enthusiasm would spill over beyond their joyless projects' – in preparation for the occasion – to the event itself.[21] In place of a system of carefully delimited patronage, whether at the exclusively royal *grand couvert*, at the dining tables of nobility or even with reference to the twenty-two seats of Grimod's supper, here the invitation was thrown open to all. Villette's vision of a million people all seated at the same table offered *égalité* by taking liberties with the livelihoods of the thousands of restaurateurs and café owners who, Villette presumed, would offer up their labour and provisions, a gesture that, unlike the work undertaken briefly by the *wheelbarrowistes* (warmed by the satisfaction of communal endeavour), was less visible and liable to be called on repeatedly until such time that a clamour for hospitality receded. Camille Desmoulins articulated these concerns, asking why Villette, having invited the world to dinner, did not first see if there was sufficient food – or sufficient funds to pay the bill.[22] The unintended consequence of this glaring oversight was to provoke much reflection on the limits of hospitality, not so much in the sense of guest and host becoming indistinguishable[23] but between hospitality predicated on friendship or kinship, and hospitality underpinned by economic exchange. The idealism expressed in the amphitheatre was matched with pragmatism in the service industry: one restaurateur offered free military music to all parties of fifty or more;

---

20 For an account of this and subsequent festivals, see Mona Ozouf, *La fête révolutionnaire, 1789–1799* (Paris: Gallimard, 1976), trans. by Alan Sheridan as *Festivals and the French Revolution* (Cambridge, MA: Harvard University Press, 1988).

21 Ibid., p. 44.

22 Camille Desmoulins, *Révolutions de France et de Brabant* (Paris: Garnery, 1790), vol. III, p. 290.

23 See Jacques Derrida, *Of Hospitality: Ann Dufourmantelle Invites Jacques Derrida to Respond*, trans. Rachel Bowlby, Cultural Memory in the Present (Stanford: Stanford University Press, 2000).

Figure E.2 Mayors' Banquet in the Hôtel de Ville, Paris. Illustration from *The Graphic* (London), 29 September 1900.

© Illustrated London News Ltd/Mary Evans.

another supplier produced refreshments to be consumed while attending the Champs de Mars; and a hotelier declared he would provide free lodging for ten guests on the understanding that they hailed from his hometown.[24] Further accounts recall acts of generosity and friendship that could be proffered without incurring hardship. The celebration of a fledgling democracy as performed in the amphitheatre, although it recalled models drawn from antiquity and anticipated an egalitarian future, inadvertently exposed the workings of democracy in the adjustments which were necessitated by an imperfect present.

Banquet of the Mayors at the Hôtel de Ville, Paris, 1900

Municipal elections in 1900 entrenched the Nationalist party in the French capital yet saw indifference or even a growth of republican sentiment in the provinces. The pre-eminence of the capital, unquestioned in the nineteenth century, could no longer be taken for granted. As an editorial in *The Spectator* of 29 September 1900 noted:

> the decay of mob power through the introduction of arms of precision, the increased prosperity of the great cities, and, above all, the improvement in the means of internal communication, had sapped the sources of metropolitan strength.[25]

Yet the hubris of the metropolitan elite, buoyed by talk of patriotism and the expansion of the capital (even going so far as to suggest a tax on celibacy to counter the declining birth rate), was exposed when, believing that to control Paris was to dominate France, M. Grebauval, President of the Municipal Council, invited all the mayors of the 36,000 *communes* of France to a grand banquet at the Hôtel de Ville. A mere 1,000 acceptances were received, with President Emile Loubet refusing even to entertain the delegation that brought his invitation.[26] The event was cancelled.[27] Yet, rather than allow this indignity to be worsened by suggestions that the time and expense of such an undertaking made it impossible, Loubet exacerbated the potential embarrassment by promptly issuing an invitation to the very same mayors. No doubt somewhat bemused if gratified at receiving not one but two invitations to lunch in the capital within a space of days, two-thirds of the number accepted the invitation and preparations began for the event.

The sheer numbers involved in facilitating the occasion were staggering. In Paris, a workforce of 4,866 was required to prepare the food in twelve kitchens around the capital. A further workforce of 20,000 waiters had to be on hand to serve the 22,965 guests, and themselves had to be fed.

24 Spang, *The Invention of the Restaurant*, p. 101.
25 'A Great Event Has Occurred in Paris', *The Spectator*, 29 September, 1900, 2.
26 Emile Loubet was president de la République Française between 1899 and 1906.
27 'Paris Nationalists Checked', *The New York Times*, 18 September, 1900.

This representative gathering of the nation in the capital – pointedly the only place in France without a municipal representative present – began to acquire trappings of a more permanent kind. These extended to means of transportation requiring walkways sufficiently broad to allow the passage of cars and bicycles to ferry food to the diners.[28]

As for the food itself, diners may have felt some disappointment that this most rare of invitations occurred at a time when the French classical menu had concluded its descent from seventeen to a mere eleven courses – with the workforce relieved that it was no longer served *à la française*.[29] The hosts, however, made full use of the occasion to produce a gastronomic itinerary that took in the wealth of the French larder. Charles-Louis Cadet de Gassicourt's *Gastronomic Map of France* of 1809 was one of many publications celebrating the culinary wealth of a nation rich in comestibles of great variety and wide distribution. Loubet's caterers, Potel et Chabot, sought to plunder this resource in order to mirror the geographic origins of the numerous guests.[30]

To accompany the food, diners were treated to a cultural programme commencing with the singing of *La Marseillaise* and then offering four dances (barbarous, Greek, French and modern) performed by *La Comédie-Française* and *L'Académie Nationale de Musique et de Danse*, implicitly identifying four stages in the progression from rusticity to enlightenment. Although details are few of the practicalities of the performance, it is evident that in an age prior to amplification, and with a text addressed to an audience arranged on 7 kilometres of tables, problems must have been many. The fact that the rousing speech delivered by Loubet was circulated in printed form suggests that the limitations were known and accepted. The audience members were thus pre-warned of moments when their vocal support of the republic was invited and, taking their cue from the noise emanating from elsewhere in the dining space, and their enthusiasm from the bottle of wine each was expected to consume, they provided Loubet with physical and vocal confirmation of his victory over the capital's tendency towards asserting its national dominance.

28 A further image shows the organiser of the banquet overseeing the preparations from his automobile, attesting both to the scale and modernity of the occasion. See www.alamy.com/ stock-photo-in-paris-the -banquet-of-the-22000-mayors-of- france-1900–49919257.html
29 In essence all at once, resulting in groaning tables and tepid or cold food. This was superseded by service *à la russe* which saw a rise in the number of courses and servers to deliver and clear each one. See Margaret Visser, *The Rituals of Dinner: The Origins, Evolution, Eccentricities and Meaning of Table Manners* (New York: Grove Press, Inc., 1991), pp. 196–210.
30 A striking front cover for the menu for the Banquet of Mayors (in the Dr Robert Wilson Collection, the National Gallery of Melbourne, Australia) is dominated by a female figure of Liberty (an image referring to the Revolution and Republic). Behind her a gold sun radiates its beams.

Reporting of the event provided national and international readers with an opportunity to marvel at the scale of the undertaking. It was empirically precise in detailing the number of rolls, chickens and other foodstuffs consumed, but at best hazy, and more often lazy, in describing partakers of the banquet. Under the headline 'Monster Feast in Paris', the *New York Times* of 23 September 1900 seems to have been unable to suppress a metropolitan sneer at the provincials:

> There was a very picturesque crowd of mayors. Several turned up in peasants' blouses and top hats. The police report tonight that three have gone mad. Unaccustomed to them, the lights and brilliancy of the gay city have been too much for the worthy peasants, who had probably never before left their native villages.[31]

Later, the uncredited reporter observes that

> there was one unpleasant incident. Max Regis, the anti-Semite Mayor of Algiers, tried to secure a hearing. But when he attempted to speak such shouts arose that he found it impossible to obtain one. The police finally intervened and led Regis from the banquet, after some of those present had thrown articles of food at his head.[32]

Somewhat later, on 27 November, the editors of Australia's *West Gippsland Gazette* settled on the headline 'Mayonnaise and Marseillaise' to accompany a piece which, having twice established early on that England would be incapable of organising such an undertaking, is more generous in its description of the attendees and makes much of the seemingly impromptu 'march of the mayors' to the Elysée Palace. Omitting any mention of official entertainments, the report goes into raptures over the spontaneity of the guests:

> The march of the mayors after dinner to the Elysée surely needed the immortalisation of a second Mendelssohn. With the 'Marseillaise' and the ballads of the Pyrenees were mingled the drinking songs of Bordeaux and the fishers' chants of Brittany; if anything marred the splendour of the sound, it was that here and there the song of an individual was interrupted by the necessity of dodging a cab or a motor-car.[33]

That the event was a propaganda coup is undoubted; the scale of the operation that attracted such interest was recounted worldwide, along with favourable commentary on the conviviality and unity of the French. Loubet

31 'Monster Feast in Paris', *The New York Times*, 23 September 1900.
32 Ibid.
33 'Mayonnaise and Marseillaise', *West Gippsland Gazette*, 27 November, 1900.

himself encouraged a permanent memory of the event, first by distributing a postcard to all diners immediately afterwards and, over two years later, a commemorative plaque. By this time a good number of mayors were no longer in office, or inevitably, as one guest somewhat morbidly remarked, the trouble with sitting with 20,000 people round the table was that at least someone would be dead within the year.

But for all its superlatives and organisational improbabilities, the Mayors' banquet highlights the inevitable failure, when those it represents are so numerous, to utilise public space as the location for performing a coherent and efficacious democracy. At best, as C.B. MacPherson writes of participatory democracy, such systems might come together into 'a pyramidal system with direct democracy at the base and delegate democracy at every level above that'.[34] Participatory democracy imposes a representative layer of the nation over the geographical co-ordinates of the capital city. This is the reverse of the infinite regression one finds in J. Louis Borges's 'Partial Enchantments of the Quixote':

> Let us imagine that a portion of the soil of England has been levelled off perfectly and that on it a cartographer traces a map of England. The job is perfect; there is no detail of the soil of England, no matter how minute, that is not registered on the map; everything has there its correspondence. This map, in such a case, should contain a map of the map, which should contain a map of the map of the map, and so on to infinity.[35]

In the instance of the banquet, the areas mapped proceed outwards from a garden in Paris to the representation of the nation – that encompasses a garden in Paris – and then to the world – that includes France – and onwards, ever more immaterially, to universal values – which derive, one can only conclude, from France.

In considering how food functions here, there is a danger of platitude, if we invoke the commensality of the table as some universal condition that engenders the very fraternity Loubet envisages. While the positive role banquets play on such occasions as the brokering of peace treaties, the conduct of negotiations or the bringing together of those of strongly differing views, it does seem imprudent to gather opponents together in the same space and give each of them a knife. Yet such political occasions are almost invariably endured if not always enjoyed, without blows being exchanged. One might argue that this is a consequence of the obligations that customarily

---

34 Joel I. Colón-Ríos, *Weak Constitutionalism: Democratic Legitimacy and the Question of Constituent Power* (New York: Routledge, 2012), p. 69.
35 J. Louis Borges, 'Partial Enchantments of the Quixote', in *Other Inquisitions* (Austin: University of Texas Press, 2000), p. 47.

exist between host and guest. The Mayors' banquet not only attested the healthy economic state of the country, but also confirmed its organisational competence as well as the refinement of its tastes (*prospérité, bureaucratie, urbanité*). The now unassailable association between France and the arts of the table ensures that both producers and consumers of food are acknowledged and recompensed. Participants in the banquet are not performers on the one hand and spectators on the other, not host and guests, but entirely performers and entirely hosts, as a consequence of bearing the cost of the meal collectively through the public purse.

****

In a period of inequality, buttressed by tiers of privilege, Grimod's banquet eliminated all but the extremes of indulgence and the depths of privation. Such a view exposes a void that cannot be sustained and thus collapses: the final incarceration of the diners serves to disabuse the privileged few of the construct created on their seeming behalf. The diners are no longer relevant to the performance in which they had, as they thought, played a leading part, being now unwatched, forgotten. The predictive qualities of the second banquet, the Feast of the Federation, envisages an ideal social order which falls short of practical realisation by failing to acknowledge the reality which dictates that shared common goals cannot necessarily accommodate individual needs. In the final example, the Mayors' banquet, forces which are technological, logistical and culinary conspire to bring the modern state to an ambitious but unstable equilibrium. Rather than relegating food to a basic and unproblematic precondition of a move towards democratic stability, or a palliative for a move in the opposite direction – towards exclusion and elitism – food is here shown to have agency in the political development of a major European nation – and a democracy.

Bibliography

'A Great Event Has Occurred in Paris', *The Spectator*, 29 September 1900, 2.

Aresty, Esther B., *The Exquisite Table: A History of French Cuisine* (Indianapolis: The Bobbs-Merrill Company, Inc., 1980).

Bober, Phyllis P., 'The Black or Hell Banquet', in Harlan Walker (ed.), *Oxford Symposium on Food and Cookery, 1990: Feasting and Fasting: Proceedings* (London: Prospect Books, 1990), pp. 55–57.

Borges, J. Louis, 'Partial Enchantments of the Quixote', in *Other Inquisitions* (Austin: University of Texas Press, 2000).

Brillat-Savarin, Jean Anthelme, *The Physiology of Taste: Or, Meditations on Transcendental Gastronomy*, trans. M.F.K. Fisher (New York, London and Toronto: Alfred A. Knopf, 1971).

Cadet de Gassicourt, Charles-Louis, *Cours gastronomique, ou les diners de Manantville: ouvrage anecdotique, phiposophique et littéraire* (Paris: Capelle et Renand, 1809).

Colón-Ríos, Joel I., *Weak Constitutionalism: Democratic Legitimacy and the Question of Constituent Power* (New York: Routledge, 2012).

Derrida, Jacques, *Of Hospitality: Ann Dufourmantelle Invites Jacques Derrida to Respond*, trans. Rachel Bowlby, Cultural Memory in the Present (Series) (Stanford, CA: Stanford University Press, 2000).

Desmoulins, Camille, *Révolutions de France et de Brabant*, vol. III (Paris: Garnery, 1790).

Etlin, Richard A., 'Architecture and the Festival of Federation, Paris, 1790', *Architectural History* 18 (1975), 23–42 and 102–108.

Ferguson, Priscilla Parkhurst, 'Writing Out of the Kitchen: Carême and the Invention of French Cuisine', *Gastronomica* 3.3 (2003), 40–51.

Grimod de la Raynière, Alexandre, *Almanach des gourmands* (Paris: Maradan, 1803).

Grimod de la Reynière, Alexandre, *Revue des comédiens: ou Critique raisonnée de tous les acteurs, danseurs et mimes de la capitale*, vol. II (Paris: Favre, 1808).

Lebault, Armand, *La table et le repas à travers les siècles* (Paris: Laveur, 1910).

'Mayonnaise and Marseillaise', *West Gippsland Gazette*, 27 November, 1900.

'Monster Feast in Paris', *The New York Times*, 23 September, 1900.

Ozouf, Mona, *La fête révolutionnaire, 1789–1799* (Paris: Gallimard, 1976), trans. Alan Sheridan as *Festivals and the French Revolution* (Cambridge, MA: Harvard University Press, 1988).

'Paris Nationalists Checked', *The New York Times*, 18 September, 1900.

Rancière, Jacques, 'The Emancipated Spectator', *Artforum* (March 2007), 270–81.

Rousseau, Jean-Jacques, *Lettre à d'Alembert sur les spectacles [1758]* (Paris: Garnier Frères, 1889).

Spang, Rebecca L., *The Invention of the Restaurant: Paris and Modern Gastronomic Culture*, Harvard Historical Studies (Cambridge, MA: Harvard University Press, 2001).

Strong, Roy, *Feast: A History of Grand Eating* (London: Pimlico, 2003).

Visser, Margaret, *The Rituals of Dinner: The Origins, Evolution, Eccentricities and Meaning of Table Manners* (New York: Grove Press, Inc., 1991).

Index

This index, compiled by Margaret Shewring with J.R. (Ronnie) Mulryne, includes the personal names and brief descriptions of those architects, landscape and urban designers, artists, performers, scenographers, writers, choreographers and composers who created or were principal participants in festivals and occasions of state as well as those who commissioned these events or were otherwise important historical or cultural figures. It lists the sites where performances were held and other named locations, architectural features that contributed to the performances and aspects of theatrical staging and dance. Types of festival events and scenic devices are each grouped in a single entry. Names mentioned in footnote references and bibliographies are not included. The names of twentieth- and twenty-first-century scholars and commentators are also omitted, with a few exceptions; all these names can be found in the extensive bibliographies which follow each chapter. Figures and plates are indicated in *italic* font.